"Settler-colonialism reveals the brutal face of imperialism in some of its most vicious forms. This carefully researched and penetrating study focuses on one of its ugliest manifestations, the forcible transferring of indigenous children, and makes a strong case for Canadian complicity in a form of 'cultural genocide'—with implications that reach to the Anglosphere generally, and to some of the worst crimes of the 'civilized world' in the modern era."

—Noam Chomsky

"Tamara Starblanket's work is confident, clear and succinct; her work is ground-breaking and provides us with new ways of looking at how the states treatment of First Nations Peoples has gone unrecognised for its genocidal affect. This work provides an excellent critique on the exclusion of cultural genocide from how genocide is defined in international law."

—Professor Irene Watson
Research Professor of Law, University of South Australia

"Tamara Starblanket's book provides a much needed examination and critique of the 'residential school' system that forcibly transferred Indigenous children from their families, communities, and nations into institutions run by the colonizer state—in this case, Canada. Despite the fact that the United Nations 1948 Convention on Genocide explicitly includes 'forcibly transferring children of the group to another group' in its definition of 'genocide,' there are those who deny that the colonial 'civilizing' project amounted to genocide. Starblanket demonstrates that the residential schools in fact aimed at destroying the most intimate level of Indigenous life—the child-parent relation—employing brutal beatings, solitary confinement and other horrible punishments, often resulting in children's deaths. The goal of the schools was to prevent Indigenous societies from perpetuating themselves. Though officially repudiated, the residential schools produced a continuing social and institutional legacy. Starblanket's work brings this history and its legacy effects to our awareness and shows that 'the road home' requires an emphasis on Indigenous self-determination."

—Peter d'Errico
Professor of Law, University of Massachusetts

"Tamara Starblanket has skillfully taken on one of the most difficult and contentious issues, genocide. With intellectual courage and determination, she has approached the issue from the perspective of a Cree woman, scholar, and attorney who has first-hand knowledge of the deadly and destructive intergenerational impacts of Canada's domination and dehumanization of Original Nations and Peoples."

—Steven T. Newcomb (Shawnee, Lenape), author
Pagans in the Promised Land: Decoding the Christian Doctrine of Discovery

SUFFER THE LITTLE CHILDREN

Genocide, Indigenous Nations and the Canadian State

by

Tamara Starblanket

Clarity Press, Inc

ISBN: 978-0-9986947-7-1

EBOOK ISBN: 978-0-9986947-8-8

In-house editor: Diana G. Collier

Cover: R. Jordan P. Santos

Photo credit: University of Alberta Libraries

Library of Congress Cataloging-in-Publication Data

Names: Starblanket, Tamara, author.

Title: Suffer the little children : genocide, indigenous children, and the
Canadian state / by Tamara Starblanket ; foreword by Ward Churchill.

Description: Atlanata, GA. : Clarity Press, Inc., 2018. | Includes
bibliographical references. |

Identifiers: LCCN 2018007845 (print) | LCCN 2018008085 (ebook) | ISBN
9780998694788 | ISBN 9780998694771

Subjects: LCSH: Indigenous children--Legal status, laws, etc.--Canada. |
Children and genocide--Canada. | Genocide (International law) | Crimes
against humanity--Law and legislation. | Convention on the Prevention and
Punishment of the Crime of Genocide (1948 December 9)

Classification: LCC KE7722.I58 (ebook) | LCC KE7722.I58 S73 2018 (print) |
DDC 342.7108/72083--dc23

LC record available at https://lccn.loc.gov/2018007845

Clarity Press, Inc.
2625 Piedmont Rd. NE, Ste. 56
Atlanta, GA. 30324 , USA
http://www.claritypress.com

TABLE OF CONTENTS

FIGURES

ACKNOWLEDGMENTS

Ay-ay kinanâskomitin to our Creation, our Mother Earth, and our Ancestors and our Future Generations. *Ay-ay kinanâskomitin* to the Elders for your love of our future generations and for your commitment to our right of self-determination as the Original Nations on our Great Turtle Island. *Ay-ay kinanâskomitin* to my late son, Kihiw, for being a guiding light and my source of inspiration when it was unbearable and immensely painful in my life. Special acknowledgement of the children who suffered and passed on in the residential institutions and to my late family. It was the tremendous loss of my late family that inspired me to study and examine the legal question of colonialism and genocide. Thank you for helping me to turn the trauma of your loss into something positive. I could not have finished this task without your help and guidance as my Ancestors.

Ay-ay kinanâskomitin, Great Spirit, for saving my life again and again, and for carrying me through the pain and deep grief with which I've lived for most of my time in this world. Thanks as well to those from the four directions of Great Turtle Island upon whose prayers and love I leaned when my task seemed impossible, and especially when I was sick in 2011 and 2014.

Ay-ay kinanâskomitin to my children and grandchildren and to my late sibling's children (my nieces and nephews) for being my inspiration when it seemed impossible. This is for your children's children.

Ay-ay kinanâskomitin to Lazare and Roberta Whiskeyjack for also adopting me as your daughter years ago, shortly after my father passed on. And to the Whiskeyjack family, all of whom prayed for and loved me during a period of tremendous pain and grief. There were truly times I doubt I'd have made it, had it not been for the care with which you've enfolded my children and me.

Ay-ay kinanâskomitin to Stan Fuller, my adopted Dad, for

adopting me as your daughter, cheering me on through the years, and caring for me like you do. God bless you for being who you are and for your kindness and strength.

Ay-ay kinanâskomitin to Uncle Paul Morin and Aunty Brenda Starblanket. for being there when things were extremely difficult and for being a rock when our family passed on to the spirit world. Your support is appreciated and does not go unnoticed for being the Elders in our family.

Ay-ay kinanâskomitin to the Daniels family for your support and prayers. In particular, to Tina, Kelly and Reanna for instructing the doctors not to take me off of life support. For your prayers and songs when I was faced with passing on, and special mention goes to Terry Daniels, Darwin Daniels, Michelle, Daniels and Jason Daniels.

I'm grateful to a number of others as well, among them Darren Cook, Curtis Ahenakew, Brian Lee, Beatrice Ironstand, Betty Thomas, Colby Tootoosis, Mylan Tootoosis, Joan Delorme, Patricia Bekkattla, Anna Flaminio, Seema Ahluwalia, Avery Ledoux and Leanna Paul and Wanita Bird for encouraging and often helping me to continue when I was ready to quit.

My gratitude extends to the Ahtahkakoop Cree Nation for funding the first part of my master of laws, and to the Native Education College for allowing me the time to complete it. In that vein, acknowledgement is due to the University of Saskatchewan, College of Law for its financial support, a matter facilitated by Professor Barbara von Tigerstrom, the Graduate Chair, and her predecessors: professors Paul Chartrand, Mark Carter, and Martin Phillipson.

Clearly, since the book has evolved from a thesis prepared in fulfilment of the requirements for a master of law degree, those from whose input I've benefitted include my thesis supervisor, Professor Dwight Newman, and the members of my advisory committee, professors Isobel Findley and Wanda Wiegers. Thank you for your tough questions. *Ay-ay kinanâskomitin* to Professor Irene Watson of the University of South Australia for your role as the external reviewer of my thesis. Your insights into the workings of "raw law" provide invaluable analytical tools for use not only by your own Nunga Peoples of Welpulprap, but those of the Great Turtle Island, and indeed all Original Nations.

As with all such efforts, *Suffer the Little Children* could not have been written without considerable input from others. First of all in this regard, *ay-ay kinanâskomitin* to Doris Greyeyes for being such a wonderful teacher and mentor. Your ability to think on so many levels and maneuvre for our right of self-determination in your work is inspiring.

No less significant were the criticisms and suggestions of the students who were part of the Aboriginal Justice Studies Program, with whom I engaged in continuous discussions during the initial drafting of my thesis. In particular, my position as a college instructor allowed me to "field test" the legal arguments herein by making them in the classroom, a form of "peer review" that led to a number of refinements. I'm deeply appreciative of the contributions made by those who participated in these processes.

At another level, there are those upon whose work I've consciously built, and with whom I've been fortunate enough to have had the opportunity to interact directly. Here, the late Cuban diplomat and law professor, Miguel Alfonso-Martinez, deserves special mention for his critical feedback and lucid explanations of the relationship between colonialism and genocide, and both in terms of their dehumanization, demonization, and consequent destruction of colonized peoples. His insights have provided much of the bedrock upon which first my thesis, and now the book, can be said to stand.

Ay-ay kinanâskomitin to Sharon Venne for your wisdom, guidance, and patience and for your work in the protection of our Treaty in international law and our right to self-determination in international law and for modelling a true Indigenous lawyer to me. You are an amazing scholar and lawyer, a mentor to many.

Ay-ay kinanâskomitin to Gordon Lee for raising the issue of "brainwashing," as evidenced by the fact that so many of our young people no longer think in our languages and speak them. Thank you for driving home the point that this specifically intended result of residential schooling is patently genocidal in its implications. Thanks as well to the "unknown man" from Treaty Four Territory who helped me identify this as a metaphor properly used in proving the case against the Canadian state.

Ay-ay kinanâskomitin to Ward Churchill for your extensive expertise on genocide and for honouring me by writing the foreword to the book. Your scholarship, too, is remarkable, and foundational to the legal and other arguments advanced herein. Thank you for the force and clarity of your work, and for inspiring me to follow your lead by never backing down.

Ay-ay kinanâskomitin to Steven Newcomb for your ground-breaking work in cognitive legal theory and its application to the domination and dehumanization of our Original Nations. Your concepts are integral to the book. They provide a powerful tool for our Peoples and Nations to critically address and challenge colonialism and genocide.

Ay-ay kinanâskomitin to Professor Roland Chrisjohn of St. Thomas University for so thoroughly refuting the victim-blaming therapeutic model known as the "Reservation School Syndrome" and reinterpreting the mental harm suffered by Indigenous children in such "total institutions" as a dimension of genocide. Thank you for providing still another cornerstone.

Ay-ay kinanâskomitin to Professor Natsu Taylor Saito of Georgia State University for your answers to my questions about customary international law, especially as it bears upon colonialism and genocide.

Ay-ay kinanâskomitin as well to Professor Peter D'errico of the University of Massachusetts for your consistent support of my work, and to University of Chicago professors John Quigley and Mathew Lippman for your answers to my queries about understandings of genocide in conventional international law.

All that said, no one named above bears responsibility for my thinking, and less still for the manner in which I've chosen to express it. While I hope and believe it will prove worthy not only of the faith those individuals and many more have placed in me, any errors or other shortcomings to be found in *Suffer the Little Children* are mine and mine alone.

Dedication

This book is dedicated to my late son Kihiw. Thank you for being my son and choosing me as your mother for a short time on this earth. You inspire forgiveness, compassion and great healing in my life.

It is also dedicated to my family who passed into the Spirit World as a result of the genocide: my late father, Baptiste, and my late mother, Irene, who was forced to attend the Prince Albert Indian Residential School, as well as my late sisters Petrina, Candace and my late brother Tuck. So, too, my late grandfather, Jonas, who was forced to attend the Thunderchild Indian Residential School; my late grandmother Annie, who was forced to attend the Birtle Indian Residential School; my late aunt, Gloria, and uncles, Vern and Clifford, all of whom were forced to attend the Prince Albert Indian Residential School. It is also dedicated to my late brother, Kevin, who found us in 1991 after being raised away from us. Finally to my late step-father, Robert, and my late adopted brother, Jeremy.

This book is dedicated to the Original Nations and Peoples of Great Turtle Island whose children were and continue to be forcibly removed from them in the name of "civilization," to the memory of the countless children claimed by brutal colonial violence during their years-long confinement in Canada's residential schools, to the victims who continue to endure the long-term impacts of their experiences in those institutions, and to their children, who now suffer the traumatic effects of their parents' intractable traumas. Such is the nature of genocide that the ravages visited upon those targeted are known to be passed along through generations. Special mention goes to our children that leave this Earth too soon. Bradley Hendry, among many other children, you will be remembered by the ones who love you. Hence, this book is dedicated most of all to our coming generations in the hope that it will contribute to creation of circumstances enabling them and their Peoples to once again know peace.

Finally, it is dedicated to the late Professor Miguel Alfonso-Martinez of Cuba, whose unequivocal commitment in asserting the inherent right to self-determination of Indigenous Peoples remains a shining beacon to us all.

| Foreword |

RECONCEPTUALIZING THE LAW AND HISTORY OF INDIGENOUS PEOPLES' GENOCIDE BY CANADA

Tamara Starblanket is the sole survivor of the ravages visited upon three successive generations of her family by the Canadian settler-state. Her life has, from its earliest moments and in the most intimate ways, been shaped by the perpetual atrocity of Canada's internal colonization not only of her own *Nehiyaw* (Cree) people, but those of every First Nation within the vast territory over which it has come to assert dominion. The effects of such subjugation have been and remain catastrophic—perhaps, in a real sense, unimaginably so to those who've not experienced them.

Resistance, like courage, takes many forms. While the iconographies of armed struggle and confrontational modes of nonviolent civil disobedience predominate in the popular imagination, the bedrock of its enactment will be found in far quieter but no less adamantly determined refusals of the oppressed to accept the impositions of their oppressors. For indigenous peoples, this has been manifested first, foremost, and indispensably in the perpetuation—despite multifaceted, sustained, and truly vicious efforts by the settler-state to expunge such knowledge—of time-honored understandings as to who they are and why, and the clarification not just of their experienced historical and present reality, but of the political and legal nature of same in a national and international context.

Starblanket's resistance has followed the latter course, undertaking the daunting task of reframing the terms and logic employed by the colonizers to disguise and purportedly legitimate their past actions and resulting entrapment of Indigenous Peoples and territories in the contemporary Canadian settler-state to provide a clear vision, both experiential and politico-legal, of Canada's culpability for the crime of genocide, as evidenced in Canada's forced removal of Indigenous children into the residential schools system.

The manner in which she employs the term "genocide" is entirely consistent with the meaning posited by Raphaël Lemkin when he coined it in 1944, i.e., any policy adopted for purposes of bringing about the dissolution of an identified human group, as such. Her usage also comports with the legal definition codified in the second article of the United Nations' 1948 Convention on Prevention and Punishment of the Crime of Genocide She necessarily restores equal weight to all five of the criteria delineated under Article II as acts of genocide—four of them nonlethal—thereby giving short shrift to the colonial intelligentsia's campaign over the past seven decades to peddle the misconception that "real" or "true" genocide is at issue only in cases where mass murder has occurred.

Starblanket's reclamation of Article II in its entirety—and in particular the genocidal acts described in subparagraphs (e) and (b)—requires her rejection of the subterfuge wherein successive generations of scholars have endeavored to reclassify the nonlethal modes of genocide enumerated therein as "ethnocide" or "cultural genocide", an ostensibly lesser and in any case uncodified offense to which no criminal culpability is formally attached. As she points out, the "qualitative distinctions" supposedly distinguishing ethnocide from "actual genocide" are a carefully contrived illusion; Lemkin coined *both* terms on the same page of his 1944 book, *Axis Rule in Occupied Europe*, while observing that they are synonyms. Far from being something different, moreover, Lemkin held that "cultural genocide," as he termed what revisionists now refer to as ethnocide, has been the crime's historically normative form, with perpetration by way of straightforward physical extermination the exception.

Further, again following Lemkin's lead, she contextualizes the crime of genocide as a necessary product of colonialism, focusing on the relationship between one nation and another (or others) and the repective claims to territory involved, rather than by the notion that the colonized must be separated from the colonizing power by an open expanse of sea water.

By deploying the words "genocide" and "colonialism" properly, Starblanket validates Sartre's 1967 insights on colonialism's inherently genocidal nature in ways and to an extent surpassing that provided by his own pioneering assessment. This obtains from her focus upon the internal and settler-state modes of colonization and the extent to which that experience replicates that of the "classic" overseas variety based on a *mission civilisatrice* and racial superiority, which has long been accepted as colonialism's *sine qua non* by imperial and anti-imperialist analysts alike.

Starblanket makes no effort to dwell on blatantly exterminatory policies such as—to cite but one example among many—Nova Scotia Governor Edward Cornwallis' payment of bounties for the scalps of Mi'kmaqs and others in 1749-50. Rather, she elects to illuminate what has been elsewhere and aptly described as "the Final Solution to Canada's Indian problem," the insidious policy of "assimilation" through which the "remnants" of First Nations were to be culturally extinguished, and their surviving populations incrementally absorbed into the steadily growing and intractably predatory population of European interlopers, while their territories and rich resources would accrue to the occupying Canadian state, for disposition as it willed.

Her legal exposition centers on Article II(e) of the Genocide Convention, which defines as genocide "any of the following acts committed with intent to destroy, in whole or in part, a national, ethnical, racial or religious group, as such" and in particular subparagraph (e), "Forcibly transferring children of the group to another group", bolstering this by an exposition of the extent to which international customary law views.

To illustrate Canada's culpability in this regard, she concentrates upon its century-long record of compulsorily removing at least 150,000 Indigenous youngsters by official count, many no more than five years of age, from their families, communities, and societies, consigning them to a complex of residential schools, state-sponsored wherein they were subjected for years on end to the degrading brutality of "deculturation" and simultaneously indoctrinated to see themselves—and reality itself—in terms imposed by their colonizers. Since the express goal of this ugly process was to deny Indigenous societies their coming generations, thus eroding their capacity to perpetuate themselves to the point that they'd ultimately "vanish," the case against Canada might considered airtight on the basis of its violation of Article II(e) alone.

Starblanket goes much further, however, demonstrating how the four nonlethal categories of genocidal policy are overlapping, often interactively so. This is to say that in violating Article II(e) as it did, Canada also and knowingly "caus[ed] serious bodily [and] mental harm to members of the [target] group" as a matter of policy, thereby violating Article II(b). Indeed, given that the forced transfer of Indigenous children occurred in the context of broader policies designed to destroy First Nations economies by expropriating their land and resources, leaving most in conditions of destitution so dire as to compel their dispersal—a process imperialist shill Samuel P. Huntington once characterized as "forced-draft urbanization"—Canada's violation of Article II(e) violation can be seen as an integral feature of its overarching violation of Article II(c): "deliberately inflicting on the group conditions of life calculated to bring about its physical destruction in whole of or in part."

This is heavy stuff, about which much more should be said, and Starblanket is unsparing in saying it. She has thereby furthered the struggle for liberation and, for that, she has earned the utmost respect of all who aspire to achieve it.

Tamara Starblanket is what is known as a brave-hearted woman, imbued with a warrior spirit. Although she is certainly young enough to be my daughter, it would be presumptuous of me to refer to her as such. Nor do we share the clan relationship necessary to my being construed as her uncle. I am, however, proud to call her sister, and to thank her.

—Ward Churchill, November 2017

This image of a child on the brick wall of the St. Michael's Residential School in Alert Bay residential school before it was demolished in 2015 depicts the trauma and the forced civilization process. The artwork captures the essence of the destruction inherent in these abominations called "schools"'. **Source: Catherine Grosson, St. Michael's Residential School, Alert Bay, BC. 2015**

THE COLONIZER'S WAY OF GENOCIDE
Confronting the Wall of Evasion and Denial

"I want to get rid of the Indian problem.... Our objective is to continue until there is not a single Indian in Canada that has not been absorbed into the body politic and there is no Indian question."
—Duncan Campbell Scott, Superintendent
Department of Indian Affairs

"The policies adopted by Canada over the years with regard to Indians are not different from the rationale employed by Nazi Germany in its implementation of what it called the "Final Solution." Residential schools were only one element.... [Overall,] the horrors experienced by Indian Nations were no less than those experienced by others."
—Harold Cardinal, survivor

Suffer the Little Children is not a product of "scholarly detachment." It was born of pain, entire lives of it, most immediately my family's and my own. Beyond that, its birth was induced by the suffering of my people as a whole, a suffering shared by each of the peoples indigenous to that portion of North America, our Great Turtle Island, now commonly referred to as "Canada." In every instance, the pain and suffering results from genocidal actions taken against us by the Canadian settler state,[1] as a matter of policy and law for well over a century. Indeed, such policy-driven actions continue at present, albeit in somewhat altered form, and the toll continues to mount.

While other aspects of Canada's "Indian policies" can be seen to fit the definition of genocide,[2] specifically at issue in this book is its century-long program of forcibly removing indigenous children from their families, communities, societies—in sum, from their *Nations*—and placing them for sustained periods in "residential schools" where the stated goal was to strip them of their cultural identities and "remake" them into "end products" deemed useful to Canada's colonizing and ever-growing settler population. To this end, children as young as four were crammed into poorly-heated and -ventilated barracks-type "dormitories," systematically demeaned and degraded, subjected to both physical and psychological torture (including wholesale sexual predation), denied anything that might be called adequate nutrition, medical care, or clothing, and typically impressed into manual labor. The effects were, and of course remain, devastating.

I am the sole member of my birth family still alive. My grandparents, maternal and paternal, as well as my late mother and her siblings, were all forced to spend their formative years in the schools, an experience from which none of them would ever recover. The consequences are perhaps best reflected in the fact that my last sister passed into the Spirit World at age 29. Were they here before me, I would tell them that I know that the immensity of the sense of loss, emptiness and sorrow by which their lives were consumed was not their fault, nor that of the countless others upon whom the same agony was inflicted.

I am a product of this genocidal reality, at least thus far, although I never personally attended a residential school. Like my late sister, however, I've lived my life with the results. And for this reason, then, I am obligated by my own *Nehiyaw* (Cree) tradition to recount the story of what has happened and is *still* happening, so that all can know it for what it was and will always remain. To do so is an honouring, an expression of my love and respect not only for my family, but for the *Nehiyaw*, and for all Indigenous Peoples, our children, their children, and for every coming generation. Accordingly, it is intended as a contribution to the revitalization, and ultimately the liberation of what the late Shuswap leader George Manuel forty years ago described as a "Fourth World" comprised of Indigenous Nations in every region of Mother Earth.[3]

Rubrics of Denial

With formal training in what is called "law", my recounting is undertaken in a particular way, often using language and arguments from that "discourse" to explain Indigenous positions and understandings. This is by no means as straightforward an endeavor as it might seem at first glance, and not simply because the values and corresponding laws embraced by Indigenous peoples are conspicuously absent from international jurisprudence and what passes as "responsible" legal scholarship. While preparing the initial draft of this book as a Master of Laws thesis, I ran head-on into the barriers erected and maintained by Canada's academic gatekeepers to prevent or at least limit exposure of the culpability attending certain actions of the Canadian state, and those of the colonial society.

The thesis-writing process up to the defence was strenuous, as I sought to explain the blocks and traps put in place by state governments to conceal the crime of genocide in the colonization of Indigenous Nations and Peoples' lands and territories. The committee ultimately conceded that genocide was proven, but resisted fundamental aspects of the legal argument. It was suggested that I drop the land issue, and the connection to genocide under the United Nations Genocide Convention (UNGC). In response, I contended that insofar as Canada unquestionably originated and developed as a British colonial project, my proposed examination of the forced transfer of Indigenous children in light of the 1948 Convention on Prevention and Punishment of the Crime of Genocide was entirely appropriate.

While my point was conceded, it was nonetheless suggested that I would be better served to frame my assessment in terms of "human rights violations" rather than genocide. On the second suggestion, I reminded the committee that human rights and genocide are different frameworks. One deals with individual rights and genocide addresses crimes against nations or human groups. It was suggested to delete child welfare from my legal analysis. My response to this proposal was "no" for reasons that should be obvious. Another critical point of contention was "law" or positive law as it is known.

Sharon Venne, Cree lawyer and author of *Our Elders Understand our Rights Evolving International Law and Indigenous Peoples*:[4] has said that colonial laws are "rules and regulations," but not laws in the true sense of the word. Colonial laws are made to be broken. Our "original laws and instruction"[5] are not to be violated, and evidence of this is provided by the changes that are taking place on the earth. For example, if fresh water is depleted by colonial greed, there will be no water left to sustain future generations of Creation. Steven Newcomb in *Pagans in the Promised Land: Decoding the Christian Doctrine of Discovery* shows that western law operates from a view of dominating the land and dehumanizing the original peoples and nations who are in the way of colonialism.[6] This view sets out the essence of colonization and genocide. Ultimately, my final thesis is a *legal* analysis. I had to contend with a thesis committee that did not understand how the positive western colonial view of the world is the problem.

Key to the last position was the claim that doing a "proper" legal analysis would require my taking into account not only international law (the Genocide Convention), but Canada's own genocide statute, and treating them as if they were "equally valid." The Nazi defendants during the Nuremberg trials had taken an identical position—i.e., whatever they'd done had been "purely legal" under Germany's domestic laws.[7] That idea had been unequivocally rejected by the Nuremberg tribunal (on which Canada, as a Commonwealth country, was represented by Britain's Lord Geoffrey Lawrence).[8]

Suffice it to say that the drafting process, as well as the days leading up to my thesis defense, was more grueling still. More than a few of the criticisms and suggestions for "improving" my argument were no less appallingly wrong-headed than those already mentioned, and every one of them had to be countered along the way. However, the committee did concede with an open mind to the legal arguments I had developed and in the end I was successful and received my degree, but by then I'd long-since gained a new appreciation for the truth of Susan Griffin's observation in *A Chorus of Stones* about there being "whole disciplines, institutions, rubrics in [settler] culture which serve as categories of denial."[9] The Canadian version of law, which falls entirely within the rubric of *colonial* law, was already high on my list of such categories, but academic institutions and their assorted disciplines, the teaching of law not least, have now earned a much higher position than they held back in the days when I was still naïve enough to believe that "the pursuit of truth" had something to do with "higher education."

There is of course far more involved in the Canadian academy's deliberate and systematic falsification of genocidal realities than the distortion of international law and legal principles. As Gayatri Chakravorty Spivak has pointed out, "The colonizer constructs himself as he constructs the colony."[10] This is true not only materially and systemically, but in terms of the colonizer's self-concept and the image of this wholly invented "self" that is officially sanctioned and projected. While examples of how the latter is undertaken are seemingly endless, a key in the context of this book is the fashionable "scholarly" contention that Canada at some mysterious point in time became a "postcolonial society."[11]

Whatever else may be meant by the term "postcolonial"—those using it can't even agree on when "the postcolonial era" should be said to have begun,[12] let alone when Canada is supposed to have entered it[13]—because of the relationship of colonialism to genocide, the pretense of Canadian "postcoloniality" clearly serves as a useful polemical tool with which to confuse the issue, providing a basis upon which to brand charges that Canada committed genocide against Indigenous Peoples "controversial," or to deny them altogether.

The technique fits hand in glove with that adopted by the Canadian government over the past twenty years (i.e., after the evidence had become overwhelming), which consists of conceding that "in the past" a limited range of "wrongs," invariably described as "tragedies" rather than as criminal acts stemming from an even more criminal policy, were in fact done to numerous Indigenous individuals, most notably children confined in the schools.[14] The crown jewel in this regard was the 2008 "apology to former students of Indian Residential Schools" delivered "on behalf of the Canadian Government" by Prime Minister Stephen Harper, wherein the treatment suffered by those who'd survived the ordeal was minimized as amounting only to "abuse" and "neglect," and an agreement arrived at two years earlier was touted as marking "a new beginning" (thereby implying that it should be seen as wiping the slate clean).[15]

As a member of his own staff later revealed, "the best that can be said of Harper's apology is that it was a strategic attempt to kill the story" of the residential schools once and for all,[16] or, failing that, to contain it. The mechanism employed for such purposes was, as Harper indicated, the 2006 Indian Residential School Settlement Agreement, implemented on September 19, 2007.[17] While the agreement's main selling point was that those who'd been forced to attend the schools would receive monetary compensation for resulting damages, the amounts paid have averaged only $26,000 per individual.[18] Predictably, in exchange for even this pittance, each recipient was required to relinquish his/her right to pursue further legal action against either the government or any of the various churches paid to run the schools.[19]

With much fanfare, the pre-existing, state-sponsored "Aboriginal Healing Foundation" was also allotted an increased subsidy with which to provide therapy to the many survivors psychologically ravaged by their experiences in the schools. Exactly what this was actually supposed to accomplish is rather mysterious,[20] since the sorts of trauma involved tend to require long-term treatment and the foundation's funding was abruptly cut off in 2010.[21] In substance, the gesture towards "healing" added up to little more than another public relations exercise of the sort often "used by colonizers [to put a] happy face on colonialism,"[22] although in this instance the idea was to reinforce the image of Canada's colonizing settler state as a "postcolonial" democracy characterized by the benevolence of its "pluralism" and concern for the wellbeing of even the most oppressed sectors of its purported citizenry.[23]

To put flesh on the bones of this governmentally-desired storyline, the Settlement Agreement included one other major component: The establishment in 2009 of a so-called Truth and Reconciliation Commission (TRC).[24] Charged with conducting the research necessary to compile a definitive record of the residential schools, detailing their effects on students confined in them, and recommending steps to be taken by the perpetrator state in order to "restore a healthy relationship" with its victims—all in a mere five years—the three-person commission was not only far too small to fulfill its lofty-sounding mandate in the time allowed, its framing of the issues has from the outset been consistent with that preferred by the government (of which it was formally a department, and upon which it was correspondingly dependent for its funding).[25]

It's therefore unsurprising that in its final report, a summary of which was recently published, the TRC adheres to the federal script in every significant respect.[26] There is, for example, no real discussion of the violation of our international Treaties by the forcible removals. Instead, Indigenous Nations are presented as if we're somehow "naturally" subparts of Canada, and "reconciliation" as requiring merely that the state permit us to "enjoy" a slightly greater degree of autonomy within the framework of its overarching authority.[27] While the recommended relationship remains unmistakably that of colonizer and colonized, it is described as "Aboriginal self-determination," thereby reinforcing the illusion of Canada's "postcoloniality."[28] The solution is to implement the "United Nations Declaration on the Rights of Indigenous Peoples" as a "framework for reconciliation."[29] The problem with this approach is that critical analysis is absent about the Canadian state's goal of the destruction of our Nations by the entrenchment of its longstanding goal of appropriating our land and affirming Canada's so-called "territorial integrity" and how it accomplishes this end by "consuming and devouring" our Nations into its colonial body politic through laws and policies framed as the achievement of "reconciliation".[30]

Similarly, the TRC trots out the term "cultural genocide" on the very first page of its summary to describe the purpose and effects of the residential schools.[31] In fact, the commissioners' recommendations lead directly *away* from genocide, since their proposed "remedies" center all but exclusively upon redressing violations of the human rights of individuals rather than of the group rights inhering in the Indigenous Nations explicitly targeted for destruction through the forcible removal of their children (which is to say, their future).[32]

It's true that the commission places a certain weight on increased federal funding to support the revitalization of Indigenous languages and cultures,[33] but nowhere is it suggested that the still-living officials who oversaw the program during its final phase should be prosecuted on charges of, say, criminal conspiracy and crimes of genocide.[34] Nor is it proposed that Canada pay anything like the sort of reparations paid by the German Federal Republic to Israel as a result of the Nazi judeocide.[35] All told, it's impossible to avoid the conclusion that, irrespective of the intentions of individual commissioners, the TRC has produced a report that is very far from the truth. Ultimately, it can only serve as yet another brick in the elaborate wall of evasion and denial behind which the Canadian settler state and the society it represents seek to conceal the reality of their genocide against the Indigenous Peoples of Turtle Island.

Beyond the Wall

This book is meant to serve as a battering ram in which to hammer through the wall of denial. In keeping with its origin as a legal thesis, it relies heavily on international law in making its case. The material upon which I've drawn is consistent with Indigenous understandings, or can and should be interpreted that way. This is to say that I've reversed the standard academic procedure of privileging "western" thinkers, invoking them only where they've attained validation through the belated realization of things Indigenous Peoples have known all along.[36]

This work is a legal analysis of the Canadian state's legislated forcible transfer of Indigenous Peoples' children from their Nations into residential schools and child welfare systems, which is culpable under the Genocide Convention.[37] The colonial destructive framework guides the state in its domination over Indigenous Nations. Colonial laws compel the forcible transferring of Indigenous children. The intent is to destroy, in whole or in part, a protected human group. It is also worded in policy as the government's goal to "absorb"[38] or assimilate the original national identities into the Canadian "body politic"[39] (state and society) by the removal of Indigenous Peoples from our land. This oppressive process is the two phase process of genocide described by Raphael Lemkin.[40] In this regard, the national pattern of the oppressed (Original Nations/Indigenous Nations) is forcibly indoctrinated into the national pattern of the oppressor (Canadian state) through massive acts of genocide. Lemkin was referring to the identity of *nations* in his analysis of genocide._

The greatest challenge to overcome in proving the crime of genocide is the oppressive dominating and dehumanizing framework internationally and domestically infested with the rubric of denial. The challenges exist in international laws that conceal the atrocities of colonial invasion globally. James

Crawford in his "Foreword" to Antony Anghie's *Imperialism, Sovereignty and the Making of International Law* determines that historical relationships between Indigenous and non-Indigenous Peoples have an "underlying pattern of domination."[41] Antony Anghie conveys how international laws "legitimized colonial exploitation"[42] and "developed many mechanisms to prevent any claims for colonial reparations."[43]

Lemkin, in his original conception of genocide, understood cultural genocide as a process of colonialism in his analysis of the Nazi occupation and invasion of the lands and territories of Eastern European countries. Given this, Lemkin's original conception of the crime did not make it to the final form of genocide recognized today. The *Travaux Préparatoires* is a compilation of the discussions and debates that took place prior to the ratification of the Genocide Convention in international law. The deletion of cultural genocide as a crime in international law reveals the domination of state interests.[44] Current claims that residential school are "cultural genocide" cannot be addressed as a crime of genocide in international law.

Integral to the legal question is the "*civilizing*" criterion that requires and purports to justify domination and dehumanization.[45] Western law and scholarship is loaded with terminology that downgrades and dehumanizes Indigenous Peoples. The invocation of words like *tribe*, *savage* and *heathen* is an attempt to dehumanize peoples and deflect attention away from our identity as Nations. Indigenous Nations are made invisible and debased rather than elevated as purported by the "civilizing" experience of colonialism. The "civilizing missions"[46] of European invaders such as Great Britain justified overrunning and claiming the lands/territories of Indigenous nations by declaring us as less than human. Designations of violent descriptors (i.e. savage) which are then used as a basis for claiming the original nations were not sovereign,[47] in turn provided the justifications for the legislated state removal and demonization of scores of Indigenous children away from loving families, communities, and ultimately their nations.

These forcible removals have led to the catastrophic trauma or long term, ongoing impacts that are prevalent in Indigenous societies and nations to this day. The main effect has been the alienation from, and, in the worst case scenario, termination of Indigenous children's distinct identities as Nations and most importantly from their territories. *Anishinaabe, Dene* and *Nehiyaw* identities, like those of other Original Nations, embody a relationship with Mother Earth, original laws, languages, cultures, spirituality and most importantly, a healthy conception of an Indigenous human identity that is directly dependent on the Earth and mandates the maintenance of that relationship. Indigenous children are the future generations of Indigenous nations and their forcible transfer facilitates the destruction of those peoples/ nations by causing them to be socialized or indoctrinated into the language, culture, and traditions of the colonizing society.

The discussions that led to the adoption of the *Convention on the Prevention and Punishment of the Crime of Genocide* (hereinafter UNGC) highlight the state government's colonial framework. As previously declared, the *Travaux* underscores that colonialism or *cultural genocide* is at the root of the odious scourge called "genocide". The Polish delegate, Mr. Katz-Suchy expressed opinion on this matter by stating that: "inclusion in the Convention of an article relating to cultural genocide… would have a far-reaching beneficial effect especially in so far as colonial and dependant peoples were concerned."[48] It was also determined that, "narrow nationalist and imperialist motives, had been successful"[49] in diminishing the concept of genocide. The diminishment of the crime has allowed for "loopholes of escape for perpetrators of the crime."[50] Domestic implementation of the Genocide Convention in its penal code has allowed the Canadian state's unabated forcible removal of Indigenous children, undetected by international scrutiny. The limited definition of genocide in the Criminal Code of Canada permits this genocide to continue as there are no legal avenues to protect those most vulnerable to the crime. The ability of the UNGC to punish and prevent destruction of Indigenous Nations by state perpetrators from the horrors of the crime of genocide is therefore called into question. Chapters One and Four will examine how this was achieved and why.

Another issue concerns the high threshold required to prove there had been specific intent on the part of the perpetrators. The advisory committee questioned me on this point, and I maintained my position by explaining that the specific intent—in addition to the outright statements of policymakers such as Duncan Campbell Scott and later acknowledgement by Prime Minister Stephen Harper—could be drawn from the massive and ongoing destruction that was its inescapably visible result. It is contended that the specific intent requirement actually serves the denial of genocide due to its difficulty to prove. As will be discussed, the high standard of specific intention thwarts Indigenous Peoples/Nations' ability to prove intention with the result of making it nearly impossible to show genocide in the non-Indigenous rule of international law. The child welfare system is a case in point. The residential school system destroyed not just the family integrity and the transmission of the national identity to the generations upon whom it was enacted, but also the ability of the succeeding "civilized" generations to parent. The direct result is the continuing forcible removals in the child welfare system. Having caused this, the state then develops the standards ("inability to parent") for removal of Indigenous children into foster care homes. Traumatized and dysfunctional parenting patterns are invoked to forcibly remove our children into the present day child welfare system.

No effort by the Canadian state is put into assisting the victims of genocide (parents) of the residential schools to re-learn *Dene* or *Anishinaabe* parenting skills before the birth of children. The result is a continuing destructive process that demonizes the Indigenous parents for lack of parenting skills through no fault of their own. Children continue to be forcibly transferred away from Indigenous parents and demonized, isolated and destroyed. Ensuing generations of these Indigenous children are then further socialized and indoctrinated into the dominant colonial society. The goal of assimilation or absorption into the colonial society or (body politic) has not changed over time and the result of the ongoing removal at this stage is still the same.

Even though cultural genocide and forced assimilation were deemed to be not criminal, this book will show how the end product of the "colonial project" serves as evidence of that crime. It accomplishes the task by unpacking the destructive colonial framework under which the forcible removals occur and by revealing the rhetorical euphemisms that conceal the genocide. The forcible transferring of Indigenous Peoples children will be examined from a "cognitive"[51] lens of domination and dehumanization that unpacks the destructive framework of colonialism that came to be embedded in international law. It is necessary because the euphemistic colonial language employed to benignly characterize as civilizing what was forcibly imposed on and horrifically experienced by Indigenous Peoples' children conceals the reality of the genocidal harm against the Original Nations in the Western Hemisphere and globally.

It should also be stated that my interpretive approach, in common with that of Indigenous Peoples the world over, is consistently and unequivocally straightforward. In effect, we rather ironically share with U.S. Supreme Court Justice Antonin Scalia the view that, "Words have meaning. And their meaning doesn't change," at least never for such cynical reasons as their deployment for political advantage or expediency.[52] This is, or should be, *especially* true with respect to the words with which law is articulated. Correspondingly, I extend no patience to those who've sought to parse, distort, and deform the meaning of the term "genocide," always for purposes of limiting its applicability and frequently to the point of twisting it into the veritable opposite of itself.

My first chapter, "Naming the Crime,"[53] therefore begins by laying out the definition codified in the 1948 Convention on Prevention and Punishment of the Crime of Genocide, which, as a recognized "peremptory norm" (*jus cogens*) of international law, is legally binding on *all* states, irrespective of their domestic statutes.[54] From there, the definition provided by Raphaël Lemkin when he coined the term in 1944 is examined, as are the ways in which it was narrowed during the process of drafting the Genocide Convention over the next four years. Finally, I review subsequent international jurisprudence as well as the unremitting efforts by state governments, such as Canada, both to nullify Lemkin's foundational explanation of "the incomparable crime,"[55] and to narrow the resulting legal definition of genocide beyond recognition.

The second chapter, titled "The Horror," provides a brief historical and present day overview of Canada's policy of systematically and forcibly removing Indigenous children from their families, communities, and Nations, what was done to them during the years of their "educational" confinement in settler institutions, and the ongoing effects of the residential schools, not only on those who directly experienced them, but on their children, their children's children, and their Nations. It also examines the present day forcible removals in the child welfare system. Each aspect of the process is assessed both on the basis of Lemkin's seminal formulation, and through the lens of the definitional criteria set forth in the Genocide Convention shortly thereafter. Canada's forced transfer of Indigenous children to the schools is also situated within the broader strategy of genocide pursued even now by the settler state against Original Nations.

The third chapter, "Coming to Grips with Canada as a Colonizing State," addresses the question of why the Canadian settler society has so persistently displayed what Robert Jay Lifton famously, though rather superficially, described as "the genocidal mentality" (and has consequently conducted itself as it has).[56] Here, the work of figures such as James Blaut, Jean Paul Sartre, Frantz Fanon, Aime Cesaire is drawn upon in ways which reinforce and sometimes amplify that of critical intellectuals like Steven Newcomb, Sharon Venne, Ward Churchill, Robert A. Williams Jr., and the late John Mohawk in identifying the nature and root cause of what the late Lenape (Delaware) scholar Jack D. Forbes termed "the wétiko disease" (or "dis-ease," as Churchill would have it).[57] In particular, to address the euphemisms and genocide denial, a model is created to explain genocide from the reality of what really went down. Thus, it compels the western reader or genocide denier to view the reality of the destruction that Indigenous children, hence entire Nations on Turtle Island, have endured at the hands of the colonizer state.

Chapter 4, "Smoke and Mirrors," is concerned with the ways in which Canada has sought to evade the burden of guilt arising from its historical and continuing perpetration of genocide. The conceptual subterfuges touched upon earlier in this introduction are explored in greater depth, and the legalistic maneuvers the settler state has undertaken for the same purpose are subjected to substantive critique. With the validity of such barriers debunked, the way is open to apply the *actual* law to Canada, a "prosecution" that takes into account several of the hurdles—e.g., the matter of "specific intent"—misguidedly established in international jurisprudence concerning genocide. These last are overcome by the recorded statements of responsible settler officials and other documents as well as international legal precedent. Canada thus stands essentially self-convicted of committing "the crime of crimes."[58]

Finally, in my conclusion, "The Way Ahead," I take stock of where we presently find ourselves and offer what I see as Indigenous Peoples' only real alternative to allowing, or assisting in, completion of the genocidal processes Canada long since set in motion. On the other hand, we can wander down the path of least resistance, acquiescing in the subordinate status assigned us by the settler-state, collaborating in the administration of our designated internal colonies while our Peoples are increasingly assimilated into the settler society and our cultures undergo a final phase of dissolution. On the other, we can refuse to engage in this sort of "autogenocide,"[59] struggling instead to assert our inherent right to self-determination, a right guaranteed to *all* Peoples under international law,[60] thereby positioning ourselves to rebuild and sustain our Nations on our own terms. The latter option, it seems to me, is the sole route to "recovery" from what has been done to us.

A Few Comments on Style and Terminology

It will have already been observed that I capitalize the words "Indigenous" and, in that connection, "People(s)" and "Nation(s)." As regards "Indigenous," I do so for the same reason that "Canadian," "Quebecois," and the like are capitalized,"[61] Were I not to capitalize the "I" in Indigenous it would thus require that I *de*capitalize all other such identifiers (e.g., "Quebeçois"). Particular rights and legal standings are recognized in international law as inhering both in "peoples" and in "nations," a fact I choose to emphasize by capitalizing the words whenever a Fourth World People/Nation is at issue.[62] Since this book is written for my people (*Nehiyaw,* and other Original Nations), at times I address them in this work. As well, I will utilize the first and third person at different times, depending on which form of communication works best.

I use the terms "judeocide" or *Sho'ah* when referring specifically to the Nazi genocide of European Jews.[63] This is because Jews were by no means the only "human group" upon whom genocide was inflicted by the Nazis. Indeed, there was a "mosaic of victims," notably the Poles and several other Slavic peoples.[64] Even in the Wannsee Protocol and subsequent directives implementing the *Endlösung* (Final Solution), Gypsies (Romani) were explicitly targeted right along with the Jews, and received the same treatment.[65] Accordingly, whenever I refer to "the Nazi genocide," my reference is to *all* those who suffered Nazi efforts to eradicate them.

It will perhaps be noticed that I use the term "Original Nations" rather than "First Nations," a unique designation which the Canadian state appears to have preferred rather than the normative "indigenous," which I use here—although Newcomb utilizes the term "Original" in his work, contending that the words "indigenous peoples" peoples mean "dominated peoples."[66] I *never* employ the word "tribe" in referring to an Indigenous People's nation.[67] Or "Native" (or "native") and "Aboriginal" (or "aboriginal"), other than in direct quotes. Nor, with regard to Peoples Indigenous to the Great Turtle Island, do

I use the terms "Indian," "American Indian," or the monstrous contraction, "Amerind."[68] On these matters, I trust that the record of anthropology, a discipline literally born of colonialism and the source of most of the terminology I reject, provides a more than ample explanation.[69]

My practice of referring wherever possible to Indigenous Peoples by their *own* nation's names rather than those assigned to them by their colonizers follows in very much the same vein. Since the book is written in English and the names are from other languages, they are italicized, other than in the relatively few instances where a People's actual name has entered standard English. Where the two differ, the actual name is in first usage, followed by the colonially-imposed term in parentheses (e.g., "*Nehiyaw* (Cree)"). At the same time, in the remainder of the book I will refrain from using the term commonly applied by Indigenous Peoples to the settlers—*moonias* —mentioning it here only to indicate that we have our own connotation-laden language with respect to the settlers.[70]

Finally, Some Anticipated Criticisms

Certain criticisms are so predicable that I feel quite comfortable in heading them off at the pass. First among these is that my comparing Canada's "Indian policies" to certain of those implemented by the Nazis against those they viewed as racial/cultural inferiors "diminishes the memory" of the Nazis' victims.[71] In effect, this is to claim that the Nazis' genocidal policies were in every respect "incomparable,"[72] and thus that the fate of those victimized is unique.[73] Any suggestion to the contrary is cast as "disrespect" for the victims.[74] My response is that any such claim to uniqueness can be made only by denying the suffering of all others, and that denial of others' pain is a *cardinal* disrespect. Clearly, it's not me who's seeking to deny either the reality or the magnitude of someone else's misery, least of all that of those victimized by the Nazis. That I acknowledge it is evident in the very fact of my making comparisons to Nazi policies.

Some or all of a range of "technical concerns" will almost certainly be voiced as criticisms, mainly in an effort to bolster the "uniqueness" argument rejoined in the preceding paragraph. To the extent that these center on questions of scale, proportionality, mode, and the like, I'm content to simply refer readers to historian David E. Stannard's essay, "Uniqueness as Denial," wherein they are thoroughly demolished.[75] Criticisms centering upon questions of whether the forced transfer of Indigenous children by Canada "really" fits the definition of genocide codified in international law, including the issue of "specific intent," will be addressed in Chapters 1 and 4, along with efforts to redefine genocide exclusively in terms of direct killing (in other words, as an especially egregious variety of mass murder).

Another line of criticism, some of which I've already heard, concerns my comparisons of Canada's residential school policies to those implemented by the United States during the same period. It should be recalled that when would-be cabinet minister Nicholas Flood Davin submitted the 1879 report that prompted Canada's policy of forcibly transferring Indigenous children to such facilities, his recommendations were made after consulting with U.S. officials and were closely patterned after their preexisting model of "Indian boarding schools" (also known as "industrial schools").[76] It's hardly necessary to take my word for this, as it was openly acknowledged by Prime Minister John A. McDonald in an 1883 address to the Canadian House of Commons.[77] That Canada is and has always been in important respects a follower of the U.S.—a junior partner, if not its *de facto* "step-child"—is simply a reality, no matter how uncomfortable it might be for the colonizer to admit. I am no more inclined to cater to their chauvinistic desire to evade this unpleasant truth than I am their efforts to deny their country's perpetration of genocide against Indigenous Peoples.

| Chapter One |

NAMING THE CRIME
Defining Genocide in International Law

"Genocide is genocide,
no matter what form it takes
and no matter what you call it."[1]
—Sharon H. Venne

Deeply contentious is the definition and concept of genocide. When the term was first being defined by Raphaël Lemkin's monumental work, *Axis Rule in Occupied Europe*[2] in 1944, the Nazi regime was colonizing Eastern Europe in its quest for territory and world domination. The *United Nations Convention on the Prevention and Punishment of the Crime of Genocide*[3] (hereinafter UNGC) was born from Lemkin's conception of the crime. The draft discussions at the United Nations leading up to the recognition of the crime in international law is quite telling. They provide the background for the legal analysis and the legal applications that will follow in a later application of the law. I will discuss the basic elements of genocide, and finally, in naming genocide and defining the crime, it will be necessary to elaborate on the colonial invasion of other peoples' lands and territories.

The anti-colonial factor and the debates leading up to the final vote of the UNGC help to define the legal concept.

Origination of the Term

Known as the "father"[4] of the Genocide Convention, Raphaël Lemkin struggled to have "his concept of genocide as a legal instrument"[5] protected despite attempts to undermine his concept. Lemkin coined the term by combining the "Greek word *genos* (race, tribe) and the Latin *cide* (killing)."[6] While the concept of genocide was created to describe Nazi occupation and invasion, Samantha Power writes that Lemkin was unwavering that "'genocide' not be equated with Hitler's Final Solution."[7] William Schabas explains that Lemkin understood the crime could only be committed against "'national groups' rather than against 'groups' in general."[8] However, the definition was broad in that it encompassed not only physical and biological destruction but also cultural destruction.[9] Genocide is directed against national identities or "nations," not at individual people. Lemkin wrote, "[b]y 'genocide' we mean the destruction of a nation or of an ethnic group."[10]

Lemkin emphasized the collective aspect of the crime: "Genocide is directed against the national group as an entity, and the actions involved are directed against individuals, not in their individual capacity, but as members of the national group."[11] Genocide is a crime against "nations."[12]

> Generally speaking, genocide does not necessarily mean the immediate destruction of a nation, except when accomplished by mass killings of all members of a nation. It is intended rather to signify a 'coordinated plan' of different actions aiming at the destruction of essential foundations of the life of national groups, with the aim of annihilating the groups themselves. The objectives of such a plan would be disintegration of the political and

> social institutions, of culture, language, national feelings, religion, and economic existence of national groups, and the destruction of the personal security, liberty, health, dignity, and the lives of the individuals belonging to such groups.[13]

Schabas remarks on the scope of genocide that Lemkin proposed: "It involves attacks on various components of the life of captive peoples."[14] The distinct identity of a national group is consumed or swallowed by the invading oppressor through various means. Lemkin's explanation of a "coordinated plan" refers to state law, policy and techniques with the ultimate objective of destruction of the national group.[15]

State policy and the role it plays in the commission of genocide "fell within the rubric of genocide"[16] even if the group physically survives. Lemkin understood the crime involved the state and the commission of genocide could only be committed by state actors: the primary perpetrator of genocide is the state. The Nuremburg Laws serve as an example of state laws applied against human groups. The German invasion can be described as a *dominating* and *dehumanizing*[17] framework of destruction. Ward Churchill explains that Lemkin took great care "to distinguish it [genocide] from being strictly associated with descriptors of literal murder..."[18] This refers to "*any* policy undertaken"[19] [emphasis original] to destroy the national identity of a human group. As Churchill emphasizes, "There is in fact every indication that Lemkin saw the physical survival of all or most members of groups subjected to genocide as being normative, their physical extermination exceptional."[20] Accordingly, Lemkin recognized that genocide occurs in two phases:

> one, the destruction of the national pattern of the oppressed group; the other, the imposition of the national pattern of the oppressor. This imposition, in turn, may be made upon the

> oppressed population which is allowed to remain, or upon the territory alone, after removal of the population and the colonization of the area by the oppressor's own nationals. [21]

Lemkin described the two phases as a "*denationalization*"[22] [emphasis added] process; however he did acknowledge that a stronger word for the denationalization process is "genocide"[23]. Power writes "[a] group did not have to be physically exterminated to suffer genocide. They could be stripped of all cultural traces of their identity. 'It takes centuries and sometimes thousands of years to create a natural culture,' Lemkin wrote, 'but genocide can destroy a culture instantly, like fire can destroy a building in an hour.'"[24] If the two phases have been implemented then genocide occurs.[25]

Schabas notes that "many of today's scholars are struck by the breadth of the definition of genocide that Lemkin proposed."[26] He explains that Lemkin acknowledged "the physical destruction of a people, but that was only a part of the larger concept.[27] The *larger concept* is the oppression of national groups in the colonization process and the destruction of those oppressed nations. Lemkin's two phases describe colonization as a process in which the oppressor swallows up the oppressed nation's identity into the colonial oppressor's state. In other words, it is the absorbing of the distinct identity of the nation into the "body politic"[28] or what is known as the process of cultural genocide. Lemkin's analysis of the German occupation of Europe involved an examination of the Hitler regime's domination of other countries.

John Cooper explains that huge areas of Eastern Europe were targeted for mass colonization efforts: "Lemkin argued, large areas of occupied Europe were incorporated into the Reich, including Western Poland, Luxembourg, and certain Yugoslav provinces, and other enormous tracts of land in the East were earmarked for colonization and the *Lebensraum* (living space) theory was invoked by the Nazis in support of this [emphasis original]."[29] Compare this to Timothy Snyder on the German invasion in *Bloodlands: Europe Between Hitler and Stalin* in which he determines that the Nazi model of colonial invasion in Eastern Europe was modelled after the colonial invasion on Turtle Island (North America).[30] Synder explains,

> Colonization would make of Germany a continental empire fit to rival the United States, another hardy frontier state based upon exterminatory colonialism and slave labor. The East was the Nazi Manifest Destiny. In Hitler's view, "in the East a similar process will repeat itself for a second time as in the conquest of America." As Hitler imagined the future, Germany would deal with the Slavs much as the North Americans had dealt with the Indians.[31]

The German invasion involved claiming territory and land and the destruction of the supplanted nations. In this regard, the two concepts of colonialism and genocide are linked and integral to one another. Cooper writes that Lemkin's purpose was to "understand through studying these occupation regulations that the Germans intended to reorganize Europe on racial lines...."[32]

"Laws of occupation"[33] are a primary feature of the dominating and dehumanizing colonial legal framework of the Nazi invasion and demonstrate the two phases of genocide. Schabas articulates that *Axis Rule* "comprises Lemkin's exacting analysis and compilation of the occupation laws which controlled millions of subjugated peoples across Europe and facilitated the occupiers' attempted annihilation."[34] Lemkin explains, "This régime is totalitarian in its method and spirit. Every phase of life, even the most intimate, is covered by a network of laws and regulations which create the instrumentalities of a most complete administrative control and coercion. Therefore these laws of occupation are an extremely valuable source of information regarding such government and its practices."[35] The "techniques of occupation"[36] describe the colonization process:

> Genocide is effected through a synchronized attack on different aspects of life of the captive peoples: in the political field (by destroying institutions of self-government and imposing a German pattern of administration, and through *colonization* by Germans); in the social field (by disrupting the social cohesion of the nation involved and killing or removing elements such as the intelligentsia, which provide spiritual leadership—according to Hitler's statement in *Mein Kampf*, "the greatest of spirits can be liquidated if its bearer is beaten to death with a rubber truncheon"); in the cultural field (by prohibiting or destroying cultural institutions and cultural activities; by substituting vocational education for education in the liberal arts, in order to prevent humanistic thinking, which the occupant considers dangerous because it promotes national thinking); in the economic field (by shifting the wealth to Germans and by prohibiting the exercise of trades and occupations by people who do not promote Germanism "without reservations"); in the biological field (by a policy of depopulation and by promoting procreation by Germans in the occupied countries); in the field of physical existence (by introducing a starvation rationing system for non-Germans and by mass killings, mainly of Jews, Poles, Slovenes, and Russians); in the religious field (by interfering with the activities of the Church, which in many countries provides not only spiritual but also national leadership); in the field of morality (by attempts to create an atmosphere of moral debasement through promoting pornographic publications and motion pictures, and the excessive consumption of alcohol) [emphasis added].[37]

Mathew Lippman explains that genocide "did not necessarily involve immediate extermination. This process, more typically, entailed a series of coordinated acts designed, and intended, to slowly suffocate a group. These actions typically were directed against a collectivity's culture, institutions, language, religion and physical integrity."[38] According to Lippman, "Lemkin ruefully observed that the practice of genocide had evolved into an almost scientific system which presented 'one of the most complete and glaring illustrations of the violation of international law and the laws of humanity.'"[39]

The Litany of Definitional Distortions

Drafting the Genocide Convention

UN General Assembly Resolution 96(1) on December 11, 1946, ordered the Economic and Social Council to undertake studies to write up a draft convention. The Economic and Social Council instructed the Secretary-General to write a convention in accordance with the resolution 96(1) put forward by the General Assembly.[40] The draft was to be completed in accordance with the spirit and aims of the General Assembly resolution. The opening comment by Peru's representative, Mr. Arca Parro, indicates the moral scope of the proposed convention in the following statement that governments are the perpetrators of the crime:

> [It] seemed impossible that genocide could be performed within a country without the backing of the government itself or of a powerful group within the government. If effective punishment was to be carried out by international action, such action would have to be directed not merely against guilty individuals, whom their governments would protect, but against the government itself.[41]

The UNGC went through three drafting stages.[42] In

1947, the Secretary General was directed by UN United Nations Economic and Social Council to undertake a draft on genocide with the assistance of experts.[43] Three experts, Raphaël Lemkin, Henri Donnedieu de Vabres, and Vespasien Pella, were commissioned to undertake the task of writing the first draft.[44] The experts drafted the first framework, entitling, it "Draft Convention on the Crime of Genocide".[45] On the Draft Convention Churchill writes that genocide was "defined in a two-fold way, encompassing all policies intended to precipitate '1) the destruction of [such] a group' and '2) preventing its preservation and development'."[46] Robert Davis and Mark Zannis, authors of *The Genocide Machine in Canada,* wrote on the separate categories of genocide:[47]

> [1. Physical] In the category of *physical* it outlined mass extermination and "slow death" measures (i.e. subjection to conditions of life which, owing to lack of proper housing, clothing, food, hygiene and medical care or excessive work or physical exertion are likely to result in the debilitation or death of the individuals; mutilations and biological experiments imposed for other than curative purposes; deprivation of all means of livelihood by confiscation of property, looting, curtailment of work, and the denial of housing and of supplies otherwise available to the other inhabitants of the territory concerned).
>
> [2. Biological] The secretariat's draft took biological genocide to mean the restricting of births in the group. It named the methods of sterilization or compulsory abortion, segregation of the sexes and obstacles to marriage.
>
> [3. Cultural] Cultural genocide was defined as the destruction of specific characteristics of a group. Among the acts specified: forced transfer

> of children to another human group; forced and systematic exile of individuals representing the culture of the group; the prohibition of the use of the national language, even in private intercourse; systematic destruction of books printed in the national language; or religious works, or the prohibition of new publications; systematic destruction of historical or religious monuments, or their diversion to alien uses; destruction or dispersion of documents and objects of historical, artistic, or religious value and of objects used in religious worship.[48]

On the three categories of genocide, Professors de Vabres and Pella accepted biological and physical genocide but disagreed with cultural genocide. They "held cultural genocide represented an undue extension of the notion of genocide."[49] Lemkin's view was that the diversity of cultures was as important as the physical integrity of a nation: "a racial, national, or religious group cannot continue to exist unless it preserves its spirit and moral unity. Such a group's right to existence was justified not only from the moral point of view, but also from the point of view of the value of the contribution made by such a group to civilization generally. If the diversity of cultures were destroyed, it would be as disastrous for civilization as the physical destruction of nations."[50] In the first draft, Lemkin's concept of genocide was maintained; however, it was "[ignored]"[51] and "met with significant and suspicious resistance by Canada and the United States."[52] The Secretary-General indicated that the draft produced at this stage was to present all viewpoints, including those of the experts, to provide a wide discussion basis for consideration.[53]

The Canadian representative stated that "the Canadian Government and people would regard with the utmost abhorrence 'any deliberate act committed with the intent to destroy the language, religion or culture of a national, racial, or religious group on the grounds of national or racial origin or religious belief.'"[54] The delegate from Canada then continued on by opposing the inclusion of cultural genocide: "It was a far cry from the unspeakable crimes which had been perpetrated at the Nazi crematoria, and which had so fundamentally shocked mankind, to the prohibition of the use of a museum cherished by some particular cultural group or other acts of cultural repression, deplorable and revolting though they might be."[55] The conclusion from Canada's perspective was that the Genocide Convention would be weakened by placing cultural and physical genocide on the same level.[56] The solution from Canada's position was to place it under the Covenant on Human Rights. Davis and Zannis state, on the downplaying of cultural genocide, that:

> The loss and human suffering for those whose culture has been healthy and is suddenly attacked and disintegrated are incalculable.
>
> One should not speak lightly of "cultural genocide" as if it were a fanciful invention. The consequence in real life is far too grim to speak of cultural genocide as if it were a rhetorical device to beat the drums for "human rights." The cultural mode of a group exterminated is genocide, a crime. Nor should "cultural genocide" be used in the game: "Which is the more horrible, to kill and torture; or, remove the reason and will to live"? Both are horrible.[57]

Canada's position throughout the drafting stages remained the same, a resounding opposition to the inclusion of cultural genocide. In fact, it was the only point that Canada disagreed with in its entirety.[58]

Ad Hoc and Sixth Committee Debates

The smoke and mirrors game continued into the Ad Hoc and Sixth Committee sessions. The debate concerned key elements of the crime such as "cultural genocide, the protection of political groups and an international tribunal for the suppression of genocide."[59] The drafting committees managed to delete almost all traces of cultural genocide. From the onset, Canada "vociferously opposed the inclusion of cultural genocide in the Convention."[60] The Canadian representative considered the Ad Hoc Committee draft acceptable on the whole, with that exception—even while it was recognized that the Canadian people were horrified at the prospect and sought action for its suppression. But then, the cultural genocide that the Canadian people ostensibly feared was not that related to Indigenous Peoples, but that potentially victimizing the two settler cultures. As Hirad Abtahi and Phillipa Webb explain the Canadian delegate, Mr. Lapointe, maintained his position:

> No drafting change of Article III would make its substance acceptable to his delegation. Yet it was true to say the Government and people of Canada were horrified at the idea of cultural genocide and hoped that effective action would be taken to suppress it. The people of his country were deeply attached to their cultural heritage, which was made up mainly of a combination of Anglo-Saxon and French elements, and they would strongly oppose any attempt to undermine the influence of those two cultures in Canada, as they would oppose any similar attempt in any other part of the world.[61]

The statement, "Anglo-Saxon and French elements" being tied to Canada's cultural heritage, is the epitome of colonial invasion, and presumption of ownership of the land that does not belong them. Such is the dominating and dehumanizing effect of being rendered "invisible"[62]or nonexistent as the Original Nations of Great Turtle Island. Does the protection of "Anglo-Saxon and French elements" include forcibly transferring Indigenous Peoples' children into residential state institutions?

Canada is a *settler*[63] state comprised of many different immigrants that have come here from abroad. While dominant among them, the French and English are but two of the many immigrant cultures, the French are from France and the English are from the United Kingdom. Is it any wonder that Canada vociferously opposed cultural genocide? In fact it was the only point they objected to. Abtahi and Webb on the Canadian delegate's objection to cultural genocide:

> His delegation was not, therefore, opposed to the idea of cultural genocide, but only to the inclusion in the convention of measures to suppress it. His delegation did not wish to limit the scope of the convention in any way, as was shown by the fact that it had voted in favour of the inclusion of the protection of the political group, but it felt that the idea of genocide should be limited to the mass physical destruction of human groups.[64]

Instead the solution Canada proposed was to recommend that the "protection of language, religion and culture within the framework of the international declaration on human rights."[65] The effect of this maneuver is to *restrict the scope* of the convention so that its coverage related to the genocide of Indigenous Nations is qualified under this approach. State concerns centered on whether the treatment of Indigenous Peoples would be construed as genocide. According to Mathew Lippman, "The United States apparently did not want to risk international recrimination for the country's continued practice of racial segregation and mistreatment of Native Americans...."[66] The standard argument against cultural genocide was that it "went too far" in the protection aspects.[67]

Venezuelan delegate Mr. Pérez Perozo felt that in principle cultural genocide "should be suppressed, since it was possible to destroy a human group ethnically without exterminating it physically."[68] The Ad Hoc Committee proponents that supported the inclusion of cultural genocide emphasized that, "there were two ways of suppressing a human group, the first by causing its members to disappear, and the second by abolishing, without making any attempts on the lives of the members of the group, their specific traits. According to this opinion, the Convention would fail fully to achieve its objects if it left out cultural genocide."[69] The other perspective against cultural genocide held that "there was a considerable difference between so-called 'physical' genocide (including biological genocide) and 'cultural' genocide. Only physical genocide presented those exceptionally horrifying aspects which had revolted the conscience of humanity."[70] According to Davis and Zannis, Lebanon's representative did not believe that "mankind was ready to take that step and would rather define genocide as mass homicide alone. 'Nevertheless, certain higher considerations led the world conscience also to revolt at the thought of the destruction of a group, even though individual members survived'."[71]

The position of the Canadian state was to equate genocide with mass physical destruction.[72] Churchill contends that scholarly and legal arguments that make genocide synonymous with mass killings warps the very understanding of the term.[73] The end result has been an obfuscation of the term by involving states/lawyers/scholars[74] that deny genocide occurs by state governments or colonial societies. Roland Chrisjohn, Tanya Wasacase, Lisa Nussey, Andrea Smith, Mark Legault, Pierre Loiselle and Mathieu Bourgeois in "Genocide and Indian Residential Schooling: The Past is Present," reflect on state maneuvering around the concept of cultural genocide:

> Privately, the federal government was well aware that, as it stood, its treatment of indigenous people would qualify as genocide. Publicly, the equation of genocide with mass homicide was a means of repudiating the proposed genocide convention in its entirety; homicide was already a punishable offence under each country's laws and as such, a genocide convention would be

> redundant. Nation-states would thus be eminently justified in choosing not to implement it. Further, the homicide interpretation would allow Canada and the United States to expropriate the moral "high ground", pointing their self-congratulatory fingers at monstrous countries committing crimes unfathomable within their own humanitarian, freedom-loving, peaceful borders.[75]

Chrisjohn et al. further observe that, "[a] comparison between the (Lemkin-driven) Secretariat and Ad-Hoc Committee's draft of the convention and the Convention ultimately adopted by the General Assembly in 1948 is horrifyingly instructive."[76] This is reflected in 1948 when the Department of External Affairs reported position of approval during the general debate, except with respect to cultural genocide and "reserved [the] right to move the deletion of Article III (on cultural genocide) at the third session of the General Assembly."[77] External Affairs claimed that the issue of cultural genocide "was neither within the Council's terms of reference nor properly included in a convention designed for the protection of human life."[78] Hirad Abtahi & Philippa Webb on the Canadian delegate (Mr. Lapointe), confirmed the state's position by "consider[ing] the draft convention prepared by the *Ad Hoc* Committee to be acceptable on the whole, but he disagreed with it on the one fundamental point of cultural genocide."[79]

The Canadian position concluded that if cultural genocide provisions were maintained then his "delegation would have to make certain reservations."[80] The excuse given was the "Canadian Constitution limited the legislative powers of the Federal Government to the benefit of the provincial legislatures."[81] By deleting cultural genocide, protection to Indigenous Nations and Peoples the world over was excluded. The relegation of human groups or national collective identities that should be protected under the UNGC—which indeed specifically addresses the protection of human groups—to an individual human rights convention such as the International Covenant on Civil and Political Rights both conceals and is unable to address legal appeals related to crimes of genocide against Indigenous Peoples.

In other words, the effect of an individual human rights framework predominates and leaves unaddressed international legal avenues to protect the collective national identities of the Original Nations the world over. It is an attempt to conceal genocide in the colonization of our lands and territories.

The restriction of the scope of genocide as a crime is in direct opposition to the moral and humanitarian objective of the UNGC. Statements made by Yugoslavia's representative, Mr. Bartos, are indicative of this view,

> [The] crime, however, was still being committed, on the pretext of "police measures", in colonial wars against oppressed peoples fighting for their freedom. The question was therefore one of great importance at the present time. It was essential to draw up as soon as possible a convention which would constitute a real code of international law forbidding genocide in general, not a text with loopholes which would prevent the punishment of many acts of genocide…"[82]

On the issue of the prevention of genocide, the draft convention "lacked sincerity, as if the draft were merely a blind to persuade the masses that the Governments detested the crime of genocide, while at the same time those governments reserved the right to organize, or at least tolerate, in their respective territories the preparations for the crime and the propaganda which preceded it."[83] Mr. Bartos explained that the draft "made no mention of the crimes of Nazism and fascism. That almost gave the impression that they were purposely excluded from direct condemnation so as to permit of their rehabilitation at some future date. Genocide had been arbitrarily disassociated from fascist and Nazi ideologies, of which, nevertheless, it was the direct result."[84] He emphasized that "in order to supress genocide, its real causes must be destroyed, namely, those doctrines of racial and national superiority…"[85] The issue, Yugoslavia maintained, was the dodging of fundamental aspects of the crime and the weakening of the preventative shield the UNGC was to maintain.[86]

The Ukrainian Soviet Socialist Republic (hereinafter Ukraine SSR) delegate, Mr. Kovalenko, expressed concern about "the undeniable link which existed between crimes of genocide and the Nazi and fascist racial theories, and expressed surprise that the draft convention now before the committee had not stressed that relationship. His delegation was of the opinion that the preamble of the draft should be amended so as to include an express condemnation of those theories."[87] On the concept of cultural genocide Mr. Kovalenko went further:

> It was generally recognized that genocide aimed at the extermination of a group of people. That aim could be attained by exterminating all the members of the group or by destroying its characteristics. In the opinion of the Ukrainian delegation, no country which was genuinely anxious to combat the crime of genocide and to prevent it as well as punish it, could oppose the inclusion of cultural genocide among the acts to which the convention applied.[88]

On the moral and legal obligations,

> Mr. Kovalenko objected to the doubts expressed by the United Kingdom delegation as to the effectiveness of an international convention on genocide to assure mankind the security to which it aspired. International treaties were not scraps of paper; a convention on genocide, like all international conventions, would have great legal and moral force for, on the other hand, it would lay down the concrete measures which the signatory States would have to take and, on the other hand, the States would be in duty bound to observe rigorously the obligations they had undertaken.[89]

The opposition to cultural genocide resulted in the entire category diminished to a form that is unrecognizable from Lemkin's conception of the crime. On October 25, 1948, the Sixth Committee rejected cultural genocide as a crime.[90]

The UNGC retained some of the integrity that Lemkin envisioned through addressing the forcible transferring of children from one group to another group.

Forced Transfer of Children

The forced transfer of children retained its life by an amendment that requested the retention of the "forced transfer of children to another human group."[91] Comments made by delegates on the forcible transferring of children are critical to understanding the crime. While the French delegate was opposed to the insertion of cultural genocide, he however determined that French

> opposition would surely not extend to the special case of the forced transfer of children, an act far more serious and indeed more barbarous than the other acts enumerated in the first draft convention under the heading of cultural genocide.... The forced transfer of children had not only cultural, but also physical and biological effects since it imposed on young persons conditions of life likely to cause them serious harm or even death.[92]

The Greek delegate, Mr. Vallindas, held that "[t]here could be no doubt that a forced transfer of children, committed with the intention of destroying a human group in whole, or at least in part, constituted genocide. The forced transfer of children could be as effective a means of destroying a human group as that of imposing measures intended to prevent births, or inflicting conditions of life likely to cause death."[93] The Greek delegation emphasized the importance of including the "'forced transfer of children', a means of committing genocide which had been used not only in the past but was still being used."[94]

The representative from Uruguay, Mr. Manini Y Ríos held that "there was reason also to condemn measures intended to destroy a new generation through abducting infants, forcing them to change their religion and educating them to become enemies of their own people."[95] Furthermore, it was determined by the Greek delegate that the forcible removal of children was not "primarily an act of cultural genocide. Although it could in certain cases be considered as such, it could be perpetrated rather with the intent to destroy or to cause serious physical harm to members of a group."[96] The Venezuela delegate Mr. Pérez Perozo stated that,

> the Committee implicitly recognized that a group could be destroyed although the individual members of it continued to live normally without having suffered physical harm. Sub paragraph 5 of article II has been adopted because the forced transfer of children to a group where they would be given an education different from that of their own group, and would have new customs, a new religion and probably a new language, was in practice tantamount to the destruction of their group, whose future depended on that generation of children.[97]

The key point is that a human group or nation depends on its children to transmit to future generations the distinct characteristics of that nation's collective identity even if the destruction experienced is not physical or mental or bodily harm. The Venezuelan delegate continued,

> Such transfer might be made from a group with a *low standard of civilization and living in conditions both unhealthy and primitive, to a highly civilized group* as members of which children would suffer no physical harm, and would indeed enjoy an existence which was materially much better; in

> such a case there would be no question of *mass murder, mutilation, torture* or *malnutrition*; yet if the *intent of the transfer were destruction of the group, a crime of genocide would undoubtedly have been committed* [emphasis added].[98]

Venezuela presupposes that a transfer would not involve mutilation, torture, or malnutrition, or mass murder; however, if the transfer causes massive acts of serious physical or bodily or mental harm against the targeted children it would be horrific. It also emphasizes that if there is no serious bodily or mental harm or no mass physical destruction but the intent is to destroy the human group, then it will constitute a crime. Despite its recognition of the destructive impact of cultural genocide even where physical conditions are positive, nonetheless, inherent in this statement is the dehumanizing ideology that characterizes state domination. The Venezuelan delegate assumes in relation to the forcible transferring of *uncivilized* peoples' children to *civilized* human groups that mass murder, mutilation, torture and malnutrition would not be a part of the experience. However, if the result causes collective serious bodily and mental harm against other peoples' children then it adds another dimension to the crime.

The comments by state delegates on the "forced transfer of children from one group to another group" shed light on the importance of retaining it as a crime. The analysis is important for clarification on aspects of the crime in past and present forcible removals of Indigenous children from their families and Nations to state residential institutions. Despite the "greatly truncated"[99] version of genocide adopted by the General Assembly there is enough latitude to determine when a crime occurs.

The UN General Assembly passed the *United Nations Convention on the Prevention and Punishment of the Crime of Genocide* on December 9, 1948. The UNGC entered into law January 12, 1951. Canada acceded to the Convention on November 28, 1949, and subsequently ratified it on September 3, 1952.[100] Despite the attempted reservation threatened by Canada there were no official reservation made:

> From the record contained in the Travaux, Canada's opposition to including cultural genocide in the Convention stands out from that of other countries in terms of its strength of its opposition and its unwillingness to compromise to any degree on the provision. Cultural genocide was not just a sticking point for Canada; it was the *only* major concern Canada appears to have expressed with regards to the draft Convention. Canada's explicit statement that it would lodge reservations regarding cultural genocide provisions were they to be included in the final text implies that Canada may not have intended to be bound by such provisions. Whether the reason for Canada's opposition relates to its domestic policies is not touched upon in the Travaux. [Emphasis original][101]

Canada took a different approach altogether when the issue is examined domestically and correlates with the previous quote that Canada did not intend to be "bound by such provisions" at all. The crime of genocide is properly in the realm of international law and the elements to prove genocide are discussed below.

Elements of the Crime

William Schabas in *Genocide in International Law: The Crime of Crimes* outlines the elements of an offence to prove a claim of genocide: "Criminal law analysis of an offence proceeds from a basic distinction between the physical element (the *actus reus*) and the mental element (the *mens rea*). The prosecution must prove specific material facts, but must also establish the accused's criminal intent or 'guilty mind'."[102] The chapeau in Article II establishes the *mens rea*, which is the "'intent to destroy, in whole or in part, a national, ethnical, racial or religious group, as such'."[103] Article II establishes the *actus reus* or the criminal acts of the offence in (a)-(e).

The principal perpetrator of the crime is a government or state. Recall that Lemkin understood genocide as a crime to be committed by state governments and officials. John Quigley, author of *The Genocide Convention: An International Law Analysis,* notes Article IX determines that a state is "[responsible] 'for genocide or for any of the other acts enumerated in Article III,' [and] makes it plain that a state may perpetrate genocide, including conspiracy, incitement, attempt, and complicity."[104] The fact that states can be held accountable for genocide and responsible for committing genocide is acknowledged in the jurisprudence. The International Court of Justice (hereinafter ICJ) in 2007 declared that individuals and state governments may commit the crime of genocide. The ICJ in the *Case Concerning the Application of the Convention on the Prevention and Punishment of the Crime of Genocide* (*Bosnia and Herzegovina v. Serbia and Montenegro*) (*hereinafter Bosnia v. Serbia*) held that the,

> Contracting Parties to the Convention are bound not to commit genocide, through the actions of their organs or persons or groups whose acts are attributable to them. That conclusion must also apply to the other acts enumerated in Article III. Those acts are forbidden along with genocide itself in the list included in Article III. They are referred to equally with genocide in Article IX and without being characterized as "punishable"; and the "purely humanitarian and civilizing purpose" of the Convention may be seen as being promoted by the fact that States are subject to that full set of obligations, supporting their undertaking to prevent genocide.[105]

Article III of the UNGC provides that, "The following acts shall be punishable: (a) Genocide (b) Conspiracy to commit genocide (c) Direct and public incitement to commit genocide; (d) Attempt to commit genocide; (e) Complicity in genocide."[106]

Schabas acknowledges the court's conclusions "that States could be held responsible for genocide, and that article IX established jurisdiction to make such determinations."[107]

Actus Reus

The *actus reus* is the physical element of a crime. Article II lists the acts that constitute the crime: To reiterate, they are as follows:

a.) Killing members of the group;
b.) Causing serious or bodily mental harm to members of the group;
c.) Deliberately inflicting on the group conditions of life calculated to bring about its physical destruction in whole or in part;
d.) Imposing measures intended to prevent births within the group;
e.) Forcibly transferring children of the group to another group.[108]

Schabas claims that "within the paragraphs there are also elements of the mental elements or *mens rea*."[109] Three enumerated acts require proof of a result. They are "killing members of the group; causing serious bodily or mental harm to members of the group; forcibly transferring children of the group to another group."[110] To show a crime of genocide "requires evidence that the act itself is a 'substantial cause' of the outcome."[111]

Causing Serious Bodily and Mental Harm to Members of the Group

Article II(b) holds that causing serious bodily or mental harm to members of the group is a crime of genocide. The text of the UNGC does not "specify that the harm caused be permanent harm, but it does use the adjective 'serious.'"[112] Schabas citing the District Court of Jerusalem in the *A-G Israel v. Eichmann* (hereinafter *Eichmann*) case found that Article II(b) "could be caused 'by the enslavement, starvation, deportation and persecution…and by their detention in ghettos, transit camps, and concentration camps in conditions which were designed to cause their degradation, deprivation of their rights as human beings, and to suppress them and cause them inhumane suffering and torture."[113]

The International Criminal Tribunal for Rwanda (ICTR) in *Prosecutor v. Akayesu* (hereinafter *Akayesu*) citing *Eichmann*, construed "serious bodily or mental harm, without limiting itself thereto, to mean acts of torture, be they bodily or mental, inhumane or degrading treatment, persecution"[114] that fall within the ambit of Article II (b). Other acts listed by the ICTR that constitute serious bodily and mental harm include beatings, threats of death, interrogations, detainment, sexual violence, mutilations, rape, "often repeatedly, often publicly, and often by more than one assailant."[115] The International Criminal Tribunal for the former Yugoslavia (hereinafter ICTY) in *Prosecutor v. Stakić* held that the term "'[c]ausing serious bodily or mental harm' in sub-paragraph (b) is understood to mean, *inter alia* acts of torture, inhumane or degrading treatment, sexual violence including rape, interrogations combined with beatings, threats of death, and harm that damages health or causes disfigurement or injury. The harm inflicted need not be permanent and irremediable."[116]

The phrase "causing mental harm" is in contention historically;[117] however, the jurisprudence establishes clarity with respect to the crime. Schabas writes, "[H]arm that amounts to 'a grave and long-term disadvantage to a person's ability to lead a normal and constructive life' is *not* sufficient to meet the terms of article II (b) of the Convention [emphasis added]."[118] However, the ICTY has said that harm amounting to 'a grave and long-term disadvantage to a person's ability to lead a normal and constructive life' has been ruled sufficient for this purpose. The ICTY in *Prosecutor v. Krajišnik* [hereinafter *Krajišnik*] clarified that,

> [t]hus, only (ii) – "causing serious bodily or mental harm" – remains somewhat open to interpretation, but a fair and consistent construction of this clause alongside the four other types of actus reus is that, in order to pass as

> the actus reus of genocide under (ii), the act must inflict such "harm" as to contribute, or tend to contribute, to the destruction of the group or part thereof. *Harm amounting to "a grave and long-term disadvantage to a person's ability to lead a normal and constructive life' has been said to be sufficient for this purpose* [emphasis added]."[119]

It would appear, therefore, that Schabas' statement is in direct contradiction to the language from the *Krajišnik* case. The case law suggests there are long term consequences to crimes that fall within the ambit of Article II(b). The trial chamber of the ICTY in the case of *Prosecutor v. Krstić* (hereinafter Krstić) held that

> In line with the *Akayesu* judgement, the trial chamber states that serious harm need not cause permanent and irremediable harm, but it must involve harm that goes beyond temporary unhappiness, embarrassment or humiliation. It must be harm that results in a grave and long-term disadvantage to a person's ability to lead a normal and constructive life. In subscribing to the above case-law, the Chamber holds that inhumane treatment, torture, rape, sexual abuse and deportation are among the acts which may cause serious bodily or mental injury. [120]

Again, Schabas' contention is that harms that amount to "a grave and long term disadvantage to a person's ability to lead a normal and constructive life" is *not* sufficient to meet the terms of Article II (b) of the Convention. If "it must be harm that results in a grave and long-term disadvantage to a person's ability to lead a normal and constructive life," then how can Schabas contend that "harm" which meets that standard is "not sufficient" to meet the terms of' that standard, namely Article II (b) of the Convention? It appears that the jurisprudence acknowledges otherwise.

Further to the above, the chamber in *Kayishema* suggests there is a distinction between bodily and mental harm. The court explained the phrase "'causing serious bodily harm'" to mean "harm that seriously injures the health, causes disfigurement or causes any serious injury to the external, internal organs or sense."[121] The ICTR in *Kayishema,* concurring with *Akayesu,* claims that the judgement "further held that acts of sexual violence, rape, mutilations and interrogations combined with beatings, and/ or threats of death, were all acts that amount to serious bodily harm."[122] A further reading of the findings in *Akayesu* shows that the court did not make this distinction between bodily and mental harm. The court found that beatings, threats of beatings, rape, sexual violence, mutilations, interrogation, and detainment, constitute "serious bodily and mental harm."[123] The trial chamber of the ICTY in *Prosecutor v. Blagojević* elaborated on mental harm:

> [T]he trauma and wounds suffered by those individuals who managed to survive the mass executions does constitute serious bodily and mental harm. The fear of being captured, and, at the moment of separation, the sense of utter helplessness and extreme fear for their family and friends' safety as well as their own safety, is a traumatic experience from which one will not quickly—if ever—recover. Furthermore, the Trial Chamber finds that the men suffered mental harm having their identification documents taken away from them, seeing that they would not be exchanged as previously told, and when they understood what their ultimate fate was. Upon arrival at an execution site, they saw the killings fields covered of [sic] bodies of the Bosnian Muslim men brought to the execution site before them and murdered. After having witnessed the executions of relatives and friends, and in some

> cases suffering from injuries themselves, they suffered the further mental anguish of lying still, in fear, under the bodies – sometimes of relatives or friends – for long hours, listening to the sounds of the executions, of the moans of those suffering in pain, and then of the machines as mass graves were dug.[124]

The chamber determined it would be a traumatic experience for anyone that witnessed the horror and destruction of their loved ones and friends. It also affirmed that one might never recover from the experience.

On the issue of sexual violence and rape the ICTR determined it would "constitute infliction of serious bodily and mental harm on the victims"[125] and "one of the worst ways of inflict[ing] harm on the victim as he or she suffers both bodily and mental harm."[126] The crime has "physical and psychological"[127] destructive consequences. The ICTR holds that:

> The Tribunal considers that rape is a form of aggression and that the central elements of the crime of rape cannot be captured in a mechanical description of objects and body parts. The Tribunal also notes the cultural sensitivities involved in public discussion of intimate matters and recalls the painful reluctance and inability of witnesses to disclose graphic anatomical details of sexual violence they endured. The United Nations Convention Against Torture and Other Cruel, Inhuman and Degrading Treatment or Punishment does not catalogue specific acts in its definition of torture, focusing rather on the conceptual framework of state-sanctioned violence. The Tribunal finds this approach more useful in the context

> of international law. Like torture, rape is used for such purposes as intimidation, degradation, humiliation, discrimination, punishment, control or destruction of a person. Like torture, rape is a violation of personal dignity, and rape in fact constitutes torture when it is inflicted by or at the instigation of or with the consent or acquiescence of a public official or other person acting in an official capacity.[128]

The chamber highlights that rape is synonymous with torture when it is committed for purposes such as the destruction of a victim through degradation, punishment and intimidation and control. Sexual violence and rape is deemed to be torture when the crime is committed by a public official or a person acting in an official capacity.

Rape is defined "as a physical invasion of a sexual nature, committed on a person under circumstances which are coercive."[129] Sexual violence includes rape, and is defined as "any act of a sexual nature which is committed on a person under circumstances which are coercive. Sexual violence is not limited to physical invasion of the human body and may include acts which do not involve penetration or even physical contact."[130] The chamber gives an example of a victim being forced to perform "gymnastics naked" in a public setting constitutes sexual violence: "The Tribunal notes in this context that coercive circumstances need not be evidenced by a show of physical force. Threats, intimidation, extortion, and other forms of duress which prey on fear or desperation may constitute coercion…[131] A compelling view of the court is the determination of rape and sexual violence as genocide if the requisite intent is satisfied. Schabas, on the determination of sexual violence as genocide, writes that it leads to the "progressive development of the law of genocide."[132]

The determination of rape as an act of torture certainly conveys that there are long term mental psychological consequences on a victim. Like torture, sexual violence is viewed as a violation against a victim's personal dignity. The court suggests that if the perpetrator is acting in a capacity as a government official with the consent or acquiescence of a public official it adds to the element of the crime. Consequently, the finding in *Krstić* and *Krajisnik* suggests a long term mental component to Article II (b). The findings by the ICTR and ICTY suggest that the long-term psychological consequences for sexual violence as well as acts of "inhuman treatment, torture, rape, sexual abuse and deportation are among the acts which may cause serious bodily or mental injury."[133]

The *Travaux* suggests that forcibly removing children from one group to another group and that the experience of "*mutilation, torture, malnutrition*" destroy the national group because of its dependence on its children to transmit the identity of that society to future generations.[134] Certainly massive acts of collective brutal violence and terror against Indigenous Peoples would cause serious bodily and mental harm and would destroy or certainly impede the ability of the children to lead healthy constructive lives as members of their nations. It is self-evident that causing serious bodily and mental harm to adults would constitute destruction; however, when children as young as four years old and for years at a time are seriously bodily and mentally harmed through atrocious acts of terror the destruction becomes certain. Of this there can be no question.

Forcibly Transferring Children of the Group to Another Group

Article II (e) declares that forcibly transferring children of the group to another group is a crime. According to Schabas it "requires proof of a result, namely, that children be transferred from the victim group to another group"[135] The term "forcibly" can also mean not only "physical force, but may include threat of force or coercion, such as that caused by fear of violence, duress, detention, psychological oppression or abuse of power, against such a person or persons or another person, or by taking advantage of a coercive environment."[136] Kurt Mundorff writes the "meaning of 'forcible' has not been directly at issue in genocide case law, though several courts and committees have opined on the issue."[137] It was broadly clarified in *Akayesu* to mean that "the objective is not only to sanction a direct act of forcible physical transfer, but also to sanction acts of threats or trauma which would lead to the forcible transfer of children from one group to another."[138] Mundorff explains that the term "'forcible' encompassed both direct force and non-direct force."[139] Later it was determined by the ICJ in *Bosnia v. Serbia* that Article II(e) requires a stricter standard in that it "requires deliberate intentional acts."[140]

Mundorff, citing scholarly opinion, suggests that two essential requirements are involved to show the transfer and this means "separating children from their group and placing them with another group."[141] However, a different perspective by Claus Kreβ indicates that the child need only be separated from their group.[142] The transfer requirement is "satisfied when the children are in another group's control."[143] Certainly state legislation or laws that force the transfer of children would satisfy this requirement.

Australia's *Bringing Them Home: Report of the National Inquiry into the Separation of Aboriginal and Torres Strait Islander Children from Their Families* (hereinafter *Bringing Them Home*) acknowledged the government policy of forcibly removing Indigenous Peoples' children to other "groups" "could properly be labeled as genocidal."[144] Australia's report concludes that "the practice of forcible transfer of indigenous children to non-indigenous institutions and families violated article II (e) of the Genocide Convention."[145] The report also concluded that the purpose of the removal of children was the "absorption or assimilation of the children into the wider, non-Indigenous, community so that their unique cultural values and ethnic identities would disappear, giving way to models of Western culture."[146] The problem with this conclusion is that forced assimilation and cultural genocide are not culpable under the UNGC. As positive as the finding appears, it does not determine that any of the acts are genocide, per se, but rather cultural genocide, which is not punishable under international law. According to Schabas, the crime of cultural genocide is not punishable unless it is related to physical or biological genocide.[147] Therefore, any claim made about cultural genocide is a non-issue in international law.

Mens Rea

Another standard of proof is the intention or *mens rea* behind the crime. Article 30 of the Rome Statute of the International Criminal Court clarifies that "'a person has intent where (a) In relation to conduct, that person means to engage in the conduct; (b) In relation to a consequence, that person means to cause that consequence or is aware that it will occur in the ordinary course of events'."[148] Knowledge is explained in Article 30 (3) of the Rome Statute as "awareness that a circumstance exists or a consequence will occur in the ordinary course of events."[149] Schabas explains that a "purpose-based" approach focuses on individual offenders, whereas a knowledge-based approach examines "the plan or policy of a State or similar group, and highlights the collective dimension of the crime of genocide."[150] Notwithstanding the academic rhetoric on the subject of intent, there is no doubt that the requirement of evidence of a state plan or policy is important for convictions of genocide.

The ICTY rulings in *Karadzić* clarified that a requirement for evidence of genocide is the existence of a "'project' or 'plan'."[151] Schabas elucidates that the ICTR in *Akayesu* "did not insist upon proof of a plan with respect to the incitement for genocide, but this may have been because the issue was self-evident. At one point in the judgment, it referred to the 'massive and/or systematic nature' of the crime of genocide."[152] In determining responsibility for genocide the court determined evidence of a plan or policy or "general political doctrine".[153] Important to proving genocide is the specific intent requirement. The ICJ in *Bosnia and Herzegovina v. Serbia and Montenegro (*hereinafter *Bosnia v. Serbia*) ruled on specific or special intent,

> …Article II requires a further mental element. It requires the establishment of the "intent to destroy,

> in whole or in part,...[the protected] group, as such." It is not enough to establish, for instance in terms of paragraph *(a)*, that deliberate unlawful killings of members of the group have occurred. The additional intent must also be established, and it is defined very precisely. It is often referred to as a special or specific intent or *dolus specialis*.... It is not enough that the members of the group are targeted because they belong to that group, that is because the perpetrator has a discriminatory intent. Something more is required. The acts listed in Article II must be done with the intent to destroy the group as such in whole or in part....[154]

Critical scholarly opinion by Quigley determines that general intention is sufficient to satisfy the mental element of genocide while a requirement of specific intent places a higher standard of evidence of the intent to destroy a group. Further, Quigley is of the opinion that intent can be proved by factual circumstances.[155] Another perspective from Mundorff explains that the standard of intention expressed leads to continuing "ambiguity" in general and "[f]or this reason, many commentators have advocated abandoning the laden language of specific intent."[156] The differences between general and specific intent are as follows:

> In a general intent offence, the only issue is the performance of the criminal act, and no further ulterior intent or purpose need be proven....[a] specific intent offence requires performance of the *actus reus* but in association with an intent or purpose that goes beyond the mere performance of the act. Assault with intent to maim or wound is an example drawn from ordinary criminal law.[157]

In this regard, the perpetrator of genocide would have to commit one of the acts with the intention of destroying the protected group.

The Matter of "Specific Intent"

There is a two-step process to establish intent: "a general intent as to the underlying acts, and an ulterior intent with regard to the ultimate aim of the destruction of the group."[158] In other words, "general intent" means that the act or acts, themselves, are intentionally perpetrated, while "ulterior intent" refers to a longer range intended outcome that is the primary purpose of the act.[159]. General intent is satisfied by evidence of the material elements of the crime, as addressed in Article II(a)-(e), and special intent is satisfied if it can be shown there is a specific "intent to destroy in whole or in part" a protected group. Schabas defines the components of specific intent as "to destroy" and "in whole or in part" and "groups".[160] In his view, the term "in whole or in part,' refers to the intent of the perpetrator, not to the result."[161] The case of *Akayesu* elaborates on specific intent:

> Contrary to popular belief, the crime of genocide does not imply the actual extermination of group in its entirety, but is understood as such once any one of the acts mentioned in Article 2(2)(a) through 2(2)(e) is committed with the specific intent to destroy "in whole or in part" a national, ethnical, racial or religious group.
>
> Genocide is distinct from other crimes inasmuch as it embodies a special intent or *dolus specialis*. Special intent of a crime is the specific intention, required as a constitutive element of the crime, which demands that the perpetrator clearly seeks to produce the act charged. Thus, the special intent in the crime lies in "the intent to destroy, in whole or in part, a national, ethnical, racial or religious group, as such.[162]

It is determined that in some instances it may be difficult to determine the mental factor, even impossible, so the court resolved this issue by examining a certain number of presumptions of fact.[163] According to Mundorff the courts have applied the finding of specific intent in *Akayesu* to other decisions.[164] On proof of intent, the trial chamber in *Kayishema* held that,

> Regarding the assessment of the requisite intent, the Trial Chamber acknowledges that it may be difficult to find explicit manifestations of intent by the perpetrators. The perpetrator's actions, including circumstantial evidence, however may provide sufficient evidence of intent. The Commission of Experts in their Final Report on the situation in Rwanda also noted this difficulty. Their Report suggested that the necessary element of intent can be inferred from sufficient facts, such as the number of group members affected. The Chamber finds that the intent can be inferred either from words or deeds and may be demonstrated by a pattern of purposeful action. In particular, the Chamber considers evidence such as the physical targeting of the group or their property; the use of derogatory language toward members of the targeted group; the weapons employed and the extent of bodily injury; the methodical way of planning, the systematic manner of killing. Furthermore, the number of victims from the group is also important. In the Report of the Sub-Commission on Genocide, the Special Rapporteur stated that "the relative proportionate scale of the actual or attempted destruction of a group, by any act listed in Articles II and III of the Genocide Convention, is strong evidence to prove the necessary intent to destroy a group in whole or in part.[165]

The finding suggests that intent is satisfied if there is a massive pattern of destruction to the proportionate scale of the actual or attempted destruction of a group. Genocide includes a dual mental component that pertains to the "group": "one directed against the immediate victims, and a second against the group."[166]

On the "[i]ntent to destroy [through] acts against [g]roup [m]embers,"[167] Quigley, citing Akayesu writes: "Thus, the victim is chosen not because of his individual identity, but rather on account of his membership of a national, ethnical, racial or religious group. The victim of the act is therefore a member of a group, chosen as such, which, hence, means that the victim of the crime of genocide is the group itself and not only the individual."[168] It means that the entire group does not have to be destroyed so long as the harm directed against the individual is intended to affect the group through the destruction against the individual as a member of the group.[169] Hence, the victim of genocide is the group itself and not the individual alone.

The court gave the example of the rape and sexual violence affecting not only the Tutsi women but the Tutsi group as a whole.[170] According to the Trial Chamber in *Krstić*, the intent to destroy a group means:

> [T]he intent to destroy a group, even if only in part, means seeking to destroy a distinct part of the group as opposed to an accumulation of isolated individuals within it. Although the perpetrators of genocide need not seek to destroy the entire group protected by the Convention, they must view the part of the group they wish to destroy as a distinct identity which must be eliminated as such.[171]

The ICTR in *Akayesu* on proving specific intent considered,

> that intent is a mental factor which is difficult, even impossible, to determine. This is the reason why, in the absence of a confession from the accused, his intent can be inferred from a

> certain number of presumptions of fact. The Chamber considers that it is possible to deduce the genocidal intent inherent in a particular act charged from the general context of the perpetration of other culpable acts systematically directed against that same group, whether these acts were committed by the same offender or by others. Other factors, such as the scale of atrocities committed, their general nature, in a region or a country, or furthermore, the fact of deliberately and systematically targeting victims on account of their membership of a particular group, while excluding the members of other groups can, enable the Chamber to infer the genocidal intent of a particular act.[172]

The ICTY in *Karadzić* found that "intent derives from the combined effect of speeches or projects laying the groundwork for and justifying the acts, from the massive scale of their destructive effect and from their specific nature, which aims at undermining what is considered to be the foundation of the group."[173] The Chamber in *Akayesu* applied the same finding.[174] The ICTY on general political doctrine and same patterns of conduct found with respect to specific intent that:

> [It] may be inferred from a certain number of facts such as the general political doctrine which gave rise to the acts possibly covered by the definition in Article 4, or the repetition of destructive and discriminatory acts. The intent may also be inferred from the perpetration of acts which violate, or which the perpetrators themselves consider to violate, the very foundation of the group—acts which are not in themselves covered by the list in Article 4(2) but which are committed as part of the same pattern of conduct.[175]

If the destruction is massive, widespread and systematic this will satisfy the specific intent requirement. In application to the law, the ICTR in *Akayesu* made the following finding with respect to intent:

> [T]he Chamber is of the opinion that it is possible to infer the genocidal intention that presided over the commission of a particular act, *inter alia*, from all acts or utterances of the accused, or from the general context in which other culpable acts were perpetrated systematically against the same group, regardless of whether such other acts were committed by the same perpetrator or even by other perpetrators.[176]

On the intent to destroy the group, the court was satisfied that the victims (Tutsi peoples) were targeted:

> Owing to the very high number of atrocities committed against the Tutsi, their widespread nature not only in the commune of Taba, but also throughout Rwanda, and to the fact that the victims were systematically and deliberately selected because they belonged to the Tutsi group, with persons belonging to other groups being excluded, the Chamber is also able to infer, beyond reasonable doubt, the genocidal intent of the accused in the commission of the above-mentioned crimes.[177]

It was determined that rape and sexual violence constitutes genocide "as long as it was committed with the specific intent to destroy, in whole or in part, a particular group, targeted as such."[178] It was held that rape and sexual violence constitutes serious bodily and mental harm and is "one of the worst ways of inflict[ing] harm on the victim as he or she suffers both bodily and mental harm."[179]

The court held that rapes and sexual violence were committed solely against Tutsi women,

> many of whom were subjected to the worst public humiliation, mutilated, and raped several times, often in public, in the Bureau Communal premises or in other public places, and often by more than one assailant. These rapes resulted in physical and psychological destruction of Tutsi women, their families and their communities. Sexual violence was an integral part of the process of destruction, specifically targeting Tutsi women and specifically contributing to their destruction and to the destruction of the Tutsi group as a whole.[180]

Given that sexual violence is akin to torture, the findings in the jurisprudence could be applied to cases that involve torture against a human group. With respect to Article II (b) to show a case of genocide, it must be shown that "one or more victims actually suffered physical or mental harm. If this act is perpetrated with the requisite mental element, the crime has been committed."[181]

With respect to the forcible transfer of children, Mundorff outlines the material elements to prove genocide.[182] He explains that for genocide to be shown the acts must be "carried out against a discernable, protected human group—not merely against a number of individuals who belong to a protected group."[183] Mundorff clarifies that under the UNGC, "actions taken against a number of individuals belonging to a group precisely because of their membership in that group still would not amount to genocide unless these actions were accompanied by the intent to destroy their group, at least in part."[184] The crime becomes genocide only when the crime is committed with the intent to destroy an enumerated protected group.

With respect to Indigenous Peoples' children, this analysis

will proceed to answer whether the crime of genocide can be properly applied to the state of Canada, in another chapter, but the remainder of the analysis here begins to deconstruct colonialism. The destructive colonial legal framework under which Indigenous children are forcibly removed from their loved ones and placed into residential institutions is central to the question of state culpability. A critical issue to examine is retroactivity and colonialism with respect to laws and policies of colonial governments. The legal application with respect to retroactivity will be applied in a later chapter. The "laws of occupation" are shaped and sustained by a vicious colonial ideology. It's the colonizer's laws that coerce and compel the transfer of Indigenous Peoples' children—and indeed invade and control every aspect of the subject Indigenous Peoples' lives. The *Travaux* highlights the "anti-colonial"[185] factor as it relates to genocide.

The *Travaux* and the Anti-Colonial Factor

Integral to the question of state crimes is the extent to which international law has served as a "dominating and dehumanizing"[186] legal framework against Indigenous Peoples and Nations. Steven Newcomb in *Pagans in the Promised Land: Decoding the Doctrine of Christian Discovery* offers a model of cognitive domination (or cognitive legal theory) that explains how language provided a framework for domination and dehumanization through the doctrine of discovery, detailing how "pagan," "savage," and other such terminological degradation was employed from the outset as a vehicle upon which to advance and justify European claims to the territories of Indigenous Nations.[187] As he subsequently observed, "the ideas used to construct and maintain such patterns of domination are not a *physical* container, nor a *physical* object; they are nothing more than mental processes. The paradigm of domination is, first and foremost, a product of the mind [emphasis original]"[188]

The framework ultimately adopted in the UNGC allows states such as Canada the impunity to continue to oppress Indigenous Peoples without any international interventions. Sharon Venne explains in *Our Elders Understand our Rights: Evolving International Law Regarding Indigenous Rights*, "[c]ustom over the last five hundred years has developed against the rights of Indigenous Peoples. Inter-state practice moved towards an accepted international law norm that Indigenous Peoples were not to be recognized as 'Peoples.'"[189] Antony Anghie in *Imperialism, Sovereignty and the Making of International Law* challenges the assertion that,

> [c]olonialism is a thing of the past. This is the broad understanding that informs the conventional narrative of international law. The principal concerns of this book are to question this assumption and to examine how this narrative sustains itself and how international law seeks to suppress its relationship with colonialism—a relationship that was, and continues to be, central to international law's very identity.[190]

In effect, as a result of colonial powers' dominance over the drafting process, international law fails to protect against the imposition of a colonial framework of destruction over Indigenous Peoples. The drafting process of the UNGC reveals the construction of this framework of domination and dehumanization. Domestically, this framework is applied against oppressed encompassed Nations to their detriment and to the advantage of the state.

Ward Churchill's *Kill the Indian Save the Man: The Genocidal Impact of American Indian Residential Schools* explains that an examination of how Indigenous Nations and Peoples are represented in scholarship and law (internationally and domestically) reveals an "exclusionary effect, establishing definitional/conceptual threshold criteria" against peoples who have been deemed to be uncivilized.[191] Martti Koskenniemi in *The Gentle Civilizer of Nations,* citing Charles Salomon, affirms that, "[n]o word is more vague and has permitted the commission of more crimes than that of civilization."[192] *Webster's Third New International Dictionary Unabridged* provides the following entry under "civilization": "the act of civilizing; esp. the *forcing* of a particular cultural pattern on a population to whom it is foreign [emphasis added]."[193] The idea that "the state" is by its very nature dominating and dehumanizing and genocidal in its interactions with Indigenous Nations and Peoples is never entertained. Instead it is deemed from the western view point that "the state" (or "European") is an agent of *civilization* in the world and therefore beneficial to the peoples/nations they encounter.

The process of one people forcing and imposing a foreign cultural pattern on another people is genocide. Koskenniemi continues, "the history of all colonies begins with violence, injustice and the shedding of blood: the result is everywhere the same; the disappearance of the native races (*des races sauvages*) coming into a contact with civilized [dominating and dehumanizing] races."[194] *Dehumanization* of the original nations and peoples gives the *dominating* state the license to destroy with impunity with no qualms or afterthought. Destructive racial theories still prevail today as is seen by the 1991 *Delgamuukw* decision wherein it was determined Indigenous Peoples' lives before colonization were "nasty, brutish and short"[195] or less than human.[196] Chief Justice Allen McEachern does not seem to conceive or care that his destructive beliefs are violent toward the original nations of the Gitksan-Wet'suwe't'en. The *Delgamuukw* decision serves as an example of the dominating and dehumanizing perspective that is inherent in colonial societies, even as it is hailed as a step forward for Indigenous Peoples.

Colonial Clause

The Genocide Convention's *Travaux Préparatoires*[197] supports the contention that cultural genocide was removed from the UNGC because of colonialism globally. It stands to reason that if the relation of colonialism to genocide has been concealed and excluded from the convention in international law, then the fact that the experience of the forcible transfer of children takes place under a destructive colonial framework is also concealed from the world at large. The debates with respect to the "colonial clause"[198] clarify ambiguities that pertain to the correlation between colonialism and genocide. The specific clause itself, in the context of the

UNGC, sheds light on the connection between colonialism and cultural genocide.[199] For clarification, the colonial clause gives a contracting state the freedom of designating to which "colonial territories" the UNGC will apply.[200] The discussions shed light on colonialism as a genocidal process.[201]

The debate concerned a "new article by the United Kingdom delegation [*A/C.6/236*] and the amendment to that article submitted by the delegation of the Ukrainian SSR [*A/C.6/264*]."[202] The United Kingdom Amendment (A/C.6/236) observed of the UK's colonies that, "[a]mong the territories administered by the United Kingdom, some were completely self-governing in their internal affairs and it would be constitutionally impossible for the United Kingdom to accept the convention on their behalf first without consulting them."[203] Mr. Kovalenko of the Ukrainian Soviet Socialist Republic (Ukrainian SSR) in rebuttal, stated that,

> he had submitted an amendment to the new article proposed by the United Kingdom delegation because he felt it was extremely important for the convention to apply to all countries and especially to non-self-governing territories. In his opinion, the peoples of non-self-governing territories were most likely to become the victims of acts of genocide because they did not possess the highly developed organs of information necessary to inform the whole world immediately of the commission of the crime.
>
> When the question had been discussed on previous occasions, the supporters of the "colonial clause" had always raised the argument that it was necessary to consult the local administrations before accepting a convention on their behalf. However, it was extremely unlikely that any non-self-governing territory would not wish to benefit from the provisions of the convention so the main argument against his amendment was not very convincing.[204]

Later, Mr. Morozov of the Union of Soviet Socialist Republics (USSR) further queried the UK's representative, Mr. Fitzmaurice. "He wished to know first how many of the territories for which the United Kingdom Government was responsible, enjoyed self-government and had the power to decide the question of adherence to the convention, and how many did not enjoy that power.?"[205] In response the UK representative answered "that he was not personally a colonial expert and was not therefore in position to give precise figures without further reference. He was, however, able to say that at least three quarters of the territories for which the United Kingdom was internationally responsible possessed systems of self-government and legislations."[206] Mr. Morozov, in response,

> emphasized that the convention on genocide was not a convention of the usual type. The question it covered could not automatically be resolved without specific reference to the position of colonial territories.
>
> Colonial policy had been a dark page in history even in pre-fascist times. The Committee did not wish to see those dark pages prolonged by a failure to extend the provisions of the convention on genocide to the colonial territories. The Committee should bear in mind that millions must not be allowed to remain outside the scope of the convention and left to the arbitrary action of the colonial Powers.[207]

The United Kingdom delegation in response rebutted that "with regard to colonial policy, which the representative of the USSR referred to as a dark page in history, the United Kingdom delegation denied the moral authority of the Soviet Union Government to make any such statement, or to set itself up as a model of conduct before the world."[208] The UK denied the concerns of the USSR and the Ukrainian SSR with respect to colonial territories, a matter important to the question of Britain's colonial invasion globally. The necessary point to draw from this debate is that colonialism is regarded as a genocidal process by the very fact that it came up in the drafting process of the genocide convention. The vicious reality of colonialism was exposed to the world governments. Important comments by the Ukraine SSR and USSR delegates and the ad hominem denial by the UK suggest its awareness of its criminal vulnerability with regard to its colonial administrations the world over.

The state position in support of retaining cultural genocide in the convention directly relates to the concern of those states that colonial policy had been a dark page in history. Although the debates about cultural genocide have been mentioned previously in the chapter, further elaboration is necessary. States, such as Poland, Yugoslavia, Ukraine SSR and the Union of the Soviet Socialist Republic, among others, contended that cultural genocide is a central tenet of the crime.[209] The strong opposition with respect to the deletion of cultural genocide concerned the understanding that "fascism, nazism and doctrines of racial superiority"[210] are at the root of genocide and should remain in the preamble to the UNGC. Abtahi and Webb on the representative, Mr. Zourek of Czechoslovakia,

> quoted numerous instances of cultural genocide, of which the Czech and Slovak peoples had been victims during the nazi occupation. Those acts were designed to pave the way for the systematic disappearance of the Czechoslovak nation as an independent national identity. Such nazi activity had been accompanied by a thorough attempt to destroy everything which might remind the people of its national past and to prepare the way for complete germanification. The Nürnberg trials had shown that the measures taken by the nazis in Czechoslovakia were merely the groundwork of a gigantic plan for the complete

> germanification of the Czechoslovak nation. It was hardly necessary to emphasize the close connexion [*sic*] between such a plan and the nazi theory of racial superiority….All of those acts of cultural genocide had been inspired by the same motives as those of physical genocide; they had the same object – the destruction of racial, national or religious groups.[211]

Given that cultural genocide had been deleted[212] the issue came to a head in the USSR amendment [A/766][213] because of its concerns related to the "loopholes which might prevent the punishment of those who perpetrated the crime of genocide or incited others to do so."[214] An earlier concern expressed by the USSR delegate on the so-called protection of cultural genocide issues under a human rights framework held that:

> A number of delegates held the view that the protection of groups against acts of cultural genocide could very well be ensured by the declaration of human rights, and that the idea of cultural genocide was not yet sufficiently developed to warrant its inclusion in the convention. The Soviet Union delegation did not share that view. It was not sufficient for the declaration of human rights to deal with the cultural protection of groups. Such protection should be ensured by the convention on genocide.[215]

Mr. Morozov emphasized his bafflement that some delegations raised objections to the

> organic connexion between fascism and racial theories and genocide being emphasized in the

> convention on genocide. Should the General Assembly accept that view, it would by that very fact demonstrate its refusal to condemn racial theories, or to admit that those theories led to genocide. It was clear that such theories were incompatible with the principles of the Charter. To say that the crime of genocide had no connexion with racial theories amounted, in fact, to a re-instatement of such theories. The USSR delegation strongly objected to such an attempt.[216]

Genocide followed "racial theories intended to develop racial and national hatreds, the domination of the so-called 'higher races' and the extermination of the so called 'lower races'. The crime of genocide formed an integral part of the plan for world domination of the supporters of racial ideologies."[217] He emphasized

> the tenor of another USSR amendment dealing with the crime of cultural genocide, which was defined as the sum total of premeditated action to destroy the religion, culture, or language of a national, racial or religious group. It included, for example, such acts as prohibiting the use of a national language and the publication of books or newspapers in that language, the destruction of libraries, museums, schools, places of worship, and generally speaking, the destruction of every building serving a cultural purpose. Even the delegations which had opposed that amendment had agreed that such acts should be suppressed, but they had claimed that they had no connexion with genocide and that they should be considered in connexion with the discussion of the rights of [oppressed peoples]. The delegation of the USSR could not agree with the view, for it regarded cultural genocide as an aspect of genocide.[218]

The USSR further highlighted another shortcoming: that "its application in Non-Self-Governing Territories was left to the discretion of the administering Powers."[219] Mr. Morozov proposed that the inadequate "resolution inviting those Powers to extend the application of the convention to the territories at the earliest opportunity"[220] it "should be replaced by a definite clause stipulating that the convention should apply not only to the signatory States, but also to the territories under their administration including all Trust Territories and Non-Self-Governing Territories."[221] Mr. Morozov drew attention to the fact that the UK objected to the provision proposed,

> on the plea that it would represent interference on the part of the metropolitan Powers in local government activities. In the opinion of the USSR delegation, the reason why the colonial Powers had pressed so strongly for the omission of such a clause, which incidentally appeared in many other conventions, was because they intended to have a free hand to ensure that colonial territories were maintained in a position of inferiority. That was contrary to the principles of the Charter and therefore the USSR delegation pressed for the adoption of its amendment.[222]

Mr. Katz-Suchy of Poland opposed the deletion of cultural genocide and not clearly linking the preamble to fascist race theories. The most important was the "recognition of the close link existing between the crime of genocide and racial theories and other similar doctrines which had been the official ideology of those countries for many years and which unfortunately was still rooted in those countries."[223] The Polish delegate continued, "If the convention were to be effective, it had to apply to colonies. The Metropolitan States had to be prepared to apply it. Genocide had often been committed in the colonies; the colonial peoples were always in danger from metropolitan

States in that respect, whether in the direct physical form or in the form of cultural genocide."[224]

The amendment (A/766) was rejected by the General Assembly; however what is important is that genocide is linked to theories of the so-called higher races over the so-called lower races. According to the USSR, the removal of cultural genocide "might be utilized by those who wished to carry out [genocide] against national, cultural and racial [human groups/nations]. Such [destruction] did exist at the present time and prevailed in certain territories and colonies administered by countries who prided themselves on their civilization."[225] The USSR further argued that, "Article XII gave the colonial Powers discretion to extend or not to extend the provisions of the convention to their colonies. The rejection of the USSR amendment providing for the extension of the convention to all Non-Self-Governing Territories diminished the value of the present text."[226]

Doctrines of racial superiority are what led to the demonization, isolation and destruction or genocide of our Original Nations in the Western Hemisphere and the world over. The racist christian doctrine of discovery is a case in point. The destruction of Indigenous Nations and Peoples is based on the designation of dehumanizing descriptors such as *savage* or *barbarian*. The discussion raised by the USSR and the rebuttal by the United Kingdom over the colonial clause and the dark history of colonization illuminates the contention that cultural genocide was deleted because of colonial invasion and racist doctrines used to claim and overrun other peoples' lands and territories. The Polish delegate's concern that "colonial" peoples were always in danger of genocide is also instructive and very telling. It was maintained that unless some provision regarding cultural genocide was included in the convention states may use this to "justify crimes of genocide."[227] From the USSR's position the colonial powers intended to make certain that "colonial" territories were maintained in a "position of inferiority".

The erasure of cultural genocide demonstrates the continuation of the colonial objective and the colonial clause debate conveys that the Original Nations of Great Turtle Island and elsewhere have not entered into a "post-colonial era."[228] The removal of the term as a legal concept in international law rendered Indigenous Peoples "invisible"[229] by masking the reality of colonial destruction. USSR's point is well taken with regard to the linkages between cultural genocide and the civilization process.[230] The notion of "civilization" itself is synonymous with "colonialism" and rooted in the destructive doctrine of discovery.[231]

Recall the genocide committed against human groups by the Nazi government. The horrors of WWII were the precursor to the codification of genocide in international law. Writers have documented the model of invasion that Hitler replicated in Eastern Europe as based on the model of colonial invasion in the Western Hemisphere.[232] The Nuremberg laws served as the "cornerstone" establishing the Nazi regime's "legalized persecution"[233] against human groups. According to the United States Holocaust Museum, "these laws embodied many of the racial theories underpinning Nazi ideology."[234] For example, identification cards were issued to identify who was or was not a Jewish person.

Mundorff examines the Nazi state program of forcibly transferring children. Heinrich Himmler, who directed the program, viewed its underlying purpose as their "indoctrination:"[235]

> I think it our duty in these circumstances to take these children, even if we have to rob them or steal them. This may painfully affect our European sensibility, and many people will say to me: How can you be so cruel as to want to take a child from its mother? To that my answer is: How can you be so cruel as to be willing to leave a brilliant future enemy on the other side who will kill your son and grandson? Either we recover this superior blood and use it ourselves or—this may seem cruel to you, gentlemen but nature is cruel—we must destroy it. We cannot

> take the responsibility of leaving this blood on the other side, enabling our enemies to have great leaders capable of leading them. It would be a crime if the present generation hesitated to make a decision and left it to its descendants.[236]

Mundorff conveys that children who were considered to be "racially valuable" were removed and placed in "German orphanages or with German families, to be raised as Germans."[237] Children from eastern occupied lands were placed in temporary "'Germanization camps,' orphanages, or foster placements."[238] Prosecutor Neely in his opening statement against Himmler declared that the fact that "these innocent children were abducted for the very purpose of being indoctrinated with Nazi ideology and brought up as 'good' Germans" [served] to aggravate, not mitigate, the crime."[239] As the horrors of the Nazi colonial invasion of Eastern Europe were revealed, the evil of genocide became acknowledged by the world at large.

Compare this to Canada's legislation with respect to Indigenous Peoples, such as the Gradual Civilization Act,[240] that is rooted in a racist colonial ideological framework. The Canadian government institutionalized racist ideologies into the legal fabric of its state and society. Theories of racial superiority and destructive colonial ideology are found in the words of many government officials. Kent McNeil author of "Social Darwinism and Judicial Conceptions of Indian Title in Canada in the 1880's" writes that the foundation for residential schools was candidly stated in parliament on May 9, 1883 by John A. MacDonald, which was to remove the children from the so-called "savage" influences of the parents.[241] McNeil elaborates on an exchange between Prime Minister MacDonald and MP Charlton further elaborates on the goal of the state. Charlton "infer[s] that the efforts to educate and Christianize the Indians, and make them good members of society, are not being attended with marked success."[242] MacDonald replied that it takes "generations for the Indians to get an aptitude for the cultivation of the soil. According to the principle of development, that must be of slow growth, not in one generation."[243] McNeil explains that government law and policy are based on theories of racial superiority or what is known as Social Darwinism.

Forcible child removals are but one of the "civilizing" programs put into place by the Canadian government. It would seem straightforward to conclude that the residential schools policy constitutes genocide; however this is not the case. The question of whether the Nazi government's conduct is *genocide* is not debatable. However, when the same question is applied to Canada the issue becomes moot. Central to an understanding of the forcible removal of Indigenous children is the unpacking of the dominating and dehumanizing experience of colonial invasion. The relevance of the Genocide Convention's colonial clause in the context of the legal issue in this book is that it demonstrates international recognition that one cannot examine the issue of genocide without looking at the destructive colonial framework under which the forcible transfer of Indigenous children was massively undertaken by the Canadian state.

| Chapter Two |

THE HORROR
Canada's Forced Tranfer of Indigenous Children

"I entered school when I was six. At 47, it took me
some time forty years before I could talk
about my experience in Residential School,
and that was just the first step.
And I have a number of steps to take
before I can consider myself a whole person.
—Residential School Survivor

The residential school system was a program designed and implemented by the state and church (from 1883 to 1996)[1] that utilized a destructive and vicious legal framework that invoked "doctrines of racial superiority"[2] —a civilizing project— to forcibly remove Indigenous Peoples' children from our Nations and ultimately from our lands and territories. Still, to this day, our children continue to be forcibly removed from our homes and families into the provincial child welfare systems with no end in sight.[3] The devastation and effects of racist colonial violence enacted upon our Nations continue to be reflected through the poverty, incarceration rates, suicides, and addictions that we suffer from, among other devastations and the most important being our relationship to our lands and territories.

The Goal of Complete Assimilation

Canadian law and policy have been expressly geared toward bringing about the complete disappearance of Indigenous Nations, as such.[4] By 1842, the Bagot Commission had declared that since "the Indians" were in an "uncivilized state," they should be compelled to assimilate into the colonial society by such means as imposing Canada's system of private property ownership and the forced transfer of children to residential facilities in which they could be compelled to view the world in eurocentric terms.[5] As Duncan Campbell Scott later put it, "our objective is to continue until there is not a single Indian in Canada that has not been absorbed into the body politic, and there is no Indian question, and no Indian department."[6] The state goal was absorption into the "body politic."[7] In other words; the objective was to destroy our Original Nations.

As John Milloy in *A National Crime: The Canadian Government and the Residential School System, 1879 to 1986* correctly contends, "the schools have been, arguably, the most damaging of the many elements of Canada's colonization of this land's original peoples and, as their consequences still affects the lives of [Indigenous Peoples] today, they remain so."[8] In 1996, the Royal Commission on Aboriginal Peoples (hereinafter RCAP Report) concluded that Canada's various assimilation policies, together with the various laws authorizing their implementation, were "designed to move communities, and eventually all [Indian] Peoples, from their helpless 'savage' state to one of self-reliant 'civilization' and thus to make in Canada but one community—a non-[Indian], Christian one," and that, especially during Scott's tenure, "education was 'by far the most important of the many subdivisions of the most complicated Indian problem.'"[9]

John A. MacDonald assigned Nicholas Flood Davin the task of touring U.S.-designed boarding schools for Indigenous Peoples' children.[10] The Davin Report of 1879 was based on the following findings by U.S. government officials. Milloy writes, "Senior American officials who Davin visited, Carl Schurtz, the

Secretary of the Interior, and E. A. Hayt, the Commissioner of Indian Affairs, evinced the greatest confidence in the efficacy of the industrial school, which was, Davin was informed, "the principal feature of the policy known as that of 'aggressive civilization,' their policy of assimilation."[11] Davin then determined that day schools were a dismal failure "'because the influence of the wigwam was stronger than the influence of the school'."[12] Davin's report highlighted that children should be forcibly removed away from their families and be "'kept constantly within the circle of civilized conditions'—the residential school—where they would receive the 'care of a mother' and an education that would fit them for a life in a modernizing Canada."[13]

It was recommended that children be removed from the "savage" influence of their parents and peoples and isolated in state-controlled residential school facilities. Based on Davin's recommendations, John A. MacDonald stated to the House of Commons in 1883:

> …the first object is to make them better men, and, if possible, good Christian men by applying proper moral restraints, and appealing to the instinct for worship which is to be found in all nations, whether ***civilized*** or ***uncivilized***.…When the school is on the Reserve the child lives with its parents, who are ***savages***; he is surrounded by ***savages***, and though he may learn to read and write his habits, and training and mode of thought are ***Indian***. He is simply a ***savage*** who can read and write. It has been strongly pressed upon myself, as head of the Department, that the Indian children should be withdrawn as much as possible from the parental influence, and ***the only way to do that would be to put them in central training industrial schools where they will acquire the habits and modes of thought of white men; so that, after keeping them a number***

> ***of years away from parental influence until their education is finished, they will be able to go back to their band with the habits of mind,*** the education, the industry which they have learned at these schools....[emphasis added].[14]

Other policy statements are instructive. RCAP cited the Minister of Indian Affairs, Frank Oliver, who in 1908 held that education would "'elevate the Indian from his condition of savagery' and 'make him a self-supporting member of the state, and eventually a citizen in good stan[d]ing'."[15] Scott affirmed that education was 'indispensable' for Indian communities and was necessary for without it "they 'would produce an undesirable and often dangerous element in society'."[16]

The intended "vision"[17] of the government looked to the young "for a complete change of condition."[18] The RCAP elucidates the intent of the Canadian state:

> Only in the children could hope for the future reside, for only children could undergo "the transformation from the natural condition to that of civilization." Adults could not join the march of progress. They could not be emancipated from their "present state of ignorance, superstition and helplessness"; they were "physically mentally and morally ...unfitted to bear such a complete metamorphosis."[19]

A "civilizing" boarding school education system held the greatest promise for the government's goal. Elizabeth Furniss in *Victims of Benevolence: The Dark Legacy of the Williams Lake Residential School,* cites the federal government's position:

> If it were possible to gather in all the Indian children and retain them for a certain period, there would be produced a generation of English-

> speaking Indians, accustomed to the ways of civilized life, which might then be the dominant body among themselves, capable of holding its own with its white neighbours; and thus would be brought about a rapidly decreasing expenditure until the same should forever cease, and the Indian problem would be solved.[20]

Doctrines of racial superiority to address the "Indian problem" were codified into the Canadian state's destructive colonial legal framework, which was really about overrunning and claiming our lands and resources. The articulation of the so-called problem and its solution was legislated into various laws and the Indian Department took as its goal "[t]ribal dissolution, to be pursued mainly through the corridors of residential schools."[21] The government invoked what Lemkin termed "laws of occupation"[22] to forcibly transfer Indigenous Peoples' children.[23] The purpose was to terminate the "Indian problem" or the national identity of the Original Nations. The legislation itself demonstrates the intent that went into designing the laws that force the transfer of the children. Milloy, on the legislative domination, noted: "[B]ehind every school principal, matron, teacher, and staff member who worked in the school system, and behind each participating denomination, stood the Canadian government and the Department of Indian Affairs, which was symbolic of Canada's self-imposed 'responsibility' for Aboriginal people set out in Section 91:24 of the British North America Act of 1867."[24]

Early state social engineering tactics are found in the 1857 Act to Encourage the Gradual Civilization of the Indian Tribes of the Province,[25] the precursor to the Indian Act. The British North American Act of 1867 (BNA Act) "legalized" the domination and dehumanization of Indigenous Peoples and Nations.[26] Section 18 of the BNA Act gave the colony of Canada power and authority to effect policies and programs that have led to genocide.[27] The relevance of section 18 is that it affirms that Canada is a colony of Great Britain. Section 91(24) gave exclusive legislative authority (control and domination) to the federal government under: "Indians, and Lands reserved for Indians."[28] This colonial legislation entrenched in law the racist view that Indigenous Peoples were incapable of governing themselves and imposed the *Indian Act* of 1876.[29] These colonial laws then forced the removal and compulsory attendance of Indigenous Peoples' children into the residential school system.[30]

Another example of a genocidal colonial framework is the White Paper of 1969 that was an attempt to assimilate Indigenous Peoples into Canada.[31] It is evident the government intent to "absorb" Indigenous Peoples into the colonial "body politic" has not changed over time.[32] The White Paper is viewed as attempt to get rid of the Treaties by extinguishing the Treaty and Inherent rights of Indigenous Peoples.[33] Colonial termination laws and policies are intended to continue to dominate and dehumanize until land issues are extinguished, and the Peoples assimilated or "digested"[34] into the fabric of the state of Canada.

Recall briefly that Prosecutor Neely in his opening statement against Heinrich Himmler declared that the fact that "these innocent children were abducted for the very purpose of being indoctrinated with Nazi ideology and brought up as 'good' Germans [served] to aggravate not mitigate the crime."[35] The Nazi government legislated into its framework laws intended to dominate and dehumanize the oppressed nations. The purpose of removing children to indoctrinate them as "good" Germans is similar to the language utilized by the Canadian government. Aptly clarified by David Wallace Adams, the residential school system became an "education for extinction"[36] plan of coordinated government action. The vision of Canadian government officials and the "language in which it was couched, revealed what would have to be the essentially violent nature of the residential school system in its onslaught on [children]."[37] The residential school system served to render Indigenous Peoples' children completely vulnerable to the forcible assimilation and indoctrination.

Forcible Transfer and Resistance

The Canadian state legislated the forcible transfer of Indigenous Peoples' children into residential institutions[38] where the children were then severely traumatized and dehumanized by the collective experience of the serious bodily and mental harm. While the policy statements have been reviewed, it is important to note again that the residential institution was designed for the purpose of destruction via forced indoctrination. The RCAP Report outlines the instructions given to officials:

> Those strangers, the teachers and staff, were according to Hayter Reed, a senior member of the department in the 1890s, to employ "every effort…against anything calculated to keep fresh in the memories of the children habits and associations which it is one of the main objects of industrial education to obliterate." Marching out from the schools, the children, effectively re-socialized, imbued [*or indoctrinated*] with the values of European culture, would be the vanguard of a magnificent metamorphosis: the '*savage*' was to be made '*civilized*', made fit to take up the privileges and responsibilities of citizenship [emphasis added] .[39]

The analysis proceeds to examine the ways in which Indigenous children as part of the government intent to "kill the Indian in the child"[40] were conditioned to "think, speak and write like white men."[41]

Laws of occupation that force the removal of Indigenous children sever the child from his or her national identity, family, community, land (Mother Earth), laws, government, kinship, language, and spirituality to indoctrinate and "absorb"[42] him or her into the oppressor society. The intent to destroy the national identities of the children is supported by policy statements or "general political doctrine"[43] and enacted into the colonial laws that force the transfer by state agents such as the Royal Canadian Mounted Police.[44] In the case of the present day child welfare system, the children are removed in similar ways through state agents such as the police and child welfare workers. Parents, families, communities and Nations resisted and continue to resist the removal of children as has been noted in many documents and stories.[45] The forced removal is traumatizing for the children, the families, and Nations.

> [W]hen [the] parents refused to send their children legislation was passed to enforce attendance.... Children as young as six or seven years old were rounded up and taken away, often in cattle trucks, to residential schools. Parents had no say. When the children got to the schools, they were isolated from their families and forbidden to speak their [Nation's] language or practice any part of their culture. The children who attended residential schools experienced every form of abuse—physical, sexual, emotional and spiritual.[46]

Parents vehemently objected to the forced transfer of their children. As Grant noted on parental resistance: "The most common form of resistance was to hide children or to refuse to return them on time."[47] At the Lebret Indian Residential School parents and grandparents camped outside of the boarding schools in hopes of seeing their children.[48] Parents and leaders alike recognized the potential for the extinction and dissolution of their identities and many objected to the residential school system.[49]

To the parents and leaders it was obvious that the removal of their children was an attack against their distinct identities as nations, an instrument of coercion and control. It was reported by the DIA that parents did not support the transfer of their children.[50] Chief Star Blanket was forcibly removed from his position of chief "for killing cattle to feed his band in spite of instructions to the contrary from Indian Affairs. In 1895 he was told by the department that it would support his reinstatement if he helped secure students for the residential schools from his reluctant band."[51] Star Blanket made an appeal requesting that schools be made on the reserves:

> In the Treaty we made then, the government promised to make a school for every band of Indians on their own reserve, but instead, little children are torn from their mothers' arms or homes by the police or government agents, and taken sometimes hundreds of miles away to large schools, perhaps to take sick and die when their family cannot see them.[52]

As it relates to the promises made to the Indigenous Peoples at the time Treaty was made between the Indigenous Nations and the Crown, Sharon Venne explains that: "A school house was to be in each community for all children. The Chiefs and Elders wanted their young people to be able to cope with the new comers, and believed the most successful way would be for the children to understand their ways."[53] Instead what transpired "was the forced education of their children into a foreign value system, and the introduction of residential schools where the language and spirituality was beaten out of them."[54] Of course parents vehemently resisted the removals by not

> allow[ing] their children to attend such schools—the children were not to be stripped of their identity by church-run schools. However, the government of Canada used the pass system, introduced in 1886, to force children into the residential schools. With the pass system, Indigenous peoples could not travel outside the reserves to hunt, and starvation became a reality among the people for the first time in their history

> (the Elders often speak of starvation as coming with the settlers). The people were forced into dependence on the Ottawa-appointed Indian agent for food rations or a pass. If the people refused to send their children to school, there was no food or no pass. It became a choice between allowing the children to starve or sending them to school where they would be fed.[55]

The parents and Nations resisted the removals of their children, but at every turn the government forced the transfers by any means necessary—such as starving people into submission. The removals are a violation of the Treaty.

The confusion and psychological trauma was evident on both parent and child.[56] One story recounts:

> When that truck did come, boy, I tell you. We had a back door and a front door and we beelined it. I didn't know exactly where they were going, but when everybody started running, I started to run too and realized the truck was there. And they literally chased us down….
>
> And the kids that are on the truck, they're all bawling because they're seeing us, you know screaming and yelling…. Of course, they're all crying because we're crying and Mum's crying and I can remember [saying], 'What'd I ever to do to you? Why are you mad at me? Why are you sending me away?'...She was really heartbroken.[57]

The stories are countless and the experience common that children were terrorized by the process of removal. One survivor, Emily Rice, remembers her first experience:

> "I clung to Rose until Father Jackson wrenched her out of my arms." Rice remembers. "I searched all

> over the boat for Rose. Finally I climbed up to the wheel house and opened the door and there was Father Jackson, on top of my sister. My sister's dress was pulled up and his pants were down. I was too little to know about sex; but I know now he was raping her. He cursed and came after me, picked up his big black Bible and slapped me across the face and on the top of the head. I started crying hysterically and he threw me out onto the deck. When we got to Kuper Island, my sister and I were separated. They wouldn't let me comfort her. Even today, all my sisters are strangers to me."[58]

Churchill writes, "[w]ith the youngsters thus isolated, and otherwise stripped of the most immediate links to their cultural identity, a deeper and more comprehensive demolition was undertaken."[59]

Destruction of the National Pattern

In the residential school or "total institution"[60], children are forcibly indoctrinated or conditioned by horrific violence and terror. Chrisjohn, Young, and Maraun (hereinafter Chrisjohn et al.) apply Erving Goffman's 1961 analysis of the total institution to the residential school system. Citing Erving Goffman's *Asylums*, they explain the objective of the total institution: "The total institution is a social hybrid, part residential community, part formal organization.... In our society, they are the forcing houses for changing persons; each is a natural experiment of what can be done to the self."[61] Goffman coined the term "total institution" and he did not know about the existence of the residential school system yet the "examples and the principles of operation he abstracted were taken from homes for the aged, asylums, private boarding schools, monasteries, prisons, concentration camps and the like. He called such places total institutions."[62] The residential school as a total institution implemented the "techniques"[63] of destruction. Further, the description of the residential school as a total institution matches the destructive experience and the two phases of genocide described by Raphael Lemkin.[64] Lemkin explains it as the destruction of the national pattern of the oppressed and the imposition of the national pattern of the oppressor. The techniques of destruction can also be characterized as the techniques of domination and dehumanization.

The children were dominated by military style order and regularity by the issuance of uniforms. The "uniforms" were viewed as "agents of discipline and thus of civilization and modernity."[65] The total institution begins the remaking process. Chrisjohn et al. citing Goffman explain the institutional tactics of total institutions:

> The recruit [*sic*] comes into the establishment with a conception of himself [sic] made possible by certain stable social arrangements in his home world. Upon entrance, he is immediately stripped of the support provided by these arrangements. In the accurate language of some of our oldest total institutions, he begins a series of abasements, degradations, humiliations, and profanations of self.[66]

The entry process into the total institution, as per Goffman:

> …typically brings other kinds of loss and mortification as well. We very generally find staff employing what are called admission procedures, such as taking life history, photographing, weighing, fingerprinting, assigning numbers, searching, listing personal possessions for storage, undressing, bathing, disinfecting, haircutting, issuing institutional clothing, instructing as to rules, and assigning to quarters….Action taken

> on the basis of such attributes necessarily ignores most of his previous bases of self-identification.
>
> ...although sexual molestation certainly occurs in total institutions, there are many other less dramatic examples. Upon admission, one's on-person possessions are pawed and fingered by an official as he itemizes and prepares for them for storage. The inmate himself may be frisked and searched to the extent —often reported in the literature—of a rectal examination. Later in his stay he may be required to undergo searchings of his person and of his sleeping quarters, either routinely or when trouble arises. In all these cases it is the searcher as well as the search that penetrates the private reserve of the individual and violates the territories of his self.
>
> Once the inmate is stripped of his possessions, at least some replacements must be made by the establishment, but these take the form of standard issue, uniform in character and uniformly distributed. These substitute possessions are clearly marked as really belonging to the institution and in some cases are recalled at regular intervals to be, as it were, disinfected of identifications...Failure to provide inmates with individual lockers and periodic searches and confiscations of accumulated personal property reinforce property dispossession. Religious orders have appreciated the implications for self of such separations from belongings.[67]

Total institutions are invariably fenced off from the world, "which 'broke down' the barriers that existed in greater society between places of work, sleep and play [or between Indigenous Nations and societies]; and which enforced and maintained an extreme power disparity between a large inmate population and a smaller supervisory staff…"[68] Chrisjohn, et al. continue, citing Goffman:

> In addition to personal defacement that comes from being stripped of one's identity kit, there is a personal disfigurement that comes from direct and permanent mutilations of the body such as brands or loss of limbs. Although this mortification of the self by way of the body is found in few total institutions, still, loss of a sense of personal safety is common and provides a basis for anxieties about disfigurement. Beatings, shock therapy…may lead many inmates to feel that they are in an environment that does not guarantee their physical integrity.[69]

While mortification of the self by way of the body is found in few total institutions it is found in the residential school system where children were tortured through beatings and shock therapy (among others techniques) that led to the personal safety of the children being dominated and dehumanized by the institution.[70] As recently as 2014, the media reported that at St. Anne's School in Ontario children were tortured with electric chairs.[71] Children were made "to feel that they [were] in an environment that [did] not guarantee" their personal safety.[72]

Many former students "testified (to the Royal commission and elsewhere) that they did not feel safe, or loved, or cared for; that they **were** or **felt they were** exposed to the predations of school staff…. [emphasis original]."[73] The vulnerability of a sense of impending doom or fear of what could happen next was a common experience for the young ones. The instilment of fear was a part of the forced conditioning process.

When examined from the perspective of a total institution, the residential school becomes visible as a process to achieve the oppressor's "civilizing mission".[74] Total institutions used as a tool for forced conditioning and social control generally met that objective.[75] Children do become forcibly conditioned into the kind of people the institution intended them to be and this is clearly indicated by government officials. Hayter Reed, senior department official, instructed staff officials to *obliterate* the identity of Indigenous children.[76] The importance of these statements and other government objectives indicating the same, convey the goal of forcing the so-called *savage* out of the Indian by the obliteration and change of identity in Indigenous children. One student recalled his experience at Kamloops Indian Residential School, "To me, the Indian school generally speaking was sort of like you were taken over by a superior force, by the government and [they] try to mould you into something else and they were very strict about it…."[77]

Total institutions serve as modes of forced indoctrination or brainwashing. Brainwashing is defined "to effect a radical change in the ideas and beliefs (of a person) esp. by methods based on isolation, sleeplessness, hunger, extreme discomfort, pain, and the alternation of kindness and cruelty."[78] The children become dominated and dehumanized by the sheer terror and unrelenting violence. John Milloy writes that "the basic premise of re-socialization was violent. 'To kill the Indian' in the child, the Department and churches aimed at severing the artery of culture that ran between Aboriginal generations. In the end, 'all the Indian there is in the race should be dead.'"[79] The goal of obliteration "took on a sharp and traumatic reality in the life of each child who was separated from parents and community and isolated in a threatening world hostile to identity, traditional ritual, and language."[80] Forced domination and dehumanization in an effort to "kill the Indian in the child" takes place through the enforced indoctrination of the child, "[b]y doing this, the total institution does not produce a **new** self, but **no self at all** [emphasis original]."[81]

The residential school system, resembling a total institution, was founded on "programs of cultural replacement with the avowed aim of westernizing the Indian children as completely as possible."[82] The Shingwauk Residential School, among other schools, operated on the model of cultural replacement.[83] In this process, cultural change is brought about by "the use of pressure by [colonizer] societies to induce [Indigenous] societies to make changes."[84] The definition referred to previously—that "civilizing" means "the *forcing* of a particular cultural pattern on a population to whom it is foreign"[85]—aptly correlates with David Nock's understandings. Seen in this light, the *civilization* of a dominated group is seen for what it really is: a violent process that is applied against another group to coerce them to adopt the invading culture that is being imposed.

Nock, citing Ralph Linton, writes: "Directed culture change will be taken to refer to those situations in which one of the groups in contact interferes actively and purposely with the culture of the other.... The processes of directed culture change can only operate in those contact situations in which there is dominance and submission."[86] Chrisjohn et al. concur, and pursue the prison analogy as follows:

> [I]f inmates become available at a young enough age, the tactics of total institutions won't merely "disrupt or defile" selves, but hinder their development in the first place. By **not allowing** the formation of "adult executive competency," the inmates are prevented from being or becoming persons **at all**. When used in this manner, total institutions are not, therefore, instruments of social engineering, intended to inculcate an alternative form of life; they are instruments genocide, meant to produce things unrecognizable **at all** as human beings [emphasis original].[87]

The full reality of these horrific places and what they represent begins to emerge for the reader. It is necessary that this be done, so that the residential institutions can be seen as an abomination. They are programs of genocide.

The *Circle Game* properly sums up the residential school as a total institution. Apart from being "subjected to the tortures, the rapes, the beatings and other merciless, sadistic acts,"[88] ordinary day-to-day life in the residential school was ruthless, consisting of:

- Religious indoctrination
- Hard labour
- Torturous infractions for speaking indigenous languages and contact with other family members
- Under-heated school buildings and floors
- Barrack-style living arrangements
- Chronic malnutrition and unfit food
- Witnessing other children being severely tortured, which served as warnings[89]

A government background paper on the subject writes, "Testimony by former students has revealed extremely harsh and hazardous living conditions at the schools, including hunger and malnutrition, poor heating and sanitation, inadequate clothing and exposure to contagious diseases. Many students suffered sexual, physical and emotional [torture] by the teachers and staff responsible for their care...."[90] Isabelle Knockwood in *Out of the Depths* portrays the experience of residential school in terms of loneliness, starvation, fear, violence and brutality as part of her experience at the Shubencadie Indian Residential School. Knockwood writes, "Day after day, week after week, month after month and year after year for seven, eight, nine or ten years, this was the atmosphere we ate our meals in—an atmosphere of fear of the unknown, the unexpected and the reality that you could be next."[91] Further to witnessing violence against other children, "…there may be occasions when an individual witnesses a physical assault upon someone to whom [one] has ties and suffers the permanent mortification of having (and being known to have) taken no action."[92]

Chrisjohn, et al. write: "Often, the climate of the Indian Residential Schools alternated between being emotionally overwhelming (on one extreme) and emotionally barren (on the other)….Children vied for the positive attentions of their custodians, who played favourites and set the children against one another with extra food, privileges and other inducements."[93]

Accordingly, "emotional devastation was built into the Residential Schools" [94] by the "initial separation from parents and family; prolonged isolation from parents, family and people; the period of adjustment to institutional rules; and the constant fault-finding and racial slurs addressed to them by staff."[95]

Forced indoctrination/brainwashing processes are possible when the child is isolated: "…confined there for a decade or more, relentlessly stripped of their cultural identities while being methodically indoctrinated to see their traditions—and thus themselves—through the eyes of their colonizers…."[96] Upon being confined and isolated, the fear, loneliness, and terror would take the place of family, security, and love.[97] Celia Haig-Brown, in *Resistance and Renewal,* explains that "[t]he fear and loneliness often were manifested in bed wetting. One person estimated that 25% of the boys wet their beds."[98] At Shubenacadie "[b]ed wetting was common and punishable by humiliation and horrible beatings."[99] Robert Simon, who was at Kamloops Indian Residential School, recalls:

> I remember what it felt like when I got to the residential school. I was frightened for a long time. There seemed to be continually new frightening things happening. I was on my own. It was the first time in my life that I had ever been separated for any length of time from my grandparents or my family or my mother.
>
> Until I got to the residential school, I had no idea about violence. I didn't understand fear. Well it's tough because you're alone and you'd been accustomed to people saying good night to you, giving you a hug, talking to you for a while, reading to you or something like that. It wasn't like that. You listen to children cry and you'd get scared because they'd be scared, not much you could do about it. So you'd lay in bed and think to yourself, "How can I ever get out of

> here? What did I ever do to get in here? Who did I offend so badly or who did I make so upset that I would be here and if it is so who do I talk to about promising that I would never do it again? You'd ask yourself all these kind of questions.[100]

Simon continues: "I'd go to sleep. Sometimes the children would still be crying and that was really sad. I'd cry once in a while, too. It was just pure loneliness....The loneliness was there when you were trying to sleep, when you went to sleep and when you got up in the morning, you were still lonely."[101] Churchill writes, "[a] consistent theme running through autobiographical material written by former students is how this procedure in particular engendered an abiding sense that they'd 'lost' themselves and were thus 'stranger[s,] with no possibilities' for the future."[102]

The entrance into the institutions is characterized as a vicious and violent process against the child's national identity. Haig-Brown affirms that upon arrival to the school "the cultural attacks began in earnest."[103] Churchill describes the routine as psychologically inhuman: "[T]he regimen was deliberately and relentlessly brutal. From the moment the terrified and bewildered youngsters arrived at the schools, designed as they were to serve as 'total institutions,' a comprehensive and carefully-calibrated assault on their cultural identity would commence."[104] The common practice was to force children to obedience by strictly disciplined behaviour through regimented conduct, submission to authority, and punishment to obtain domination.[105] Churchill explains how, upon first entering the institution: "For boys and girls alike, this began with a thorough scrubbing and 'disinfection'—alcohol and kerosene were among the astringents used for the latter purpose—often accompanied by staff commentary about 'dirty Indians.'"[106] The practice of cutting hair was common: "Long or braided hair, which had spiritual significance for many students, was often cut short"[107] as it was representative of the uncivilized savage. For boys, the admission procedure involved the mortifying experience of having their "heads shorn, military-style."[108] Young girls had their hair cut short.[109] The children's clothing was removed and "[i]n exchange, they were issued uniforms expressly intended to separate them from their 'excessive individualism' of their own traditions by reducing them to sameness, to regularity, to order."[110] English names replaced the names in the original languages of the children.[111] It was a common experience for the children to be given numbers.[112] The entire foundation of the residential school system is characterized as a violent conditioning process through an onslaught against the national identities of the children.

Children were ruthlessly dominated by English language indoctrination. The children were taken apart by the dehumanizing and continuous attacks against their spirituality. One student recalls, "…we were not allowed to speak our language; we weren't allowed to dance, sing because they told us it was evil. It was evil for us to practice any of our cultural ways."[113] The government understood the language was vital in the transmission of the culture from one generation to the next so all efforts were put in place to "stamp out [Indigenous] languages within the schools and in the children."[114] Children experienced humiliation and shame through this process.

One student recalls: "...I was not really allowed to speak Cree, but they didn't know' cause we just switched to English every time we saw a supervisor coming or something like that. There was not one single native tradition in the school. They just took you away, where you left everything, all the Indian-ness back there…."[115] Children were forced to adopt the christian religion in place of their culture and spirituality through this process of demonizing the original languages. J.R. Miller explains what was told to a student from Oblates' St. Phillip's school by the staff officials:

> '[O]ur language belonged to the Devil,' as did all the Saulteaux religious observances. 'They told us that our parents, our grandparents, all our people, out there whenever they have these things going, they were chanting to the devil.'

> And if they could hear the drum begin nearby on the reserve, 'they'd all tell us to go inside so we won't listen to them drums because you're chanting to the devil.' Inside, 'we'd all kneel down and pray that our people would change.' At school she was taught that all the things she had learned at home were 'ugly' and 'meant for the devil, with the result that she 'became ashamed of being Indian.'[116]

This goal was the norm; child after child was subjected to the demonization of their mother tongue.[117] Milloy on the quashing of the language:

> [T]he department and churches understood consciously that culture or, more particularly, that the task of overturning one ontology in favour of another was the challenge they faced is seen in their identification of language as the critical issue in the circle. It was through the language that the child gained its ontological inheritance from its parents and community. The word bore the burden of the culture from one generation to the next. It was the vital connection.[118]

The annihilation of the original languages was implemented through torturous acts of punishment as children were beaten for speaking their tongue.[119] Churchill explains that staff and school officials were assigned the task of "preventing pupils from 'using their own languages', even in private conversations (or prayer). Doing so, of course, meant that the children had to be placed under virtually continuous surveillance."[120] The original languages are the life force of Indigenous Nations and Peoples because our spiritual laws are encoded in our languages and contribute to a healthy conception of a human identity. As a result of the forced indoctrination of the colonial language, the youngster is forced to view the world from a reality that instils fear, self-loathing, and trauma.

Imposition of the National Pattern

Upon state-legislated control and isolation, the children were rendered vulnerable as they were dominated and brutalized through various means. The staff, teachers, nuns, and priests inflicted "torture, predatory sexual acts, forced slave labour, and starvation"[121] on the innocent. These violent acts were exacerbated by the constant attack and denigration of their culture, people, history, language, laws, and way of life. The regime was brutally enforced against the young ones to obtain their complete submission.

Obedience and domination was maintained as the national pattern of the oppressor was imposed through regimented order and socialization.[122] Children were given uniforms as their own clothes and dress was disregarded: "We wore blue tunics, white blouses, Oxford shoes, and undies provided by the school, all the years of school."[123] One student recalls: "Everything that was done in the school was done in an army-like fashion. A bell rang—we all lined up; a whistle blew—we all came in for the evening duties; another kind of bell rang for meals—the children lined up again. We were so well-trained regimentally that we didn't have to think anymore."[124] Children were forced to obey under all conditions:

> Yes, learning that white was right and that we and our parents were all wrong. I began to learn rather quickly that we had to obey and almost worship those white staff that were in charge of us. I remember one early experience I had that same fall. The children were all coming down with measles and the flu and so most of the windows were darkened in the dormitory and the beds were filled with sick children. I was one of them. I hadn't eaten for two days and I had a high fever. The matron forced me to eat but I vomited it out onto the floor. She ordered me out of bed and told me to clean it up. My head was spinning and my knees were shaking.[125]

The colonial violence and terror against the children rendered them vulnerable to the cognitive conditioning that would occur via the vicious propaganda about their culture, history, peoples and nations in the context of christian[126] and classroom indoctrination. The so called superiority of the christian worldview, culture and spirituality was emphasized by dehumanizing attacks against the national identity of Indigenous Peoples' children.[127] Another survivor maintains that "it was masterfully drilled into me that I was a 'heathen savage.'"[128] Indigenous children were forced to believe their peoples and nations were inferior and less than those of Europeans, consistent with the oppressor's goal of "killing the Indian in the child."[129]

The demonization would commence in the classroom as the children were told their peoples were wandering barbarous savages and "weren't *really* 'people,' but rather formed the 'forces of evil' that had to be overcome...."[130] It was imbedded in the children that their people were in a *savage* state with no form of society, laws, or government. Children were conditioned to believe that their people were incapable of living in a so-called *civilized* manner or that their way of life was a "real, living culture."[131] Instead the children were led to believe their culture was inferior or "archaic and undesirable."[132] On indoctrination, Haig-Brown noted, "when a culture is being attacked in an effort to dominate it or to replace it with an alternative way of life, an effective tactic includes lack of acknowledgment of that culture's history."[133] Churchill questioned

> [w]hat indigenous students were to make of the fact that their own people—and thus they themselves—had not 'crossed the sea' to get to America.... Small wonder that the children came to identify far more with the mythic legions of noble white men populating their textbooks and classroom lectures than they did with the grossly distorted caricatures of their own ancestors and traditions presented therein.[134]

On the ontology of children Milloy writes: "Parts of the programme of studies would disorient children and then attempt to re-orient them in a place filled with European 'meaning.'"[135] The techniques of destruction to impose the national pattern of the oppressor were accomplished as the young ones were beat, starved, whipped, sexually violated, rendered sick through deplorable health conditions, slave laboured, pitted against each other, and the methods go on to "obliterate"[136] their distinct national identities.

Churchill's classifications of the destruction in its reality and the ascription of the designation "total institution" to residential schools by Chrisjohn et al. are critical to proving genocide as it moves past Canada's colonial rhetoric and euphemisms that conceal the genocidal nature of the acts the children suffered by the hands of the state and church and staff officials. Chrisjohn et al. explain these rhetorical games as "word-magic."[137] The euphemistic language employed by the colonizer through government report or scholarship erects a tremendous hurdle to advancing claims—whether in law or to the public at large—that Indigenous children's experience is genocidal when the colonizer's choice of words tones down that experience, enabling the coloniser to conceal the full reality of the brutal horror. As the issue of rhetoric will be discussed in another chapter this explanation will suffice. Churchill and Chrisjohn et al. describe the destruction these abominations called "schools" represent. Churchill accurately classifies the destruction as "slow death measure of starvation", "indirect killing by disease", "slow death measure of forced labour," "torture" and "predation."[138] In other words, the title of "the parenting presumption: neglect and abuse"[139] employed by Milloy in *A National Crime* does not accurately portray these places for what they truly are: indicators of genocide.

It is impossible to segregate what are often overlapping experiences under the headings of *Death and Disease, Torture, Forced Starvation, Forced Labour,* and *Sexual Predation*. Some cases in point: in Elizabeth Furniss' *Victims of Benevolence*, children died while running away and had planned pact suicides.[140] Children were, for obvious reasons, running away from the brutal treatment and terror. The experience of torture by starvation and being beaten for not eating rotten, bug-ridden food is a consistent theme at the Williams Lake Residential School.[141] Solomon Pooyak, who was at the Thunderchild School, was beaten to death for speaking Cree.[142] Another example is that physical force would be applied to control and dominate the children such as rape as a mode of torture to force domination.[143] A horrific variation on rape involved a pregnant girl being beaten nightly in an attempt to determine who the father was. In the end she succumbed to the beatings and died. It was later speculated by fellow classmates that it was "likely a staff member."[144] Chrisjohn, et al. on the subject of the destruction write that the violations "cannot, occur in isolation from one other."[145] Further to this, short of death, the onslaught of the vicious conduct employed daily and for years on end will no doubt cause destruction. As Grant contends, "Not all deaths are believed to be from illness or accidents. The reports of students being beaten and then hospitalized come from all over the country."[146]

Death and Disease

The obliteration was accomplished with the young ones forced to live under dangerous health and sanitation conditions.[147] The lives of children were devalued. One story is recounted by Simon Baker who attended the Lytton School about his brother that died of meningitis. Simon pleaded with staff officials to take him to the hospital but when they finally did he died:

> A coffin was ordered from Kamloops, and the next day the principal told me I had to go with him to put my brother in a coffin....
>
> [We] washed him and put some clothing on him, but the coffin was to short, and that's the thing I couldn't believe, they wouldn't order another coffin. He had been dead for twenty-four hours, so we had

> to break his knees to put him in the coffin. It was so hot out, so the body started to smell. When I got back to the school, I could smell that odour. It stayed with me for a while.[148]

It was known by government officials that the residential schools were "entirely unfit for human habitation."[149] Dr. P.H. Bryce, former Chief Medical Officer of the Indian Department, released a report in 1907 slamming the Canadian government for the unfit health conditions in which he held that, "[a] trail of disease and death has gone on almost unchecked by any serious efforts on the part of the Department of Indian Affairs."[150] Milloy, referencing S.H. Blake, a lawyer on the horrendous conditions brought to the public by Dr. Bryce, determined that "[t]he 'appalling number of deaths among the younger children' was the result of removing children" from their people.[151] Blake in a straightforward response to Minister Frank Oliver stated that: "'The appalling number of deaths among the younger children appeals loudly to the guardians of our Indians. In doing nothing to obviate the preventable causes of death, brings the department within unpleasant nearness to the charge of manslaughter'."[152] Churchill, on the Bryce Report writes,

> ...[O]f the 1,537 children who had attended the sample group of facilities since they'd opened—a period of ten years, on average—42 percent had died of "consumption or tuberculosis," either at the schools or shortly after being discharged. Extrapolating, Bryce's date indicated that of the 3,755 native children then under the "care" of Canada's residential schools, 1,614 could be expected to have died a miserable death by the end of 1910.[153]

Milloy explains that Dr. Bryce condemned the "[d]epartment for its failure to act in the face of the white plague, tuberculosis."[154]

The disease and death created by unsanitary living conditions were well known to staff officials in the schools and the government apparatus.[155] As for responsibility, "The cause of that tragic 'trail of disease and death' lay in the construction, administration and funding of the residential school system after 1879."[156] These facts were aggravated by the Canadian government's refusal to address the deplorable health and living conditions our children were forced to live under.

According to the RCAP Report, "While a few officials and churchmen rejected Bryce's findings and attacked him as a 'medical faddist', most had to agree with him, and no less an authority than [Duncan Campbell] Scott asserted that system wide, '*fifty percent of children who passed through these schools did not live to benefit from the education which they received therein'* [emphasis added]."[157] Further to this, "[t]he death rates among children confined in such facilities was, after all, as high or higher than that prevailing in some of the nazis' more notorious concentration camps."[158] Churchill aptly sums it up:

> To place this startling proportion in proper perspective, it should be borne in mind that the death rate at the infamous nazi concentration camp at Dachau was 36 percent, mostly from disease. At Buchenwald, another notorious example, the rate was nineteen percent. At Mauthausen, described by historian Michael Burleigh as exhibiting 'the harshest regime of all the concentration camps,' the death rate was 58 percent (again, mostly from malnutrition and attendant disease). [159]

The government, churches and staff officials were aware of the appalling conditions, yet the residential schools were allowed to exist year after year with the same horrific standards. Exact records do not allow a count of the actual number of deaths; however, it is clear that department officials forced the children to live under these conditions as nothing was done to correct the situation.[160] Media reports render the number of children who died while in the residential school system in the thousands.[161] The relevance of the death rates to the legal issue of genocide at question relates to Article II(c) of the Genocide Convention: "Deliberately inflicting on the group conditions of life calculated to bring about its physical destruction in whole or in part". Aside from the fact that children who witnessed the massive death toll will be mentally harmed and traumatized by the experience of witnessing their friends and family dying off.

Torture

Acts of atrocious and vicious violence [162] were employed by staff, teachers, nuns, and priests. They inflicted beatings, whippings, and other sadistic acts such as "locking children in closets"[163] or rooms for prolonged periods.[164] Other acts of brutal violence include the "administration of beatings to naked or partially naked children before their fellow students and/or institutional officials"[165] and "using electrical shock devices on physically restrained children."[166] Other so-called "'corrective measures'"[167] include "forcing sick children to eat their own vomit"[168] and "withholding medical attention from individuals suffering the effects of physical abuse."[169]

All of the above and more not mentioned "went beyond the unusual standards of 'cruel and unusual punishment.'"[170] One story accounts: "I saw kids dragged out from their beds into the bathroom. They were dragged in there you could hear them getting beat up. You could hear them crying and screaming. Either because they pissed their bed or they were talking after the lights were out and stuff like that."[171] On being scolded for not getting subtractions and additions right one young girl stated, "I remember her using the whip on our knuckles. I remember my knuckles being black and blue and sore."[172] Another child recounts, "The sisters scold me all the time—they gave me bad food—the beef was rotten—I couldent [*sic*] eat it—they kept it over and gave it to me next meal—they tied my hands and blindfolded me and gave me nothing to eat for a day."[173] Chrisjohn, et al. list the ways in which torture was inflicted against our children. Some but not all are classified as follows:

- Sticking needles through the tongues of children, often leaving them in place for extended periods of time;
- Inserting needles into other regions of children's anatomy;
- Burning or scalding children;
- Beating children into unconsciousness;
- Beating children to the point of drawing blood;
- Beating children to the point of inflicting serious permanent or semi-permanent injuries; including broken arms, broken legs, broken ribs, fractured skulls, shattered eardrums and the like;
- Shaving children's head (as punishment);
- Segregation of the sexes;
- Performing public strip searches and genital inspections of children
- Eliminating any avenue by which to bring grievances, inform parents, or notify external authorities of abuses.[174]

Milloy supports this description of the overall brutal experience as children were "overworked, underfed, badly clothed, housed in unsanitary quarters, beaten with whips, rods and fists, chained and shackled, bound hand and foot, locked in closets, basements and bathrooms, and had their heads closely shaved or hair closely cropped."[175]

Children defended themselves and were often severely beaten for doing so. Churchill writes: "Another boy, upon being cracked across the skull with a cane by a staff thug named Skinner at the Red Deer School, seized the cane and hit his assailant back; shortly thereafter, the youngster was beaten so badly that he was required to undergo cranial surgery."[176] The brutal treatment was "regularly reported to Scott, but, other than the release of a vacuous 1921 assertion that such abuse would not be condoned, no particular action was ever taken"[177] and this would continue "on a system-wide basis, decade after decade, until the very end."[178] Chrisjohn, et al. shed light on the failure of the government to address the repugnant conduct as part of its "[f]ailure to adequately inspect or otherwise maintain effective supervision of institutions into which their legal wards had been placed."[179] The department allowed the conditions to continue in "the face of the many cases of egregious [torture] and examples of incompetent or cruel staff" reported to government officials.[180] Milloy confirms that the "Department turned its back on its own wards and refused to hear or support the children's real parents when they protested conditions in the schools and the treatment of their children."[181] The horror that children endured in the total institutions was amplified by the witnessing of violence and death of their family and friends. Not being able to come to their aid or defense for fear that they could be next was also a common experience, likely psychologically numbing on the young ones and certainly holding lifelong consequences.

A gruesome example is the story of the children from the Battleford Industrial School. On November, 27, 1885, the Canadian government orchestrated the greatest mass public execution of eight Cree men and one Assiniboine man for defending their people against starvation which was a violation of the Treaty. The government forced the young ones to witness the mass execution to serve as a reminder that they could be next. The *Saskatchewan Indian* newspaper documents that day: "The day the hangings took place all the Indian students at the Battleford Industrial School were taken out to witness the event. The reason for this was to remind them what would happen if one made trouble with the crown and to provide a lasting reminder of the white man's power and authority."[182] One can only imagine the sheer terror that the young ones felt as they were forced to watch their Elders and people massively hung:

> The scaffold stood in the barrack square. The platform, 20 feet by 8 feet, 10 feet above the ground with railing enclosing the trap was reached by a

> stairway. From the beam hung 8 hempen ropes in readiness for the grim task. It was 8 o'clock in the morning, silence suddenly fell on the whispering groups of civilians. The death chant from the doomed Indians ceased abruptly as a squad of N.W.M.P. rifles at support, marched up to form a cordon about the foot of the scaffold. Then came Sheriff Forget dressed in black, followed by the clergymen. Hodson, the executioner preceded the prisoners. There they came, hands tied behind their backs, with a policeman before, behind, and on either side of each. The only sound was the measured steps of the sombre procession. Sheriff, Clergymen, Interpreter, and hangmen mounted the scaffold. At the foot of the stairs the escort stepped aside and the prisoners ascended to the platform through a gate in the railing. The gate was closed and the prisoners took their places. While Hodson strapped ankles, the doomed were granted 10 minutes in which to speak if they wished, all doing so but Wandering Spirit. Then all was ready. Black hoods were lowered; ropes adjusted, a deadly silence fell as Hodson stepped behind the line. The grating of iron; 8 bodies shot through the trap; and all was over. Some of the prairie's greatest braves had passed to the land of their fathers.[183]

To be forced to witness the events of that day would certainly cause serious mental harm on the little ones. It is an act of torture, and should be termed rightfully so.

Forced Starvation

The issue of starvation was a systemic problem and department officials did not address the issue though they clearly could not have been unaware of it. The devastation of hunger was a common experience.[184] Children were starved as punishment.[185] Nutrition levels were well below what is required "for normal growth and subsistence."[186] It was also common that the food provided was spoiled and unfit for human consumption.[187] Students were offered worm-ridden food, rancid meat, improperly cooked meat such as liver, soggy bread, and unpasteurized milk.[188] According to Haig-Brown, "[w]hat better way to work at indoctrination than to take hungry children early in the morning and to subject them to a harangue on the evils of their family's way of life. It certainly appears to be an impelling way to create change."[189]

In 1902, at the Williams Lake Residential School, the inquest into the death of eight-year old Duncan Sticks who ran away from the school and was found dead the next day reveals some telling information about the conditions the children were living under. Furniss explains that the young ones gave consistent information with respect to being "forced to eat rotten food, being constantly hungry, and being whipped for not following orders."[190] Ellen Charlie testified that,

> I ran away four times because the sisters and the Fathers did not treat me good; they gave us bad food which was fit only for pigs, the meat was rotten, and had a bad smell and taste…when I did not eat it they gave it to me again for the next meal….They would sometimes make me kneel down for a half an hour or hour. They once kept me locked up for a week…They sometimes whipped me with a strap on the face and sometimes stripped me and whipped me.[191]

It was a common theme that children were starved and force fed food unfit for human life. Christine Haines explained that the sisters "gave me rotten food to eat and punished me for not eating it—the meat and the soup were rotten and tasted so bad they made the girls sick sometimes…they shut me up in a room by myself for 3 days and gave me bread and water…."[192] Edward B., a boy at Onion Lake Indian Residential School, wrote of his treatment:

> We are going to tell you how we are treated. I am always hungry. We only get two slices of bread and one plate of porridge. Seven children ran away because there [sic] hungry….I am not sick. I hope you are same too. I am going to hit the teacher if she is cruel to me again. We are treated like pigs, some of the boys eat cats and wheat. I never ask anyone to give me anything to eat. Some of the boys cried because they are hungry. Once I cry to [sic] because I was very hungry.[193]

The late George Manuel (Secwepmec visionary and leader) remembers that "hunger is both the first and last thing I can remember about that school. I was hungry from the day I went into the school until they took me to the hospital two and a half years later. Not just me. Every Indian student smelled of hunger."[194]

Massive hunger and starvation was aggravated by the fact that staff spent "monies budgeted to feed students on luxury items for themselves."[195] Examples of these items include, "marmalade, sardines, lemons, oranges, shelled walnuts, icing sugar, lunch tongue, canned salmon, toilet cream, bananas….*none* of which was shared with the youngsters subsisting on meals of 'bread and drippings [emphasis original].'"[196]

The stories overflow with "bug-ridden and spoiled foodstuffs…."[197] At the Kamloops School a young girl was forced to eat porridge that contained a big worm and "was instructed by the staff member on hand, a Sister Caroline, to 'eat it anyway [and] be thankful' (another student, professing hunger, did in fact eat the vermin.)"[198] The results of the poor diet and health were obvious to staff. Milloy citing Reverend A. Lett of St. George's School on the conditions in 1923 wrote:

> the Children were lean and anaemic and T.B. glands were running in many cases. Energy was at its lowest ebb. Five minutes leap frog was the most I could get out of the boys at once. In examining the Bill of Fare I found that here lay a great deal of the trouble in the health and welfare of the children. They were not getting enough to eat.[199]

But the hunger issue gets worse than this. The government not only failed to provide sufficient food to Indigenous children: it conducted studies on the effects of so doing. It was reported by Bob Weber in *The Globe and Mail* in 2013 that the "Canadian government withheld food from hungry aboriginal kids in 1940s nutritional experiments."[200] Government documents revealed that at least 1300 Indigenous peoples, mostly children, were involved in "a long-standing government-run experiment that came to span the entire country."[201] Weber, referring to Ian Mosby's research paper, found that "[i]n 1947 plans were developed for research on 1,000 hungry aboriginal children in six residential schools in Port Alberni, B.C.; Kenora, Ont[ario]; Shubenacadie, N[ova] S[cotia]; and Lethbridge, Al[berta]."[202] One institution "deliberately held milk rations for two years"[203] and another school "depressed levels of vitamin B1 to create another baseline before levels were boosted. A special enriched flour that couldn't legally be sold elsewhere in Canada under food adulteration laws was used on children at another school."[204] Weber wrote, citing Mosby, "They knew from the beginning that the real problem and the cause of malnutrition was under funding. That was established before the studies even started and when the studies were completed that was still the problem."[205] Interestingly, the experiments were carried out at the same time that the Nuremberg Code was established in 1947. Evelyne Shuster explains the Code was formulated "by American judges sitting in judgment of Nazi doctors accused of conducting murderous and tortuous human experiments in the concentration camps."[206] If this was not horrific enough, forced starvation was exacerbated by the slave labour conditions imposed over the young ones.

Forced Labour

The experience of forced labour was the norm.[207] Milloy writes that, "[a]ll too often, the needs of the school rather than those of the children were paramount. Graham wrote in 1930 of the St. Mary's and St. Paul's school farms on the Blood Reserve: 'The boys are being made slaves of working too long hours...'"[208] Churchill explains that "[a]mplifying the debilitating effects of continuous anxiety and stress, malnutrition and the near-total absence of basic sanitation in the fostering of rampant disease among residential school students was the substantial work regimen imposed in most such institutions."[209] Ralph Sandy, who was at Kamloops Indian School, recalls, "In the school, if you didn't work, do the job that they asked you to do, you got punished for that or got a whipping. Especially during tomato harvest, everybody has got to be out there when it's ready."[210] For the student the day consisted mostly of work,

> You go to school only three hours a day and the rest of the time you're out working, milking cows. You had to be up at five o'clock in the morning. Work until eight o'clock, then there was the breakfast. Some went to classes, some went to work, so by age ten and eleven I was working out there like a slave. You figure it out when you're nine, ten and eleven and working and slaving out there, it's very hard for a person. I didn't go to bed until after midnight, out there flooding rinks and if I didn't do it, I'd get punished for it. People used to get punished for everything that we didn't do.[211]

To make up for the shortfall of revenue from the department, "the labour fell to the boys to the detriment of their education."[212] The children were not just working; they were being overworked. Children were used as slave labour to run the farms of the residential schools; that, one staff member of the Birtle School in 1936 openly acknowledged, "The farm should be operated for the school—not the school for the farm."[213] Another disturbing point is raised by Churchill: "Hence, rather than working to feed themselves, or to acquire such 'luxuries' as adequate clothing, the children were collectively harnessed to the task of paying staff salaries and otherwise underwriting their own confinement by providing a low-cost diversity of foodstuffs and other commodities enhancing to the quality of life enjoyed by surrounding white communities."[214] In effect the children were indeed treated as "slaves"[215] and became a commodification of free labour for the oppressor.[216]

Sexual Predation

As if it was not enough to be rendered defenceless by the forced starvation, death and disease, torture, and forced labour, the children faced sadistic predatory acts by staff officials, priests, and nuns. It was a common experience for children to be sexually exploited and preyed upon in the system: "A wide range of sexual molestation, ranging from fondling to rape and sodomy occurred in the schools."[217] A former supervisor, Arthur Plint of the Port Alberni school, was sentenced to eleven years in 1995 for the sexual assault of fifteen boys from 1948-1968.[218] Grant writes, "[t] he sentencing judge called the supervisor a 'sexual terrorist' and described the Residential school system as 'nothing but a form of institutionalized pedophilia.'"[219] J.R. Miller in *Shingwauk's Vision* explains that in 1988 a police investigation into the Williams Lake School showed "widespread sexual abuse by priests."[220] Another young girl, Emily Rice, had to endure reconstructive vaginal surgery, twice, from the sexual torture she endured in her time at the Kuper Island Indian Residential School.[221] Suzanne Fournier and Ernie Crey in *Stolen From our Embrace* explain that "By the time Emily Rice left Kuper Island in 1959, at the age of eleven, she had been repeatedly assaulted and sexually abused by father Jackson and three other priests, one of whom plied her with alcohol before raping her."[222] Still another student recalls that,

"There were times when I saw girls that were abused downstairs in that one room in the annex. There used to be mattresses there [and] you could hear what they were doing. The supervisors would be there too you know."[223] Chrisjohn et al. summarize the overall experience of sexual violence and dehumanization:

- Sexual assault including forced sexual intercourse between men or women in authority and girls and/or boys in their charge;
- Forced oral-genital or masturbatory contact between men or women in authority and girls and/or boys in their charge;
- Sexual touching by men or women in authority of girls and/or boys in their charge;
- Performing private pseudo-official inspections of genitalia of girls and boys;
- Arranging or inducing abortions in female children impregnated by men in authority.[224]

The record shows that sexual violence of children was "widespread and long-standing"[225] from the beginning of the system to when the last school closed in the 1990s. The RCAP Report notes the department's acknowledgement in the 1990s it "recognized that the 'serious psychological, emotional and social sequelae of child sexual abuse are well established' and that 'there was a need to address these problems among former victims... their families and communities."[226]

The repugnant practice of the department to do nothing to correct the horror our children suffered at the hands of the perpetrators was a norm throughout the system.[227] Their excuses for this failure include "budgetary constraints". Churchill explains:

> There is a certain superficial truth to this. Offering bottom dollar for jobs often situated in "remote" and "backward" locations is a sure recipe for attracting the dregs of any "mainstream" (white) labour pool —i.e., the misfits, incompetents and

> sociopaths deemed unfit to work in other settings — and it was *always* implicit that the threshold criteria for employment in the schools was that those hired be white.[228]

But, Churchill continues,

> [t]he notion that such outcomes can be somehow separated from official intent breaks down upon being subjected to even minimal scrutiny, however. Both budget allocations and hiring preferences are obviously matters of policy. So, too, then, are the results ensuing from them, especially when the policies at issue are sustained over a long period and, as has already been demonstrated to have been the case with respect to the residential schools, in full view of the consequences.[229]

Budget constraints and hiring practices are issues of policy and aptly stated "no such corrective actions were ever forthcoming."[230] Those staff, who did oppose the atrocious conditions, were "quietly transferred' or simply fired."[231]

Reports to the department that concerned issues of callous treatment, including sexual pedophilia were "hushed up."[232] Milloy, on an incident in 1914 in which a farm instructor was reported for sexually violating two young girls, wrote: "Scott, newly appointed as Deputy Superintendent General did no more than 'suggest' that McWhinney 'be sent at an early date to some other field of work,' and then he let the matter drop."[233] Churchill illustrates one such reported encounter: "a female staff member at the Anglicans' Moose Factory Indian Residential School (Ontario) who 'would take showers with the younger Cree boys, ordering them to scrub her breasts and pubic area while she moaned.'"[234] At the Schubenacadie Residential School boys ages "nine to eleven were bathed. They were beaten if they resisted sexual overtures so they soon learned not to resist."[235] Children as young as 4 years old for an average of ten years endured brutalities that are unimaginable.

From sexual violence and rape, forced starvation, to torture and violence of every kind imaginable, the total institution devastated the well-being and the national identity of Indigenous Peoples' children. Upon being unmade, and then remade into the "civilized" vision the government intended, the results of this calculated and vicious attack against the national identities of Indigenous Peoples has produced a cataclysmic fallout. Caused by the massive and widespread violence and terror against the immediate survivors, the generations that follow bequeath an ongoing horror that has never stopped. The immense pain and sorrow that is transmitted onto further generations, such as the inability to parent, is the recipe for the further and ongoing forcible removals in the child welfare systems. What are the long term effects of the forcible transferring of Indigenous Peoples' children?

Immediate and Long-Term Effects

The impact "not only remains undiminished but may in some respects have intensified during the decades since the last survivors were released from the facilities in which the initial damage was done."[236] The *Travaux* underscores the views of state representatives during the drafting of the UNGC that the forcible transferring of children would destroy the ability of the national group (nation) to survive because of its dependence on future generations. The legislation (laws of occupation) that forces the transfers of Indigenous peoples' children results in the demise of those nations "in a relatively short time."[237] The disastrous effects are transmitted over successive generations. Hence, entire Indigenous Nations and Peoples are collectively and seriously bodily and mentally harmed as each generation passes these destructive patterns on to further generations. The most destructive impact is the inability to function as a healthy human with the characteristics that embody, say, a healthy *Nehiyaw*, *Anishanaabe*, *Dene* (to name a few) national identity. The immense pain from one generation to the next is exacerbated by the fact that many Indigenous Peoples today speak, think and write in the colonial language that was grossly imposed over our Original Nations on Turtle Island.

The prevailing "psychological" or medical model, as noted in the *Circle Game,* tends to "pathologize" and label the victims of residential school as "sick" or in need of therapy.[238] It is a maneuver that diverts attention from the culpability of the state and society that created these institutions by moving the focus to the victims rather than the perpetrators. There is even a contention that the "residential school syndrome" is a travesty.[239] But as Chrisjohn et al. ask:

> Who pretends to find it hard to believe that someone who was raped, beaten, and in effect, imprisoned during his or her childhood, all because of the "unfortunate accident" of being an [Indigenous] person, might grow up to have some personal problems....[o]r, perhaps most generally, once the Residential School era is recognized as unbridled genocide, is there some point or purpose in undertaking to show that at least some of the people who **went through** it **suffered from** it." [Emphasis original][240]

Why would it be necessary to prove the effects of such treatment when same are known to exist, for example in our present understanding of the "psychological consequences of torture" or "concentration camp syndrome" or "the psychology of colonial domination."[241] Accordingly it is rightfully contended that "virtually nothing attributed to [Indigenous] Peoples in the way of symptoms falls outside what has already been found for **any group of human beings subjected to severe and prolonged oppression and exploitation**." [Emphasis original][241] Chrisjohn et al. explain:

> When pretending to wonder whether or not Residential School had a negative impact on at least some Aboriginal individuals, there are some notable blind-spots in evidence anecdotally called forth. Few people if any, for example, have noted the similarities between the informal symptomology literature that is developing with respect to the former Indian Residential Schools attendees and the symptomology of Holocaust survivors, Japanese prison camps inmates, victims of torture and physical abuse, colonially oppressed peoples, and similarly aggrieved groups.[243]

There is no doubt that children that have suffered brutalities such as whippings, beatings, confinement, sexual violence, and many more such brutal acts of terror would be severely and perhaps permanently and fundamentally altered to view the world not from a "civilized" but from a traumatized and dehumanized point of view. The neural circuitry structuring of the brain would become wired for the trauma, thus, rendering the child vulnerable to the dehumanizing messages that would be repeated again and again to him or her through words such as *savage*, *devil worshipper* and *dirty Indian*. Churchill explains:

> When the trauma begins at an early age, the process of cognitive integration is usually distorted and, at least in many cases observable alterations in brain structure result. Although a variety of longterm therapeutic approaches offer the prospect of compensating for certain aspects of the damage—it is important to note in this connection that what is at issue are psyhcoemotional *wounds*, not "illnesses"—none are known to "heal" it.[244]

The point is that where other human groups were subjected to "severe and prolonged oppression," such as the Jews, "[w]as there ever a suggestion that the world hold off judgement about what the Nazis had done to the Jews until there was some psychosocial accounting made?"[245]

The collective oppression and terrorizing experiences endured in the residential schools are similar to the experiences of victims of the Nazi government.[246] The symptoms of Residential School Syndrome (RSS) and Concentration Camp Syndrome (CCS) are similar in every regard.[247] Wendy Grant John, former Musqueam leader has referred to residential schools as "…nothing but internment camps for children."[248] Churchill expands on the denial of officials and researchers:

> The motive of officials and "responsible" researchers alike in insisting that the Residential School Syndrome be treated as though it were something new and distinct can thus be viewed as little more than a desire to dodge the implication that if RSS and CCS share a common symptomology, they would all but inevitably share certain commonalities in causative conditions as well.[249]

The collective trauma and sorrow that characterize the present-day impact of the residential school system are manifest in many debilitating conditions.[250] High suicide rates, drug and alcohol addictions, debilitating social conditions, collective low self-esteem, trauma and dysfunction, to name a few, are squarely attributable to the effects of this genocide.[251] The immediate and long term impacts of these in turn are obvious.

The children were conditioned to view their original spiritual, physical and conceptual worldview through a lens that demonized and dehumanized their previous existence as belonging to the Original Nations of the Western hemisphere. The value and sanctity of this original worldview was destroyed and they were then conditioned or brainwashed/indoctrinated to remove any sense of their national identity and rather identify with the dehumanizing conceptions and derogatory lies that are forcibly imposed over them. The government objective was to "condition native people to" [252] believe the lies and to think, speak and write like 'white man'. If this did not work as a method of destruction, then "the goal was to render them to all intents and purposes dysfunctional (i.e., psychologically/ intellectually incapable of coherent resistance)."[253] Compel a child to see her people as inferior by disgusting designations such as "squaw" or "dirty Indian" and she will come to believe it. Torture and starve a child while she is told these belittling words and she will have contempt for her people. Sexually defile her and she will be destroyed. Now multiply this fact that these are children of Nations and what we have is a catastrophe Unable to parent, let alone function as healthy *Nehiyaw* adults, Indigenous Peoples exhibit symptoms of the after-effects of genocide.

The catastrophe becomes exacerbated because those children are from distinct national identities. Over all, the Original Nations of Great Turtle Island collectively exhibit symptoms of genocide. The forcible indoctrination process rendered Indigenous children isolated from their families, communities, national identities (*Nehiyaw*, *Nuxalk*, *Anishinaabe*, *Dene*, and so on), from their spiritual laws, languages, clans, kinship, cultures and most importantly, from Mother Earth (land). Indigenous children exit out of this horrific totality, who later as adults, exhibit traumatic parenting skills. The forced transfer of Indigenous children has deadly consequences:

> Understanding the situation of this continent's native people for what it is thus requires that the acuity with which each individual lost was/ is experienced by those closest to him or her be extrapolated in such a way as to calibrate the impact of losing *all* such individuals, collectively, upon our communities, our societies, our cultures, and thus the possibilities inherent to our future.[254]

The Canadian state would like to have the world believe this is something of the past. However, the reality is that what Prime Minister Harper described as Canada's "sad chapter"[255] is more like an ongoing horror story because the genocide continues unabated in the child welfare system.

Forcible Removals in the Child Welfare Systems

Racist and destructive theories are the cornerstone of the legalized persecution against Indigenous Nations and Peoples.[256] Colonial laws forced the removal of our children into the residential school system and continue the removals into the child welfare systems. The residential school system destroyed the ability to parent by the massive and widespread violence imposed on our children. The direct result is the child welfare system. The traumatic impact, specifically the lack of parenting skills, is the basis on which state oppression is maintained. It is the state that develops the standards ("inability to parent") for forcible removal of Indigenous children into foster care homes away from their own families, Nations and homelands under a further destructive framework. Forcible removals in the child welfare systems are sanctioned by the force of provincial law. The legal authority is found in the division of powers under the British North America Act, 1867, and the 1982 Constitution Act. More specifically, section 88 of the 1951 amendment to the Indian Act, bestowed colonial legal authority to forcibly remove Indigenous children to the provincial child welfare systems.[257]

Fournier and Crey explain that the conditions created by the residential school rendered Indigenous Peoples vulnerable to the next waves of "child abductions".[258] The genocidal impact in the one system goes on to cause the catastrophic removals in the child welfare system. The horror continues to be manifested by the inability to parent, let alone function as a healthy whole being. Traumatic parenting patterns created by the residential school system are massive and widespread. The "sixties scoop"[259] as coined by Patrick Johnston should be more accurately termed the mass removal of Indigenous children from the 1800s into the

2000s. Venne sheds light on the nature of the ongoing horror: "The child welfare system is worse than the residential school system because unlike the children who had each other to comfort one another in the boarding schools, a child in the child welfare system is isolated and alone from his/her family, people, and the Nation."[260] Fournier and Crey support this point:

> Residential schools incarcerated children for ten months of the year, but at least the children stayed in an aboriginal peer group; they always knew their First Nation of origin and who their parents were, and they knew that eventually they were going home. In the foster and adoptive care system, aboriginal children typically vanished with scarcely a trace, the vast majority placed until they were adults in non-aboriginal homes where their cultural identity, their legal Indian status, their knowledge of their own First Nation and even their birth names were erased, often forever.[261]

A child isolated in a foster care home with no comrades or friends is vulnerable to the same horrific violent acts that children in the residential school system suffered. The effects of the forcible indoctrination at this stage would be a nightmare even more so than the residential school phase because they are alone.

It has been said that the transfer rate of children in the child welfare system is a direct result of the residential school era.[262] Indeed, the rates of removal are *higher* than they were at the height of the boarding school system, with roughly three times the number of Indigenous children "in care" today as when the schools were at their peak.[263] A recent media outlet reported that of the 10,501 children in care in Manitoba that 9,205 are Indigenous children.[264] A recent study completed by Statistics Canada shows that, "while Aboriginal children represented 7% of all children in Canada in 2011, they accounted for almost half (48%) of all foster children in the country."[265] Further to the abductions, Fournier and Crey write:

> University of Manitoba researchers Brad McKenzie and Pete Hudson concluded in a study published in 1992 that aboriginal children were taken away in hugely disproportionate numbers less for reasons of poverty, family dysfunction or rapid social change than to effect a continuation of the "colonial argument": that is, "the child welfare system was part of a deliberate assault on Native society designed to make changes in Native people." The white social worker, following hard on the heels of [the government], the missionary, the priest, and the Indian agent, was convinced that the only hope for the salvation of the Indian people lay in the removal of their children.[266]

In her article, "Residential Schools: Creating and Continuing Institutionalization among Aboriginal Peoples in Canada," Julia Rand illustrates how the child welfare system, like the residential schools, is a total institution:

> Child welfare, while not having a physical location like a jail or shelter, does exhibit some of the characteristics associated with a Total Institution. A Total Institution is characterized by isolation from the community. A child taken into care will likely be isolated from his or her community while parents of an apprehended child are forced to deal with the child welfare staff, generally outside the community, as opposed to seeking guidance from Aboriginal elders and members of the Aboriginal community. A Total Institution is characterized by an extreme power differential between staff and inmates. In the child welfare

> system, there is an extreme power differential between parents and child welfare staff. Parents involved with child welfare must demonstrate their competencies as parents to child welfare staff who ultimately decide whether or not their child should be apprehended and placed into state care.[267]

The techniques of removal, imposition of a foreign identity and destruction described in the residential school phase can be applied in the same manner to the forced removal of our children into present times. The legislation enables the forcible removal of the Indigenous children whose experiences then range from the collective loss, to serious bodily and mental harm in the system:

> The homes in which our children are placed range from those of caring, well-intentioned individuals, to places of slave labour and physical, emotional and sexual [torture]. The violent effects of the most negative of these homes are tragic for its victims. Even the best of these homes are not healthy places for our children. Anglo-Canadian foster or adoptive parents are not culturally equipped to create an environment in which a positive Aboriginal self-image can develop. In many cases, our children are taught to demean those things about themselves that are Aboriginal. Meanwhile, they are expected to emulate normal child development by imitating the role model behaviour of their Anglo-Canadian foster or adoptive parents. The impossibility of emulating the genetic characteristics of their Caucasian caretakers results in a identity crisis unresolvable in this environment....The Aboriginal child simply cannot live up to the assimilationist expectations of the non-Aboriginal caretaker."[268]

One survivor on the torture: "The fourth foster mother found for George and his brother Jack by Alberta social services confined George to the basement, forced him to scavenge for food and beat him savagely, finally causing him to be removed at the advice of a doctor when he was only four…his brother Jack was left behind with the woman who had beaten George."[269] Our Nations' children in the child welfare system experience the same rates of racist violence that their predecessors in the residential school endured. The suicide rate is pandemic for children in care.[270] Our Nations' children are sexually preyed on while in the care of the system.[271] The death rates of children in care are at an all-time high. Some examples include Tina Fontaine, aged 15, who was killed after she ran away from a hotel where she was in government care in Manitoba.[272] Another young person, aged 18, Alex Gervais, in British Columbia, jumped out of a hotel window and died.[273] Gervais was housed in the hotel room unsupervised by the ministry. The residential schools and child welfare systems have devastated our communities and Nations.

The stories are similar to the experiences of children in the residential school system. Indigenous children experience sexual violence, forced labour, torture, starvation and death.[274] The effects include "psychological and emotional problems."[275] The removals of children in the system create "tremendous obstacles to the development of a strong and healthy sense of identity…"[276] One of the worst effects on future generations of Indigenous Peoples is the inability to parent according to a *Nehiyaw* or *Dene* worldview.

Traumatic Parenting Patterns

Patrick Morrissette, in the article entitled "The Holocaust of First Nation People: Residual Effects on Parenting and Treatment Implications," notes that "'[w]hole generations of aboriginal children lost their sense of identity and were denied the opportunity to acquire parental skills'."[277] Linda Bull, in the paper "Indian Residential Schooling: The Native Perspective," supports the claim that parenting issues are linked to the residential schools, Students who were brought up in these institutions did not have familial models, nor exemplars to emulate. They replicated the dysfunctional relationships of the school, and many of the families of this generation became dysfunctional. Most of the students from this generation who eventually had families, but who had not any role models during their young and impressionable growing-up years, experienced difficulty in parenting.[278] Bull explains further,

> there was a break in the continuity of maintaining family ties and the care and nurturance that is vital in the development of fragile and complex interpersonal bonds between the child and parent, in essence, the physical and psychological (emotional) needs of the child in order to establish familial bonds critical to every child's growth and development.[279]

The system "disrupted the intricate patterns of the extended families, of relationships between children, parents and elders; the schools disrupted what is in essence the most fundamental and central social aspect of Indian life, the family unit."[280] Rosalyn Ing on acculturation and the effect on parenting: "Acculturation took place amid all this confusion between two cultures which left children changed. Most of the change they underwent was not of their own doing. In the process of acculturation, a person is changed and is never the same again."[281] Ing continues, "Guilt feelings and inadequacy are associated with acculturation. Not being able to parent effectively is the result, as Natives who are products of these schools do not know which child-rearing patterns to respect and use."[282]

Oral child rearing practices and values were destroyed by the removal.[283] Residential schools modeled parenting "based on punishment [torture], coercion, and control."[284] The result of the forcible transfer of Indigenous children away from their loving families into the residential school system is the cause of the decline and in some cases outright disappearance of traditional child rearing patterns.[285] Ashley Quinn writes, "Children in residential schools did not experience healthy parental role models and without appropriate parenting models, many Aboriginal parents lacked the necessary knowledge to raise their own children."[286] Robert, who attended residential school recalls his experience on parenting:

> Before residential school life, parents did not do this, leave children unsupervised. Even siblings were given this responsibility as my sisters looked after me when my mother worked in town. Now leaving children alone is common. This is something they learned at residential school and they continue to live their lives like this....Before Native parents raised their children the way they were taught or observed their parents. This was traditional. That is the reason why they were so strong. But when the white man took it upon himself to give us an education by their system we became very confused. We lost our good ways.[287]

On being able to pass something good to his children, Robert recalls:

> They taught me how I should think about some things, but the staff erased those good things my parents taught me about caring and sharing. I never believed I was a good person. I had to steal food to survive, and I learned to lie and swear to protect myself. I felt I had nothing substantial to pass onto my children."[288]

He continues, "[T]hat's why I didn't show them or teach them my parents' traditional ways. I lost those teachings of my parents while I was at school."[289] This story highlights the cognitive conditioning or forced indoctrination that many children endured about their national identities. A further but important point articulated by Ing is the identity that is formed by the language: "The culture and the language possessed by the Natives enabled them to pass down child-rearing patterns that are necessary and worth preserving if the family, as a socialization agent, is to continue to exist."[290] It is obvious that children who experience massive and collective serious bodily and mental harm will not have the ability to parent according to their traditional systems of parenting and child-rearing let alone function as healthy human beings. The traumatic impacts of the residential school system are seminal to the high rates of removal of children into the child welfare system—and then after that, of those children's children into the child welfare system, as well. There is no distinguishing one residential institution from the other as one directly feeds off the other one. So the forcible removals in the child welfare systems is a continuation of the genocide against our Original Nations and based on vicious racist beliefs and concepts maintained by the state and society. This is the face of colonization that continues to this day, the "domination and dehumanization"[291] of our Nations.

The residential institution looks more like a prison concentration camp than a "school" in the true sense of the word.

View of the facade of the Edmonton Indian Residential School, St. Albert, Albert, date unknown.

Source: Canada. Dept. of Interior / Library and Archives Canada / PA-040761

The state and church forced Indigenous Peoples' children to view the world from a European Christian worldview. The photo of the young Thomas Moore conveys the forced conditioning process. "Thomas Moore, before and after tuition at the Regina Indian Industrial School, ca. May 1874, NL-022474." **Source: Library and Archives Canada**

Parents camped outside of the residential schools with the intent of seeing their children.
Distant view of Fort Qu'Appelle Indian Industrial School with tents, [Red River] carts and teepees outside the fence, Lebret, Saskatchewan, [May 1885?]. **Source: O.B. Buell / Library and Archives Canada / PA-182246**

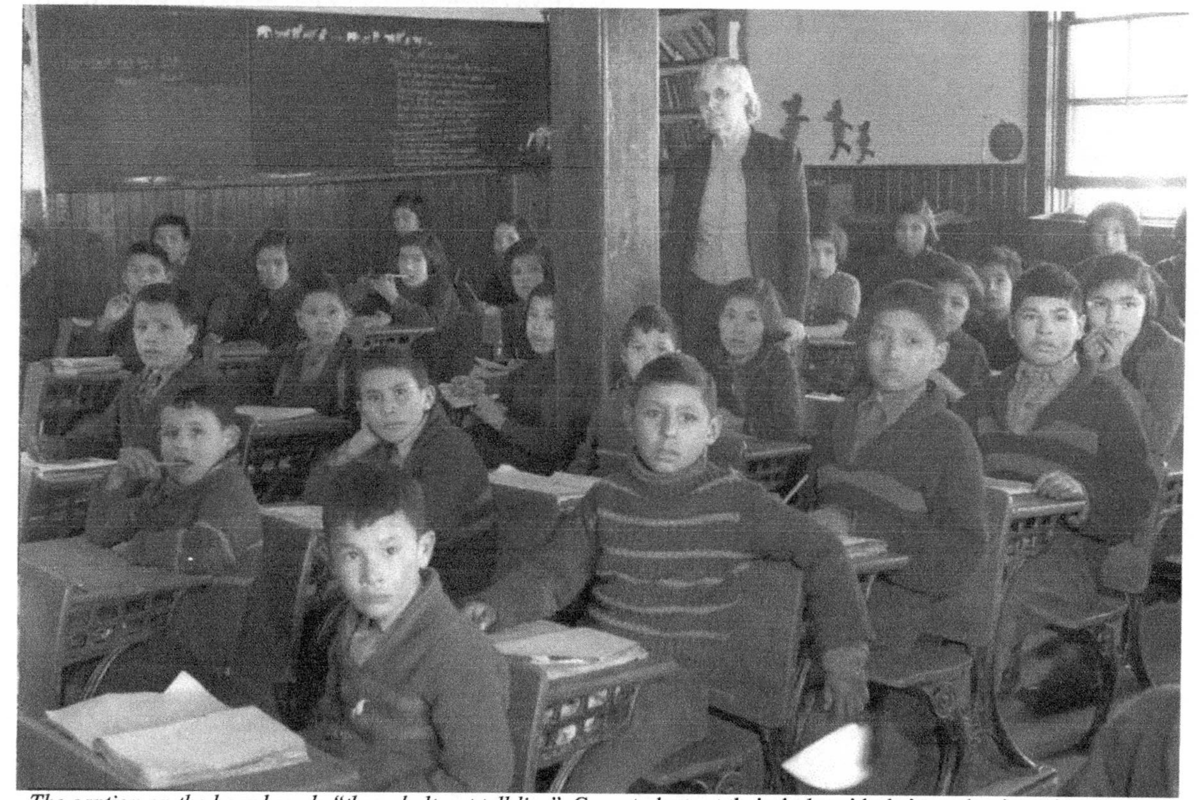

The caption on the board reads "thou shalt not tell lies". Cree students at their desks with their teacher in a classroom. All Saints Indian Residential School, Lac La Ronge, Saskatchewan, March 1945. **Source: Bud Glunz / National Film Board of Canada. Photothèque / PA-134110.**

This picture captures the loneliness and despair. A group of nuns with Aboriginal students, CA. 1890.
Source: H.J. Woodside / Library and Archives Canada / PA-123707.

Forcible indoctrination was accomplished by christian worship as the students were forced to give up their own spiritual beliefs. " Prayer Time, Junior Girls Dormitory, Cecilia Jeffrey Residential School, Kenora, Ontario, c.1950-1953" – Forcible indoctrination was accomplished by Christian prayer as the students were forced to give up their own spiritual beliefs.

Source: The Presbyterian Church in Canada Archives, G-5475-FC-77·

*The caption reads that children were being transported to church; however, it was common in the early years of the residential schools that children were transported via cattle trucks***.** "Students being transported to St. Luke's Church, Oct. 11, 1953" ***Source: Grace Reed fonds***

The fear is evident on the faces of the children. **Source: MSCC - Old Sun School, Gleichen, Alta. - Senior classroom, 1945**

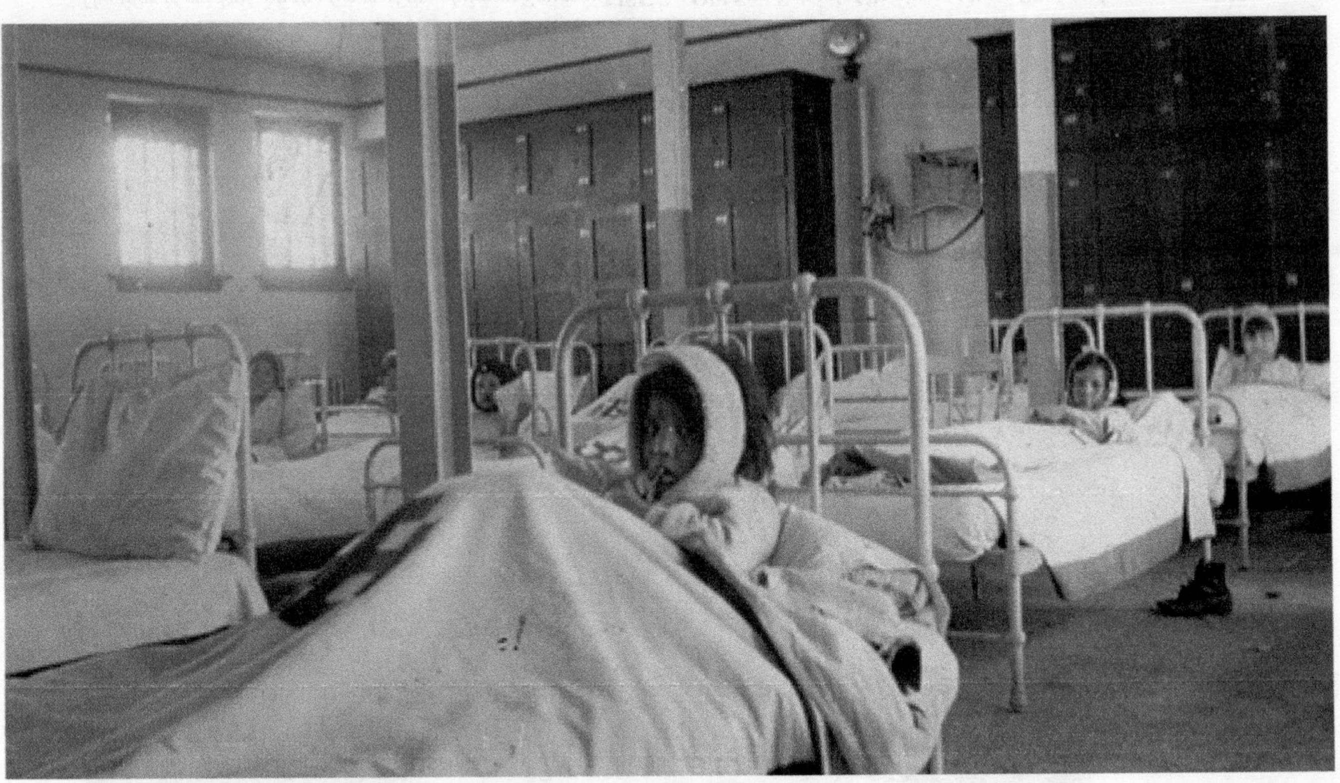

Old Sun School, Gleichen, Alberta - Hospital room and “Mumps” cases, 1944 **Source: MSCC**

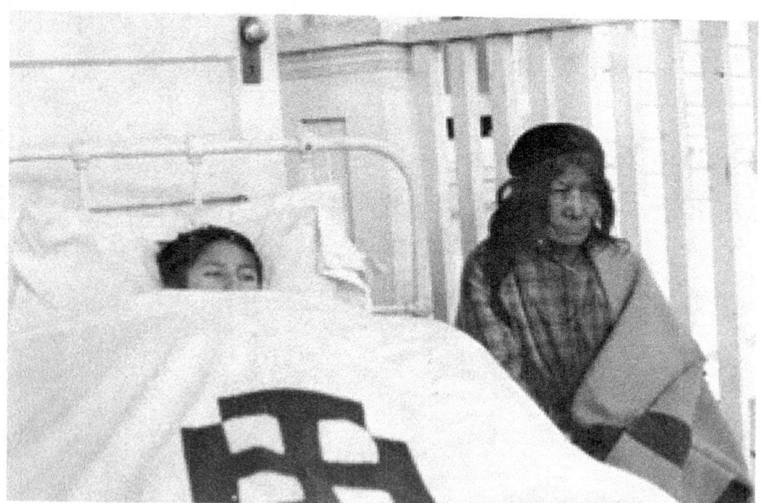

“Alex” and his grandmother, Sarcee Hospital - Sarcee Reserve, AB, 1920
Source: MSCC.

MMMN EP339: Students working in the school garden in Brandon MB, 1904-7. **Image courtesy The Manitoba Museum**

The photo captures the 'predator body politic' as explained by Steven Newcomb in Pagans in the Promised Land Decoding the Christian Doctrine of Discovery.Photograph of students reading in a classroom, ca. 1945. **Source: Edmund Metatawabin Collection, 2012-001-001 (023), Shingwauk Residential Schools Centre, Algoma University.**

In 1885, the Canadian government orchestrated the greatest mass public execution of eight Cree men and one Assiniboine man for and forced the Battleford students to witness it This is a photo of the Battleford students in front of the Battleford Industrial School at Battleford. Photograph shows the new east wing added in 1889. **[PH-2001-64] courtesy of the Saskatoon Public Library**

COMING TO GRIPS WITH CANADA AS A COLONIZING STATE

The Creator Knows Their Lies and So Must We[1]

"Our objective is to continue until
there is not a single Indian in Canada
that has not been absorbed into the body politic,
and there is no Indian question, and no Indian department
and that is the whole object of the Bill."
—DuncanCampbell Scott
DeputySuperintendent General of Indian Affairs, 1920[2]

The Colonial Framework

In the words of Prime Minister Stephen Harper, Canada has "no history of colonialism. So we have all of the things that many people admire.... Canada is big enough to make a difference but not big enough to threaten anybody."[3]

Yet as this work demonstrates, Canada does have a colonial history—less visibly so because its colony is internal to the United Kingdom framework of colonial invasion globally that imposed itself on lands its settler population occupied, lands belonging to the Original Indigenous Nations and Peoples.

A forced transfer of Indigenous children from one group (their Nations and Peoples) to another group (dominating or oppressor society) took place in Canada (and still does); this much has achieved public recognition. But what is not widely understood is that this policy took place within, and reflects Canada's ongoing imposition of, a destructive colonial framework. The root of what is known as the so-called "Indian Problem"[4] lies in this very fact, with which Canada has as yet failed to come to grips.

It is important to view the reality of the destruction that Indigenous children suffered through a lens that enables the realization that what has occurred on Turtle Island is criminal. The significance of Canada's institution of the residential school system is minimized by the colonial society as being misguided, albeit benignly, and resulting in the "abuse", "woeful neglect," and serious "mistreatment" of various sorts[5] Canada is, in short, passing the policy off as a "bad apple" amid many others that were well-intended. The standard rationalization of such *abuse* is that its underlying motives were ultimately benevolent and intended to "raise" those against whom it was applied. As Peter d'Errico points out in the Foreword to Steven Newcomb's *Pagans in the Promised Land: Decoding the Christian Doctrine of Discovery*, it is important not to engage in "whitewashing our language to make it politically correct."[6]

The oppressive reality that Indigenous Peoples endure is far removed from the way that it is characterized in a colonial society such as Canada.

At this juncture, it is important to explain the significance of cognitive legal theory and Steven Newcomb's critically important work in *Pagans in the Promised Land* in which he explains that "[c]ognitive science studies the mind by investigating the conceptual system of thought."[7]

He utilizes cognitive legal theory to challenge what he terms the "paradigm of domination".[8] Cognitive legal theory enables us to understand *not just that* the Original Nations of Great Turtle Island have been collectively and forcibly conditioned to view the world from a western christian perspective and *how it was done*; this theory validates the counter-application of a different cognition—that of Indigenous Peoples themselves—to remove the colonizer's disguise of objectivity. A study of cognitive legal theory is clearly outside the scope of this book and previous thesis (as it once was). However, it is necessary to the legal issue of colonialism and genocide and the deconstruction of our conceptual experience of colonialism. Cognitive legal theory provides a way to turn the language of the colonizer on its head through the use of metaphors. For example, Newcomb accomplishes this reorientation of understanding via the metaphor that "civilization" is the "transplanting" of "colonists."[9]

As such, it implies that civilization is synonymous with colonialism. He explains:

> Price's metaphor CIVILIZATION IS A PLANT is a use of inferences about plants (source domain) to reason about civilization (target domain). In this instance, the idea of civilization is being thought of and unconsciously experienced as it were a plant, such as a vine, that once planted, takes root and spreads outward. In this conception, civilization is thought of something that is "planted" and "grows" to "fruition." This cognitive pattern is also partly motivated (made sensed of) by the metaphor IDEAS ARE PLANTS that is embedded in the understanding of the relationship between the tradition of books (repositories of ideas) and Western civilization. Price's metaphor conceptualizes the spread of civilization in terms of cultivation by planting or transplanting people (colonists) from one location to another.[10]

In his preface, he explains that he "learned the

importance of metaphors and metaphorical frameworks in the social construction of reality."[11] If tackled in the same vein, the imposed oppressive reality can begin to be viewed in a realistic and truthful way.

With respect to the issue of genocide as a state crime, a different approach to characterizing the reality that Indigenous Peoples' children suffered in the residential institutions is required.[12] The colonizers understood that by characterizing (disguising) the legal claim with euphemisms, it would hinder, and even block a successful legal argument for state culpability. On the other hand, I learned that it might hurt my legal argument if I were to characterize the legal claims with euphemisms, and hinder, and possibly even block, a successful argument. But cognitive legal theory provided the key to understanding how to counteract that: with a counter model and metaphors that enabled the Indigenous Peoples' truth to find expression. Further to an elaboration on the application of cognitive legal theory, here is the timeline as to how the counter metaphor developed in this chapter was born. This understanding will bring clarity to the reader on how cognitive legal theory is being utilized.

In 2008, in a meeting on Treaty issues, an Elder and expert in Cree laws and the language insisted that critical to the issue of genocide is the extensive brainwashing of our young (Cree) people who do not speak and think in our *Nehiyaw* language. It was understood that "brainwashing" was the term that would be utilized to characterize the destruction.

In 2009, the late Miguel Alfonso-Martinez, Cuban lawyer and diplomat, characterized the global colonial invasion of Indigenous Peoples' lands as a project to "demonize, isolate and destroy." I understood that I would describe our oppressive experience of colonial invasion by utilizing these concepts. The concepts, put together, would comprise the Indigenous standpoint or narrative that describes the brutal destruction our Original Nations have endured since invasion began all over the globe.

In 2010, at the Treaty Four Governance Centre, I was instructed by an Elder to make a diagram for my workshop on "Genocide." This led to the creation of the "Brainwashing Machine" that is utilized later in this chapter. It was not until 2012 when I began drafting the dissertation that I had the good fortune of finding Newcomb's groundbreaking work in cognitive legal theory and discovering that a powerful metaphor had been developed to turn the tables on the western reader or "denier" of genocide. In this regard, Newcomb's cognitive theory is foundational and the cornerstone to this chapter that provides another way of examining the legal issue of genocide.

Indigenous Peoples, it is argued, obviously needed to be raised from the degradation embodied in their "barbarous" and "uncivilized" ways of life, to the "saving civilization" of Europe.[13] The colonizers' conceptions of what is civilized and uncivilized have been applied against the Original Nations of the Western hemisphere and globally are a central feature of the colonial experience. The Indian problem as defined by Canadian government officials, typical of any colonial society, is framed with descriptors that dehumanize Original Nations. John A. MacDonald's address to the House of Commons in 1883 is typical:

> …the first object is to make them better men, and, if possible, good Christian men by applying proper moral restraints, and appealing to the instinct for worship which is to be found in all nations, whether ***civilized*** or ***uncivilized***…. and the only way to do that would be to put them in central training industrial schools where they will acquire the habits, modes and thought of white men….[emphasis added].[14]

Cognitive legal scholar Steven Winter cites Roberto Unger to make the point that every branch of doctrine must rely "tacitly if not explicitly upon some picture of the forms of human association that are right or realistic in the areas of social life" with which it deals.[15] What was the picture of what was "right and realistic" from the viewpoint of white christian Canada? That "the Indians" as "national groups" *should be made to go away* by socializing and acculturating or indoctrinating Indigenous Peoples' children, the lifeblood of their own national groups, into the body politic of Canada. The intention to make those Indian national groups "go away" by destroying them matches Raphaël Lemkin's definition of genocidal intent. Bear in mind: Raphaël Lemkin felt it necessary to address colonialism and referred to the identity of *nations* in his analysis of genocide.

But as we have seen, despite Lemkin and others' efforts, cultural genocide was prevented from being encoded as a crime in international law, thereby increasing the difficulty of proving this form of genocide based solely on government statements expressing an intended destruction of this nature—even when intent is expressly again admitted in the very apology Prime Minister Harper issued to Indigenous Peoples, acknowledging that Canada had sought to "kill the Indian in the child,"[16] i.e. to absorb the national pattern of the oppressed (Original Nations) into the national pattern of the oppressor (Canadian) society.[17]

Here, the analysis will amplify the foregoing admissions of intent by challenging the attempted blocks or "loopholes"[18] built into the Genocide Convention, arguing not only that the forcible transfer of children is an indicator of genocide (as per the Convention), but also that forcible transfer causes collective, massive and widespread bodily and mental harm to Indigenous Peoples' children, thereby facilitating the forcible indoctrination. The legal application in international law will be shown in the following chapter. Intent is conveyed by the general political doctrine and colonial laws that forced the transfer and caused the massive, systemic, widespread serious bodily and mental harm against the children.

This chapter will explore the so-called "Indian problem" by unpacking the dehumanizing experience known as colonial domination. It will be shown that colonialism is integral to the so-called civilizing process premised on theories of so-called racial superiority over Indigenous Peoples, a circumstance that has led legal analyst Martti Koskenniemi, for one, to describe the "spread of Western civilization" as an *inherently* criminal enterprise.[19] It will deconstruct the forced transfer of Indigenous children, using a "cognitive" lens,[20] and, through various metaphors, lead the reader through the process by which Indigenous children were deliberately, systematically, forcibly, and often brutally conditioned to see themselves, one another, and the world itself, in terms preferred and imposed by Euro-Canadian settler colonists.

The "intent to destroy in whole or in part a human group, as such"[21] will be conveyed by viewing the reality of the indoctrination experienced by Indigenous children in state-controlled residential institutions. The colonial objective of forcing a cultural pattern from conditions of *uncivilized* to *civilized* criteria is translated into judicial rectitude by colonial laws and policies. This chapter develops an explanation of what colonial invasion entails and how the indoctrination of colonial systems, institutions, doctrines, values, beliefs—or more specifically the *civilization* process that Indigenous children forcibly suffer—takes place. It unpacks the Original Nations of Great Turtle Island's brutal experience of colonial invasion and then the forcible transferring of Indigenous children. The experience is characterized by *demonization, isolation* and *destruction.*

Civilizing Discourse

The forced transfer of Indigenous children followed theories of racial superiority that were expressed and codified into government law and policy. Lemkin termed these colonial legal frameworks as "laws of occupation."[22] Integral to understanding the experience from a cognitive lens is to unpack the experience via a lens capturing the processes of domination and dehumanization. The "Indian problem" as it is framed in colonial law is about "obliterating"[23] the distinct identity of Original Nations and Peoples by "absorbing" them into the colonial "body politic".[24] The "Indian problem" is the "barrier"[25] to the colonial state's illegitimate development of our land. The barrier is the fact that the Indigenous Peoples/Nations existed and still exist in organized societies with land, laws, and governments prior to European invasion and after. They were not in a "state of nature" as purported in theories of superiority such as those found in Thomas Hobbes' *Leviathan* in which it was determined that people in a state of nature are in an uncivilized state.[26]

Designations of racial inferiority such as *savage*, *pagan*, and *heathen* applied against Indigenous Nations justified the colonial claim on Indigenous lands by deeming them to be in a primitive state.[27] The dehumanizing designation of *savage* to the Original Nations of Great Turtle Island then justified the formation of laws and policies that maintained domination and oppression. These destructive doctrines and theories applied against the Original Nations of the western hemisphere (and the world) have led to the demonization, isolation and destruction of these original human societies and nations. Legal scholar Kent McNeil observes that early conceptions of the development of colonial law were premised on Social Darwinism.[28] While colonialism is presently not considered a crime in international law, international law does declare the "doctrine of discovery"[29] and conquest and dehumanizing descriptors such as *civilized* and *uncivilized* criteria as invalid to justify the taking of other Peoples and Nations lands and territories.[30] So the forcible transferring of Indigenous children under a colonial destructive framework using *uncivilized* and *civilized* criteria is similarly invalid.

Let us take a brief but necessary digression to address the methods used to deconstruct or unpack the colonial experience. Given that we have already discussed cognitive legal theory some further clarification is necessary with respect to the forcible conditioning of our Nations on Turtle Island.

Cognitive Conditioning

Our analysis unpacks the unseen assumptions in colonial law, scholarship and society about the Original Nations by employing the use of metaphors: "Cognitive theory enables us to realize that [western] law is the result of non-indigenous cognitive processes, social practices and conventions, and cultural patterns, and of the way that members of the dominating society imaginatively project taken-for-granted categories and concepts onto indigenous peoples"[31] of which the "overall effect has been the traumatic intergenerational domination of [Indigenous Peoples] existence."[32]

Winter's book, *A Clearing in the Forest: Law, Life, and Mind*, explains how law reasons or "how we are rational."[33] Building on Winter's cognitive legal theory, Newcomb employs the theory to deconstruct the conceptual domination system imposed on the Original Nations of the western hemisphere. Newcomb explains that "[c]ognitive science and cognitive theory are efforts to empirically examine human phenomena, such as language, in order to better understand the inner workings and structure of human conceptual systems."[34] For example the derogatory concepts of *barbarian* or *savage*, "have come to be objectified and reified as 'the law.'"[35] In this regard, colonial law is a "product of the [colonizer's] human imagination."[36] Kent McNeil's article on "Social Darwinism and Judicial Conceptions of Indian Title in Canada" demonstrates that racist beliefs guided the judiciary in the development of the law with respect to Indian title to the land.[37]

Another example: the term "Indigenous peoples" itself connotes "dominated peoples."[38] Newcomb explains in his article entitled "The UN Declaration on the Rights of Indigenous Peoples and the Paradigm of Domination" that "[t]he phrase 'paradigm of domination' refers here to a systematic use of concepts and categories that construct and maintain 'an order' of domination (often called 'civilization') within which nations and peoples termed 'Indigenous' are deemed by the dominating society to exist."[39] He continues,

> Thinking in terms of 'Indigenous peoples' existing *within* [emphasis original] a conceptual framework of domination involves metaphorically thinking of ideas and conceptions *as if* they were some sort of 'container'. To think of a set of ideas

> as 'a container' is to also conceive of those ideas *as if* [emphasis original] they were 'an object'. *The fact, remains, however, that the ideas used to contrast and maintain such patterns of domination are not a physical container, nor a physical object; they are nothing more than mental processes. The paradigm of domination is, first and foremost, a product of the mind* [emphasis added]."[40]

He instead utilizes the term "original nations" to convey the idea of peoples who enjoyed an existence free and independent of Christian European domination prior to colonialism. This chapter utilizes the terms "Original Nations" and "Indigenous Nations and Peoples" interchangeably, however Newcomb makes an important point about Indigenous nations in the international context of the United Nations being defined as dominated peoples, or peoples under dominance.[41] Newcomb on Antony Anghie's book *Imperialism Sovereignty and the Making of International Law* writes that the "origin of modern international law is predicated on imperialism and colonialism, as well as racist, religious and cultural superiority."[42] He further elaborates that racist religious and cultural superiority has a "profound implication for the international framework of 'states', and state claims of authority *over* peoples termed 'Indigenous' [emphasis original]."[43]

Cognitive legal study explains the "paradigm of domination"[44] or from the perspective of this book, the forced indoctrination that Indigenous Peoples' children have forcibly undergone in the residential institutions.[45] Patterns of domination are maintained through an imposed colonial language system over the Original Nations by brutal acts of violence. Newcomb argues that the colonial language has the effect of ensnaring the original peoples because the language itself is encoded in a paradigm of domination and dehumanization.

Newcomb's writing examines the dehumanizing language of domination encoded in western law to categorize Original Nations and Peoples.[46] Discussing René Maunier's *The Sociology of Colonies*, Newcomb observes that,

> Maunier wrote in a way that made it abundantly clear that our original nations and peoples have been subjected (from the Latin, *subjectum*, 'to throw under') to mental and behavioral patterns of domination. The conceptual roots of that system are expressed by *dom* and *sub*, and anyone who has mastered that language system can use it to maintain a sub order (lower order) status for original nations and peoples, while maintaining a *dom*inant (higher order) status for the invading and colonizing populations. Colonization is domination, and Maunier made this crystal clear.[47]

Cognitive legal study explains how the Original Nations are compelled to argue for self-determination in an imposed conceptual legal framework that has the effect of entrapping them and supporting their colonization. The young ones are forced to conceptualize the world in a way that dehumanizes their original national identity. Newcomb explains:

> Present-day indigenous nations and peoples of this hemisphere are now compelled to utilize the language and conceptual system of the dominating society as a means of thinking, speaking, and writing about our own existence while challenging certain negative, oppressive, and dominating concepts that have been mentally and, from an Indigenous perspective, illegitimately imposed on our existence.[48]

The indoctrination process utilized to compel thousands upon thousands of Indigenous children in residential institutions to conceptualize the world through a Western lens (dominating and dehumanizing their traditional views) is brutal and un-nuanced: torturing a child as young as four while a residential school staff official tells the child his/her people are *savages* will no doubt indoctrinate that child in what to him/her are personally destructive beliefs but held as normal and self-evident in the language, culture and worldview that is being forcibly imposed. Cognitive theory,

> enables us to focus on the fact that our categories and concepts form an essential part of our *experience* of the world. In other words, we experience the world, and indeed, our own lives, largely by means of our categories and our concepts. A tremendous amount of what we experience is shaped, structured, and enabled by metaphors and other cognitive or mental operations, which are products of our imagination and dependent on the kinds of bodies we have.[49]

In this way, it affects our physical world because "[a]s humans, our metaphorical experience is a result of the way we use both our embodiment and the imaginative processes of our minds to interact with our physical and social environment."[50] The way that human beings perceive their reality conditions how they will behave and interact in the social, physical and spiritual environment in which they live. In other words, Indigenous children who were forcibly conditioned to view the world from a western mind frame by having undergone violent and traumatic experiences will view the world from this traumatic reality, rather than simply assimilating Western culture as if it were their own natural and normal orientation. It follows that the trauma of the children will not only destroy the ability of the nations to carry on their distinct national identities to future generations, but also transmit traumatic and dysfunctional patterns over successive generations into the Indigenous nation itself. The once-healthy national identity of the original nation itself becomes debilitated.

Metaphors and Models

The colonial language dominates Original Nations. In this

regard, the colonizer's language is central to how information is conveyed about an oppressed nation or indeed, about its oppressor. The language of the oppressor is vital to the colonization process. Integral to this is the use of language that has the effect of concealing the reality of the experience children underwent in the residential school system.

Prime Minister Harper's *Apology* on behalf of the Canadian state amply demonstrates the sort of "word-magic"[51] employed to obscure the issue, carefully restricting its characterization of the pervasive and terrifying offenses perpetrated against students in the schools to such relatively benign terms as "abuse," and "neglect." Indeed, "neglect" is the very antithesis of the intent manifest in the simple fact of the government's having maintained a continent-wide system of residential schools for fully a century, effecting measures at every turn to compel Indigenous children's placement in such facilities with the intention of removing their existing cognitive framework (via their culture) and replacing it with that of the colonizer nation (brainwashing). Words like "abuse" and "mistreatment" don't begin to describe the severity of the crimes committed against virtually every student in every facility, generation after generation. As Chrisjohn, Young, and Maraun observe, such semantic manipulation is designed to distort and minimize the degree of institutional culpability involved.[52] Not coincidentally, "minimization" is a method used by neoNazi judeocide deniers eager to absolve the Nazis of *their* genocide.[53]

The ways in which law and policy frame Indigenous Peoples serve to exert control over their own and wider public understanding of their experience, "physically and conceptually".[54] First, the physical constraints that arise from colonial laws of occupation describe the tearing of the children from their families—some of whom have interpreted it as kidnapping—as "the transfer of Indigenous children". Their forced confinement takes place in "residences"; reconditioning camps become "schools". The overall experience is characterized in its worst moments merely as "abuse," which is far less than the reality of the destruction experienced by Indigenous children.[55]

An accurate classification or term to describe the experience would be not just physical but mental *torture*. Recognizing that the colonial language and words have the "ability to colonize the present for Indigenous nations and peoples; it can be used to maintain a particular kind of reality that benefits states and to the continued detriment of Indigenous nations and peoples,"[56] here, the model employed will be to move past the colonial rhetoric and convey its reality from a perspective that takes into consideration the colonial language as a tool of destruction.

In the practice of law, models and metaphors are used to explain facts and evidence when conveying a case: a model explains the process and the result. In this chapter, a model is developed depicting how when the process is colonialism, the result is genocide. It attempts to employ the use of metaphors to deconstruct the way in which Indigenous Nations and Peoples experience genocide as a product of colonial invasion. Newcomb explains that "dominating forms of reasoning"[57] are found in western law that apply "certain categories, concepts, metaphors, and other thought processes to [Original Nations and Peoples], some of which, through time"[58] have come to be been seen as the norm and imbedded in the colonial systems, institutions, and fabric of the state. The model will take the reader past what is deeply imbedded and taken for granted in Western (oppressor) society about the peoples/nations it encounters in the colonization of other peoples' lands and territories. Important to the model developed are some definitions.

Definitions

Dehumanization involves a process of rendering oppressed peoples as less than human. The *Concise Oxford Dictionary* defines dehumanize as, "deprive of human characteristics [or] make impersonal or machine-like."[59] Colonialism is defined as the "policy and practice of a power in extending control over weaker [dominated] peoples or areas [of land]. Also called: imperialism."[60] Colonialism involves phases such as "indoctrination". Indoctrination is defined as "to teach (a person or a group of people) to systematically accept doctrines, esp. uncritically."[61] A synonym for indoctrination is "brainwashing".[62] Genocide, as defined by Raphael Lemkin is the "destruction of a nation or an ethnic group."[63] The purpose in highlighting Lemkin's definition is that he clearly understood that genocide is a crime against national groups.

Colonialism and Genocide

Original Nations the world over are dominated and dehumanized in the process of colonial invasion and occupation.[64] As previously addressed the "colonial clause"[65] debate during the drafting of UNGC reveals the colonial destructive framework in international law. The Union of Socialist Soviet Republics (USSR) and Yugoslavia, among other states, argued the retention of cultural genocide was necessary to retain the integrity of the Genocide Convention. From the record in the *Travaux* the "dark colonial" history was a bone of contention among state governments. The debates reveal that colonialism and cultural genocide are the same. Jean-Paul Sartre determined that colonialism "is by its very nature an act cultural genocide. Colonization cannot take place without systematically liquidating all the characteristics of the native society."[66] Given that cultural genocide was removed from the final definition of the crime recognized in international law it is important to deconstruct the oppression maintained by colonialism. As a result, international law or (western law) as it presently stands is an oppressive framework that benefits colonial states to the continued detriment of Indigenous Nations.

Chrisjohn, Young, and Maraun define the "Indian problem" as the fact that the People and Nations existed on the land prior to the European invasion, and still exist on it afterwards[67] with a resultant ownership claim on the land and its resources. Europeans (United Kingdom) invaded territories in the Americas, Asia, Africa, the Pacific and Australia. The "laws and policies" created by the state or the colonial invader oppress the Original Nations' land, laws and formation of systems of government.[68] In his "Foreword" to *Imperialism, Sovereignty and the Making of International Law*, James Crawford acknowledges the "underlying pattern of domination and subordination" during the different epochs in international law.[69] International legal frameworks served state interests in maintaining their pattern of colonial domination. Crawford continues,

> From the beginning, international law was not exclusively concerned with the relations between states but, and more importantly, with the relations between civilizations and peoples. Moreover these were relations of *domination*. Colonization and Empire were present at the creation, and the apologetic use of universalist ideals has never been abandoned, whatever new forms it may have taken [emphasis original].[70]

The idea that the state is genocidal in its interactions with the original nations and peoples is never entertained in a western perspective. Instead it is presupposed, reflecting the viewpoint of the colonial oppressor (state), that states are agents of civilization in the world, the sole source of law creation, custodians of international law, and therefore are, by their very nature, beneficial. However, this view point can only be maintained by disregarding the destructive and genocidal effect that states have had on Indigenous Nations and Peoples globally. This reality plays out internationally and domestically as colonial states justify their continued domination and dehumanization of Peoples and Original Nations.

Consider the view that the forcible transferring of Indigenous children is committed with "mixed intentions or benevolent motivations."[71] The paradigm of benevolence in the colonial discourse absolves perpetrators of crimes in the "civilization" process. Another disconcerting perspective relates to the idea that death is absolute and the only form of genocide that should be recognized. Kurt Mundorff, citing Colin Tatz, contends that "the Genocide Convention does not account for '[g]rades or levels' of genocide, 'for all of us, death is absolute: serious bodily or mental harm is something else; children forced into conversion may well become coerced Catholics or Muslims, but they live.'"[72] Tatz and Mundorff's analysis on the forcible transferring of Indigenous children reveal the pattern of domination and dehumanization. It never occurs to the state or oppressor or (western thinker) that its actions are destructive and harmful to the people and nations they encounter in the civilizing process.

In his *Discourse on Colonialism*, Aimé Césaire writes that paradoxically, "[c]olonization works to *decivilize* the colonizer, to *brutalize* him in the true sense of the word, to degrade him, to awaken him to buried instincts, to covetousness, violence, race hatred, and moral relativism [emphasis original]."[73] The western scholar or oppressor state does not view its actions as being violent or destructive against the peoples/lands it is invading or the children they are kidnapping and forcibly removing in the name of civilization. The oppressor who engages in the exercise of justifying the domination and dehumanization of peoples that are subordinated in the colonization process reveals the sickness or disease that is rampant not just in the civilization process, but in the so-called civilizer.

It's this model, explained here as demonization, isolation and destruction, that guides the state or western thinker in law and scholarship. Consider the example of Colin Tatz claiming because Indigenous children did not die from physical destruction, at least they still live physically after suffering from atrocious acts of serious bodily or mental harm. Scholars who engage in this reductive discourse are a part of the problem as it maintains a perspective that conceals the reality of genocide. Charles Salomon affirms the violence of colonialism involves "the disappearance of the native races (*des races sauvages*) coming into contact with civilized races."[74] State advocacy for termination of the Indian problem is justified and grounded in a destructive racist discourse.

Recall that doctrines of racial superiority are at the root of genocide. European colonizers, such as the United Kingdom's colonial laws and doctrines, rationalize violence and the systematic legal application of what are effectively epithets such as *heathen* and *pagan* against human beings and nations. This oppressive discourse sought to justify the formation of "newly-formed"[75] states such as the United States, New Zealand, Australia, and Canada over lands that belong to the Indigenous Nations. It is necessary to review some of the discourse to see the patterns of demonization, isolation and destruction prevalent globally, and then review the discourse or policy statements in Canada. The legal and academic discourse that downplays the violent nature of colonialism is articulated by Sharon Venne in the "Introduction" to *Perversions of Justice: Indigenous Peoples and Angloamerican Law* writes,

> This continent has not entered a "postcolonial era." Native North America remains occupied by invaders from abroad, settlers who have appropriated our land and resources for their own benefit. Indigenous Peoples who conducted themselves as sovereign nations since time immemorial continue to be forcibly subordinated to the self-assigned "governing authority" of recently established settler states both north and south of an arbitrary boundary separating the United States and Canada. It is thus patently obvious that we, the indigenous nations of North America, have not been decolonized. Until we are, the idea of "post colonialism" has no relevance to us. Indeed, the term, now quite fashionable in academic discourse, serves only to render us *invisible*, masking the reality of our circumstance [emphasis added].[76]

It will be seen that this problem of *invisibility* is really a pattern that exists all over the world where human societies and nations have undergone colonial invasion and endured the imposition of a "civilizing" colonial framework based on racial superiority.[77] The deleterious effect allows genocide against Indigenous Peoples and Nations to continue unchecked because of the masked illusion that Indigenous Nations have neither valuable, self-sustaining cultures nor a valid claim to remain free from colonial control and domination. Newcomb writes, "[g]iven that our respective [Indigenous Nations] were originally free and independent of the European mind and mental processes for thousands of years in this hemisphere, now known as the Americas, how did it come to be considered virtually 'self-evident' that our very existence as [original nations]"[78] merits being controlled by a conceptually dominating and dehumanizing system.

"Colonization" as Domination and Dehumanization

It is interesting to recall that Lemkin undertook an extensive study of the laws of occupation across Europe. The Axis powers invaded territories and destroyed national identities in their quest for world supremacy. Lemkin explained that the colonizing "régime is totalitarian in its method and spirit. Every phase of life, even the most intimate, is covered by a network of laws and regulations. Therefore these laws of occupation are an extremely valuable source of information regarding such government and its practices."[79] These laws were the instruments entrenching a demonizing, isolating and destructive experience for the victims of the Nazi invasion. The Nuremberg laws served as a mechanism that gave the Nazi government's racist ideology legal force and served as the foundation of its "legalized persecution".[80] The nations that survived the physical and biological genocide were dominated and dehumanized under the Nazi government laws of occupation.

Colonization is implemented by completion of the two phases of genocide and "[t]his imposition, in turn, may be made upon the oppressed population which is allowed to remain, or upon the territory alone, after removal of the population and colonization of the area by the oppressor's own nationals."[81] Lemkin described the colonization process through studying the invasion of Eastern Europe, however "he did not intend for 'genocide' to capture or communicate Hitler's Final Solution."[82] In this regard "[a] group did not have to be physically exterminated to suffer genocide. They could be stripped of all cultural traces of their identity."[83] Consider the colonial invasion of other human groups/nations around the world. It has been determined the Nazi invasion and planned colonization of Eastern Europe was modeled after European precedents established *vis-à-vis* Indigenous North America.[84] It is necessary to examine what colonialism is, as seen from this view point.

Davis and Zannis contend that "[t]he nature of colonialism is central to a study of modern genocide."[85] The authors correspondingly hold that the imposition and maintenance of a colonial system is in itself a manifestation of genocidal intent. Colonialism and genocide are related in the following manner: "Whether the purpose of colonialism is to destroy groups can be answered by examining the relationship between the colonial *power* (the nature of the control exercised) and the dependent people. The purpose served by making independent people dependent should be considered."[86] The methods utilized to force national identities or human groups under a regime of domination are relevant: "The very nature of colonialism is systematic and is characterized by a methodical approach to all its activities. Colonial empires arise from the systematic application of power; they do not arise haphazardly."[87] The colonizer's system "inherently"[88] results in genocidal outcomes.[89] To expand upon Sartre's views, quoted earlier:

> Indeed, colonization is not a matter of mere conquest as was the German annexation of Alsace-Lorraine; it is by its very nature an act of cultural genocide. Colonization cannot take place without systematically liquidating all the characteristics of the native society.... For the subject people this inevitably means the extinction of their national character, culture,

> customs, sometimes even language. They live in an underworld of misery like dark phantoms ceaselessly reminded of their subhumanity.[90]

With the arrival of Europeans in the Americas, Asia, Africa, Australia and the Pacific, not only the people but thousands of years of accumulated knowledge were completely wiped out completely in many territories. Power quotes Lemkin as observing that, "'It takes centuries and sometimes thousands of years to create a natural culture.... but genocide can destroy a culture instantly, like fire can destroy a building in an hour.'"[91] In this connection, it must be born in mind that the Indigenous population of North America was reduced by European invasion and colonization from eighteen million or more in 1500 to not more than a third of a million four centuries later, with any number of peoples/cultures eradicated in the process.[92] As historian David Stannard puts it, "it is impossible to know what transpired in the Americas during the sixteenth, seventeenth, eighteenth and nineteenth centuries and not conclude that it was genocide."[93] Lemkin's conception of the crime is the two-phase colonization process which matches the cultural genocide process.

The Osage scholar George Tinker, in "Tracing a Contour of Colonialism," his preface to Ward Churchill's *Kill the Indian Save the Man,* affirms that "only the most comprehensive sort of assimilation posed a viable alternative to the campaigns of physical extermination."[94] Churchill, quoting Sartre, observes that "[e]ventually, if the colonizer's system functions as intended, the colonized 'do not need to be exterminated anymore. No, the most urgent thing... is to humiliate them, to wipe out the pride in their hearts, to reduce them to the level of animals. The body will be allowed to live on but the spirit will be destroyed. Tame, train, punish: those are the words that obsess the colonist.'"[95] In effect, while colonially-oppressed peoples may remain *physically* alive, they are reduced to what political philosopher Giorgio Agamben, relying primarily on the example those consigned to the Nazis' ghettos and camps, referred to as "bare life," a condition devoid of those attributes associated with humanity (i.e., rights, dignity, a genuine sense of self, and so on).[96] Sartre refers to the internalized terror and violence that colonized peoples are forcibly conditioned to live with after colonization by the oppressor nationals. These oppressed peoples live *physically*; however, the experience of colonialism renders the *spirit* destroyed. In other words, the body is alive but the essence of the human spirit or culture has been extinguished.

Consider that John A. MacDonald in 1883 held that the goal of the Canadian colonial government was to force Indigenous Peoples to change from *savagery* to people who will "acquire the habits, modes and thought of white men."[97] The children that emerge from "government and religious boarding 'schools'" are intended to have internalized the conceptual cognitive traumatic reality with which they were indoctrinated.[98] To reiterate, on domination, Newcomb explains that the "phrase 'paradigm of domination' refers here to a systematic use of concepts and categories that construct and maintain 'an order' of domination (often called 'civilisation')"[99] that are imposed upon the minds of Indigenous children. So the success of the colonial enterprise depends on the degree of indoctrination imposed upon the colonized peoples.[100] Indoctrination is prominent among the "techniques of occupation" described by Lemkin.

Indoctrination

Recall that according to the *Collins English Dictionary*, indoctrinate means to "teach a person or a group of people) to systematically to accept doctrines, esp. uncritically." The synonym for indoctrination, according to *Webster*, is "brainwashing." Brainwashing is defined by *Collins* as meaning "to effect a radical change in the ideas and beliefs (of a person) esp. by methods based on isolation, sleeplessness, hunger, extreme discomfort, pain, and the alternation of kindness and cruelty."[101] Viewing colonialism as a system requiring the conditioning of children, Ngũgĩ wa Thiong'o in *Decolonising the Mind: The*

Politics of Language in African Culture points out its most significant aspect: "But its most important area of domination [is] the mental universe of the colonised, the control, through culture, of how people perceived themselves and their relationship to the world. Economic and political control can never be complete or effective without mental control. To control a people's culture is to control their tools of self-definition in relationship to others."[102]

Thiong'o explains further, "[t]he domination of a people's language by the languages of the colonising nations was crucial to the domination of the mental universe of the colonized."[103] A child who experiences colonial conditioning via the imposition of a foreign language will see himself or herself as the colonizer views the child and her people: "Since culture does not just reflect the world in images but actually, through those very images, conditions a child to see the that world in a certain way, the colonial child was made to see the world and where he stands in it as seen and defined by or reflected in the culture of the language of imposition."[104] It becomes worse when a child is forcibly conditioned to see "images of his world as mirrored in the written languages of his coloniser. Where his own native languages were associated in his impressionable mind with low status, humiliation, corporal punishment, slow-footed intelligence and ability or down right stupidity, non-intelligibility and barbarism"[105] the results would be devastating.

When a child suffers the imposition of a colonial language by acts of violence and terror and is brainwashed by the methods of torture, starvation, forced labour, sexual predatory acts and other methods that compel his/her domination and dehumanization, that child will be traumatized for life. Indoctrination involves the termination of Indigenous Peoples' distinct national identities and healthy characteristics. Essentially all characteristics of Indigenous human cultural and national identity become "systematically liquidated";[106] "the body will be allowed to live on but the spirit will be destroyed."[107] Thiong'o affirms that, "[t]he images of this world and his place in it implanted in a child take years to eradicate, if they ever can be."[108] The effect on children of living under a violent state regime that demonizes their national identity and people, isolates them for years at a time from loving families and nations, and destroys their spirits with methods that are morally and legally repugnant, will be lifelong.

Tinker encapsulates the forced transfer of Indigenous children/indoctrination/civilization process:

> Taken, often by force, from their homes at ages as young as four, transported to facilities remote from their families and communities, confined there for a decade or more, relentlessly stripped of their cultural identities while being just as methodically indoctrinated to see their traditions—and thus themselves—through the eyes of their colonizers, chronically malnourished and overworked, drilled to regimental order and subjected to the harshest form of corporal punishment, this was the lot of one in every two native youngsters in North American for successive generations.[109]

Churchill explains that the need to establish a "residential school system is *inherent* for any successful order of colonialism," and that for colonialism to be successful it "can only be accomplished by a violent subjugation."[110] Sartre describes this process as being "internalized by the colonized as a form of terror."[111] The process of obliterating the national identity or the spirit is successful, "if the colonizer's system functions as intended."[112] Churchill, citing Sartre on dehumanization, writes:

> Colonial violence does not only aim to keep the enslaved people at a respectful distance, it also seeks to dehumanize them. No effort will be spared to liquidate their traditions, substitute our language for theirs, destroy their culture without [admitting them to] ours; they will be

> rendered stupid by exploitation. Malnourished and sick, if they continue to resist, fear will finish the job: the [natives] have guns pointed at them; along come civilians who settle [upon their] land and force them with the riding crop to farm it for them. If they resist, the soldiers [or police] will shoot and they are dead men; if they give in, they degrade themselves and they are no longer human beings; shame and fear fissure their character and shatter their personality. The business is carried out briskly by experts: "psychological services" are by no means, a new invention. Neither is brainwashing.[113]

Forced indoctrination processes cause mental disorders in the oppressed. Writing in *The Wretched of the Earth* on the psychological disorders created by colonization, Frantz Fanon describes imperialism as "sow[ing] seeds of decay"[114] from which there is little cure, so long as the colonial environment persists:

> ...the psychiatric phenomena, the mental and behavioural disorders emerging from [colonialism] have loomed so large among the perpetrators of "pacification" and the "pacified" population. The truth is that colonization, in its very essence, already appeared to be a great purveyor of psychiatric hospitals. Since 1954 we have drawn the attention of French and international psychiatrists in scientific works to the difficulty of "curing" a colonized subject correctly, in other words making him thoroughly fit into a social environment of the colonial type.[115]

The indoctrination or "colonialism forces the colonized to constantly ask the question 'Who am I in reality?'"[116] On the inability to recover from colonial terror and violence, Sartre explains, "these imperious characters, panic-stricken by their omnipotence and the fear of losing it, only dimly remember that they were human beings....Three generations? By the second generation, scarcely had the sons opened their eyes when they saw their fathers being beaten; in psychiatric terms, there they were, 'traumatized'—for life."[117] The fallout from this colonial invasion is shattering on the mind, body and spirit.

Tinker illustrates this point: "[t]he only remaining task was, when- and wherever possible, to condition native people to be not only accepting but embracing of their circumstance. Where this was not possible, the goal was to render them to all intents and purposes dysfunctional (i.e., psychologically/intellectually incapable of coherent resistance).[118] " So genocide was in fact a "means to an end":[119] the milking of the colonized nations' resources and seizure of their lands.

An important question asked in *The Circle Game* concerns the mindset of the colonial people that forcibly remove Indigenous Peoples' children to residential institutions—the practice of pathologizing the survivors of genocide and viewing them as sick, when in fact the oppressor never examines its own conduct and role in the act of genocide. Chrisjohn, Young, and Maraun conclude that, "whatever else it might be, the experience of Residential Schooling is not a 'disease,' and yet RSS [residential school syndrome] squarely places our efforts to understand the episode within the medical model. This is a **rhetorical** move and not a scientific one [emphasis original]."[120] This move puts the onus on healing, on the need of the individual to "recover" from what has been and continues to be a collective colonial attack against the survivor's national identity. Or in other words the shift focuses away from the perpetrators of genocide by making it a "**problem of specific individuals** [emphasis original]."[121] In this manner the survivor of the experience of genocide becomes further demonized with destructive terms employed in relation to sickness.

The people that require help are the ones who designed and

created these institutions. Those scholars, medical practitioners, social workers and greater society that deny the genocidal experience and colonial destruction suffered by Indigenous Peoples' children as causal factors of their malaise are effectively complicit with the state governments that designed the residential school institutions. According to Chrisjohn, Young, and Maraun, this is the "real" "residential school syndrome."[122] Perhaps a better way to frame the syndrome is the ongoing commitment to engaging in the colonization-civilization "supremacist task of rationalizing and legitimizing [the Canadian state]."[123] The government and society that operates from a dominating and dehumanizing premise of racial superiority is rooted in a destructive and hypocritical (even schizophrenic?) discourse of civility, unable to face the full reality of their own deeds. Césaire in studying colonization and civilization makes an interesting point in relation to the so-called civility of European invasion by examining the violent nature of European imperialism. On the defensibility of colonial rule:

> The fact is that so called European civilization—"Western" civilization—as it has been shaped by two centuries of bourgeois rule, is incapable of solving the two major problems to which its existence has given rise: the problem of the proletariat and the colonial problem; that Europe is unable to justify itself either before the bar of "reason" or before the bar of "conscience"; and that, increasingly, it takes refuge in a hypocrisy which is all the more odious because it is less and less likely to deceive. *Europe is indefensible* [emphasis original].[124]

The main point is "that no one colonizes innocently, that no one colonizes with impunity either; that a nation which colonizes, that a civilization which justifies colonization—and therefore force—is already a sick civilization, a civilization that is morally diseased, that irresistibly, progressing from one consequence to another, one repudiation to another, calls for its Hitler."[125] Césaire's point is that colonization is the product of a *sick* and *destructive* people and this becomes transmitted as each nation it colonizes is destroyed in the civilization process. The analysis is important to the discussion of civilization and the proliferation of theories and laws that seek to justify and support the so-called civilizing missions of European imperialism. The oppressor designates or labels Indigenous Peoples as *sick* or *savage*; however, the sickness and savagery "resides in the minds and hearts of the people who planned, designed, [and] implemented"[126] these programs of genocide, whose reality they themselves cannot admit to.

Doctrines of Racial Superiority

The global terrorization of colonialism was facilitated by the so-called best colonial thinkers, such as Hobbes and Locke, who were

> hopelessly mired in the intellectual/moral morass of trying to frame Europe's blood-drenched reality in terms of an 'unparalleled advancement' in actualizing the loftiest of ideals. Far from offsetting or countering the vulgarities of Europe's imperial pretension, Enlightenment philosophy served as the intellectual engine empowering its expansion to global proportions. Theories of racial superiority exist across all colonial societies and in their academic discourse.[127]

Eurocentric theories place Indigenous Peoples as "voiceless, nameless, and faceless demon[s]"[128] with no form of social, political, and legal organization. Their discourse contextualizes Indigenous Peoples as the noble savage and romanticizes colonial terror, violence and destruction.[129] Stannard in an unequivocal manner explicates that:

> The destruction of the Indians of the Americas was, far and away, the most massive act of genocide in the history of the world. That is why as one historian aptly has said, far from the heroic and romantic heraldry that customarily is used to symbolize the European settlement of the Americas, the emblem most congruent with reality would be a pyramid of skulls.[130]

The "birth of the modern" which occurred during the late-eighteenth and early-nineteenth centuries was marked by the predominance of a theory known as "legal positivism" developed a bit earlier by philosophers such as Thomas Hobbes and John Locke,[131] and devoted in no small part to "proving" that "Western civilization" was in every respect superior to all others and thus "justified" in asserting dominion over them.[132] This was especially so with regard to Indigenous societies, which were all but invariably cast as "primitive" or "savage," and thus lacking the capacity even to formulate laws or govern themselves.[133] Hobbes in fact is "credited" with having popularized the notion that, since they existed in a "state of nature," the lands of "savage peoples" were by definition *terra nullius*—that is, "ungoverned territories," belonging to no one—and could thus be rightly claimed by any Europeans desiring them.[134]

Locke in particular applied the theory to Indigenous Nations in the Western Hemisphere, describing our territories as "waste lands" demanding "domestication" by "civilized men" (i.e., Europeans).[135] As Robert A. Williams, Jr., concludes in *The American Indian in Western Legal Thought*, "Locke's discourse thus legitimated the appropriation of the American wilderness as a right, even as an imperative, under natural law."[136] The colonial discourse of racial superiority had "hardened into the assumptions of ideological argument" and the continuity of colonial destruction "had been completely integrated into the 'common sense' of late–eighteenth-century English Americans."[137]

To quote Nigel Joseph, "it is the state of nature debate

that first establishes this way of thinking about the relationship between Western societies and indigenous peoples. Once we have convinced ourselves that a society is primitive or inferior, it becomes much easier to justify taking away their land, or refusing to share natural resources with them."[138] Further, as James (Sákéj) Youngblood Henderson points out, the "state of nature *remains* the prime assumption of modernity, a cognitive vantage point from which European colonists can carry out experiments in cognitive modeling and engineering that inform and justify modern Eurocentric scholarship and systematic colonization. Indigenous Peoples have experienced this concept in slavery, colonization and imperialism [emphasis added]."[139]

Demonization is accomplished through the categorization of Indigenous Peoples and Nations as *uncivilized heathens*. Consider the case of *Regina v. St. Catharine's Milling* of 1885. The court determined that "Indian Peoples were found scattered wide-cast over the continent, having, as a characteristic, no fixed abodes, but moving as the exigencies of living demanded. As heathens and barbarians it was not thought that they had any proprietary title to the soil, nor such any claim thereto as to interfere with the plantations, and the general prosecution of colonization."[140] The belief that Indigenous Nations are *less human* than Europeans illegitimately justifies the oppressor taking action to isolate Original Nations from their land, laws, government, and most importantly their children. The result is destruction in the name of civilization. The end product is always genocide. Churchill, following Sartre, affirms that colonization is intrinsically genocidal.[141]

Juridical analysis in present day legal thinking reveals this destructive line of reasoning in the case of *Delgamuukw et al v. The Queen*.[142] The Gitksan-Wet'suwe't'en Nation made a claim of ownership and jurisdiction in their traditional territories. Chief Justice McEachern, quoting Thomas Hobbes, determined that "Aboriginal life in the territory was, at best, 'nasty, brutish and short.'"[143] The view that Indigenous Peoples and Nations are *primitive* and do not have *laws* is foundational in western legal thought. It is commonly held that because Indigenous

Peoples did not utilize lands according to European practices (viewed as establishing optimal standards for land utilization)[144] or circumscribe its ownership, this rendered the land a free for all. It becomes clear that Hobbes' analysis of the primitive savage as applied by the judiciary in colonial law dominates and dehumanizes. European colonial invaders then crafted fictitious legal doctrines such as the doctrine of discovery. Williams on Western legal systems:

> The conquest of the earth is not a pretty thing when you look into it too much. The history of the American Indian in Western legal thought reveals that a will to empire proceeds most effectively under a [colonial] rule of law. In the United States, and in other Western settler-colonized states, that rule begins with the Doctrine of Discovery and its discourse of conquest, which denies fundamental human rights and self-determination to [original nations] peoples. For the native peoples of the United States, Latin America, Canada, Australia and New Zealand, therefore, the end of the history of their colonization begins by denying the legitimacy of and respect for the rule of law maintained by the racist discourse of conquest of the Doctrine of Discovery.[145]

Therefore, "the Doctrine of Discovery was nothing more than the reflection of a set of Eurocentric racist beliefs elevated to the status of universal principle–one culture's argument to support its conquest and colonization" or domination and dehumanization over the original nations of the Western hemisphere and globally.[146] Theories of racial superiority have had genocidal consequences for Indigenous Peoples and their relationship with Mother Earth.[147] The doctrine of discovery, which is for all intense purposes a Doctrine of Theft, is rooted in a destructive frame of mind that seeks to dominate the Earth and Nations who stand in the way. The *Travaux* supports the contention that Western ideals of "civilization"[148] and "doctrines of racial superiority"[149] are foundational to genocide.[150]

The Invention of "Civilization"

The definition of "civilization" offered in *Webster's Third New International Dictionary* includes "the act of civilizing; esp. the *forcing* of a particular cultural pattern on a population to whom it is foreign." Newcomb describes the civilization-colonization process as *necessarily* being one of "imperial expansion by means of colonists, colonies, and a host of colonial and empire-expanding activities" for purposes of asserting dominion over the "land, population, wealth and power" of Others, especially those comprising Indigenous Nations.[151] In substance, the effect—in many cases real, and always intended—is to reduce those Others to the level of "bare life,"[152] a thoroughly dehumanized or "subhuman" condition conveyed in terms like "primitive" and "savage."[153]

As is exemplified by the Nazis' depiction of Slavic peoples as *untermensch*—"subhumans," or, more literally, "under men"[154]—the vernacular itself serves to "rationalize" and ultimately "justify" not only the expropriation of the lands and other "property" of Indigenous Others in the minds of the colonizers, but eradication of their original societies (as necessary, by outright extermination of all or a vital portion of the people themselves).[155] Historian James Blaut links the outlook to "the notion that European civilization—'The West'—has had some unique historical advantage, some special quality of race or culture or environment or mind or spirit, which gives this human community a permanent superiority over all other communities, at all times down to the present."[156]

Some analysts have diagnosed this narcissistic cultural self-concept, known as "eurosupremacism," as a collective pathology akin to megalomania in individuals, born of a deep-seated, acute, and abiding sense of cultural inadequacy which drives those afflicted to try and compensate by demeaning, degrading, and destroying Others, all the while systematically appropriating that which was and remains theirs, both materially and intellectually.[157]

Such an interpretation is certainly consistent with the narcissism and megalomania reflected in "eurocentrism," i.e., "The West's" conception of itself as comprising the veritable center of the universe. Blaut summarizes the eurocentric view of the world:

> Europe eternally advances, progresses, modernizes. The rest of the world advances more sluggishly, or stagnates: it is "traditional society." Therefore, the world has a permanent geographical center and a permanent periphery: an Inside and an Outside. Inside leads, Outside lags. Inside innovates, Outside imitates.[158]

Demonization begins with the destructive fallacy that Indigenous Peoples/Nations (non-Europeans) are less than Europeans in human development, technological, social, political, economic, agricultural, and legal systems. The colonizer believes the "folklore"[159] they have created about European history and the civilization process globally. But there were hundreds of millions of Peoples and Nations organized on Great Turtle Island and other regions globally with national identities, land, laws, governance, languages, and cultures since the beginning of time.[160] The recent over 525-year invasion of Europeans into the Western Hemisphere does not invalidate the existence of Original Nations that were and still exist on Turtle Island and other parts of the globe.

International law supports the position that the discovery doctrine is an instrument of domination and dehumanization. The International Court of Justice advisory opinion in the *Western Sahara* case determined that the doctrines of discovery and conquest are invalid to dispossess peoples of land.[161] The *Western Sahara* case affirms that theories of racial superiority are invalid to affect the rights of Indigenous Peoples' rights to their land and territory. Venne on the finding by the ICJ in the *Western Sahara* case: "the degree of civilization was no longer a valid criterion for determining if a territory inhabited by Indigenous Peoples is *terra nullius* but rather it is a question of whether such peoples have social and political organization."[162] It was determined that the "absence of settled towns and villages did not preclude Indigenous Peoples from having the right to self-determination in their territory."[163] If theories of racial superiority are declared invalid to justify the taking of land then similarly colonial doctrines of racial superiority should be equally invalid to justify the forcible removal of other peoples' children. The ICJ proclaimed that the only way a foreign state is able "to acquire any right to enter into territory that is not *terra nullius* is with the freely informed consent of the original inhabitants through an agreement."[164] On this most important finding by the ICJ it is also imperative to point out that, "Indigenous governments do not have to emulate European governmental structures to have sovereignty over their territory. European colonizing states could gain access to lands only through an agreement with the full consent of the Indigenous Peoples."[165] Treaties made between Indigenous Nations and the Crown affirms the Nation-to-Nation relationship that was accepted at the time of their making.

Forced Transfer Affects Our Nationhood

Early in the colonization of Great Turtle Island, several Peace and Friendship Treaties were made between the Indigenous Nations and the Crown of Great Britain.[166] The Treaty affirms the *Creation-given* inherent authority of the Original Nations on Great Turtle Island to their *nationality, land, laws* and *governments*.[167] The integrity of Treaties is internationally protected by the Vienna Convention. For the state of Canada to claim that our treaties are "sui-generis" (i.e. not of the same order as other nation-to-nation—international—treaties) is but another instance of the colonially-induced permeation of law with tenets based on doctrines of racial superiority. Miguel Alfonso-Martinez in the Treaty Study explains:

> the dominant viewpoint—as reflected, in general, in the specialized literature and in State administrative

> decisions, as well as in the decisions of the domestic courts—asserts that treaties involving indigenous peoples are basically a domestic issue, to be construed, eventually implemented and adjudicated via existing internal mechanisms, such as the courts and federal (and even local) authorities.[168]

He further emphasizes,

> It is worth underlining, however, that this position is not shared by indigenous parties to treaties, whose own traditions on treaty provisions and treaty-making (or on negotiating other kinds of compacts) continue to uphold the international standing of such instruments. Indeed, for many indigenous peoples, treaties concluded with European powers or their territorial successors overseas are, above all, treaties of peace and friendship, destined to organize coexistence in —not their exclusion from—the same territory and not to regulate restrictively their lives (within or without this same territory), under the overall jurisdiction of non-indigenous authorities. In their view, this would be a trampling on their right to self-determination and/or their other unrelinquished rights as peoples.[169]

The Elders affirm that the treaties are ones of peace and friendship.[170] This means that the land was to be shared with the settlers to the "depth of a plough."[171] In the article entitled "Understanding Treaty Six," Venne emphasizes that, "The Chiefs and Elders *could not have sold the lands to the settlers* as they could only share the lands according to the Cree, Saulteaux, Assiniboine and Dene Laws [emphasis added]."[172] In "Treaties Made in Good Faith," she further observes that Lord Denning affirmed in the *Indian Association of Alberta v. the Foreign and Commonwealth*

Secretary, "[n]o parliament or legislature can change the Treaty without the consent of the Treaty Peoples."[173]

Canada as a colony of Great Britain (successor) inherited the obligations to implement the Treaties according to the original Spirit and Intent.[174] Indigenous laws guided and instructed the negotiations:

> Actually, all of North America is Indigenous land. At the time of the treaty-making, Indigenous Peoples never gave up the land. When Indigenous Peoples talk about the land and the making of treaty, we are talking about our life and the life of the future generations. Land is central to the process. We have a relationship with our Creation based on a legal system designed to protect and honour the land. These are the laws that guided Cree Peoples when the chiefs negotiated and concluded Treaty Six in 1876.[175]

The Treaty provides for two parallel legal systems that are intended to co-exist, each party respecting the authority of the other. With respect to governance, Indigenous Nations' did not consent to the oppression of our laws, our way of life, and the forced removal of our children. Elder Alex Bonais stated the case at the International Meeting on Treaties held in Onion Lake Cree Nation in 1989: "This land was given to us. We were to stay here and nothing is going to destroy our land as long as the sun shines. ... The whiteman came across the ocean to destroy us and take away our children. Now our people are crying out from all over this land."[176] The responsibility and obligation to protect the land and their children was never relinquished at the making of the Treaties.

As established British policy in the colony of Canada was not a policy of war, "the 'ordinary' genocide of [Indigenous] Peoples grew out of Canada's need to extinguish"[177] Indigenous Peoples' relationship and "title to the land, without violating the letter and the spirit of established British policy. How to do this was, and continues to be, the 'Indian problem'."[178] One of the greatest violations of Treaty is the government's forcible transferring of Indigenous Peoples' children to the residential schools and child welfare systems. The Original Nations recognized their dependence on their future generations for the continuance of their distinct national identities. Chief Starblanket vehemently opposed the removal of children:

> In the Treaty we made then, the government promised to make a school for every band of Indians on their own reserves, but instead, little children are taken from their mothers' arms or homes by the police or government agents, and taken sometimes hundreds of miles away to large schools, perhaps to take sick and die when their family cannot see them.[179]

The effects are catastrophic and incalculable as successive generations transmit oppressive and traumatized characteristics. Children are forcibly conditioned into speaking, writing and thinking in the colonial language that dominates their national identity. Elder Bonais explained that "[a]s soon as children are born, they say 'hello' in English. They do not speak their own language. It seems to me that we do not believe in our Elders and what they have told us in the past."[180] As an instance, children do not learn that we have names in our original languages that identify our land and territories.[181] The Indigenous laws that instruct Indigenous Nations to protect and honour Mother Earth become severely impeded, and in the worst case scenario terminated. Indigenous Peoples' children and future generations do not understand their Treaty obligations and responsibilities.[182]

The collective ignorance that is passed down through the generations about Treaty rights contributes to the destruction of Indigenous Peoples and Nations because the Treaty affirms their distinct identity as Nations. In this regard, it is generally not understood that the effects of the forced transfer lead to collective destruction. The state of Canada individualizes the collective experience of the residential school system seeking in this manner to avoid the greater implications of collective devastation to the Nations themselves.[183] The peoples of Indigenous Nations become collectively indoctrinated to disparage rather than demand the right to their collective identities through the massive and widespread serious bodily and mental harm that occurs in the residential school.

The program of the residential school was "shaped and sustained by the representation of department officials and churchmen of the character, circumstances and destiny of the nation's [so called] Aboriginal population."[184] Given all of the above, the analysis will implement the traumatic experience of civilization into the model. Seen through this lens, it will be conveyed that colonial invasion is a genocidal process. An important note is that the model will be proven in the proceeding chapter in the legal application. The model is not the legal application *per se* but an input of the forced civilization and colonial invasion into the model.

Model of Dehumanization and Domination

Dominating and dehumanizing laws and policies are implemented to demonize, isolate and destroy Original Nations through a forced civilization-indoctrination process. Also known as "laws of occupation", these laws serve as the cornerstone of the legalized persecution and oppression of Indigenous Nations in the colonizer's quest for land. Colonial domination justified by the dehumanizing Western doctrine of racial superiority is vital to the process of genocide. The experience of genocide for Indigenous Nations is characterized in a model that explains the destructive framework of colonial invasion on a global scale. The model shows that *colonialism* and *genocide* are inextricably linked.

Certain sectors of academic discourse and society have downplayed the destructive nature of colonialism and deny that genocide occurs in this process.[185] It has been claimed that because Indigenous children were not intended to be physically wiped out "genocide" did not occur. Mundorff contends that, "[a[s Colin Tatz put it, though the Genocide Convention does not account for '[g]rades or levels' of genocide, 'for all of us, death is absolute: serious bodily or mental harm is something else; children forced into conversion may well become coerced Catholics or Muslims, but they live.'"[186] Tatz, and even Mundorff, appear to promote the idea that "[w]hatever these programs' effects, they were not constructed to kill individuals—an important distinction."[187] The claim that serious bodily and mental harm (which the UNGC itself defines in Article II(b) as genocidal) is not as horrific as death reveals the inability of such scholarship to come to grips with the full devastation of the genocidal experience of Indigenous Peoples' children as we have attempted to make visible, here.

From a cognitive legal lens, does a claim of what is right from the perspective of the colonial denier, such as Tatz—who claims even though children suffered serious bodily and mental harm, children forcibly indoctrinated and coerced into a catholic worldview is not as horrific as death—make it true? Does it lessen the horror that children endured at the hands of the state? Newcomb, building on Winter's cognitive legal theory, provides a powerful mechanism to challenge the genocide denial in this regard:

> Steven L. Winter points out that the revolutionary findings of cognitive theory provide us with a refreshing new insight into "the issues of meaning and autonomy in human affairs." Because of the history of U.S. government [Canadian government] officials imaginatively imposing their thoughts and ideas on our respective peoples in the name of "law," we as Indian people have been socialized into the habit of thinking of non-Indian law *as if* it were kind of an external physical force "or authority that rules over us." Yet Winter points out that what is called law is "but one consequence of more pervasive cultural processes of meaning-making."[188]

He further holds by citing a quote from Adolf Hitler that "One cannot rule by force alone. True, force is decisive, but it is equally important to have this psychological something which the animal trainer also needs to be master of his beast. They must be convinced that we are the victors."[189] The oppressive narrative of genocide denial that is deeply entrenched in the state and colonial society is a product of its colonial imagination. Newcomb continues, "[we] as indigenous nations and peoples have the ability to assume the cognitive and psychological position that the [genocide denier] is not the victor [or even truthful]."[190] It might be claimed that our analysis here is a product of the indigenous imagination; however, the evidence of massive and widespread violence and terror that children endured at the hands of the state is not imaginary but factual, though the colonial imagination may have to be overcome to digest it.

In this regard, Lemkin's framework on genocide had to do with state perpetrators of the crime trying to disestablish that which holds a nation or people together collectively (linguistically, culturally, psychologically, and spiritually) with the objective of making that nation or people no longer exist. It seems that "killing the Indian in the child"[191] or "kill the Indian, save the man"[192] (in the US context) encapsulates the intention test for genocide because it provides a concise verbal formulation of the intention to destroy ("kill") that which holds the Indigenous nations together as a cohesive whole. That does not have to only consist of physical death. MacDonald's address to the House of Commons in 1883 supports the contention here that the goal was to ensure that "Indian" people no longer existed as national identities by being compelled to "acquire the habits, modes and thought of white men."[193]

The methods used to coerce young people to speak, think, and write like white men exhibit massive patterns of violence and terror.

Further, Tatz's analysis assumes not only that the forcible transfer of children is not as destructive as death but that it will not result in death. The assertion is questionable, given the reports of starvation experiments performed on Indigenous children.[194]

The media reported in March 2014 that "the death records of tens of thousands of First Nations children who died during the time residential schools were operating in Canada have been handed over to the Truth and Reconciliation Commission."[195] More recent estimates by the TRC put the number to at least 6000.[196]

However, as early as 1907 Dr. Peter Bryce concluded that children were dying off at catastrophic rates. Milloy on Dr. Peter Bryce, concludes that "When the File Hills ratios are applied to Bryce's sample of 1537 children, it results in an increase from twenty-four percent to forty-two percent as the percentage of those children who died from their school experience" from the deplorable health and living conditions. He continues,

> Assuming that these ratios were constant, and projecting them throughout the system in 1907, when there were 3,755 students in the school, would mean that some 1,614 of those children would die prematurely. And every year more children came into the schools and became more infected.[198]

Further to this, "[t]he death rates among children confined in such facilities was, after all, as high or higher than that prevailing in some of the Nazis' more notorious concentration camps."[199] So the numbers that are concluded by the TRC are questionable at best.

The destruction brought against children throughout the history of the system was known by state officials, yet nothing was ever done to rectify or change the atrocious conditions that Indigenous Peoples' children were living under.[200] Duncan Campbell Scott openly acknowledged that "system-wide 'fifty percent of the children who passed through these schools did not live to benefit from the education which they had received therein."[201] In spite of Bryce's medical report to the Department of Indian Affairs, no action was taken to address the atrocious conditions. Another aggravating factor is the most recent reports of starvation experiments performed on Indigenous children. Dr. Ian Mosby confirms the government knew that underfunding was the cause of the malnutrition before the experiments were conducted.[202] This action by government officials begs a serious question as to their intent in this regard.

Another issue is specific intent. The state of Canada ensured that forced assimilation or cultural genocide measures were not recognized as a crime of genocide in international law. This explains why the state invokes the loopholes[203] it created when drafting the crime because of the awareness that the conduct it was engaging in would be genocide under international law. The state regards its genocidal conduct as "cultural genocide"[204] as per the loophole in the treaty itself, resulting from TRC final conclusions. The statement by the Canadian Civil Liberties Association to the Hate Propaganda Committee that the forcible removal of Indigenous children would be genocide is instructive.[205] The Hate Propaganda Committee (and therefore, Canada) knew by the instruction from the Civil Liberties Association. Given the attempted loopholes created by the omission of cultural genocide from the UNGC, the "civilizing" mandate was nonetheless accomplished contrary to UNGC Article II(b)—by the widespread and massive experience of the serious bodily and mental harm against Indigenous Peoples' children. How does the state account for this widespread atrocity? It was known through the history of the system that children underwent atrocious acts of violence, starvation, forced labour conditions, and appalling death rates.[206]

Yet government inaction throughout the residential school system to address its wrongs was a norm. Did the state of Canada, having been aware of what was happening and indeed its likely results, seek to rectify the problems and/or stop the system in its tracks and return the children back to their loving parents, families, communities, and nations? Did the government do anything to rectify the destruction committed against innocent children? No. These facts certainly negate any argument that the intention behind the system was "*benevolent*." Certainly having knowledge of the conditions and violence children were living under aggravates, not mitigates, the specific intent requirement. It allowed the massive and systemic serious bodily and mental harm to continue unabated.

Another issue concerns whether or not the purpose of the residential school system changed over time. The answer is no. The goal of absorbing the national identity of Indigenous Peoples has not changed over time. If the goal to destroy the national identity of the *Nehiyaw, Anishinaabe, Dene, Nuxalk,* has not changed then the effects will not change either.

Prime Minister Harper, in his so-called apology downgrades a genocidal experience for Indigenous Nations collectively. The experience is minimized as adding up to no more than "tragic accounts of the emotional, physical and sexual abuse and neglect of helpless children."[207] The use of a model challenges the "genocide denial"[208] that occurs globally about Indigenous Peoples and Nations experience of colonial invasion.

The model employs the use of a metaphor to deflect understanding of the destructive colonial framework that explains the residential school as an intentional genocidal process. It will be shown that the effects of the residential school are in the child welfare system. The way that the child welfare system operates continues the effects of the residential school system. The metaphor of a machine will be used to convey this experience. The colonizer justifies its genocidal actions in colonial law, policies, scholarship, institutions, and society to resolving the so called "Indian problem." out of existence. For example, scholarship downplays the experience of genocide in the residential schools by calling it *abuse*. Terming it abuse minimizes the reality of the destruction by framing it as something much less than *genocide*. The model allows the reader to see a reality that is hidden in plain sight.

Demonization, Isolation, and Destruction

In the colonizing process, genocide takes place through three stages: 1) demonization, 2) isolation, and 3) destruction of Original Nations or Indigenous Peoples and Nations. All of these elements come together as the oppressor implements the "two phases" of genocide described by Lemkin. Figure 1 displays the domination and dehumanization through a metaphor. The model describes the colonial body and the tools of this body or colonial society. Missing from this model is the "body politic" or "colonizing body."[210]

The metaphor of the "machine" or "engine"[211] is used to explain the process of genocide. For clarity, the use of the terms machine or engine metaphorically explains the process of indoctrination or the serious bodily and mental harm that occurs as a result of the forced transfer. It explains the process Indigenous Nations have collectively undergone through the forced transfer of their children from one group (their own family/community/Nation) to another group (via residential institutions expressly intended to "assimilate"" them into colonial society).[212]

Clarification is necessary because genocide is a *human decision*. The use of the word "machine" is by no means an attempt to diminish the human decision of genocide. Human beings plan, create and drive the machines they construct. The model explains not just the act but the colonizing "state of mind" behind the act. The metaphor of the machine is used to explain the residential school system as a dominating and dehumanizing process. The figure itself represents symbolically a washing machine or more specifically a "brainwashing" machine that explains the process of genocide.

The term "brainwashing" is not meant to dehumanize or disrespect the experience of Indigenous Peoples' children's collective terror and violence. It conveys the reality of the collective experience of the forced indoctrination through the serious bodily and mental harm committed against the children. The forced indoctrination process brutally conditioned children to think, speak, and write like the "civilized" society it was being transferred to through brutal methods. The model explains the violent process of conditioning innocent children into viewing the world from a westernized christian perspective.

The work of Ward Churchill's *Kill the Indian Save the Man*[213] and Chrisjohn, Young, and Maraun's *The Circle Game*[214] is utilized to explain how the forcible transferring of Indigenous

Figure 1
Domination and Dehumanization of Original Nations

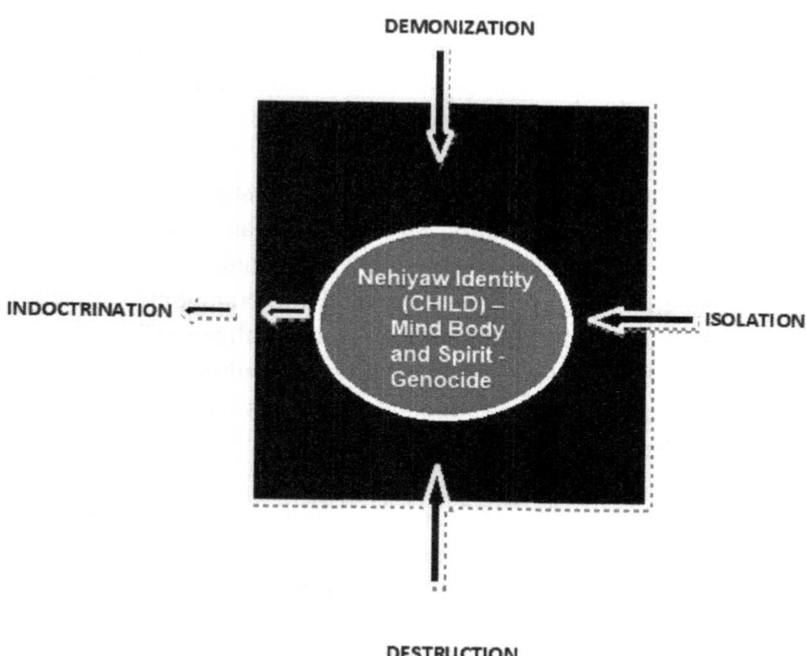

Peoples' children causes the collective serious bodily and mental harm. Churchill explains Indigenous children were forced to see themselves through the eyes of the colonizer.

Churchill juxtaposes photos of a young Cree named Thomas Moore as he appeared at the time of his arrival at the Regina Indian Industrial School in 1910 and another of Moore as he appeared three years later.[215] The cover photo cover of this book, *Suffer the Little Children,* shows children at the Holy Angels Boarding School in Fort Chipewyan praying to a recently arrived statue to the school. Easily misinterpreted as children engaged in humble prayer, the actuality it captures is their torturous religious indoctrination. While such "before and after" imagery was frequently used by government propagandists as "graphic evidence of the 'progress' made by children committed to residential institutions,"[216] what it actually provides is stunningly powerful visual evidence of genocide's "two phases," i.e., the deliberate and systematic "destruction of the national pattern of the oppressed group" and "imposition of the national pattern of the oppressor."[217] As Churchill explains,

> …regardless of whether church or state was ascendant in operating the schools at any given moment or location, the result was the same. Even as they underwent a harsh and thoroughgoing process of deculturation (or "denationalization") the children were systematically "reenculturated" to function in psychointellectual terms as "little white people."[218]

Macdonald's address to the House of Commons in 1883 provides evidence of this intended goal of forcibly "re-enculturating" the children into "little white people."[219]

Insofar as children were forcibly dominated and dehumanized by torture, starvation, disease, forced labour, and sexual predatory acts,[220] Churchill's analysis supports the brainwashing machine analogy by his accurate classification of the destruction rendered against the children.

The young ones were rendered unable to fit into either the colonial world or their own societies and were forcibly indoctrinated with terror, self-loathing, and destroyed in this process as the successive generations of children transmitted the terror, trauma, confusion, sorrow, and debilitating social conditions. These are known as the long-term impacts of genocide.[221] Children that physically survived the residential school system suffered both bodily and mental destruction. The young ones were individually and then collectively as Nations brainwashed by the methods utilized to "kill the Indian in the child."[222] Again: the survivors witnessed their friends, brothers, sisters, (family and people) being tortured, raped, starved, and slave-labored, sometimes to death. The children were compelled to live under deplorable living and health conditions, which also led to death.

This experience supports Sartre's view that colonialism produces internalized violence and terror in the colonized.[223] The long-term impacts were transmitted to several generations and "[t]he profundity of their destructive effects upon native people, both individually and collectively, not only in the immediacy of their operational existence but in the aftermath as well, was and remains by any reasonable estimation incalculable."[224]

Chrisjohn, Young, and Maraun's explanation of the "total institution"[225] supports the metaphor of the machine that forcibly conditions a child that 'thinks, speaks and writes'[226] like the oppressor. The authors demonstrate the process of being taken apart and reassembled into the intended vision of the government.

> [i]n the name of efficiency, total institutions "*unmake*" the people over whom they gain control. It matters little how old an inmate is when he or she is placed under the institution's thumb; whoever that person **is**, and how he or she defends and asserts it, must be *taken apart and reassembled* enough to allow what remains to operate in accordance with the intuitional requirements [emphasis original and added].[227]

They further add that, "[b]y doing this, the total institution does not produce a **new** self, but **no self at all** [emphasis original]."[228]

The total institution or machine or engine dehumanizes the child. The Canadian Oxford Dictionary defines "engine" as "a thing that is an agent or instrument of a desired end or achievement (drive the engine of progress faster.)"[229] Recall that "dehumanize" is defined as, "deprive of human characteristics [or] make impersonal or machine-like."[230] The process de-spirits the children by rendering them machine-like or severely traumatized. Consider this further definition of "engine," as "a machine or instrument esp. a contrivance used in warfare or torture."[231]

The oppressor employs the "tools," "machinery," or "engine" to produce the desired result that absorbs Indigenous children into the "body politic."[232] The metaphor of the "colonial body" or "artificial man" explains the "state."[233] Newcomb writes about this colonial body as a

> collective body (composed of individual humans interacting in their social and cultural lives) arrives to a "new" continent with a colonizing, ravenous "hunger" (desire) for land. From an indigenous perspective, this collective colonizing body can be metaphorically thought of as predator that pursues its indigenous spoil and prey; it sets out to catch, devour and consume everything in sight (this correlates with the common expressions "this is a consumer society" and "we're in the belly of the beast").[234]

He demonstrates that colonization is a metaphor for eating through "the conception of the image of an empire, state, or common wealth as a collective body or metaphorical person."[235] The colonizing body engages in the "process of 'seizing,' 'eating,' and 'swallowing' indigenous lands."[236] In this sense, "colonization can also be understood metaphorically" as process of "digestion or assimilation."[237] According to Newcomb, the "imagery makes sense of U.S. policies to assimilate Indians 'into' the social and political body of the United States [and Canada]."[238] Churchill in the same vein, "the weight of policy in the U.S. and Canada alike has been placed on 'assimilating'—'digesting' might be a better word—the residue of survivors."[239]

The colonial body is a "predator" that "pursues its spoil or prey."[240] Newcomb explains, "[The] concept of the predator makes sense of Wheaton's statement in his *Elements of International*

Law that 'the heathen nations of the other quarters of the globe were the lawful spoil and prey of their civilized conquerors'."[241] The predator swallows, engulfs, devours and consumes Original Nations and their lands into its colonizing body politic. To reiterate, Scott openly declared that "our objective is to continue until there is not a single Indian in Canada that has not been *absorbed into the body politic* [emphasis added]."[242] The state policy and law of this same colonizing body (from the U.S. side) was said, in the words of Theodore Roosevelt, to be a "mighty pulverizing engine to break up the tribal mass."[243] The metaphor is seen as a "pulverizing engine," conveying that the prey are being prepared for consumption into the colonial body.

The national identities of Indigenous children are consumed or destroyed by the torture, sexual predation, starvation, forced labour and in all too many instances, death.[244] The total institution forcibly indoctrinates or "unmakes" and remakes Indigenous children through massive colonial terror and violence. In other words, through a civilization process, in which children are forced to "acquire the habits and modes of thought of white man."[245] To repeat, the metaphor of the machine conveys the collective serious bodily and mental harm against the innocent. The total institution explains how children were forced to acquire these *thoughts* of white men.

The model expresses the predator's machine that prepares the prey for "consumption" into the colonizing body as it devours everything in sight. The prey is designated as land and the peoples indigenous to the land (Original Nations).[246] The brainwashing/indoctrination machine (total institution) is the mechanism designed to dominate and dehumanize through methods that demonize, isolate and destroy children and Nations. An important aspect of the model is the language or cognitive conditioning imposed on Indigenous children in the indoctrination process.[247]

The imposition of an alien language at the expense of their own served to deny the young ones any viable sense of themselves as being *of* their Nations/Peoples, and thus of a true understanding of the corresponding spiritual and cultural traditions, thereby paving the way for their acceptance of the colonial worldview in which all things Indigenous, including the children themselves, were demeaned to the point of dehumanization.[248]

Forced transfer severs Indigenous Peoples' relationship with their lands and territories and ultimately their identities as Nations because the child becomes an "enemy"[249] of his/her own people, having been trained to view them as inferior. Churchill recounts one student's experience at Oblate's St. Phillips School in Ontario: "Long before she'd completed her schooling, she learned to hate, not simply the people who oppressed her, but herself and her race as well."[250]

The spiritual relationship embodied in Creation's laws with Mother Earth (Great Turtle Island) becomes severed in the residential school. An example is an Indigenous language (name) designated to identify a territory. The *Nehiyaw* language contains spiritual laws that embody how people are to relate in a beneficial way to that land or territory. Spiritual laws are encoded into Indigenous languages.[251] The dominating society forces another language (e.g., English) onto children and as a result those children never learned or do not remember either the nature of their relationship with their land, or the reasons for it.[252] It becomes a deliberate process to isolate children from their land. Newcomb writes:

> From a cognitive science perspective [the dominating conceptual system] have become part of the neural circuitry and structuring of our brains. As a result, non-Indian strands of meaning have become interwoven into our social and cultural lives as Indian people, thereby making the constraints of [the dominating system] an integral part of the fabric of our own imaginations and an integral part of the daily social interactions of Indian people in Indian communities.[253]

As a result, Indigenous children that have undergone

forcible indoctrination will not have been raised *Nehiyaw* and so in what way can the children claim to be reared by their families, communities and Nations? The spiritual laws embedded in the language become severed by not being passed on to new generations.[254] The young ones are now a product of the dominating society's language and culture and not their own society's culture and language. The fallout for successive generations of Indigenous children is catastrophic.[255] Indigenous children become dominated and dehumanized through the methods employed in the total institutions. The isolation from loving families, communities and nations render children vulnerable to the forced indoctrination. The end product is destruction in the name of "civilization."

In other words, the forced transfer of Indigenous children causes the young ones serious and bodily mental harm. Denigrating a child's history, people, culture, or way of life causes destruction to that child. Tell a child his/her people are "worthless savages" and it is likely that the child will come to see herself or himself through the eyes of the colonizer.[256] The situation becomes exacerbated by torture such as poking needles through tongues, whippings, and beating children into submission.[257] As an example, the "insertion of a needle"[258] into or "dry ice"[259] on the tongue to force an Indigenous child to not speak her own language, but to speak the colonizer's language instead, will cause serious bodily mental harm and compel that child to speak and think in the language being forcibly imposed. The child becomes unmade and then remade to think speak and write like the colonizer in this process of colonial destruction.

Add the experiences of starvation, forced labour and untold death by disease and other methods and the oppressor society creates a child that has been conditioned into something that is "unrecognizable"[260] to the parents and families from whom the young one was kidnapped. Take the situation further and sexually prey upon a child and that child becomes utterly destroyed in the process. The effect is shattering as collectively the trauma, sorrow and grief becomes transmitted from generation to generation. The collective trauma brought about by the residential school phase is then used by very dominating society that created that trauma (dysfunction) to justify the child welfare system phase of the process.[261] The state uses its imposed standards of judgment to create the institutions (residential schools) that create the destructive conditions, and then use its standards of judgment to forcibly steal another generation of children in the child welfare system. It is well acknowledged in academic scholarship and government reports that the forcible removals in the child welfare system is a direct effect of the residential school system by the inability to parent and further by the state and societies on-going racist dominating and dehumanizing beliefs about Indigenous Peoples.[262] The rates of removal are appalling in the child welfare system.[263] It is reported that in some provinces eighty percent of children in care are aboriginal, yet they make up only five percent of the total population of Canada.[264] The collective trauma and dysfunction affects entire Original Nations on Great Turtle Island.

Let us turn again to the debates during the drafting of the crime in international law. The Venezuelan delegate affirmed: "[T]he forced transfer of children to a group where they would be given an education different from that of their own group, and would have new customs, a new religion and probably a new language, was in practice tantamount to the destruction of their group, whose future depended on that generation of children."[265] Greece's position on the forcible transferring of children is instructive, "The forced transfer of children had not only cultural, but also physical and biological effects since it imposed on young persons conditions of life likely to cause them serious harm or even death."[266]

The children who witness and/or experience brutalities like mass hangings, forced labour, beatings, rape, and the like, are severely traumatized and become remnants of their former selves. What are transmitted to the next generation are not the Nations' healthy characteristics but—over successive generations—traumatized and destructive patterns.[267] Collective trauma, suicides, drug and alcohol addiction, traumatized parenting patterns and so forth are transmitted onto future generations of children, hence Indigenous Peoples as entire Nations are destroyed in the process.[268] The genocidal effects include dispossession of their lands and territories as Nations as they unknowingly and sometimes knowingly enter into agreements intended to cede and surrender their lands (nationhood) to the colonizing body or colonial state.[269]

The ability to transmit to the next generation the healthy characteristics of that society in terms of its land, laws, worldview and nationhood becomes severely impeded and, in the worst case scenario, terminated. The state agenda of termination imposed on Indigenous Peoples collectively becomes the residential school and the child welfare systems. Instead of healthy characteristics of nationhood, patterns of destruction are transmitted to successive generations. In the worst case scenario, the residential school and the effects destroy entire Nations as the children that come out cannot relate to their identities as nations, laws, languages, spirituality, cultures, families, and most importantly an identity that embodies a relationship with Mother Earth. The continuance of this identity is crucial to the survival as a national identity or *Nehiyaw*, *Anishinaabe*, and *Nuxalk* to name a few.

This reality is concealed by the colonizer state, as every effort has endeavored to render Indigenous Peoples as invisible. By this concealment, the colonizer state individualizes the collective experience of genocide that Indigenous Nations encounter in the colonization of their lands and territories. Indigenous Peoples' experience of genocide as Nations is not recognized because of maneuvers put in place to mask the reality of colonialism.[270] The characterization of genocide from a dominating and dehumanizing lens explains the experience as *demonization, isolation* and *destruction* in the context of the UNGC. The analysis will now proceed to prove this model in international law.

| Chapter Four |

SMOKE AND MIRRORS
Canada's Pretense of Compliance with the Genocide Convention

"They are committing the greatest indignity human beings can inflict on one another: telling people who have suffered excruciating pain and loss that their pain and loss were illusions."
— Elie Wiesel, *Night*[1]

Controversy

There is an ongoing and often bitter "controversy" in Canada as to whether the state perpetrated genocide in its implementation of laws, policies and programs under which several successive generations of Indigenous children were consigned to a state-wide system of residential schools for the express purpose of forcing their assimilation into the Eurocanadian "settler" society[2]—a colonial project which continues to this day with the extensive seizures of Indigenous children into the provincial child welfare systems. The previous chapters have examined the removal of cultural genocide from the definition of those acts which comprise genocide as detailed in Article II of the Genocide Convention, and the implications of this removal as related to avoiding international recrimination for colonialism. This has special application to the legal issue in question, in so far as this removal seeks to exculpate the destructive colonial framework in which the forcible transfers of our children occur into present times. The analysis has shown that colonialism is implicated in the crime of genocide. The consequences for world governments such as the United Kingdom are great. Canada, as a colony of Great Britain, went hand in hand with it to ensure that cultural genocide was deleted from the 1948 Convention on Prevention and Punishment of the Crime of Genocide (hereinafter, UNGC).

Once again, it is important to bear in mind how genocide is defined in international law: Article II of the UNGC frames it as being "any of the following acts committed with the intent to destroy, in whole or in part, a national, ethnical, racial, or religious group, as such:"

a) Killing members of the group;
b) Causing serious bodily or mental harm to members of the group;
c) Deliberately inflicting on the group conditions of life calculated to bring about its physical destruction in whole or in part;
d) Imposing measures intended to prevent births within the group;
e) Forcibly transferring children of the group to another group.[3]

It is deemed to be genocide when *any* of the enumerated acts is committed "with intent to destroy, in whole or in part"[4] a protected group. The Genocide Convention advocates the protection of "national, ethnical, racial or religious groups."[5] But Canada excludes key elements of the UNGC in implementing this treaty into its Criminal Code.[6] The relevant sections that are not included in the Canadian Criminal Code are articles 2 (b), (d) and (e). Why?

What is the legal effect of the Criminal Code when Canada has continued to forcibly and in large numbers[7] remove Indigenous children from their families, communities, and nations which according to the Genocide Convention constitute an act of genocide? Canada cannot absolve itself of acts that are deemed to be in violation of customary international laws.[8] Can Canada continue to commit what is an enumerated act of genocide by the UNGC and excuse itself by continuing to say that it is *not intending* what the Genocide Treaty recognizes as *the result* of such an act—even as its former Prime Minister admits that Canada did indeed intend to "kill the Indian in the child? Insofar as the Canadian government's legislation attempts to thwart the domestic application of the definitional acts of genocide entered into its Criminal Code by the UNGC, seeking thereby to immunize itself from culpability for possible government violations and conduct by the omission of any such enumerated criminal acts in the Criminal Code, might this rather be seen as the reverse: an indication of awareness of Canada's vulnerability to such claims?

Irrespective of any reservations Canada might have made to the UNGC (but didn't), or any omissions in its implementation into its own Criminal Code, Canada cannot absolve itself of acts that are criminal.[9] Given this most important question, an examination of Canada's domestic legislation and its limited definition of genocide from a customary international law perspective is important to the overall question as to whether Canada is criminally culpable for crimes of genocide. If genocide is the crime of crimes, aren't states under a duty and obligation to refrain from committing genocide? Further, if a state has acceded to the UNGC does this not impose a greater duty on states to refrain from genocidal conduct? The convention was submitted to signatory states for ratification and to enact the necessary domestic implementing legislation. The criminal legislation superficially supposes that Canada enacted the entire body of the convention into its *Criminal Code*, but it did not.

The following analysis examines two questions: Whether the Canadian state violates customary international laws and whether, if so, is it culpable for genocide. The answers to these questions are found in turn by reviewing the Advisory Opinion on *Reservations to the Convention on the Prevention and Punishment of the Crime of Genocide*. The drafting process, beginning from the Draft Convention to the final form of the UNGC, reveals the extent of denial about important elements of the crime. We will scrutinize the Canadian *Criminal Code* and its exclusion of key elements of international law. Canada's efforts at concealment and obfuscation is a theme that runs through the draft discussions and is manifest in the way that the Convention was implemented into domestic law, including the rhetoric that is utilized by the government and society that renders the residential school system experience as benign or less than genocide.

Forcibly transferring Indigenous children into residential schools created an ongoing intergenerational impact and the conditions for further child removal via the child welfare system. Child removals in the provincial systems continue with no end in sight. The government's forcible transferring of Indigenous children from their Nations can be best understood by examining, in addition to the colonial project and the international laws on genocide, the humanitarian and moral principles and universal scope of the Convention as envisioned by the United Nations General Assembly, and Canada's inclusion of a limited definition of genocide within its *Criminal Code*. It is general practice to refer to the text of the Genocide Convention in proving genocide; however, this analysis takes a different approach by utilizing both a textual approach (the UNGC) and an examination of the issue from a moral and humanitarian or a customary international law stand point.[10] The ability of the UNGC to protect Indigenous Peoples' children (ultimately Indigenous Nations) comes into question for the reason that the forcible transferring of children continues unabated into the present.

Genocide in Public International Law

In interpreting genocide in public international law Article 38 of the Statute of the International Court of Justice[11] provides three primary sources for deriving what is international law: international conventions; international custom; and general principles of law, with a fourth being scholarly opinion. The Genocide Convention and the Vienna Convention on the Law of Treaties[12] (hereinafter Vienna Convention) are the pertinent conventions in the context of genocide. Articles 31 and 32 of the Vienna Convention are identified by the ICJ to "guide interpretation of the Genocide Convention."[13] Article 31 declares that "a treaty shall be interpreted in good faith in accordance with the ordinary meaning to be given to the terms of the treaty in their context and in the light of its object and purpose."[14] Article 32 of the Vienna Convention declares that,

> Recourse may be had to supplementary means of interpretation, including the preparatory work of the treaty and the circumstances of its conclusion, in order to confirm the meaning resulting from the application of Article 31, or to determine the meaning when the interpretation according to Article 31:
> (a) leaves the meaning ambiguous or obscure; or
> (b) leads to a result which is manifestly absurd or unreasonable.[15]

The *Travaux Préparatoires*[16] (hereinafter *Travaux*) will be utilized to clarify ambiguities concerning Article II(e) forcibly transferring of children from one group to another group as there exists little jurisprudence that addresses this specific section of the UNGC. Fortunately, there is case law that provides clarity and a broad application to the forcible transferring of children that causes the serious bodily or mental harm to members of the group and it will be utilized to provide a broader-based understanding. The *Travaux* will be utilized to provide answers to ambiguities that concern the forcible transferring of Indigenous children from their families and nations into state-controlled residential institutions. Again, the second source is reflected in genocide case law and "serves as evidence of the customary international law of genocide."[17] The third source is general principles of law. General Principles of law refer to general principles of law recognized by "civilized nations." Venne writes "general principles of law rest on the common attitudes and approaches of different municipal legal systems."[18] The fourth source of law is scholarly opinion.

The "Made in Canada" Approach to Genocide

David MacDonald and Graham Hudson in "The Genocide Question and Indian Residential Schools in Canada," refer to the monist and dualist approaches to international law in which, "[m]onists hold that international law should be recognized in domestic courts unless it irreconcilably conflicts with domestic legislation. Dualism states that international laws have no standing unless implemented by Parliament through statute."[19] The "fence-sitting"[20] approach by MacDonald and Hudson does not address the Canadian state's culpability for crimes of genocide with regard to the application of customary international law. However, the paper does raise revealing points with respect to the lack of application of customary international laws on genocide in Canadian jurisprudence.[21]

According to MacDonald and Hudson, it is acknowledged that, "[t]o date, the Canadian courts have refused to give effect to the UNGC in private law settings and have had few occasions to consider it in criminal proceedings."[22] The omission in Canada's Criminal Code of the international law (UNGC) definition specifying what are to be considered acts of genocide has "had important ramifications for what [Indigenous] peoples can claim as genocide in Canadian courts."[23] The limited definition is in violation of international customary laws on genocide, given that there is the glaring legal question of state involvement with respect to Article II(e), the forcible transferring of Indigenous Peoples' children. With respect to the case of *Re Residential Schools* the authors note,

> This judgment highlights a fairly common and contestable judicial attitude towards the UNGC as a "political" or moral standard and not, absent legislation to the contrary, a legally binding document. It also ignores legal doctrine that makes international customary law an automatic part of Canadian common law, independently of legislative implementation."[24]

The legislative omission allows the state of Canada to argue against the application of international laws to its own conduct.

Domestic ratification of the UNGC allowed each state to enact the enabling legislation, however, Canada took advantage of this process and defined genocide in a way that does not encompass the portrayal of the crime in international law. During the 1952 Senate debates, Arthur Roebuck stated on the enforcement of the crime:

> In Article V the contracting parties undertake to enact—and note this language—in accordance with their respective constitutions the necessary legislation to give effect to the provisions of the convention, and to provide effective penalties for persons guilty of genocide and its associated crimes. So far as Canada is concerned, this is simple procedure, for there is on file a letter from the Deputy Minister of Justice, Mr. Varcoe, stating that Canada has already on its statutes books the prohibitions necessary to the implementation of the convention.[25]

Citing the legal opinion given by the Minister of Justice, Roebuck further held that he could not "conceive of any act of commission or omission occurring in Canada as falling within the definition of the Crime of Genocide in Article II of the Convention, that would not be covered by the relevant section of the Criminal Code."[26] On enforcement Roebuck affirmed the limitations of the UNGC to make government officials accountable:

> In view, honourable senators, of the possibility that for years there will not be any international tribunal with penal or criminal jurisdiction, it follows logically from that article that in practice only private individuals may be prosecuted for

> the crime of genocide, and that they must be prosecuted according to the laws of the state in which they live or in which the crime is committed. *The governments in most countries are not likely to submit their acts to the judgement of their own courts, nor are they likely to submit to those courts the question of the guilt of their high officials, whose criminal acts may have been in accordance with government policy. The truth is that this convention lacks teeth* [emphasis added].[27]

The acknowledgement by Senator Roebuck that involving state governments will not lead to their holding their own government officials accountable begs a serious question raises. Why go to great effort to have genocide recognized as a crime in international law, then render the integrity of the crime inapplicable within domestic state borders? It shows that Canada understood the loopholes left open for the implementation process. The limited definition of the crime in domestic laws would later render any possible government conduct of genocide as impossible or moot in a Canadian court.[28]

According to Davis and Zannis, "Canada serves as an example of the importance of the watering down process. The actual ratification sailed through Parliament with no problems, accompanied by the proper pious speeches about the horror of Nazi atrocities and due gratitude that such things 'could never happen here."[29] Then, in its domestic implementation, the government "redefine[d] genocide in a way so as to ensure that it could never become an embarrassment to anyone."[30]

The discussions in 1952 in the House of Commons shed light on the matter. Mr. L.D. Crestohl announced that states such as Nazi Germany and Japan had committed crimes and sought to avoid culpability: "[u]nder the guise of its being a matter of domestic jurisdiction, these crimes were repeatedly committed while civilization stood aghast and shouted 'shame', but unfortunately did nothing more."[31] With respect to the "theory of non-intervention in a matter of so-called domestic jurisdiction,"[32] Crestohl stated:

> [I]s no longer tenable with respect to crimes which are universally acknowledged as inhuman and immoral, and this notwithstanding the fact that traditionally criminal law has been considered as an expression of the right of a state to define and punish acts, which in its judgement are contrary to public order within its borders. International law of modern times has recognized certain crimes which it declared to be international, and regards them as directed against public order not of any one given country, but as against public order of the entire family of nations.[33]

Crestohl later announced that, "[i]t is, of course, not difficult to conceive that a criminal court of any particular state might have a problem in trying its ruler, leader, statesman or anyone else. Domestic courts can unfortunately be tampered with or neutralized by legislation, as we see in the case of South Africa today."[34] Whether or not Crestohl also took into account the Canadian situation, his point is clear: it is unlikely any state will admit to the possibility of their state committing such crimes, let alone hold itself accountable for crimes of genocide in its own domestic legislation or courts.

Lester Pearson, then Minister of External Affairs, piously declared "the possibility of the crime of genocide being committed in Canada seems to me to be extremely remote. I stress the fact that the broad purpose of this convention is to bring the law throughout the world up to the standard which I think we may say without boasting happily exists already in our own country."[35] Pearson, after receiving a legal opinion from the deputy minister of justice, concluded that the crimes enumerated in Article II could not apply to Canada.[36]

Nonetheless, when the Canadian state's ratification process is examined, it reveals a concerted effort to warp the integrity of the *already* limited definition of the crime of genocide to a form that is barely recognizable in international law. Pearson further distorted the definition of the words "mental harm" to mean "physical injury to the mental faculties."[37] Schabas acknowledges that Pearson's interpretation of mental harm is not supported by "either the Convention text or the *Travaux*."[38]

Another smokescreen was the effort to equate genocide with mass killing or physical destruction. In 1965, Canada's Special Committee on Hate Propaganda (Hate Propaganda Committee), advocated for restricting the definition of genocide to the physical killing aspect of the crime:

> For purposes of Canadian law we believe that the definition of genocide should be drawn somewhat more narrowly than in the international Convention so as to include only killing and its substantial equivalents—deliberately inflicting conditions of life calculated to bring about physical destruction and deliberately imposing measures to prevent births. The other components of the international definition, viz., causing serious bodily or mental harm to members of a group and forcibly transferring children of one group to another group with intent to destroy the group *we deem inadvisable for Canada – the former because it is considerably less than a substantial equivalent of killing in our existing legal framework, the latter because it seems to have been intended to cover certain historical incidents in Europe that have little essential relevance to Canada, where mass transfers of children to another group are relatively unknown* [emphasis added].[39]

The Committee also deemed the inclusion of articles 2(b) and (e) as "inadvisable for Canada". Churchill noted, in *Perversions of Justice* on the domestic legislation, that:

> The subterfuge in this case was to write domestic implementing legislation in such a way as to excise from the country's "legal understanding" those classifications of genocidal policy in which Canada was actually engaged, retaining only those involving "physical destruction…killing, or its substantial equivalents" (that is, Article II (a), (c) and (d) of the 1948 Convention).[40]

Churchill continues,

> no [state], of course, whether it be Canada or the U.S. or Nazi Germany, holds a legitimate prerogative to pick and choose among elements of international law, electing to abide by some and others not. Less, does it possess a right to unilaterally "revise" the Laws of Nations in conformity with its own preferences.[41]

The Hate Propaganda Committee further suggested that the forced transfer of children be left out because mass transfers of children in Canada are "unknown". The assertion that mass transfers are "unknown" indicates a denial that is little more than a lie. The government was well aware of the residential schools as indicated in the following statement made by the Canadian Civil Liberties Association (hereinafter Civil Liberties Association) to the Hate Propaganda Committee:

> Section 267A (e) would make it an offence to advocate for forcibly transferring children of one group to another group, with the intent of destroying the group. Could it be argued that the proposals to impose integrated education upon the children of Doukhobors or Indians for example, might fall within this prohibition?[42]

The concern from a Civil Liberties stand point indicates the awareness that the forcible transferring of Indigenous children would constitute genocide. Davis and Zannis continue:

> The risk contained in this sub-section is that a court might be persuaded that the proposal to transfer children in such a way is intended to "destroy" a culture, i.e. a group. Clearly whatever one thinks of compulsory integrated education, the advocacy of it in such circumstances should not constitute a criminal offence. In our view, the concept of genocide should be limited to *physical* (emphasis theirs) destruction.[43]

Declarations by the Civil Liberties Association demonstrate the concerted effort by the government to limit the crime, and civil society complicity. It was understood the forcible transferring of Indigenous children would be deemed culpable. The Hate Propaganda Committee then artfully held with respect to the narrowing of the crime to physical destruction, that,

> because existing Canadian law already forbids most substantive aspects of genocide in that it prohibits homicide or murder vis-à-vis individuals, and because it may be undesirable to have the same acts forbidden under two different legal categories, we deem it advisable that the Canadian legislation which we urge as a symbol of our country's dedication to the rights set out in the Convention…"[44]

Rather it was maintained that because legislation addressing one aspect of the crime—killing/murder—already existed in the Canadian Criminal Code, further legislative efforts should be restricted to address "'*advocating and promoting' genocide*, [emphasis added] acts which clearly are clearly not forbidden at present by the Criminal Code."[45]

The government ratified the UNGC in 1952; however, it was nearly twenty years later, in 1970, that the warped definition of genocide was implemented into Canadian laws. Canada enacted "genocide" into its domestic Criminal Code under the guise of "hate propaganda" Section 318 reads as follows:

> (1) Everyone who advocates or promotes genocide is guilty of an indictable offence and liable to imprisonment for a term not exceeding five years.
>
> (2) In this section, "genocide" means any of the following acts committed with intent to destroy in whole or in part any identifiable group, namely,
>
> (*a*) killing members of the group; or
>
> (*b*) deliberately inflicting on the group conditions of life calculated to bring about its physical destruction.
>
> (3) No proceeding for an offence under this section shall be instituted without the consent of the Attorney General.
>
> (4) In this section, "identifiable group" means any section of the public distinguished by colour, race, religion, ethnic origin or sexual orientation.[46]

The Genocide Convention was redefined to a "made in Canada" approach. Why was the crime of genocide reduced to a hate crime? From the record contained in the *Travaux*, the authors in *Genocide Reinterpreted* maintain that Canada's efforts to evade and deny cultural genocide cannot be tied to what was happening domestically. However, "causing serious bodily mental harm to members of the group"[47] and the "forcible transferring of children from one group to another group"[48] and "imposing measures intended to prevent births within the group"[49] did not make it to the final cut.

With respect to these crimes excluded from the Criminal Code, "two are directly relevant to Residential School practice and the other has yet to receive serious historical study with respect to Aboriginal Peoples."[50] Canada's criminal domestic legislation avoids any possible investigations into whether or not Canada has committed genocide within its domestic borders. The effect has consequences, forestalling any ability to submit a claim of genocide in a Canadian court as applied to the potential Canadian state conduct of genocide.

What is the recourse for Indigenous Peoples when all doors have been slammed shut?[51] Before proceeding to that analysis, it is critical to unveil the smokescreen that can be and is created by the deployment of certain words rather than others. In the practice of law, words matter, and in this regard it is imperative to clarify the use of the *word game*.

Separating Rhetoric from Reality

The *word game* the state utilizes to separate its conduct from the horrific truth is imperative to absolving itself of criminal responsibility. The settler state and society, as part of the denial they engage in, characterize state domination, and the theft of our lands and our territories, and the forcible removal of our children, in benign terms. With respect to the residential school, Chrisjohn, Young, and Maraun explain that "the [s]tandard account…disposes neatly of all problems associated with Indian residential schooling."[52] While Canada has been involved in "official, longstanding continuing policy"[53] of genocide, there has also been a longstanding use of myths, "rhetoric" or "euphemisms" that convey the residential schools as less than genocide.[54] Euphemisms conceal from the public at large that the act of forcibly transferring Indigenous children from one group to another, with the intended destruction of that group, is an act of *genocide* in international law. Statements such as "inadequately fed" show the reality of the serious bodily and mental harm experienced in the residential schools system through the classification of forced starvation. Concealing actuality through *words* even as the subject is discussed with apparent openness is one of the ways the oppressor upholds and can maintain its continued and on-going genocide against our Nations.

The forcible transfer of Indigenous children was not merely "profoundly negative," and therefore "wrong," as Prime Minister Harper so blandly put it in his apology to former residential school students. "Wrong" is a far cry from "criminal," which, unlike "wrong", implies the possibility of legal recourse and remedy, or indeed should raise questions as to why there has been—can be—none. Terms that characterize the harm as an "assault," "neglect," or "abuse" do not capture the reality experienced by Indigenous children in the residential institutions.[55] "Words have a history," as Steven Newcomb observes. "Words from the past have the ability to colonize the present. Words shape and create reality."[56] Genocide is occluded by the use of words such as causing the "woeful mistreatment, neglect and abuse of many children"[57] when the woeful mistreatment is more accurately depicted as torture, starvation, disease, forced labour, and endemic sexual predation.[58] The term *neglect* implies that what happened was not even an action to which intent might be adduced, but a non-action, reinforcing the notion that it was accidental or not intended. *Neglect* projects a euphemistic inversion of the intent to destroy the Original Nations (national identities) by forcibly taking Indigenous children which is accurately termed in the UNGC as an act of *genocide*.

Similarly, terming the harm intended as based on the objective of *assimilation*[59] rather than what the residential institutions were designed for—which was to *disassemble* or destroy Indigenous Nations as such—also minimizes the destruction experienced by Indigenous children. As Venne explains "[g]enocide is genocide, no matter what form it takes and no matter what you call it."[60] Calling an apple an orange will never make an apple an orange. So terming *genocide* as *assimilation* will never change the reality of the destruction experienced by children and the effort to destroy national groups, meaning Indigenous Nations.

As Chrisjohn, Young, and Maraun point out, "words do hurt people, and so effectively that knowledge of how the word-magic works is a closely guarded secret. When the subject of

Indian Residential Schools arises, the word-magic (better known as *rhetoric*) kicks into overdrive, but so smoothly and effortlessly that we scarcely notice that we're headed toward Never-Never-Land at warp speed [emphasis original]."[61] So "[g]etting a grip on the rhetorical devices deployed against a clear understanding of Indian Residential Schooling is therefore essential."[62] On that note, the term "sixties scoop," as is fashionably used in the media, academic, and government discourse about the forcible removals of our children in the child welfare system during the period of the "60s" implies that the policy was limited to that time period. It is an ongoing and present genocide taking place against our national identities via the child welfare system.

Once the *reality* behind the *rhetoric* is discerned, other statements contained in the Apology support our views herein. For example, stories are "far overshadowed by tragic accounts of the emotional, physical and sexual abuse" experienced by children.[63] The Apology acknowledges the contention of the destruction as torture and the sexual predatory acts experienced by children. Furthermore, the RCAP Report and other sources such as John Milloy's *A National Crime* supports rather than limits the ability of the evidence as the euphemistic language becomes revealed to the reader.

Finally, on the "regrettable" admission by the government that "many former students have died and are no longer with us,"[64] the death rates at certain periods of the residential school system were catastrophic.[65] The use of the term *regrettable* does not suffice as the necessary acknowledgement of "death," particularly when not addressed in its proper context, which is the effort of Canada to destroy the Original Nations. Children that witnessed the destruction and deaths of their brothers, sisters, and friends in the boarding schools caused the serious mental harm to children by instilling "terror and fear." Survivors of the residential school have described the fear and terror as a result of being seized from their parents and forcibly confined in residential institutions by an alien, dominating nation which was seeking to reprogram their minds.[66]

Reserving the Right to Commit Genocide

Canada has been embroiled in a long standing denial of the destruction it has engaged in, both long before and ever since Canada ratified the UNGC in 1952. The government cannot admit that customary international law, too, is applicable to its conduct with respect to Indigenous Nations and Peoples. The Criminal Code legislation gives the Canadian government the impunity to determine whether its actions are genocidal, since there exists no enumerated crime that makes Articles II(b), (d), and (e) of the UNGC a crime in Canada's domestic laws. In other words, there is no domestic access to a claim of genocide against the state and there are no checks in international law that prevent genocide and protect Indigenous Nations and Peoples from the revolting threat caused by colonial invasion. But given that the convention embodies a norm of *jus cogens*, the limited definition in the Criminal Code may violate the Vienna Convention. These actions can be viewed as an implied Canadian reservation to the UNGC. Although there is no definition for an *implied reservation* the term will be explained in the following section. If Canada did not agree that Articles II(b), (d), and (e) would be applicable to its Criminal Code, it was under an obligation to publicly declare this intention in a reservation. Reservations can be made when a treaty is signed, ratified, accepted, approved or acceded to. But Canada made none.

The Vienna Convention defines a reservation to mean, "a unilateral statement, however phrased or named, made by a State, when signing, ratifying, accepting, approving, or acceding to a treaty, where it purports to exclude or to modify the legal effect of certain provisions in their application to that State."[67] In the drafting stages, commentary by the Secretariat considered it "unthinkable' that, for example, States could pick and choose among the groups to be protected under the Convention."[68] The Secretariat further believed that "reservations of a general scope had no place in a convention that did not deal with the private interests of a State, but rather the preservation of an element of an international order."[69] And that the former were trumped by *jus cogens* norms of the latter.

Given that Canada's action does not involve a "reservation" as traditionally understood in international law, this investigation contends that Canada's limited definition of genocide in its Criminal Code is an implied reservation. Although there is no official definition for an *implied reservation* the term will be expanded upon. If Canada did not agree that Articles II (b), (d), and (e) would be applicable to its Criminal Code, it was under an obligation to publicly declare this intention when it was drafting the crime from 1946-48. There should have been an official reservation prior to Canada becoming a signatory to the convention. The source for this contention is found in the peremptory norm in the UNGC that there are "certain fundamental, overriding principles of international law, from which no derogation is ever permitted."[70]

We will now examine the International Court of Justice Advisory Opinion on Genocide, which describes the purpose and object of the Genocide Convention, in the context of the issue of reservations to the UNGC.

The 1951 ICJ Advisory Opinion

The ICJ in its 1951 Advisory Opinion entitled *Reservations to the Convention on the Prevention and Punishment of the Crime of Genocide* (hereinafter Advisory Opinion) examined questions with respect to reservations to the UNGC. The Advisory Opinion does not address the internal implementation of the convention in domestic law; however, the court establishes several principles in the international rule of law pertaining to the object and purpose of the convention. The purpose and object are found in the intention of the United Nations General Assembly which affirmed that genocide is a crime under international law, and invited Member States "to enact the necessary legislation for the punishment and prevention of this crime."[71] This provides a starting point with respect to addressing state legislation and genocidal practices. The purpose was to affirm that there are moral and humanitarian principles that are integral to the international rule of law. In other words, the UNGC it called for was to embody principles of customary international law as it concerned genocide.

The ICJ was mandated by a General Assembly Resolution of November 16, 1950 to examine the following legal questions that then arose:

I. Can the reserving State be regarded as being a party to the Convention while still maintaining its reservation if the reservation is objected to by one or more of the parties to the Convention but not by others?

II. If the answer to question I is in the affirmative, what is the effect of the reservation as between the reserving State and:
   (a) The parties which object to the reservation?
   (b) Those which accept it?

III. What would the legal effect as regards the answer to question I if an objection to a reservation is made:
   (a) By a signatory State which has not yet ratified?
   (b) By a State entitled to sign or accede but which has not yet done so?[72]

The ICJ determined there is a "generally recognized principle that a multilateral convention is the result of an agreement freely concluded upon its clauses and that consequently none of the contractual parties is entitled to frustrate or impair, by means of unilateral decisions or particular agreements, the purpose and *raison d'être* of the convention."[73] Contractual parties to the convention are not entitled to weaken the purpose and object of the convention.

The court acknowledged a need for flexibility from the traditional approach which was linked to the "notion of the integrity of the Convention as adopted, a notion which in its traditional concept involved the proposition that no reservation was valid unless it was accepted by all the contracting parties without exception, as would have been the case if it had been stated during the negotiations."[74] Reasons for a flexible approach are found in the universal character of the United Nations and the wide degree of participation envisioned.[75] However, the flexible approach does not give a contracting state the unfettered authority to frustrate or impair "the purpose and *raison d'être* of the convention."[76] The court answered the first question by examining the special characteristics of the UNGC as solutions in resolving the legal questions at issue.[77] Solutions to the legal question of reservations are found in the purpose and object of the convention. The ICJ acknowledges that the origin of the convention is found in the intention expressed by "the United Nations to condemn and punish genocide as 'a crime under international law' involving a denial of the right of existence of entire human groups, a denial which shocks the conscience of mankind and results in great losses to humanity, and which is contrary to moral law and to the spirit and aims of the United Nations."[78] There are two consequences arising from the intention of the United Nations. The first is the affirmation that the "principles underlying the Convention are principles which are recognized by civilized nations as binding on States, *even without any conventional obligation* [emphasis added]"[79] The second "is the universal character both of the condemnation of genocide and of the co-operation required 'in order to liberate mankind from such an odious scourge'."[80]

The object and purpose imply a balance between the two approaches seeking 1) universal participation and 2) condemnation and punishment of genocide. Moral and humanitarian principles are fundamental to this approach. The court acknowledges:

> It is indeed difficult to imagine a convention that might have this dual character to a greater degree, since its object on the one hand is to safeguard the very existence of certain human groups and on the other to confirm and endorse the most elementary

> principles of morality. In such a convention the contracting States do not have any interests of their own; they merely have, one and all, a common interest, namely, the accomplishment of those high purposes which are the *raison d'être* of the convention. Consequently, in a convention of this type one cannot speak of individual advantages or disadvantages to States, or of the maintenance of a perfect contractual balance between rights and duties. The high ideals which inspired the Convention provide, by virtue of the common will of the parties, the foundation and measure of all its provisions.[81]

The court explains that the "object and purpose of the Genocide Convention imply that it was the intention of the General Assembly and of the States which adopted it that as many States as possible should participate."[82] However, the goal could not have "intended to sacrifice the very object of the Convention in favour of a vain desire to secure as many participants as possible. The object and purpose of the convention thus limit both the freedom of making reservations and that of objecting to them."[83]

It was also maintained that any State entitled to become a party to the Genocide Convention had the unfettered authority to make the reservation it chooses by virtue of its sovereignty. But the court did not share this view and held, "It is obvious that so extreme an application of the idea of State sovereignty could lead to a complete disregard of the object and purpose of the Convention."[84] In other words, state sovereignty cannot trump or impede the moral and humanitarian principles which are the basis of the convention. With the purpose and object of the convention being considered as the guiding principle on questions 1 to 3 the court answered in the following manner:

> *On Question I*:
> by seven votes to five,

that a state which has maintained a reservation which has been objected to by one or more of the parties to the Convention but not by others, can be regarded as being a party to the convention if the reservation is compatible with the object and purpose of the Convention; otherwise, that state cannot be regarded as being a party to the Convention.

On Question II:
by seven votes to five,

(a) that if a party to the Convention objects to a reservation which it considers to be incompatible with the object and purpose of the Convention, it can in fact consider that the reserving State is not a party to the Convention;
(b) that if, on the other hand a party accepts the reservation as being compatible with the object and purpose of the Convention, it can in fact consider that the reserving State is a party to the Convention.

On Question III:
By seven votes to five,

(a) that an objection to a reservation made by a signatory State which has not yet ratified the Convention can have the legal effect indicated in the reply to Question I only upon ratification. Until that moment it merely serves as a notice to the other State of the eventual attitude of the signatory State;
(b) that an objection to a reservation made by a State which is entitled to sign or accede but which has not yet done so, is without legal effect.[85]

The protection of human groups and the morality of

the convention are important factors in determining whether a reservation is valid. Possible divergent views on reservations are "mitigated by the common duty of the contracting States to be guided in their judgment by the compatibility or incompatibility of the reservation with the object and purpose of the Convention. It must clearly be assumed that the contracting States are desirous of preserving intact at least what is essential to the object of the Convention."[86] It was further stipulated by the court that, "should this desire be absent, it is quite clear that the Convention itself would be impaired in both its principle and in its application."[87]

An important principle the ICJ articulates is found in the distinguishing characteristic which establishes in customary international law the moral and humanitarian principles of the UNGC. It also suggests the reservation must be compatible with the purpose and object of the convention. If the purpose is to maintain the moral and humanitarian scope, then the question remains concerning the domestic ratification of the convention in Canadian laws. Does a flexible approach allow the state to reinterpret or circumscribe genocide in domestic laws? What does it mean if a state can maneuver the process by fostering an illusion of acceptance at the international level and engage in crimes of genocide in its own back yard? Can a state pardon itself of genocide by limiting the crime in its domestic laws? The question is worthy of an investigation as otherwise there is no recourse for Indigenous Peoples' children whether in Canada or any other colonized state.[88]

On this question, it was determined in the Human Rights and Equal Opportunity Commission report, *Bringing Them Home: Report of the National Inquiry into the Separation of Aboriginal and Torres Strait Islander Children and Their Families*, that a state "cannot excuse itself by claiming that the practice was lawful under its own laws or that its people did not (or do not) share the outrage of the international community."[89] The obligation required by customary international law creates a responsibility of state governments not to engage in the crime or to circumscribe genocide in its domestic laws.[90] The following UNGC provisions are not included: "causing serious bodily or mental harm to members of the group," "imposing measures intended to prevent births within the group," and "forcibly transferring children of the group to another group." Under the semblance of a so-called genocide law termed "hate propaganda" the current definition of genocide includes only "killing members of the group" and "deliberately inflicting on the group conditions of life calculated to bring about its physical destruction." Canada's actions can be viewed as an implied reservation.

The state's domestic implementation excludes crimes that it is actively participating in and furthermore calls into question its intent to comply with the UNGC intent to protect "national, ethnical, racial or religious groups."[91] If Canada intended to have entire sections of the convention excluded from its domestic laws, it was under an obligation to make a formal reservation. The enactment of a limited definition of genocide in the Criminal Code is indicative of Canada's awareness of its vulnerability to claims of genocide under the UNGC definitional acts which it refused to encode. While Canada was drafting the UNGC from 1946-48 it was engaging in crimes against Indigenous Peoples' children and the Canadian state's effort to remove cultural genocide during the drafting stages of the crime in international law shows its earlier efforts of denial and obfuscation where it claimed not to know that destruction of this kind was occurring in Canada. The forced transfer of Indigenous children was but one of the crimes it was engaging in against the Indigenous Nations.[92] What is the recourse?

Article 18 of the Vienna Convention on the Law of Treaties

The remedy is found in Article 18 of the Vienna Convention.[93] This section holds the following:

> A state is obliged to refrain from acts which would defeat the object and purpose of a treaty when:
>
> (a) it has signed the treaty or has exchanged

> instruments constituting the treaty to ratification, acceptance or approval, until it shall have made its intention clear not to become a party to the treaty; or
>
> (b) it has expressed its consent to be bound by the treaty, pending the entry into force of the treaty and provided that such entry into force is unduly delayed.[94]

A criticism against invoking Article 18 concerns the purported "vagueness and ineffectiveness"[95] of this section. However, it is then admitted that Article 18 is a norm of customary international law.[96] Another criticism in Palchetti's view is that the "purpose and object"[97] is difficult to determine. The response to this question is found in the ICJ's Advisory Opinion that clearly identifies the purpose and object of the UNGC. Another critical point is that the purpose and object is in reference to the crime of crimes. Palchetti goes on to contend that "whether an act of a state may be regarded as defeating the object and purpose of a treaty must be assessed taking into account the specificity of each treaty or category of treaties."[98] The *Travaux* also contains answers to the moral obligation of states to adhere to the UNGC. In this regard, an Article 18 analysis is necessary.

International scholars Laurence Boisson de Chazournes, Anne-Marie La Rosa, and Makane Moïse Mbengue determine that Article 18 pursues the objectives of "legal security", "legal transparency", and "good faith".[99] The authors provide an insightful analysis of legal legitimacy, stating that "Article 18 of the Vienna Convention pursues the objective of legal security necessary for the stability and viability of international treaties. For this reason, States are able better to assess all of the legal implications of the different steps of the conclusion of a treaty."[100] The text of Article 18 with respect to the UNGC in the context of legal security demands that "States refrain from acts contrary to an international treaty even before it has begun to apply. A multilateral or bilateral treaty should translate the common aspirations of the States which partook in its negotiations."[101] Further, "[i]n order to guarantee a minimum of legitimacy for the process of transforming these aspirations into legal norms, States must in return be required to comply with a minimum standard of conduct in relation to the treaty."[102]

Boisson de Chazournes, La Rosa and Mbengue provide this explanation on legal transparency: "Article 18 offers true scope for reflection on the mechanisms to be developed for promoting and guaranteeing information on the position of states in respect of an international treaty."[103] The authors suggest that in the case of a state that does not wish to be bound by the obligation in a treaty, "it still remains under a transparent obligation"[104] to report its issues with respect to the treaty.

On the question of good faith obligations, Boisson de Chazournes, La Rosa and Mbengue attest that, "Article 18 allows the legal framing of the particular relation that binds a State to a treaty. In other words, the obligation implicitly arises for every state to make its future behavior in relation to a treaty public and objective instead of taking advantage of the inviolable prerogative of State."[105] The "conception of the principle of good faith finds its legal expression in Article 18 (b) of the Vienna Convention in respect of States having expressed their consent to be bound being from this moment parties to the treaty in question."[106] The significant legal effect of the principle of good faith is in "Article 18 of the Vienna Convention, which creates an obligation for the signatory state (outside the contractual link) to refrain from acts contrary to the object and purpose of a treaty as long as it has not expressed its intention not to be bound by it."[107] To reiterate, this means that states must be transparent about their intentions with respect to the treaty (in this case the UNGC) and refrain from conduct that is contrary to an "international treaty even before it has begun to apply."[108] It is also imperative that there be an obligation upon States to make their future conduct and behavior in relation to a treaty "public and objective instead of taking advantage of the inviolable prerogative of the State."[109] The question is whether Canada violates Article 18.

Applying the Law to Canada

Article 18 Application

The United Nations General Assembly (hereinafter General Assembly) passed Resolution 96(I) on December 11, 1946, in which it was declared that genocide was a matter of international concern: "Genocide is a denial of the right of existence of entire human groups, as homicide is the denial of the right to live of individual human beings; such denial of the right of existence shocks the conscience of mankind, results in greater losses to humanity in the form of cultural and other contributions represented by these human groups."[110] The General Assembly affirmed that "genocide is a crime under international law which the civilized world condemns and for the commission of which principals and accomplices—whether private individuals, public officials or statesmen…are punishable."[111] The UNGC was established to punish the vilest forms of violence and to protect and prevent destruction against human groups. The crime is committed against "a national, ethnical, racial or religious group"[112] or collective national identity, not against individuals.

The ICJ in its Advisory Opinion on Genocide with respect to the question of whether "any State entitled to become a party to the Genocide convention may do so while making any reservation it chooses by virtue of its sovereignty"[113] answered no to this question. The court did not share this view and held, "It is obvious that so extreme an application of the idea of State sovereignty could lead to a complete disregard of the object and purpose of the Convention."[114]

The ICJ, referring to General Assembly Resolution 96(1), declared the UNGC would be an instrument that would "condemn and punish genocide as 'a crime under international law' …. and which is contrary to moral law and the spirit and aims of the United Nations."[115] The General Assembly resolution is a source of "international law"[116] on genocide, and further to this, the moral and legal underpinning of the law.[117]

The purpose of the UNGC is to maintain the moral and

humanitarian principles on the basis of which it first entered into international law. Schabas explains that,

> [r]eference by the Court [ICJ] to such notions as "moral law" as well as the quite clear allusion to 'civilized nations' suggest that it may be more appropriate to refer to the prohibition of genocide as a norm derived from general principles of law rather than a component of customary international law. On the other hand, the universal acceptance by the international community of the norms set out in the Convention since its adoption in 1948 means that what originated in 'general principles' ought now to be considered a part of customary law.[118]

Schabas explains with regard to the 2006 ICJ decision in *Democratic Republic of Congo v. Rwanda* that the "prohibition of genocide was 'assuredly' a peremptory norm (*jus cogens*) of public international law, the first time it has ever made any declaration about any legal rule."[119] The ICJ "reaffirm[ed] that 'the principles underlying the [Genocide] Convention are principles which are recognized by civilized nations as binding on States, even without any conventional obligation' and that a consequence of that conception is 'the universal character both of the condemnation of genocide and of the co-operation required 'in order to liberate mankind from such an odious scourge.'''[120] Schabas notes on the 2007 ICJ decision in *Bosnia and Herzegovina v. Serbia and Montenegro* (hereinafter *Bosnia v. Serbia)* in which it held "the affirmation in Article I of the Convention that genocide is a crime under international law means it set out 'the existing requirements of customary international law, a matter emphasized by the Court in 1951.'''[121]

The significance of the ICJ's decisions in 2006 and later in 2007 affirmed the UNGC as having reached the status of *jus cogens* and emphasized the "moral and humanitarian principles which are its basis."[122] The *jus cogens* norm refers to "certain fundamental, overriding principles of international law, from which no derogation is ever permitted."[123] Venne, on the legal significance of the rule, explains that this refers to "...the creation of peremptory international norms that are binding on all states and can only be changed by the development of a different peremptory norm."[124] The *jus cogens* norm implies that state governments are subject to customary international laws on genocide. A question to be examined later is whether member states that acceded to the UNGC can violate international customary laws concerning genocide. The UNGC's purpose and object is to maintain the moral scope envisioned by the General Assembly. Does the UNGC impose a responsibility and obligation on states not to create the illusion of their acceptance of the norms of customary international laws on genocide, and further their non-acceptance of the definition of genocide in domestic laws, and most importantly, not to engage in genocide within their domestic borders? It would appear the answer is yes.

The ICJ highlights the legal and moral cooperation required of states to liberate humankind from genocide. The finding by the ICJ affirms the Genocide Convention is binding and a peremptory norm of customary international law. Venne, citing Article 53 of the Vienna Convention, on the *jus cogens* rule, explains:

> A treaty is void, if at the time of its conclusion, it conflicts with the peremptory norm of general international law. For the purposes of the present Convention, a peremptory norm of general international law is a norm accepted and recognized by the international community of states as a whole as a norm from which no derogation is permitted and which can be modified only by a subsequent norm of general international law having the same character.[125]

Based on Article 53, Canada is not above international customary laws and not able to exempt itself from it. Accordingly, the Vienna Convention supports the claim that states are to act in good faith with respect to a treaty by not engaging in conduct that is contrary to the *jus cogens* on which it is based.

The significance of Article 18 of the Vienna Convention to the question at issue with respect to the UNGC is that states should not be engaging in criminal conduct (genocide) prior to entering into a treaty addressing that conduct (the UNCG) and then continue with that prohibited (genocidal) conduct after the treaty is ratified by the state. At the time of its drafting, Canada was already a near century deep into the seizure and confinement of Indigenous children, with policies and effects as described above. And even then, in 1947, Dr. Ian Mosby confirms in his critical report that Canada was engaging in "nutritional experiments"on—which is to say, the deliberate starvation of—Indigenous children in the residential school system.[126] The importance of the date (1947) is that Canada was significantly involved in drafting the UNGC. To be engaging in "nutritional experiments," conduct that is contrary to the treaty. Even at that time, as reflected in the General Assembly Resolution 96(1), it was a matter of common acceptance that genocide was *jus cogens*. Accordingly, Canada was in violation, not only of the requirement that it cease any practices prohibited by the genocide treaty in the process of formation, but also of international customary laws on genocide.

The responsibility under customary international law creates an obligation on states to refrain from acts of genocide.[127] A state government cannot escape its culpability for criminal conduct by creating loopholes internationally in the drafting of the UNCG and domestically via its implementation of the UNCG via omitting Articles 2(b), (d) and (e) of the UNGC from its Criminal Code.[128] The limited definition of genocide in Canada's Criminal Code seeks to conceal the state's culpability with respect to the forcible transferring of Indigenous children from their Nations into residential institutions and other genocidal laws and policies with respect to Indigenous Peoples—but instead reflects its awareness of that culpability, and its intent to evade it. By excluding crimes it is actively engaged in from its penal laws, Canada sought to be able continue the crime (which it did for a further 50 years before terminating the program) unabated from international scrutiny. If Canada intended to have entire sections of the convention excluded from its domestic laws it was under an obligation to make a formal reservation—but that would have highlighted the crime, of which it professed ignorance, and its awareness of it.

Article 18 of the Vienna Convention articulates that "a state is obliged to refrain from acts which would defeat the object and purpose of a treaty when: (a) it has signed the treaty or has exchanged instruments constituting the treaty to ratification, acceptance or approval, until it shall have made its intention clear not to become a party to the treaty."[129] Based on this clause Canada was under an obligation not to engage in conduct that defeats the purpose and object of the UNGC. The object and purpose is affirmed by the Advisory Opinion of 1951 which declares the moral and legal objective of the UNGC to protect human kind from this odious scourge.[130] The Advisory Opinion also declared that state sovereignty could not impede the object and purpose. The declaration by the ICJ in 2006 and 2007 that the UNGC has achieved the legal status of *jus cogens* affirms the moral and legal objective of the convention. Article 18 requires that states maintain good faith and refrain from acts that are contrary to a treaty prior to accession and after.

According to Chazournes, La Rosa, and Mbengue, the legal effect of the principle of good faith "finds its expression in Article 18 (a) of the Vienna Convention, which creates an obligation for the signatory state (outside the contractual link) to refrain from acts contrary to the object and purpose of a treaty as long as it has not expressed its intention to be bound by it."[131] An analysis of article 18 (a) with respect to the UNGC seems to require that states must make it known publicly to the other state parties that prior to accession it intends to have certain fundamental aspects of the crime inapplicable to domestic laws on genocide. The Government of Canada was under an obligation to be transparent about its intentions to have fundamental components of the convention inapplicable to domestic legislation. The limited definition impedes the ability of the state to be held criminally accountable in its own domestic laws. Certainly MacDonald and Hudson's view that Canadian laws and courts do not apply international laws of genocide to questions of state culpability supports this contention that the state did not intend to be bound by the UNGC.[132]

Canada's refusal in the drafting of the UNGC to accept cultural genocide as a crime is instructive. Why go to great efforts to reject the entrenchment of the legal conception of cultural genocide as crime in international law? Then, go through a further process domestically that circumscribes or guts critical sections of the crime in Canadian legislation? It demonstrates the effort the state has undertaken in its endeavor to ensure it does not get caught up in the international crime of genocide. The government's actions certainly leave it open to the question of its culpability of genocide for its destructive colonial legal framework under which the forcible transferring of Indigenous Peoples children took place, not just prior to 1952, but after accession to the UNGC. The Canadian government was under an obligation to make it known that it objected to Articles 2(b), (d) and (e). Certainly, the excuse by the government that the crimes excluded are "unknown" is not adequate. Furthermore, the Criminal Code legislation conveys that it sought to supercede international law by reserving the right to exclude critical components of the crime of genocide from its domestic legislation, and thereby absolve itself of the crime.

Another supporting point on the question of good faith is worth reiterating for purposes of the legal application that "Article 18 requires the legal framing of the particular relation that binds a State to a treaty. In other words, the obligation implicitly arises for every state to make its future behavior in relation to a treaty public and objective instead of taking advantage of the inviolable prerogative of State."[133] Chazournes, La Rosa, and Mbengue explain:

> In other words, the fact of refraining from acts that would defeat the object and purpose of a treaty turns out to be a manifestation of the principle of good faith. In the case of ratified treaties, it strengthens the rule of *pacta sunt servada*. The parties of a treaty oblige themselves to act in good faith in the context of the agreement they have concluded.[134]

This principle of good faith finds its legal expression in Article 18(b): to be bound by the treaty. On this point, the ICJ in its Advisory Opinion on Genocide did not support the authority of the state to pick and choose which aspects of the UNGC a state could reserve itself from based on its sovereignty. It is clear that such an application of state sovereignty would undermine the object and purpose of the convention. So this finding by the ICJ and Article 18 means that the State of Canada does not have the unfettered authority by virtue of its sovereignty to determine which aspects of the UNGC might apply to its criminal conduct. Again, it is most critical to highlight to the reader that we do not accept that the colonial so-called state has sovereignty over our lands and territories. This analysis on state sovereignty is necessary to the application of international laws to the colonial state's conduct with respect to genocide.

Certainly, the UNGC attaining the status of *jus cogens* affirms the legal and moral obligation on states not to engage in genocidal conduct such as the forcible transferring of other peoples' children. The illusion of an acceptance of the criminality of genocide at the international level and then a further smokescreen of acceptance with the purported implementation of the UNGC in Canadian laws is intended to allow the state to evade the applicability of the UNGC to possible state conduct of acts of genocide against Indigenous Peoples' children. Furthermore, the state is not allowed to pick and choose which acts are to be defined as genocide in its domestic laws and which not, given that there is the issue of state culpability concerning genocide.

In its attempts to evade the charge of genocide for its conduct, Canada has violated international laws by implying a reservation in its Criminal Code. The list of crimes not included in the final cut is instructive. Insofar as a state must refrain from acts of genocide while drafting genocide in international law and the forcible transferring of Indigenous Peoples' children in Canada had occurred long before the drafting of the UNGC (1946-1948) and up to present times, the legal opinion by the Deputy Minister of Justice in 1949 on whether any of the acts enumerated in the convention could be applied to any situation in Canada, and all efforts to create an illusion of acceptance, indicate an obfuscation of the highest kind.[135] The Criminal Code legislation contradicts this important point, worth reiterating:

> A multilateral or bilateral treaty should translate the common aspirations of the States which partook in its negotiations. In order to guarantee a minimum of legitimacy for the process of transforming these aspirations into legal norms, States must in return be required to comply with a minimum standard of conduct in relation to the treaty.[136]

By purposefully excluding critical sections of the UNGC, Article II, Canada is not complying with a minimum standard of conduct when engaging in a UNGC-defined act of genocide—the forcible transferring of Indigenous children from one group (Indigenous families, communities and Nations) to another group (Canadian society)—through the residential schools and child welfare systems.

The significance of this date (1946-1948) is that Canada was involved in drafting genocide legislation, and to be engaging in so-called "nutritional experiments," (1947) conduct that is contrary to the Genocide Convention, challenges the ability of the convention to protect Indigenous Nations and Peoples. Mosby also confirms the government knew that underfunding was the cause of severe malnutrition before the experiments were conducted.[137] The principles established in international law provide a legal and moral obligation on state government not to engage in genocidal conduct, especially against other peoples' children. Further it provides a legal and moral responsibility not to take "advantage of the inviolable prerogative of the State."[138]

With respect to the claim that a treaty's prohibited conduct cannot be made retroactive, the question is answered by Canadian conduct in violation of Article 18 of the Vienna Convention. The question is whether crimes that fall under the UNGC are retroactive. Schabas in *Unimaginable Atrocities* writes that while, "as a general rule international treaties do not operate retroactively (or retrospectively), there are exceptions. Indeed, most of the treaties dealing with international criminal prosecution have been given a retroactive effect."[139] Schabas elaborates further, "The International Court of Justice has made a couple of tantalizing comments to the effect that there is no express temporal limitation in the Genocide Convention to prevent it from having a retroactive effect."[140] Given that colonization is an issue that has a retroactive aspect, "claims based on colonialism, racial [violence] discrimination and the slave trade retain some salience."[141] It should be highlighted at this juncture, the forcible removals in the child welfare system is a crime that is on-going, as has been demonstrated. This on-going genocide exacerbates the Canadian state's conduct and any potential criticism of the claims we are making in this analysis. A rogue state cannot make a claim of retroactivity considering that it went to great efforts to avoid its actions getting caught up in the international definition of genocide.[142] It attempted to change what would be defined as a criminal act, both internationally and domestically. Further to this, Canada was engaged in genocidal acts against Indigenous Peoples' children both before, and after, the UNGC entered into law. The violent and brutal genocidal domination and dehumanization committed against Indigenous children in the residential school in an effort to "kill the Indian in the child" caused the catastrophic collective trauma and dysfunction that are currently exhibited in

Indigenous Nations and that forcible removals continue unabated in the child welfare system.

The *Travaux* portrays state perspectives with respect to the crime of forcibly transferring children of the group to another group. It was declared the forcible transferring of children is a crime that was to be maintained in the convention. Jamie Herschkopf and Julie Hunter explain that delegates "agreed that forced transfer of children was the most serious and indeed 'barbarous' act enumerated under the separate category of cultural genocide."[143] The Greek delegate, Mr. Vallindas, held that "The forced transfer of children could be as effective a means of destroying a human group as that of imposing measures intended to prevent births, or inflicting conditions of life likely to cause death."[144] The Greek delegation emphasized the importance of including the "'forced transfer of children', a means of committing genocide which had been used not only in the past but was still being used."[145] It was explained further that, "It was not primarily an act of cultural genocide. Although it could in certain cases be considered as such, it could be perpetrated rather with the intent to destroy or cause serious physical harm to members of a group."[146]

To exclude the crime would be in contravention of the moral and legal obligation to prevent genocide. This is for obvious reasons as human groups depend on their children or future generations for their survival as distinct national identities. Venezuela explained that forcibly transferring a human group's children to another group would result in the destruction of that group whose future depended on that generation of children.[147] The Uruguay representative said the process, "educat[es] [children] to become enemies of their own people."[148] Uruguay and Venezuela's analysis correlates with the contention that children forcibly indoctrinated through a total institution that forces the labour, tortures, starves, sexually preys, and causes death will destroy the ability of Indigenous children to transmit to future generations their national identities such as *Nehiyaw*, *Anishinaabe*, *Dene*, among those of many other Original Nations.

Forcibly transferring children is committed with the intent

to destroy the collective group (or Nations) of Indigenous Peoples as they depend on their children for their continued survival as Nations. The fact that national groups depend on their children is emphasized by the representative of Venezuela. The moral and humanitarian integrity of the UNGC is compromised when Canada's Criminal Code is analyzed according to this perspective.

When, indeed, these destructive effects become manifest, as was forecast, the government then invokes the results (traumatic parenting patterns) it created to justify the further mass removal of children into the child welfare system. So the way the child welfare system operates continues the effects of the residential school system. The provincial legislation is forcing the transfer of our children at calamitous rates.[149] The oppressor uses the trauma, sorrow, and debilitating conditions it created in a manner that continues to demonize, isolate and destroy Indigenous Nations and Peoples' children. The "colonizing mentality of child welfare agencies"[150] uses the conditions that were created in the residential school system to continue the mass removal of children into present times.

The Canadian State, among other state governments, wiped out cultural genocide from the UNGC and undermined the original intention indicated in the UN Resolution 96(1) which determined that cultural losses were as important as other losses in the commission of the crime.[151] The *Travaux* reveals the great effort state governments undertook to warp Lemkin's understanding of the crime. Colonialism is at the heart of Lemkin's concept of genocide and the overrunning and claiming of other peoples' lands and territories. Colonizing countries such as the United Kingdom, and its colonial settler states such as Canada, diminished Lemkin's concept of the crime by creating loopholes that deny that the root of genocide is in "fascism, Nazism, and doctrines of racial superiority."[152] Theories of racial superiority are foundational to the domination of Indigenous Nations and Peoples, manifested and promoted through a dehumanizing state framework. The issue of a limited definition of genocide in Canada's Criminal Code is indicative of a bigger problem. The problem is that Canada is a perpetrator of genocide, and not just a perpetrator of genocide, but remains a colonial—not post-colonial—state, the latter giving rise in an ongoing manner to the former. What is the recourse?

Application of the UNGC

The Canadian state codified into its framework legislation that serves as the cornerstone of the legalized persecution against Indigenous Peoples. Doctrines of racial superiority are "institutionalized" into the legal fabric of the colonial state and society. The Canadian government imposed the *Indian Act* of 1876 which dismantled traditional systems of government and our Indigenous laws that had instructed our Nations since the beginning of time.[153] The colonial laws of occupation then forced the massive removals of our children.[154]

This analysis will apply the UNGC to the Canadian State's forcible transferring of Indigenous Peoples' children into residential institutions (residential schools and child welfare systems). It has been shown that the forcible transferring of our children into residential schools first "unmakes" the children and then forcibly indoctrinates them by brutal acts of dehumanizing violence.[155] The forced transfer of Indigenous children has severely impeded the ability of Indigenous Peoples to transmit the healthy characteristics of their national/cultural identities to subsequent generations, while causing "serious bodily and mental harm" and inflicted as part of a process expressly intended to destroy Indigenous "national groups" "in whole or in part."[156]

Intention is satisfied by numerous official statements of policy, the Apology[157] and the "widespread and massive"[158] serious bodily and mental harm experienced by children in the residential institutions. It was acknowledged in the early drafting stages of the crime of genocide in international law that forcing the transfer of children would cause the eventual "disappearance" of the group.[159] The application will conclude with an examination of the long-term effects of genocide that arise from the forcible transferring of Indigenous children into residential schools, viewing the child welfare system as reflective of an ongoing crime against Indigenous Peoples and Nations which is a direct effect of the residential school system.

The following analysis will set up the rule of law, issue, facts, and application of the law. The application of the law to show beyond a reasonable doubt, to say nothing of a preponderance of evidence, that the Canadian government is culpable for crimes of genocide. The facts are supported by the massive forced transfer of Indigenous children that causes the systemic and widespread serious bodily and mental harm. The many books, reports and personal stories show this common experience. This section will lay out the facts and set up the issue according to the UNGC.

Given that the rule of law has been discussed and reviewed previously the application will briefly reiterate the findings in genocide law. For genocide to be shown, the application requires that the *mens rea* and *actus reus* elements are satisfied according to the text of the Genocide Convention. The *actus reus* is the physical act of genocide outlined in Article II of the Convention. The *mens rea* element requires an intention to destroy in whole or in part a group. Two elements of intention are required to be shown: "a general intent as to the underlying acts, and an ulterior intent with regard to the ultimate aim of the destruction of the group."[160] The ICJ in *Bosnia v. Serbia* said this about specific intent: "Article II requires a further mental element. It requires the establishment of the 'intent to destroy, in whole or in part, . . . [the protected] group, as such'[161] In other words, the act or acts must be intended. The other is a further specific intent regarding the group. Here, the perpetrator is the State of Canada and this intent refers to a Canadian state plan or policy.[162] With respect to "state intent," the case law suggests that a massive, common and widespread experience of destruction can suffice to satisfy the standard of specific intent.[163]

The International Criminal Tribunal for Rwanda (hereinafter ICTR) in the case of *Prosecutor* v. *Akayesu* (hereinafter Akayesu) found that "On the issue of determining the offender's specific intent, the Chamber considers that intent is a mental factor which is difficult, even impossible to determine. This is the reason why, in absence of a confession from the accused, his intent can be inferred from a certain number of presumptions of fact."[164] It is important to reiterate the finding by The ICTR that,

> [I]t is possible to deduce genocidal intent inherent in a particular act charged from the general context of the perpetration of other culpable acts systematically directed against that same group, whether these acts were committed by the same offender or others. Other factors, such as the scale of atrocities committed, their general nature, in a region or a country, or furthermore, the fact of deliberately and systematically targeting victims on account of their membership of a particular group while excluding members of other groups, can enable the Chamber to infer the genocidal intent of a particular act.[165]

The International Criminal Tribunal for former Yugoslavia (hereinafter ICTY) in *Radovan Karadzić, Ratko Mladic* (hereinafter *Karadzić*) similarly determined that intent can be satisfied by the general political doctrine and patterns of same conduct.[166] The chamber in the *Karadzić* case held that "[t]his intent derives from the combined effect of speeches or projects laying the groundwork for and justifying the acts, from the massive scale of their destructive effect and from their specific nature, which aims at undermining what is considered to be the foundation of the group."[167] The destruction must have been intended against a protected human group. With respect to "destroying a group in whole or in part," it is not necessary that the entire group be destroyed so long as the destruction directed against the individual affects the group through the violation against the individual as a member of the group.[168]

The ICTR found the accused in *Akayesu* guilty of genocide based on the following finding of intent: "[I]t is possible to infer the genocidal intention that presided over the commission of a particular act, *inter alia*, from all acts or utterances of the accused, or from the general context in which other culpable acts were perpetrated systematically against the same group, regardless of whether such other acts were committed by the same perpetrator or even by other perpetrators."[169] The widespread, systemic, and massive sexual destruction against Tutsi women was enough to satisfy specific intent.

The chamber in ICTR ruled serious or bodily or mental harm to mean "acts of torture, be they bodily or mental, inhumane or degrading treatment, persecution."[170] Under the ambit of serious and bodily mental harm the ICTY in *Prosecutor* v *Krstić* (herenafter Krstić) held the same finding as the ICTR.[171]The *Eichmann* ruling held that "serious and bodily and mental harm" could be caused through the "enslavement, starvation, deportation and persecution[…]and by their detention in ghettos, transit camps, and concentration camps in conditions which were designed to cause their degradation, deprivation of their rights as human beings, and to suppress them and cause them inhumane suffering and torture."[172]

The ICTY in the *Prosecutor v. Stakić* case held that genocide could be accomplished by "acts of torture, inhumane or degrading treatment, sexual violence, including rape, interrogations combined with beatings, threats of death, and harm that damages health or causes disfigurement or injury. The harm inflicted need not be permanent and irremediable."[173] The trial chamber of the ICTY in *Prosecutor v. Blagojevic* gave examples of serious mental harm such as witnessing the grave harm against loved ones, being forcibly separated from family and friends, witnessing the death of relatives and friends, and mental anguish from listening to the moans of those suffering in pain.[174] The court held these traumatic experiences and the "utter helplessness and extreme fear for their family and friends' safety as well as their own safety, is a traumatic experience from which one will not quickly—if ever—recover."[175]

The ICTR in *Akayesu* determined that sexual violence or rape is as destructive as torture and would cause serious bodily and mental harm. The court determined that rape and sexual violence can result in "physical and psychological destruction."[176] It was held that sexual violence would cause destruction to the families and communities and to the group as whole.[177] The findings by the ICTR and ICTY seem to suggest that the long-term consequences for sexual violence as well as acts of "inhuman treatment, torture, rape, sexual abuse and deportation are among the acts which may cause serious bodily or mental injury."[178] The case law suggests there are long-term consequences to these crimes that fall within the ambit of Article II (b).[179] Given this brief review of the law, we will now apply the facts to Canada.

The legal issue is whether the Canadian state is culpable for crimes under the UNGC, which embodies customary international law, by its forcible transfer of Indigenous children into residential institutions in an admitted policy intent to "kill the Indian in the child." Given the government's position on the "Indian problem"[180] and its assumption of legal authority to force the transfer of children, residential institutions (residential schools and child welfare systems) are used to demonize, isolate and destroy Indigenous Nations and Peoples. Genocide occurs in two phases: (1) the destruction of the national pattern of the oppressed and (2) the imposition of the national pattern of the oppressor.[181] The two acts of genocide giving rise to these two phases can be framed as follows:

1) The forced transfer of Indigenous Peoples' children into residential institutions causes destruction of the national pattern.
2) The forced indoctrination of colonial laws, ideologies, values, beliefs, laws, systems and institutions designed to destroy Indigenous Peoples' children, spirituality, cultures, laws, and relationship with the land (Mother earth) via brutal violence and terror causes serious physical and mental harm to members of the group.

Article II(b) and (e) of the Genocide Convention correlate with Lemkin's two phases of genocide. The articles of the two phases are framed in the following manner:

e) Forcibly transferring children of the group to another group.
b) Causing serious or bodily mental harm to members of the group.

The legislation that forces the transfer causes the forcible indoctrination of Indigenous children into the oppressor state and society by the collective massive and widespread serious bodily and mental harm. The issue is not "assimilation," it is in the forcible **indoctrination** as the young ones become seriously mentally and/or bodily harmed by the indoctrination process.

Kill the Indian Save the Man and *The Circle Game* explain the program of genocide in a clear and concise manner that moves past the rhetoric. Both sources help to candidly illustrate the residential school system where children were brutalized by colonial violence and horror. Children were dominated and dehumanized by methods such as torture, forced labour, sexual predation, forced starvation, deplorable health and living conditions that were used to forcibly indoctrinate the young ones. Dr. Peter Bryce in the early 1900s documented the deplorable health and living conditions. Churchill shows the genocidal impacts of the residential school system.

Figure 2 (following page) illustrates the process in order to convey to the reader that the legislated forced transfer of children into the residential school system is an abomination. Short of death, the sexual predatory acts, torture, the slow death measure of starvation, and forced labour cause serious bodily and mental destruction. Being witness to loved ones and friends dying off would certainly cause mental destruction, and even bodily destruction as the child becomes conditioned to believe if they do not submit to the perpetrator he/she could be next. *The Circle Game* supports *Kill the Indian Save the Man's* classification of the destruction. Chrisjohn, Young and Maraun's (hereinafter Chrisjohn) illustration of the total institution explains the residential school system as an institution designed to unmake or forcibly condition children. Children were cognitively conditioned

FORCING THE TRANSFER OF CHILDREN
↓ - legislation and forced removal by state

DESTROYING THE NATIONAL PATTERN OF THE OPPRESSED GROUP
↓ - comprehensive and carefully calibrated assault on the children's identity

IMPOSING THE NATION PATTERN OF THE OPPRESSOR
↓ - denationalization or re-enculturation by the following methods

1. Slow Death Measure of Starvation
2. Indirect Killing by Disease
3. Slow Death Measure of Forced Labour
4. Torture
5. Sexual Predation

WORLDS OF PAIN
↓ - Long term impacts of genocide

Figure 2:
Churchill's Illustration of Genocide, ***Kill the Indian Save the Man***

to view reality from a "white man's view of the world" or a lens of domination and dehumanization. Further to this, children were subjected to horrific disease-infested and unsanitary living conditions in the residential school system and died at alarmingly high rates. Reports by the media confirm that thousands of children died while in the residential school system.[182]

Indigenous children have been destroyed by the "techniques of occupation"[183] discussed by Churchill and Chrisjohn. In this manner it has been shown that the forced transfer of children into state-controlled residential institutions is destructive. Children who endure serious bodily and mental harm will exit the residential school destroyed. The common experience of the destruction experienced by the children can be categorized under the headings of *death and disease, torture, forced starvation, forced labour, and sexual predation*. The residential school system as a total institution destroyed children, first, through the forced transfer, second, by the forced "deculturation (or 'denationalization')," [184] and third, by the techniques of imposition. The psychological attack employed against children was a careful and systematic attack instilling fear and self-loathing by denigrating their national identity in the process of removing any traces of it, and by destroying their spiritual beliefs.

The residential school system as a total institution forced the indoctrination and the total "swallowing"[185] up of that child's identity into the "body politic".[186] Once residential schools are understood in this light, it becomes clear that "their very existence…constituted an abomination."[187] Indigenous children were systematically destroyed by their forced removal from their loving, nurturing and caring environments into institutions designed for the destruction of that environment: "There can be no question whether the transfer of children upon which the residential school depended was coercive, that it was resisted by parents and other adults—and often, to the extent they were able, by the youngsters themselves—or that physical force was used to overcome that resistance."[188] Grant writes that "[a] common misconception is that Indian people simply accepted the Residential school regime. Though resistance to it was difficult and largely futile, Indian parents did resist, and they never stopped trying to change the system."[189]

Theories of racial superiority are the bedrock of the legal framework. Kent McNeil writes that, "[t]here can be no doubt that the evolutionary theories of human societies prevalent in the latter half of 19th century influenced government policy toward Indigenous Peoples."[190] It was held by some states during the drafting of the UNGC that theories of racial superiority are at the root of genocide. Given this, it is worth mentioning again that theories of racial superiority were institutionalized into German laws and it was these laws that facilitated German destruction against non-German human groups. With regard to Canada, doctrines of racial superiority were enshrined within a colonial legal framework justifying destruction against Indigenous children—hence entire nations—by their forcible removal. Moreover, the residential schools were a well thought-out "coordinated plan of different actions" designed to address "the Indian problem".[191]

So, does Canada violate the UNGC by the forcible transferring of Indigenous Peoples' children that causes collective serious bodily and mental harm against the Original Nations of Great Turtle Island? Entire Nations are affected as the forcible transferring of children affects the ability of Indigenous Peoples to transmit the healthy characteristics of those societies on to further generations. The *Travaux* confirms that the forcible transferring of children affects the ability of the human group to survive. Since the material elements to show a case of genocide requires a "basic distinction between the physical element (the *actus reus*) and the mental element (the *mens rea*), the prosecution must prove specific material facts, but must also establish the accused's criminal intent or "guilty mind."[192]

Forcible Transferring

On the issue of the forcible transferring, it must be shown that the children are in the control of the oppressor.[193] This enumerated crime "requires proof of a result, namely, that children be transferred from the victim group to another group."[194] The ICTR in *Akayesu* clarified that

> [w]ith respect to forcibly transferring children of the group to another group, the Chamber is of the opinion that, as in the case of measures intended to prevent births, the objective is not only to sanction a direct act of forcible physical transfer, but also to sanction acts of threats or trauma which would lead to the forcible transfer of children from one group to another.[195]

Force can also mean not only the use of physical force, "but may include threat of force or coercion, such as that caused by fear of violence, duress, detention, psychological oppression or abuse of power, against such person or persons or another person, or by taking advantage of a coercive environment."[196] In application to the facts, children were forced using the above criteria; colonial laws sanctioned the transfer. Parents were coerced and forced to hand their children over to the Canadian government through the legislation by threats of punishment, fines, and imprisonment. The pass system introduced in 1886 and starvation were tactics used by the state to compel parents to hand their children over to the government.[197] Vicki Trerise writes:

> Amendments to the *Indian Act* in 1880 established the Department of Indian Affairs [DIA], and in 1886 further amendments provided for the establishment of schools for Indian children off the reserves, and authorized strong penalty provisions up to imprisonment for failing to send one's children to school, and for "the arrest and conveyance to school, and detention there, of truant children and of children who are prevented by their parents or guardians from attending, … Another new section in the 1886 amendments

> specifically authorized the establishment of industrial or boarding schools for Indian children, with provisions to enforce attendance. This was reinforced by amendments in 1894 which extended the penalties for refusal to send children to school specifically to industrial or boarding schools off the reserves, and introduced a regulatory regime whereby the DIA would operate the schools both on and off reserve.[198]

Children were forcibly removed via colonial legislation or "laws of occupation."[199] The legislation provided the so-called legal authority for the forcible physical transferring of Indigenous Peoples' children away from families and nations into residential schools. Further to this there were the threats of penalties if Indigenous Peoples did not abide by the Indian Act legislation.[200] Other threats and acts of trauma included leaders being deposed of leadership. Chief Star Blanket was removed from his position of leadership until the children of his nation were given over to the government for removal.[201] It was found in the case of *Eichmann* that deportation, enslavement, starvation, and persecution are crimes of genocide.

Forcing the transfer of Indigenous children through cattle trucks, RCMP police, and child transportation vehicles (in present times) and other measures to force the transfer certainly constitute deportation and enslavement and facilitate the forcible transferring of children. Further to this, the legislation threatened sanctions of "the arrest and conveyance to school, and detention there, of truant children and of children who are prevented by their parents or guardians from attending"[202] the residential schools. Certainly the Indian Act would qualify as the legal instrument of persecution against Indigenous children, parents and the Nations who resisted the forcible removal. According to the facts laid out parents and children were faced with threats or trauma if children were not given over to the colonial state for the forcible confinement into residential schools. The forced removal was a massive and common experience.

Serious Bodily and Mental Harm

Indigenous children become seriously harmed, both physically and mentally, by the transfer and indoctrination processes alike. The serious bodily and psychological destruction resulted from their common, massive and widespread experience of practices fitting the classification of torture, starvation, sexual predation, death and disease, and forced labour. These classifications of serious bodily harm in the *Eichmann* ruling constituted serious bodily mental harm through the "detention in ghettos [and] concentration camps in conditions, which were designed to cause their degradation, deprivation of their rights as human beings, and to suppress them and cause their inhumane suffering and torture."[203] The residential school or total institution serves as the place where Indigenous children were dominated by their detainment and enslaved for years at a time leading to their dehumanizing and inhumane suffering, starvation, tortures, and the sexual predatory acts that the children endured by staff officials. The standard ages children were isolated and detained began from the ages of four-five and lasted until they were fifteen-sixteen.

The facts established show that the forcible transferring into the total institution causes the physical detainment. The physical detainment leads to the massive serious bodily and mental harm. The destruction identified such as "needles" in the tongue for periods of time, "burning or scalding", "beating children to the point of drawing blood", "beating children into unconsciousness" among other torturous acts would certainly inflict serious bodily and mental harm.[204] This destruction was a common experience and well established in the reports and writings of the residential schools.[205] Other acts listed by the ICTR that constituted serious bodily and mental harm included beatings, threats of death, interrogations, detainment, sexual violence, mutilations, and rape, "often repeatedly and often publicly, and often by more than one assailant."[206] The ICTY in *Stakić* found that torture, inhumane or degrading treatment, sexual violence, including rape, interrogations combined with beatings, threats of death, and harm that damages health or causes disfigurement or injury are acts that would cause serious bodily or mental harm.[207]

The news media reports of electric chair torturing of children in St. Anne's Residential School in Ontario would certainly satisfy the serious bodily and mental harm requirement for genocide to be shown.[208] Other examples of terror and violence that children endured includes being locked in small spaces, inserting needles into other regions of their anatomy, "beating children to the point of inflicting serious permanent or semi-permanent injuries, including broken arms, broken legs, broken ribs, fractured skulls, shattered eardrums and the like, shaving children's head as punishment", "segregation of the sexes", "performing public strip searches and genital inspections of children" and so forth.[209] The ones listed and many other forms of violence occurred in a massive and widespread fashion.

Moreover, on the issue of starvation and the recent revelation of state experiments indicates that 1300 Indigenous children were subjected to "nutritional experiments." An important point concerns the knowledge the government had about underfunding before conducting the experiments. According to Mosby, "They knew from the beginning that the real problem and the cause of malnutrition was under funding. That was established before the studies even started and when the studies were completed that was still the problem."[210] The experiments took place in 1947 which is an important date as the Canadian government was involved in discussions leading up to the adoption of the UNGC in international law at the very time the government was conducting the experiments. Accordingly, the Nuremberg Code stipulates that a human subject should have the legal capacity to give consent to the experiments being conducted.[211] Indigenous children were obviously not in a position to give consent. Another point is that the experiment should be conducted as to avoid all unnecessary physical and mental suffering. Suffice it to say that starvation will indeed cause physical and mental suffering. These factors all serve to aggravate not mitigate the crime of genocide.

The court in *Akayesu* found that genocide culpability

could be established as a result of sexual violence and rape. The court found that "rape and sexual violence certainly constitute infliction of serious bodily or mental harm on the victims…"[212] The sentencing judge in Canada's *Plint* case "called the supervisor a 'sexual terrorist' and described the Residential school system as 'nothing but a form of institutionalized pedophilia'."[213] Sexual violence against Indigenous children is a massive and common experience.[214] The ICTR found with respect to the crime, that rape and sexual violence was "one of the worst ways of inflict[ing] harm on the victim as he or she suffers bodily and mental harm."[215] The crime of sexual violence has destructive physical and psychological consequences on the group.[216] With respect to the young ones sexual violence and rape would have devastating consequences. Of this there can be no question.

Another aspect of Canada's culpability for causing serious bodily and mental harm that is satisfied from the facts is the long-term destruction against Indigenous Peoples' children. The case law suggests that there are long-term consequences to crimes that fall within the ambit of Article II(b).[217] The effects must lead to conditions that render the victims of genocide unable to live a normal constructive life. The ICTY clarified that "harm amounting to 'a grave and long-term disadvantage to a person's ability to lead a normal and constructive life' has been said to be sufficient for this purpose."[218] There is no doubt that the forced transfer of Indigenous children has caused intergenerational patterns of trauma and debilitating sorrow.

Children who were starved, whose labour was forced and who endured massive acts of rape and sexual violence became dehumanized by the torturous acts and destructive beliefs imposed on them. Think about it: tell a child that her people are savages and less than human while she is shackled and chained to a bed, or beaten up, or while she is being raped, then far from assimilating in any healthy manner into another culture, that child will develop a brutalized worldview, leading to his/her dysfunctionality in society.

Children will come to see the world through the traumatic worldview that is imposed on them. Indigenous Peoples exhibit symptoms of peoples who have endured prolonged suffering under genocidal programs. One example is that suicidal thoughts are linked to the residential schools.[219] In fact, it's been observed by *The Globe and Mail* that "[p]revious studies have suggested suicide and self-inflicted injuries are among the leading causes of death"[220] for Indigenous Peoples. As Emily Alston O'Connor observed, "[t]he forced removal of children and youth from their Native communities has been linked with social problems such as 'high suicide rate, sexual exploitation, substance use and abuse, poverty, low educational achievement and chronic unemployment.'"[221] The fallout from the physical and mental harm is further evidenced in the massively disproportionate percentages of Indigenous Peoples in prisons, hospitals and rehab centers.

But perhaps the greatest effect as it relates to the survival into the future of Indigenous Nations is the inability to parent according to traditional child rearing methods. Indigenous parents have a responsibility to transmit Indigenous laws about Creation and the land (Mother Earth), in the languages that embody these understandings, their cultures and spirituality on to further generations. This is an integral feature of traditional child rearing. Instead, traumatized patterns of parenting are passed from generation to generation. The long-term impacts lead to the massive and widespread collective breakdown of Indigenous Peoples' Nations because they depend on their children for survival. Over all the ability of Indigenous Peoples to carry on the distinct and healthy patterns of their national identities becomes terminated over successive generations.

The greatest destruction is the disconnection to the land (Mother Earth) through the languages and spiritual beliefs or national identity of so many Original Nations on Great Turtle Island. The great trauma and sorrow and the confusion caused by the massive and wide spread violence and horror would certainly sever the young from his or her identity by not being able to speak or think in their own original languages. The consequences would be devastating on the young ones, hence entire Nations because they depend on their children.

Intent

The United Nations discussions highlighted in the *Travaux* affirm that forcibly transferring children would affect the ability of the targeted "group" to survive.[222] The effect is that Indigenous children are forcibly conditioned into "speaking, thinking and writing"[223] like the oppressor through the massive patterns of serious bodily and mental harm inflicted against them in the residential institutions. Indigenous peoples were not just *assimilated* into the "modes and thoughts of the white man" they were ***collectively seriously bodily and mentally harmed*** by the crimes of torture, forced starvation, forced labour, sexually predatory acts and death that were committed against their children. The young ones were forcibly indoctrinated individually and collectively that their Nations, Peoples, laws, languages, spirituality, and so forth were inferior and this has resulted in the transference of collective serious bodily and mental harm onto further generations.

On the subject of a state plan, Schabas on *Akayesu* writes, the court "did not insist upon proof of a plan with respect to the incitement for genocide, but this may have been because the issue was self-evident. At one point in the judgment, it referred to the 'massive and/or systematic nature' of the crime of genocide."[224] Further to this, it was also determined that there did not have to be one, but many perpetrators of genocide.[225] In the Canadian context, we are looking at a destructive colonial framework imposed by successive governments for over a century, first evidenced by John A. MacDonald's address to the House of Commons in 1883.[226]

Recall that the "Indian Problem" refers to the land and the inconvenient truth as to who are the owners of the land on Great Turtle Island. The Treaties made between Indigenous Nations and the Crown affirm that the Original Nations have an inherent Creation-given legal responsibility to protect the land. Successive Canadian governments' responses to the so-called Indian Problem were legislated into various colonial laws which all reflected the Indian Department's goal of "[t]ribal dissolution, to be pursued mainly through the corridors of residential schools."[227] In this manner the government targeted Indigenous Peoples' children. The legislation is a testament to the government's concerted effort in designing the colonial laws that forced the transfer of other nations' children into residential institutions.

It might be argued that statements like the ones expressed by John A. MacDonald, Hayter Reed, and Duncan Campbell Scott are not enough to show the specific intent requirements. However, the chamber in *Akayesu* citing the ICTY in the *Karadzić* case clarifies that policy may help to determine criminal culpability by the "same pattern of conduct"[228] through factors such as "general political doctrine which gave rise to the acts possibly covered."[229] The chamber of the ICTR established that "intent is a mental factor, which is difficult, even impossible, to determine. This is the reason why, in the absence of a confession from the accused, his intent can be inferred from a certain number of presumptions of fact."[230]

The ICTY in *Karadzić* supports the view that policy statements that shed light on the general political doctrine reflect expressed specific intent by Scott, Reed and MacDonald among others. Hayter Reed instructed staff officials "to employ 'every effort…against anything calculated to keep fresh in the memories of the children habits and associations which it is one of the main objects of industrial education to *obliterate* [emphasis added]"[231] the Indian from the child. This, and other statements expressing the same, clarifies and support specific intent, along with the massive and widespread serious and bodily harm children suffered as a result of the residential institutions policy. The violence that children suffered follows from the destructive intent expressed in government law and policy.

Harper's *Apology* shows specific intent by the statement, "kill the Indian in the child."[232] It shows that the government intended to harm Indigenous Peoples by destroying that which is distinctly *Indian.* The *Akayesu* trial chamber determined destroying a group to mean: "The victim is chosen not because of his individual identity, but rather on account of his membership of a national, ethnical, racial or religious group. The victim of the act is therefore a member of a group, chosen as such, which, hence, means that the victim of the crime of genocide is the group itself and not only the individual."[233] Certainly the expression "kill the Indian in the child" is an expression of the intent to destroy. Over all, the instructions requesting the *obliteration* of distinct elements of Indigenous Peoples' children national identities and the Apology, satisfy this requirement, as does the statement made by John A. MacDonald in 1883 to the House of Commons declared that children should be removed from parental influence and removed to residential institutions.[234]

As was reviewed in previous chapters the children were forced to "acquire the habits and modes of thought of white men."[235] The children were not just assimilated; they were forcibly indoctrinated by the massive and widespread acts of colonial violence and destruction wreaked upon them. As mentioned earlier, the Chamber in *Akayesu* found the accused guilty of genocide based on the widespread harm selectively committed against the Tutsi:

> Owing to the very high number of atrocities committed against the Tutsi, their widespread nature not only in the commune of Taba, but also throughout Rwanda, and to the fact that the victims were systematically and deliberately selected because they belonged to the Tutsi group, with persons belonging to other groups being excluded, the Chamber is also able to infer, beyond reasonable doubt, the genocidal intent of the accused in the commission of the above-mentioned crimes.[236]

The system-wide serious bodily and mental harm reveals patterns of the same massively destructive conduct; this is enough to show specific intent. The sexual predatory acts along with the widespread torture, forced starvation, forced labour and deaths were certainly a massive onslaught against Indigenous children.

The violence and horror would certainly impede the ability of Indigenous Nations to transmit the healthy characteristics of their national identities onto further generations. In this regard, the forcible removal to the residential institutions contributes to the destruction of the group as a whole, as Indigenous Nations depend on their children. The Venezuelan delegate during the drafting of the crime supports the finding that the forcible removal contributes to the destruction of the Indigenous Nations whose future depended on those generations that were stolen.[237]

The *Travaux* confirms that forcibly removing children would make them enemies of their own people.[238] In application to the facts by the massive and widespread serious bodily and mental destruction that caused the forced indoctrination Indigenous children come to self-loath their national identity. Indigenous Peoples come to identify in the colonizing language rather than their own languages. Spiritual laws are encoded in Indigenous Peoples' languages. The original languages are critically important to the national identities of Indigenous Nations. Further, the Original Nations are drawn into modern day land claims agreements and other colonial processes that terminate their distinct national identity through the severing or surrendering of the land to the colonial state.

Indigenous Peoples' depend on their land and territories for the continuance of their national identities. The land is paramount to the identities of the Original Nations on Great Turtle Island. This contributes to the destruction of the group as a whole. Furthermore, if the success of the colonial project depends on the extent of indoctrination and identity confusion, then those Nations that enter into modern day land claim agreements or other destructive arrangements are doing so at the expense of their future generations. By not being raised in accordance with an original national identity (i.e. *Nuxalk*, *Anishinaabe*, *Nehiyaw* or *Dene*) the long term effects of genocide are manifest.

The destruction is directed against Indigenous children because they are children of Indigenous Peoples and Nations. According to the Trial Chamber in *Krstić*, the intent to destroy a group means that the perpetrator must "view the part of the group they wish to destroy as a distinct entity which must be eliminated as such."[239]

In application to the facts and the "group" requirement, it is obvious that Indigenous children were targeted because of their national identities such as *Nehiyaw* or *Dene* (or in government terminology, their *Indian* identity). The legislation openly targeted Indigenous Peoples' children for the forcible removal. The comment by John A. MacDonald in 1883 openly targeted Indigenous children to be removed away from the parental influence. Further to this, the fact there was massive and widespread "institutional pedophilia" and tortuous violence of every kind against Indigenous Peoples' children aggravates the governments conduct in these matters.

It could be contended that the government did not intend to destroy the children the way it is articulated in this book; however, the government was aware of the destruction and never corrected the atrocities and the repugnant acts of violence against the children. The many autobiographical stories, books and government reports support this fact.[240] One example is the report made by the chief physician of the Department of Indian Affairs in 1907. Dr. P.H. Bryce declared that the atrocious dilapidated and living conditions that children were forced to live under in the residential institutions was in a state of emergency. The government was aware at this point and did nothing to address the problem.

Scott openly admitted that more than half of the children who passed through the institutions did not survive. Did the government stop the system in its tracks and return the children to the parents and Nations? The inaction by the government aggravates, not mitigates, its conduct. Further to this, the enrollment rates went up with the 1920 amendment to the *Indian Act*, which mandated that parents who kept their children away from the schools be imprisoned or fined and that the children could be "arrested without a warrant and conveyed to the school by the truant officer."[241] This further legislated action demonstrates aggravated government intent, and supports the requirement of specific intent called for under international law.

Like the finding in *Akayesu*, it is obvious that rape or sexual violence was committed solely against Indigenous Peoples' children. On the issue of serious bodily and mental harm, sexual violence and rape was determined to be a crime of genocide because sexual violence was an integral part of the process of destruction that specifically targeted Tutsi women and this contributed to the destruction of the Tutsi group as a whole. [242]

With respect to specific intent concerning sexual violence and rape, the case of *Akayesu* found that, "the rape of Tutsi women was systematic and was perpetrated against Tutsi women and solely against them."[243] The court went on further and held that '[s]exual violence was a step in the process of destruction of the [T]utsi group – destruction of the spirit, of the will to live, and of life itself."[244] The jurisprudence suggests that sexual violence and rape is genocide if it is massive and widespread.

In application to the facts, scores of Indigenous children were seriously bodily and mentally harmed by massive sexual violence and rape.[245] The crime of sexual violence has physical and psychological destructive consequences on the group. Similarly torture may also have destructive psychological consequences on a "group" according to the finding in *Akayesu*. It was acknowledged by the government that positive stories are "far overshadowed by the tragic accounts of the emotional, physical and sexual abuse"[246] The massive and widespread brutal violence in its various forms against the children would indeed cause great destruction to the ability of the young ones to be successful and healthy citizens of the Nations from whom they were forcibly removed. Children that suffered widespread sexual violence, torture, starvation, forced labour, and witness the massive death rates will exit out of the residential school traumatized by the collective devastation of serious bodily and mental harm of their peers.

Given these were ***children*** that endured years and years of inhumane suffering from an early age of human development and were terrorized by many methods there is no doubt that a child will come out traumatized and psychologically shattered by the serious bodily and mental destruction inflicted upon them collectively. For some children, the terror went on from the time they were detained to the time they were discharged. The total institution pummeled the national identity out of the children: "[b]y **not allowing** the formation of 'adult executive competency,' the [children] are prevented from being or becoming persons **at all.** When used in this manner, total institutions are not, therefore, instruments of social engineering, intended to inculcate an alternative form of life: they are instruments of genocide, meant to produce things unrecognizable **at all** as human beings [emphasis original]."[247]

The residential institutions dominate and dehumanize Indigenous Peoples' children by demonizing, isolating, and destroying the ability of the Original Nations to pass on healthy characteristics of those nations onto further generations. Shauna Troniak, researcher for the government writes, "The traumas of physical and sexual abuse, social and emotional dislocation and cultural loss have manifested, for many survivors and their communities, in after effects such as substance abuse, violence, and family breakdown. Many survivors' descendants have experienced and continue to experience inter-generational effects as a result of this unresolved trauma."[248]

Forcible Transfers into the Child Welfare Systems

Colonial laws forced the transfer of Indigenous Peoples' children into the residential school system and it is these laws that continue the removals into the child welfare systems today. The earlier system destroyed the ability to parent by the widespread destruction imposed against Indigenous Peoples collectively. The government caused the "inability to parent" and extensive traumatic genocidal effects and then used these as the rationale for forcible removal of Indigenous children into foster care homes away from their own families, Nations and homelands under a further destructive child welfare framework. Forcible transfers are sanctioned by the force of provincial laws.[249] The removals of our children in the child welfare system feed off the genocide caused by the residential schools.[250] So there is no distinguishing one destructive system from the other.

The inability to parent according to traditional healthy parenting and child rearing practices is caused then prolonged by the ongoing genocidal trauma.[251] Evidence of the genocidal trauma is supported by the collective serious bodily and mental destruction children underwent in the residential school system over the entire period. Oral child-rearing practices and values were devastated by the removal.[252] Residential schools compelled and embedded "parenting models based on punishment, [torture], coercion, and control."[253] The result is the decline and in some cases disappearance of traditional child rearing patterns.[254] Indigenous Peoples that endure brutal violence and horror will not parent according to their traditional child rearing methods, let alone exhibit the healthy characteristics of a *Nehiyaw* or *Dene* national identity.

Further to this, there has been the so-called **Apology.** Stephen Harper, Prime Minister of the Canadian state, apologized for attempting to "kill" the Indian, by forcibly removing children into residential schools, where everything distinctive about their identity was to be removed, and acknowledged the destruction of the ability to parent:

> We now recognize that it was wrong to separate children from rich and vibrant cultures and traditions, that it created a void in many lives and communities, and we apologize for having done this. We now recognize that, in separating children from their families, we undermined the ability of many to adequately parent their own children and sowed the seeds for generations to follow.[255]

But has the Canadian state put effort into assisting the victims of the residential schools to re-learn traditional parenting skills before the birth of children? Has the state stopped the forcible removals in the child welfare system? All of this aggravates not mitigates the Canadian government's conduct.

Indigenous Peoples' children are again being forcibly transferred and deprived of the socialization and enculturation process within their own Nations that enables them to become an integral part of their Nation or Peoples' distinct national identity. In other words, these new generations of children will not have been raised *Nehiyaw* or *Lil'wat* or *Nuxalk* or *Anishinaabe*, and so in what way can the children claim to have been socialized or raised within their families, communities and nations or represent and transmit their spiritual laws, norms and values? They cannot because they are now a product of the dominating society's language, culture, and christian religion and not their own languages, cultures and spiritual beliefs. This time around the Canadian state cannot claim they do not know that this is the end result of transferring children away from their families and nations because the government already apologized for having done this when the target destination of the children was the residential schools as "residence." Now the target destination is the non-Indigenous residence, or child welfare home.

The techniques of removal, imposition and destruction described in the residential school phase are applied in the same manner to the forced removal of our children into present times. The legislation mandates the forcible removal of Indigenous children who then experience the collective serious bodily and mental harm in the system. Our children in the child welfare systems endure the same patterns of the serious bodily and mental destruction endured in the previous system.[256]

Indigenous children in the child welfare system experience racist violence like that their predecessors endured. The suicide rate is pandemic for children in care.[257] Our Nations' children are sexually preyed upon while in the care of the system.[258] According to *The Globe and Mail,* the report by the BC Representative for Children and Youth found: Indigenous children "sexually abused in care; social workers who did not report abuse to police; provincial guidelines that are not audited for compliance; foster children abusing foster children, including a case in which the teenage perpetrator was simply shuffled to another placement;

instances in which there was no evidence that social workers or health care-care staff offered supports of any kind to children who had just disclosed sexual abuse; and foster fathers being the perpetrators in one-quarter of the 28 incidents that occurred in the home."[259] In fact, Indigenous children are "four times as more likely to be victims of sexual violence."[260]

The death rates of children in care are at an all-time high. Some examples include Tina Fontaine, aged 15, who was killed after she ran away from a hotel where she was in government care in Manitoba.[261] Another young person, aged 18, Alex Gervais, in British Columbia, jumped out of a hotel window and died.[262] Gervais was housed in the hotel room unsupervised by the ministry. The residential schools and child welfare systems have devastated our communities and Nations.

The horrors are similar to the experiences of children in the residential school system. Indigenous children experience sexual violence, forced labour, torture, starvation and death.[263] The effects include "psychological and emotional problems."[264] The child welfare system creates "tremendous obstacles to the development of a strong and healthy sense of identity."[265] One of the worst effects on future generations of Indigenous Peoples is the inability to parent according to a *Nehiyaw* or *Dene* worldview.

The residential school system destroyed the ability to parent. The result is a further destructive process that once again demonizes the Indigenous parents for lack of parenting skills, though this is through no fault of their own. The result is an ever-deepening vicious cycle: children are forcibly transferred away from Indigenous parents and isolated and destroyed; then ensuing generations of Indigenous children are seized from their parents due to the resultant inability to parent, only to be further isolated, conditioned and socialized by non-Indigenous foster care, and then at 18 years of age, often after a series of caregivers, they are abandoned into the dominant colonial society to fend for themselves without family or national roots. The goal of their absorption or assimilation into the colonial society or (body politic) has not changed over time and the result of the removals at each stage is the same. The same arguments that were applied to fulfill the international legal requirement of a specific intent to commit genocide are applicable in relation to Canada's contemporary child welfare system as demonstrated and satisfied by the massive rates of removal and widespread destruction experienced by Indigenous Peoples' children processed through that later system, and its maintenance despite its evident failure

Despite the high threshold of proof required, this legal application has shown that a genocidal colonial process occurred and continues to occur in Canada as evidenced by the past forcible removals of Indigenous Peoples and Nations' children via the residential school system that continue, albeit through a different governmental program (the child welfare system), into present times.

THE WAY AHEAD
Self-determinaton is the Solution

"In the past before the whiteman came to this continent, this island, the Indian People were able to determine for themselves their daily lives and were also able to govern themselves."
—Elder Pete Waskehat, Frog Lake First Nation (1989)

"It is not possible to undo all that has been done... but this does not negate the ethical imperative to undo (even at the expense, if need be, of the straightjacket imposed by the unbending observance of the "rule of [non-indigenous] law") the wrongs [crimes] done both, spiritually and materially, to the indigenous peoples."
—Miguel Alfonso Martinez (1999)

This book has shown that the Canadian State is responsible and accountable on two fronts. First, it has shown that the Canada has violated the Genocide Convention and the norms of customary international law with respect to the UNGC. Second it has shown the government is culpable for crimes of genocide deriving from the colonization process. If the reader remains in denial about this fact a reminder is that the state continues to forcibly remove our children into present times via the ongoing colonial imposition of its own child welfare laws upon Indigenous Peoples. After the rhetoric has been revealed for the whitewash that it is, the conclusion is not a fairy tale ending.

There is no sugar coating genocide. The language employed by the colonial oppressor tends to minimize the atrocity of the past and present. The reality is that genocide destroys Indigenous Peoples and Nations. The reality is that "children" were forcibly transferred and detained in a residential "total institution" for years where brutal and unspeakable horrors and violence were committed against the innocent. The reality is that the government intended this destruction of Indigenous Peoples and, this is framed in policy statements concerning the so-called "Indian problem." International law supports claims of genocide based on the acts it defines as such, and if the destruction is widespread, intention can be shown. This work has satisfied these requirements, demonstrating how the state targeted the children of the Original Nations of Great Turtle Island and codified into a legal framework the forcible removals that caused the disastrous trauma and dysfunction into present times.

Loopholes were justified and created by colonial states during the United Nations drafting of the Genocide Convention that removed cultural genocide from its Article II definition of acts of genocide with the goal of removing any safeguards for Indigenous Peoples and Nations against whom they were practicing it—before and during the drafting process and thereafter. The Canadian State then enacted legislation that did not include all of the acts determined by Article II of the Genocide Convention to be genocidal. The crime of genocide was in fact so limited in its implementation in the Canadian Criminal Code that it renders it impossible for any Canadian court to address the issue of whether or not the Canadian State engages in genocide based on Canadian law. Accordingly, to date the courts have not applied international law or the concept of genocide to issues involving the residential school or child welfare systems and state culpability,[1] despite the increasing frequency of discourse that the impact was genocidal.

Given this point it makes one wonder if a court of the oppressor would be able to fairly determine the issue of genocide in the colonization process, even were the Article II acts of genocide in the UNGC to be fully domestically implemented. The Canadian government is not above international laws, and would not be so regarded, especially given that it is the perpetrator of genocide against other peoples' children. The fact that the Canadian government perpetrated and continues to perpetrate the crimes against innocent children unchecked aggravates, not mitigates, its atrocious conduct, and amplifies the urgency of international legal intervention.

It is obvious from the facts that forcibly removing children from loving families and nations and physically detaining them for years at a time would be enough to cause widespread trauma. However, the fact that children were brutally dominated and dehumanized by torture, forced starvation, forced labour, sexual predatory acts, and untold death by disease and dilapidated living conditions and other methods makes it crystal clear the result would devastate not just the well-being of the children but the continuance of their distinct identities as Nations. Given that this destruction occurred over successive generations it is obvious the fallout would be catastrophic. And indeed it has been. The catastrophe plays out in many ways and in many forms. Children grow up into adults. If they are collectively dominated under a dehumanizing legal framework and not allowed to form healthy conceptions of their national identities then those children will exhibit the traumatic and painful symptoms of peoples that have lived under prolonged conditions of genocide.

This analysis raises an important question about government culpability for its conduct with respect to extending its colonial practices into present times. The forcible seizure of Indigenous children is enacted into contemporary government laws still formulated in the context of a destructive colonial framework. Most people do not understand how brutal colonialism has been for Indigenous Peoples and Nations in the Western hemisphere and globally. The paradigm of benevolence that western scholarship utilizes to facilitate the denial of colonial state genocide contributes to the ongoing genocide of the Original Nations. Scholars who debate whether residential schools were "really" genocidal are contributing to state genocide. The claim that mass physical destruction is worse than the horrors outlined in this book is an example of the repugnancy often found in western academia.[2]

At the Colonial Genocide in Indigenous North America Conference in 2012 some, not all scholars who were present, engaged in this sort of destructive dialogue.[3] I reminded the participants that the purpose of genocide scholarship is to *prevent* genocide and call it out when it is taking place—not to be engaging in genocide denial. The claim that mass physical destruction is the only form of genocide that should be recognized is an example of the failure to come to grips with the full scope of the international legal *jus cogens* prohibition, and the magnitude and depth of the destruction perpetrated that scholar deniers or gatekeepers have in this area of research. The non-indigenous scholar is unable to conceive of his/her complicity in the brutal or destructive nature of colonialism, and furthermore cannot conceive that the problem exists in the society that allows horrific acts of violence against the innocent to continue to the extent that it does.

To that end, a reminder about Dr. Bryce and his alarming message to the government and society in 1907 and again in 1922 that our children were dying off at disturbing rates: It is worth reiterating that "the mechanics of death in the schools was laid bare and responsibility placed squarely on Duncan Campbell Scott,"[4] yet despite this information responsible officials approved Scott's drive to substantially increase enrollment. The condition worsened over time and in 1920 it was reported by a government physician on dying children:

> The condition of one little girl [eight years old] found in the infirmary is pitiable indeed. She lies up curled in a bed that is filthy, in a room that

> is...dirty and dilapidated, in the northwest corner of the building with no provision of...sunshine or fresh air. Both sides of her neck and chest are swollen and five foul ulcers are discovered when we lift the bandages. This gives her pain, and the tears from her fear of being touched intensifies the picture of her misery.[5]

The colonial society through these actions has allowed the State of Canada to continue to forcibly remove Indigenous Peoples' children under a genocidal, dominating and dehumanizing discourse.

Most people in this oppressor colonial society do not understand or seem to care about the extent to which forcible transferring of Indigenous children affects the ability of the Original Nations' of Great Turtle Island to survive with their distinct national identities intact into the future. Yet, the destructive effects of Canada's efforts to wring them out is evident for all to see in the resultant and ongoing trauma leading to Indigenous Peoples' disproportionate suffering from suicides, drugs and alcohol abuse, adult and youth incarceration, poverty, detrimental health issues, and the immense pain and sorrow that follows one generation to the next. The state and society feed off[6] of the genocidal effects they created and continued by the ongoing forcible seizures.

It is acknowledged in international jurisprudence there does not have to be physical genocide for the crime to occur and in fact every single member of an oppressed human "group" can survive physically and genocide can still take place.[7] This legal research and argument has explained the most important aspect of genocide that Raphaël Lemkin attempted to portray when the crime was being defined in international law.[8]

It is hypocritical for the state of Canada and Canadians to pretend to Indigenous Peoples and Nations and to the world at large that they are "sorry" when it's obvious the Canadian state, at least, is anything but. An admission of an apology requires the perpetrator to be honest about the full extent and ramifications of conduct it engaged in against the victims it has destroyed —and to cease that conduct. Furthermore, there is no "apology" that would undo or make the atrocious crimes it has engaged in "forgivable". It is a smokescreen designed by the colonizer to absolve itself of the crimes it knowingly engages in against the innocent.

It would have been viewed as absurd for any other regime engaging in crimes of genocide against other peoples' children to evade its crimes internationally and domestically and then, as the perpetrator, to set up another destructive process that purported to investigate the issue and seek to resolve it. But such was the so-called Truth and Reconciliation Commission, a body set up by the perpetrator government. A question put to me in my defense of my master's dissertation was, "What if the TRC makes a finding of *genocide*?"[9] My response was: "How likely is it that Hitler's régime or any other régime engaging in genocide be legally able to create the body (state commission) to examine its conduct?" The committee replied that it was a good answer.

Canada, like other regimes that have engaged in crimes of genocide, should be held accountable as have other regimes in times past. This book has demonstrated that state accountability for crimes in the colonization of our lands and territories is fundamentally legal and moral and just—and indeed the only way—to address its criminal conduct against our Nations. So-called state solutions cloaked in euphemisms and rhetoric such as "reconciliation" only further the colonial agenda.

"The root word is *re* which means *to do again* or *to repeat*." Thus, Newcomb points out that reconciliation "is premised on the idea of [previously] good relations [conciliation] that broke apart and are to be put back together or mended through a 'reconciliation' process. Where is the history of good relations that are to be mended through such a process?"[10] For Indigenous Peoples who have undergone genocidal acts, reconciliation is an oxymoron. The illusion that Indigenous Peoples are now achieving justice must be dispelled. Words like *reconciliation* are premised on a constructive legal framework. But is this the case, here?

> Words have a history. Words from the past have the ability to colonize the present. Words shape and create reality. Reconciliation has a history; it has the ability to colonize the present for Indigenous nations and peoples; it can be used to maintain a particular kind of reality that benefits states and to the continued detriment of Indigenous nations and peoples.[11]

Here, the term *reconciliation* proposes that the issue has now been dealt with satisfactorily and relations have returned to a former purportedly favorable state. It is key to an ongoing extension of the intended genocide (assimilation) of Indigenous Peoples into the fabric of the state, implying that all past issues have been dealt with and the victims' grievances satisfied—even though the intended ends are still being pursued under another legal regime, the child welfare system. Indigenous Nations are forced to acquiesce to both a history and a present that is genocidal. They are forced to *reconcile* a brutal past with a future that looks even more brutal because the perpetrator continues its crimes of genocide and fails to acknowledge them as such. George Tinker explains:

> While the notion that native people can somehow heal wounds opened up by knives that continue to be twisted in our bowels may be self-evidently grotesque, it is no more so than the premise that our healing might in any sense be contingent upon, much less synonymous, with our "reconciling" with the knife-wielders. The proposition is as disgusting as it is blatantly false. It might be contended with equal merit that the "best thing" for a rape victim, psychologically-speaking, would be to reconcile with her rapist while she is being raped.[12]

As grim as this may be to the reader it describes the genocidal reality that Indigenous Nations and Peoples have been compelled to accept. Why do Indigenous Nations have to accept a further dehumanizing process?

Colonial invasion and the crimes that take place in this process are deemed to be allowable because globally, in the Western colonizer's view, the *civilization* process rendered it acceptable to destroy other peoples and nations if they are declared to be less than human. The colonial process also made it acceptable that other peoples' children can be demonized, isolated and destroyed under brutal colonial viciousness. How can a society that traumatizes and dehumanizes children over successive generations claim to be civilized? Perhaps Aimé Césaire and Roland Chrisjohn, Sherri Young and Michael Maraun are correct in their assertion that the civilization process itself is necessarily destructive.

The civilization process renders the colonizers inherently violent against the colonized peoples and nations. Indigenous Peoples and Nations are the most recent Nations that have been afflicted by this odious scourge called genocide. Again if there is doubt as to the legal research into the extent of the destruction endured in this book then the reader need only examine the residential school system and the child welfare system in its proper context. This will help clarify how it can be argued that when children are forcibly seized from their families, incarcerated in institutions, massively tortured, sexually preyed on, forcibly starved, and forced into labour with a view to erasing their original identity and indoctrinating them into foreign one, this is a crime of genocide according to international law.

Cultural genocide was deleted in the drafting process of the UNGC because it reflected the legal issues arising from the colonial invasion of Original Nations' land and territories globally. The statements made by delegates demonstrate this concern as many state representatives favoured narrowing the concept of genocide in favour of state interests.[13] Since 1492 the legal issues arising from the domination and dehumanization of Original Nations have been characterized by the demonization, isolation and destruction of those Nations.

The invasion and colonization of other peoples' land was rationalized and "justified" under the doctrine of discovery, the basis of which is founded on dehumanizing theories of racial superiority. The destructive framework under which the forcible transferring of Indigenous children took place was based on these dehumanizing doctrines applied against Indigenous Peoples. Moreover, the discussions presented in the *Travaux* underscore the awareness that destructive theories of racial superiority are at the root of genocide. The designation of savage, heathen and pagan were applied to the Original Nations of the western hemisphere to justify the destructive colonial framework that has led to crimes of genocide.

With respect to Canada, a relatively new *state*, Indigenous Peoples were and are rendered *indistinguishable* and *invisible* as Nations by means of colonial processes, language, laws, designed to conceal this reality. The illusion of invisibility allows the forcible transferring of Indigenous Peoples' children to continue. The dominating nature of the oppressor's language contributes to the concealment by the use of the word magic.

If there is no proper contextual and truthful analysis of the forcible transfers of Indigenous children away from their loved ones and Nations, then the whitewashing of this atrocity will go down as the greatest illusion Canada and other colonizer states ever created. The illusion that Canada's laws and policies have not had a devastating impact on the Original Nations must be dispelled and understood in its entirety for true healing and justice to be achieved. If the truth is not told for our children that suffered and passed on, and the victims and the generations who live with the fallout of genocide, and who as a result are threatened with extinction[14] through various means, then perhaps Canada's solution to the "Indian problem" will have been achieved.

The success of the colonial enterprise depends on the success of the indoctrinated oppressed peoples. By kidnapping our children and committing brutal acts that conditioned our peoples and nations collectively to see the world through a western-conditioned lens, many Indigenous Peoples (who are now far removed from their national, spiritual and cultural identities) enter into processes such as "land claims" and "reconciliation" and other destructive processes that will see the eventual and complete swallowing up and devouring of our national identities and our lands into the Canadian body politic.[15] It is criminal and the effects of genocide include this inconvenient truth that many people do not want to admit.

Finally, if you are non-indigenous, and find yourself reading these words, then you cannot say you have not been exposed to the truth and are not therefore accountable. It is up to you to finally be the generation of settlers that stands up against the crimes that are committed against the Original Peoples and Nations of this Western hemisphere and the world.

SELF-DETERMINATION IS THE SOLUTION

The most obvious first step in the solution to the ongoing destruction is that the Canadian state must cease its longstanding goals of genocide and its colonial laws and policies that seek to accomplish that end. Canada must return our children, our lands, and our resources that have been illegally claimed and illegitimately appropriate by the colonial invading state. Another obvious resolution is that the colonial state stops the genocide in its various forms, such as the current child welfare systems.

The Peace and Friendship Treaties made between Indigenous Nations and the Crown must be implemented. Indigenous Nations "agreed to share the top soil to the depth of the plough. Indigenous Peoples never surrendered, sold or otherwise alienated the land, water, trees, mountains, resources above and below the ground, animals, bird, fish and all other living things. The Chiefs, Headmen and the citizens are the caretakers of the land, the resources and all livings for the future generations."[16] Sharon Venne explains:

> Sharing lands is not selling the land. When the Indigenous Peoples agree to share the lands the

> non-indigenous people agree to provide certain benefits to the landlords for as long as the sun shines and the water flows. These are referred to as the Treaty promises and Treaty commitments. The Indigenous Peoples agreed to share the lands and to live in peace with the non-indigenous settlers. The Indigenous Peoples have never reneged on their obligations. The same cannot be said for the non-indigenous people.[17]

But non-Indigenous people have never been peaceful toward our Nations and at every turn have undermined the obligations and promises made in the Treaties. The forced transfer of our children into colonial residential institutions into present times is one of the gravest violations of the Treaty. We depend on our children to transmit the healthy aspects of our *Nehiyaw* and other national identities into further generations. The Treaty affirms our national identities.

The late UN Special Rapporteur on The UN Treaty Study, Miguel Alfonso Martinez, wrote on self-determination that "Indigenous Peoples, like all other peoples on Earth are entitled to that inalienable right. Article 1 of the Charter of the United Nations gives blanket recognition of this right to all peoples (enshrining it as a principle of contemporary international law)."[18] Self-determination is a Creation-given (inherent right). Martinez also believed that our Nations are subjects of international law: "In the case of indigenous peoples who concluded treaties or other legal instruments with the European settlers and/or their continuators in the colonization process, the Special Rapporteur has not found any sound legal argument to sustain the argument that they have lost their international juridical status as nations/ peoples."[19]

Our Nations on Great Turtle Island were given "laws set by the Creator"[20] to live according to in our relationship with all of Creation (Mother Earth). It is those laws that were severed with the forcible transferring of Indigenous Peoples' children onto residential institutions. Our Peoples and Nations have been forced to enter into destructive processes that denigrate our Nations and future generations. We depend on our Mother Earth for life and the life of our future generations. We depend on our children to transmit the healthy aspects of our Nehiyaw and other national identities onto further generations of our peoples

Indigenous Peoples have been forced to "utilize the language and conceptual system of the dominating society as a means of thinking, speaking, and writing about our own existence while challenging certain negative, oppressive and dominating concepts that have been mentally and from an indigenous perspective, illegitimately imposed on our existence."[21] But we as Indigenous Peoples must also begin to take responsibility and accountability by learning our languages, reclaiming our national identities, cultural and spiritual beliefs and practices, and most importantly by not accepting or conceding to state control and domination which some unfortunately do.

We must see that our responsibilities and obligations are geared toward our future generations so that they will have a chance to be *Anishinaabe*, *Kainai*, *Dene*, *Nehiyaw*, *Mohawk* and on the other side of the fictitious border the *Lakota*, *Lenape*, *Navajo*, *Pauite*, *Shawnee*, and many other Original Nations and Peoples.

Churchill reminds us that, "we shoulder the burden, *whatever* it may entail, of ensuring that the order of colonialism at last is shattered, never to be restored. Most importantly, we owe it, all of us, to our coming generations, seven deep into the future, to bequeath unto them lives free of the nightmarish reality in which ourselves remain so mired."[22] If the *Original Nations* on our Great Turtle Island are to recover and heal it is our inalienable right and responsibility to live according to Creation's laws in our lands and territories. The road home entails the right of self-determination as subjects in international law, which is a fundamental aspect of healing and recovering our way of life. In fact, it is the only solution for peace and for true justice.

GENOCIDE AND THE CHILD WELFARE SYSTEM

A Snapshot of Media Reporting on the Foster Case System in Canada

Indigenous children over-represented in child welfare by Yasmine Mayne *Spruce Grove Examiner/Stony Plain Reporter*, July 21, 2016

"The separation from our mother was really difficult."

"It was difficult to understand as a child why you couldn't be with your family."

"Being taken away from your family feels terrible ... it's like being transported to an alien country."

These are quotes from a video by the Office of The Child and Youth Advocate Alberta (OCYA) in light of a recent report published by the Auditor General's office on the delivery of child and family services to indigenous youth.

According to the report, almost 70 percent of children in care are Aboriginal, even though only 10 per cent of children in the province are Aboriginal."

'Tragic' number of aboriginal children in foster care stuns even the experts. By Michael Woods & Sharon Kirkey, *Postmedia News* May 8, 2013

"Nearly half of children under 14 in foster care in Canada are aboriginal children — a number that exceeds even the grimmest estimates of a leading First Nations' child welfare advocate. Newly released data from the National Household Survey suggest that, of the approximately 30,000 children in care in Canada in 2011, 14,225 were aboriginal."

"An 18-year-old aboriginal youth who fell to his death from a fourth-floor hotel window last week had been in government care and placed in the budget hotel in contravention of B.C. policy." **Justine Hunter, Troubled teen died in care while placed at hotel against B.C. policy, *Globe and Mail*, September 24, 2015**

"According to an Edmonton Journal-Calgary Herald investigation, 145 children in Alberta have died in foster care since 1999. Of the 145, the provincial government lists ethnic information for 94 children, including 74 who were aboriginal."

Darcy Henton, Deaths of Alberta aboriginal children in care no 'fluke of statistics' *Calgary Herald*, 01/08/2014

"Elders from the Wabaseemoong First Nation in north-western Ontario remember the bus that drove around their reserve picking up children and shuttling them to a waiting plane for a 345 kilometre…. Such mass apprehension of children from troubled Wabaseemoong, including those flights in the 1970s, have been draining the reserve of its youth for decades…"

'A lost tribe': Child welfare system accused of repeaing residential school history, Adrian Humphries, *National Post*, December 15, 2014

"Worse yet, Tina Fontaine had been under the province's care at the time of her death, in the custody of Manitoba's Child Welfare system. And she's hardly the only indigenous youth to have fallen through the cracks of the province's Child and Family Services. In March, a girl was brutally beaten and sexually assaulted.... also while in its care."

Anna Maria Tremonti, Aboriginal kids in Manitoba's care finally have advocate, CBC Radio, The Current, June 15,

Foster kids not treated as 'human' by Manitoba: First Nations advocate, China Puxtley, Metro News Canada The Canadian Press, June 9, 2015

"Manitoba doesn't treat children in care and their families as "human." Cora Morgan, who was appointed by the Assembly of Manitoba Chiefs last week, said the province's child welfare system is broken. Child and Family Services are taking children into care too quickly and it's virtually impossible for parents to regain custody. Children in care are being put up in hotels and languishing in jail without a proper support system for families in crisis that would prevent kids from being apprehended in the first place, she said. "There is a lack of humanity in the way that CFS operates," Morgan told The Canadian Press. "These children in care and these families, I don't see that they're being recognized as human… Every single individual needs to feel loved. Where do you find that growing up in a hotel room?" Manitoba has more than 10,000 children in care and the vast majority are aboriginal. The system has been under scrutiny for years following several high profile deaths and assaults of children in care."

WHY THE CHILDREN?

Sharon H. Venne

Why the children? Is it a process of the colonizers to push Indigenous Peoples to write and perform for them? In any discussion about ourselves, we are asked to frame our discussions or writings within the vision as promoted by the colonizers. When Indigenous Peoples want to tell our story from the beginning with our Original Instructions, we are discouraged and belittled to bring the story into line with a preconceived notion of what is needed to amuse and entertain the colonizers. This is colonization and destruction of our way of telling our stories. The colonization process wants us to have our stories written in a way that will bring comfort to the reader. Indigenous Peoples have to entertain the reader so that the true story of the colonization process can be sanitized and reconciled. But, how can you have true reconciliation when the truth remains hidden?

In the seven years that I witnessed Tamara Starblanket struggle with the writing of this book—she questioned herself. She questioned her ancestors. She struggled to make sense of colonization and genocide from the perspective of confusion. Why have we been left with this unexplained pain in our hearts? Our ancestors have left for the spirit world in such terrible conditions. Why? Many a phone call from Tamara came in the middle of the night with questions about the continued genocide of our Peoples. The universities wanted the discussion framed in a way that takes the human out of the picture. However, genocide is a human issue. It is not an academic discussion. It is not in the past. It is happening right now right across Great Turtle Island. These were real struggles that Tamara had to face. There was the university professor who wanted her to forget the past and write something else. However, the voices of her ancestors were pushing her to tell the truth. The truth can be hard to tell. It needs to be told.

We can write about statistics on the number of deaths like an accounting entry. We could write about the horrors of the starvation and deaths while in the custody of the state/Christian church-run institutions. This kind of writing on this topic merely brings peace to the reader—this does not bring peace to the spirits who left our Mother Earth to return to the Creation. Those spirits left us without a proper acknowledgment. Should this afterward mention that in the province of Manitoba—named after Manitou—Great Spirit—the province is seizing an Indigenous Child a day for placement in a foster home? These children are being seized at the hospital shortly after their birth as written in the newspapers on the 1st of September, 2015.[1] What happens to their placenta? Is it taken care of and returned to our Mother Earth? Are the ceremonies done for the naming of that child? Is the belly button taken care of and are the songs sung for this child who is seized at birth and removed from our Peoples? Our future – our future power?

This is the tangible result of genocide. It is an ongoing and persistent issue in our nations. Our children are the targets. What about the two-year-old boy who was beaten and left in a garage where he froze to death when the temperature dropped to minus 40C? What about him? Was the death song sung? Did his body get washed and prepared for his journey back to the Creation? Which four people spoke for him as per our Original Instructions? What message did he bring to the Creation about his treatment while on Mother Earth? It must not have been a good report.

Article 2(e) of the Convention on the Prevention and

Punishment of the Crime of Genocide as adopted by Resolution 260 (III) A of the United Nations General Assembly on 9 December 1948 defines genocide as "forcibly transferring children of a group to another group" with the intent of destroying in whole in in part a national, ethnical, racial or religious group.

There is no need to question the intention of the government of Canada as their intention clearly stated in the 1920s by then Deputy Minister of Indian Affairs Duncan Campbell Scott:

> The happiest future for the Indian race is absorption into the general population, and this is the object and policy of our government… Our objective is to continue until there is not a single Indian in Canada that has not been absorbed into the body politic and there is no Indian question, and no Indian Department.[2]

The state of Canada targeted our children by removing them from our homes and families, by placing them in residential schools, and then into care via the child welfare system which has been documented by Tamara Starblanket. What is the result of these actions? Many children never came home, having died in custody. The ones who returned home had been stripped of their identity and responsibilities, our relationship to the lands and resources having been taken along with our languages. It is the languages that link our People to the spirit of the lands. Why target the children? The colonizers wanted to have access to our lands and resources. In order to accomplish this task—the colonizers needed to have no one able to speak for the land and the resources. This is our obligation and responsibility as Indigenous Peoples. The Canadian court system decides cases on the ability of the Indigenous Peoples to document their history and relationship to their territories. Those Indigenous Peoples who cannot document their relationship are found to have no rights to the lands and resources.

When we come from the Creation, we come with our

instructions. All things that are on Mother Earth have instructions; leaves on the trees breathe in the carbon dioxide and turn it into oxygen for humans to use. The water continues to flow so that our bodies can have it to survive. Nothing alive can survive without water. The animals, the birds, the fish and all things on our Mother Earth have instructions for the survival of each other. When one disappears forever, the balance is interrupted. We can see on a daily basis the effects of an unbalanced earth. We feel that same way about the loss of the children and their gifts brought from the Creation.

From the time before the conception of a child, there are ceremonies being done for the health of the child who is going to visit us from the Creation. This child is our future. At every stage of our lives—there are ceremonies and teachings related to our life. We are born into a clan—our clan tells us how to conduct our lives. These teachings were lost to most Indigenous Peoples. There is a struggle to remember and to live those obligations and responsibilities. At this time, many of our Peoples are walking bodies without any instructions. This is an ongoing result of the acts of the state. The problem for the state is the spirit of our Peoples has survived but not without the suffering of our children. The child welfare system is state sponsored terrorism. The child is defenceless. The suffering continues—many of these children dying in care. It remains for us who remember to do the ceremonies for their spirits to return to the Creation. This is our Great Turtle Island that cannot be owned by the colonizers. The crime should be still punished by the international community. Colonization and genocide go hand and hand. It is not cultural genocide—it is genocide period. For Indigenous Peoples, there is no other conclusion to be drawn. Indigenous Peoples did not create the word—but we are living it on a daily basis – another child was seized today and another tomorrow, and so on and so on. Genocide is a crime.

ENDNOTES

Introduction

1 For background on the formation of settler-states, see, e.g., Lisa Ford, *Settler Sovereignty: Jurisdiction and Indigenous People in America and Australia, 1788-1836* (Cambridge, MA: Harvard University Press, 2011). For analyses of the results, see Lorenzo Veracini, *The Settler Colonial Present* (New York: Palgrave Macmillan, 2015); Emma Battell Lowman and Adam J. Barker, *Settler: Identity and Colonialism in 21st Century Canada* (Black Point, NS; Winnipeg, MB: Fernwood, 2015).

2 Canada's program of involuntarily sterilizing indigenous women is one example. See, e.g., Karen Stote, *An Act of Genocide: Colonialism and the Sterilization of Aboriginal Women* (Black Point, NS; Winnipeg, MB: Fernwood, 2015).

3 The term was adopted to distinguish Indigenous Nations from the so-called Third World. See George Manuel and Michael Posluns, *The Fourth World: An Indian Reality* (Toronto: Collier-Macmillan, 1974). Also see Peter McFarlane, *Brotherhood to Nationhood: George Manuel and the Making of the Modern Indian Movement* (Toronto: Between the Lines, 1993).

4 Sharon H. Venne, *Our Elders Understand our Rights: Evolving International Law Regarding Indigenous Rights* (Penticton, BC: Theytus Books Ltd., 1998).

5 See Sharon Venne, ed., *Honour Bound Onion Lake and the Spirit of Treaty Six: The International Validity of Treaties with Indigenous Peoples* (Copenhagen, Denmark: International Working Group for Indigenous Affairs, 1997), 6-7.

6 See Steven T. Newcomb, *Pagans in the Promised Land: Decoding the Christian Doctrine of Discovery* (Golden, CO: Fulcram Publishing, 2008).

7 The phrase "purely legal" was used in the argument advanced during the so-called Economic Trial at Nuremberg by defense counsel Helmuth Dix with respect to the use of slave labor by those accused. This was because, as defense counsel Hermann Jahrreiss put it during the main Nuremberg trial in 1946, the fundamental question was not simply one of international law, but whether the accused were being prosecuted for adhering to the "national criminal law which was binding on the defendants at the time of the deed." Viewed from the latter perspective,

their actions were indeed lawful, given the legal force accorded "Führer Decrees" in Germany after 1933, a development strongly endorsed by such imminent political/legal theorists as Carl Schmitt. Dix is quoted in Devon O. Pendas, "The Fate of Nuremberg: The Legacy and Impact of the Subsequent Nuremberg Trials," in Kim Christian Priemel and Alexa Stiller, eds., *Reassessing the Nuremberg Tribunals: Transitional Justice, Trial Narratives and Historiography* (New York: Berghahn Books, 2012), 255. For the Jahrreiss quote, see his excerpted trial statement in Jay W. Baird, ed., *From Nuremberg to My Lai* (New York: D.C. Heath, 1972), 90. On Schmitt's avid embrace of the "sovereign 'order-creating decision[s]'" embodied in Führer Decrees, see Michael Stolleis, *The Law under the Swastika: Studies on Legal History in Nazi Germany* (Chicago: University of Chicago Press, 1998), esp. 97.

8 "The Tribunal said that individuals could be held responsible for criminal acts even if committed on behalf of their states 'if the state in authorizing action moves outside its competence under international law.' Furthermore they could not shelter themselves behind a plea of superior orders if 'moral choice was in fact possible.'" Quincy Wright, "Law of the Nuremberg Trial," *The American Journal of International Law* 41, No. 1 (January 1947): 55.

9 Susan Griffin, *A Chorus of Stones: The Private Life of Wars* (New York: Doubleday, 1992), 162.

10 Gayatri Chakravorty Spivak, *A Critique of Postcolonial Reason: Toward a History of the Vanishing Present* (Cambridge, MA: Harvard University Press, 1999), 203.

11 Canadian settler-scholars have not only claimed "postcolonial" status, but to exemplify it. University of Manitoba professor of cultural studies Diana Brydon, for example, has asserted that anyone "truly interested in post-colonial literatures and perspectives…will come to us." By "us," of course, she means the settler intelligentsia of which she is a member in good standing. Diana Brydon, "New Approaches to the New Literatures in English: Are We in Danger of Incorporating Disparity?," in Hena Maes-Jelinek, Kirstin Holst Peterson, and Anna Rutherford, eds., *A Shaping of Connections: Commonwealth Literatures, Then and Now: Essays in Honour of A.N. Jeffares* (Sydney: Dangaroo Press, 1989), 95.

12 It appears to be a general consensus among those embracing the idea that the "postcolonial era" began with decolonization of most Third World countries during the period 1945-1975. The independence of most colonized South and Central American countries as well as Canada was gained during the nineteenth century, however, and that of the U.S. earlier still. As critics have noted, moreover, while the term "postcolonial" implies that colonialism, per se, has ended, this is true only with regard to certain forms, in certain places. Both internal colonialism and settler-state colonialism are very much ongoing, as

is readily apparent in the situations of Indigenous Peoples around the world. Rather than simply abandoning the term as ill-considered, some proponents have sought to "backdate" it so that it "begins the moment that the colonizing power inscribes itself onto the body and space of its Others," a rather peculiar maneuver that leaves "postcolonialism" indistinguishable from colonialism itself. For one of the better critiques, see Ella Shohat, "Notes on the Post-Colonial," in Padmini Mongia, ed., *Contemporary Postcolonial Theory: A Reader* (London/New York: Arnold/Oxford University Press, 1997), 321-34. The passage used to illustrate the backdating maneuver is from Stephan Slemon's "Modernism's last post," quoted in Patrick Williams and Laura Chrisman, "Colonial Discourse and Post-Colonial Theory: An Introduction," in their co-edited *Colonial Discourse and Post-Colonial Theory: A Reader* (New York: Columbia University Press, 1994), 12.

13 Presumably, this would date from passage of the British North America Act on July 1, 1867, establishing Britain's Canadian settler colony as a nominally independent state. Only the *colonists* gained independence in this arrangement, however. Those actually colonized—which is to say, the Original Nations of the Maritime Provinces, Québec, and Ontario—remained so. The same pattern prevailed in each area into which the supposedly "postcolonial" state thereafter expanded, a circumstance remaining very much in effect at present. The implications of Canada's ongoing colonization of Indigenous Peoples have therefore been consistently minimized, or simply ignored in the settler intelligentsia's assertions of Canadian "postcoloniality." For Indigenous arguments along this line, see as examples, Thomas King, "Godzilla vs. Post-Colonial," *World Literature Written in English* 30, No. 2 (1990): 10-16; Lee Maracle, "The 'Post-Colonial' Imagination," *Fuse* 16, No. 1 (Fall 1992):12-14.

14 "One aspect of our [past] relationship with Aboriginal people that requires particular attention is the Residential School system.... The Government of Canada acknowledges the role it played in developing and administering these schools.... *Tragically*, some children were the victims of physical and sexual abuse.... Particularly to those *individuals* who...suffered this *tragedy* in the residential schools, we are deeply sorry [emphasis added]." "Address of the Honorable Jane Stewart, Minister of Indian Affairs and Northern Development, on the occasion of the unveiling of *Gathering Strength—Canada's Aboriginal Action Plan*" (Ottawa: Department of Indian Affairs and Northern Development, January 7, 1998), 4.

15 Canada, Office of the Prime Minister, *Statement of Apology to Former Students of the Indian Residential Schools,* (Ottawa: June 11, 2008).

16 See Paul Bunner, "The 'genocide' that failed," *C2C Journal* (October 26, 2013), http://www.c2cjournal.ca/2013/10/the-genocide-that-failed/. Bunner was one of Harper's top speech writers.

17 The case settled was *In Re Residential Schools Class Action*, brought

by the Assembly of First Nations against the Canadian government and the churches which were authorized and funded by the state to actually run the schools. The latter included the General Synod of the Anglican Church of Canada, the Dioceses of the Anglican Church of Canada, the United Church of Canada, the Methodist Church of Canada, and "various Catholic entities." See "The Indian residential schools settlement has been approved," available online at <www.residentialschoolsettlement.ca>

18 The formula for compensation was $10,000 for the first year (or portion thereof) spent in a school, and $3,000 per year for each year thereafter. See Kathleen Mahoney, "The Indian Residential School Settlement: Is Reconciliation Possible?," *ABlawg.ca* (June 26, 2013), 1, https://ablawg.ca/wp-content/uploads/2013/06/Blog_KM_Settlement_June2013.pdf.

19 Provision was made for survivors wishing to press additional claims arising from specific and especially egregious physical/sexual abuses to do so through an "Independent Assessment Process." Each such claim had to be proven according to Canadian standards of jurisprudence—meaning, among other things, that it would be contested by attorneys representing the state and any individually-accused parties—a matter compelling claimants to hire attorneys of their own, to provide direct testimony as to what they'd suffered, and to endure humiliating cross-examinations about their most traumatizing experiences. Public exposure of what had been done to them often compounded the abiding sense of degradation instilled by the original assaults. Under such circumstances, few victims availed themselves of the "opportunity," and the even fewer who did so successfully received "on average, $110,000 per claimant." See Mahoney, "Residential School Settlement." See especially Jorge Barrera, "Ottawa mulls review of how its lawyers handled Indian residential school cases" *APTN National* News (5 October 2016), http://aptnnews.ca/2016/10/05/ottawa-mulls-review-of-how-its-lawyers-handled-indian-residential-school-cases/.

20 Actually, the proposition that genuine healing might occur under present circumstances is absurd. See Ward Churchill, "Healing begins when the wounding stops: Indian residential schools and the prospects for 'truth and reconciliation' in Canada," *Briarpatch* 37, No. 4 (June/July 2008): 19-24.

21 The foundation was created in 1998 and $125 million was allotted to it under the 2006 Settlement Agreement, and its services were supposed to be provided until 2014. Even that would have been inadequate, given the kinds of "Complex PTSD". On Complex PTSD, see Judith Herman, *Trauma and Recovery: The Aftermath of Violence—From Domestic Abuse to Political Terror, rev. ed.* (New York: Basic Books, 2015).

22 Stuart Christie, *Plural Sovereignties and Contemporary Indigenous*

Literature (New York: Palgrave Macmillan, 2009), 9.

23 To be clear, every Indigenous person in Canada is, or should be, a citizen of at least one Original Nation. Whether any of us wish to *also* be citizens of Canada is always *our* choice to make, *never* Canada's. Given that it has constructed itself on *our* territories, and using *our* resources, the Canadian settler-state's obligations to us remain unchanged, either way. Far from demonstrating its "postcoloniality," the "pluralism" to which it purports by virtue of unilaterally imposing its citizenship upon us serves only to *complete* its system of colonial domination.

24 It would perhaps be more accurate to say that the TRC was created in June 2008. By January 2009, however, all three of the original commissioners had resigned, citing "political interference," Replacements were appointed, effective July 1, 2009, and operations began shortly thereafter. *Truth and Reconciliation Commission of Canada: Interim Report* (Winnipeg, MB: Truth and Reconciliation Commission, 2012), 2.

25 "The decision…to establish the Commission as a federal government department—as opposed to a commission under the *Inquiries Act*—was made prior to the appointment of the current Commissioners, and is not one with which they would have concurred." TRC, *Interim Report*, 2. As a federal department, the TRC received some $60 million in federal funding. The sham nature of what it was actually intended to accomplish is perhaps best illustrated by the fact that in 2012 the commission had to sue to finally receive several million documents the government was required by the settlement agreement to provide. On funding, see Mahoney, "Residential School Settlement." On the withholding of documents from this supposedly official "fact-finding body," see Gloria Galloway, "Ottawa taken to court over release of residential school documents," *Globe and Mail* (December 3, 2013); "Ottawa ordered to provide all residential school documents: Truth and Reconciliation Commission took federal government to court over denial of millions of documents," *CBC News* (January 30, 2013); Gloria Galloway, "Commission to chart map of rocky road to reconciliation," *Globe and Mail* (May 31, 2015).

26 Truth and Reconciliation Canada, *Honouring the Truth, Reconciling for the Future: Summary of the Final Report of the Truth and Reconciliation Commission of Canada* (Ottawa: Truth and Reconciliation Commission of Canada, 2015).

27 TRC, *Final Report*, 183-91.

28 Canada is hardly alone in playing such games with the right to self-determination where Indigenous Peoples are concerned. See Ward Churchill, "A Travesty of a Mockery of a Sham: Colonialism as 'Self-Determination' in the UN Declaration on the Rights of Indigenous Peoples," *Griffith Law Review* Vol. 20, No. 3 (2011): 526-56.

29 TRC, *Final Report*, 190.

30 Newcomb, *Pagans*, 16. See for his discussion on the colonial body politic and the metaphors he reveals to the reader. This will be discussed in greater detail in chapter three.

31 "Physical genocide" and "biological genocide" are also mentioned on the first page of the summary, but there is no hint that either category might be in any sense applicable to the record of Canada's actions targeting Indigenous Peoples. In actuality, *both* are evident. On the biological mode, see, e.g., Stote, *Act of Genocide*. As for physical genocide, see, e.g., Tom Swanky, *The Great Darkening: The True Story of Canada's "War" of Extermination on the Pacific* (Burnaby, B.C.: Dragon Heart, 2012).

32 As Hitler put it, "He alone, who owns the youth, gains the future." Adolf Hitler, speech at the 1935 Nuremberg rally, quoted in Office of United States Chief of Counsel for Prosecution of Axis Criminality, *Nazi Conspiracy and Aggression*, 10 vols. (Washington, D.C.: U.S. Government Printing Office, 1946) Vol. 1, 320.

33 TRC, *Final Report*, 152-57.

34 Under the heading "Justice," the commissioners quite properly complain that there have been "fewer than fifty" criminal prosecutions of former residential school staff members resulting from the lodging of "nearly 38,000 claims of sexual predation and serious physical abuse" by the victims, and the RCMP's dismal investigative record on such matters. More importantly, however, they say nothing to suggest that Canada's policy of forcibly transferring Indigenous children to the facilities in question may have been a crime under international law, or that responsible officials should be prosecuted accordingly. TRC, *Final Report*, 166.

35 The reparations paid to Israel—which, unlike Indigenous Nations in Canada, had not even existed at the time the crime occurred—were *in addition to* compensation paid to individual survivors of the judeocide for their pain, suffering, and loss of property, income, and so on. Such property as was recoverable—real estate and works of art, as examples—was and is still being restored to the rightful owners or their heirs. See generally, Nicholas Balabkins, *West German Reparations to Israel* (New Brunswick, NJ: Rutgers University Press, 1971).

36 Arguably, what I've described in this paragraph is indicative of Indigenous thinking, per se. In other words, so far as I know, the formation of Indigenous knowledge is always "interdisciplinary"—not least because Indigenous knowledge systems are invariably relational, and therefore not be subdivided into "disciplines"—and designed to integrate or reject new information to the extent that it is consistent with what is already known of the whole. See Linda Tuhiwai Smith, *Decolonizing Methodologies: Research and Indigenous Peoples* (London: Zed Books, 1999), esp. 111-26; Donald L. Fixico, *The American Indian Mind in a Linear World: American Indian Studies and*

Traditional Knowledge (New York: Routledge, 2003), esp. 1-20, 41-61.

37 *Convention on the Prevention and Punishment of the Crime of Genocide,* 9 December 1948, 78 UNTS 277, (entered into force 12 January 1951, signed by Canada 28 November 1949, accession by Canada 3 September 1952).

38 See E. Brian Titley, *A Narrow Vision: Duncan Campbell Scott and the Administration of Indian Affairs in Canada* (Vancouver: University of British Columbia Press, 1986), 50.

39 Ibid.

40 Raphaël Lemkin, *Axis Rule in Occupied Europe: Laws of Occupation, Analysis of Government, Proposals for Redress* 2nd ed. (New Jersey: The Lawbook Exchange, Ltd., 2008), 79.

41 James Crawford, "Foreword" in Antony Anghie, *Imperialism, Sovereignty and the Making of International Law* (Cambridge England: Cambridge University Press, 2005), xi.

42 Anghie, Imperialism, 2.

43 Ibid.

44 Hirad Abtahi & Philippa Webb, *The Genocide Convention: The Travaux Préparatoires* (Leiden, Netherlands: Martinus Nijhoff Publishers, 2008) Vols. 1 & 2 The extensive two page volume details the discussion from the Draft Convention to the Sixth Committee; also see United Nations General Assembly, Two Hundred and Eighteenth Meeting, Draft Convention on the Crime of Genocide, U.N. Doc. E/794, E/794/Corr. 1 and E/AC. 27/1, (26 August 1948).

45 See Steven T. Newcomb, "The UN Declaration on the Rights of Indigenous Peoples and the Paradigm of Domination," *Griffiths Law Review*, Vol. 20, No. 3 (2011): 578-607 for his analysis on domination and dehumanization.

46 Anghie, *Imperialism*, at inside cover. Anghie explains this as "the project of governing non-European peoples."

47 Ibid., 29. Anghie explains "...the one distinction which Vitoria insists upon and which he elaborates in considerable detail is the distinction between the sovereign Spanish and the non-sovereign Indians. Vitoria bases his conclusion that the Indians are not sovereign on the simple assertion that they are pagans. In doing so he resorts to exactly the same crude reasoning which he had previously refuted when denying the validity of the Church's claim that the Indians lack rights under divine law because they are heathens."

48 U.N. Doc E/794, E/794/Corr. 1 and E/AC. 27/1, 713.

49 U.N. Doc E/794, E/794/Corr. 1 and E/AC. 27/1, 709.

50 U.N. Doc E/794, E/794/Corr. 1 and E/AC. 27/1, 710.

51 See Newcomb, *Pagans* for a review of his analysis on cognitive legal theory.

52 See Jennifer Senior, "In Conversation: Antonin Scalia," *New York Magazine* (October 6, 2013), http://nymag.com/news/features/antonin-scalia-2013-10/.

53 In 1941, "Winston Churchill called genocide 'the crime without a name.'" William A. Schabas, *Genocide in International Law: The Crime of Crimes,* 2nd ed.(Cambridge, UK: Cambridge University Press, 2009), 17; erroneously citing Leo Kuper, *Genocide: Its Political Use in the Twentieth Century* (New Haven, CT: Yale University Press, 1981), 12. Kuper mentions Churchill only once in his book, on page 21, and not in the manner Schabas indicates. The quote is nonetheless accurate, Churchill having used the phrase to describe what would soon be known as "genocide" during a radio broadcast on August 24, 1941. See Caroline Fournet, *The Crime of Destruction and the Law of Genocide: Their Impact on Collective Memory* (Burlington, VT: Ashgate, 2013), 3.

54 "The term '*jus cogens*' means 'compelling law' and, as such, a *jus cogens* norm holds the highest hierarchical position among all norms and principles. As a consequence of that standing, *jus cogens* norms are deemed to be 'peremptory' and non-derogable.... The legal literature discloses that the following international crimes are *jus cogens*: aggression, genocide, crimes against humanity, war crimes, piracy, slavery and slavery-related practices, and torture." M. Cherif Bassiouni, "International Crimes: *Jus Cogens* and *Obligatio Erga Omnes*," *Law and Contemporary Problems* 59, No. 4 (Autumn 1996): 67, 68; citing, among other sources, "Report of the International Law Commission on the work of its eighteenth session," in *Yearbook of the International Law Commission, 1966: Vol. 2* (New York: United Nations, 1967): 248; Draft Code of Crimes Against Peace and Security of Mankind: Titles and Articles on the Draft Code of Crimes Against Peace and Security of Mankind adopted by the International Law Commission on its Forty-Eighth Session (U.N. GAOR, 51st Sess., U.N. Doc. A/CN.4L.532 (1996), *revised by* U.N. Doc. A/CN.4L.532/Corr. 1 and U.N. Doc. A/CN.4L.532/Corr. 3; Crimes Against U.N. Personnel). The latter is included in M. Cherif Bassiouni, ed., *International Criminal Law Conventions and Their Penal Provisions* (Leiden: Martinus Nijhof, 1997), 230-241.

55 The phrase on quotes is appropriated from Roger Manvell and Heinrich Fraenkel's *The Incomparable Crime: Mass Extermination in the Twentieth Century: The Legacy of Guilt* (New York: G.P. Putnam's Sons, 1967). As a description of genocide, the main title is excellent, although the book itself is abysmal. Having gratuitously redefined genocide exclusively in terms of "the mass murder of a racial, national, political or religious group" on the first page, the authors spend the rest of the book representing even *that* exclusively in terms of the Nazi judeocide. No mention is made of the mass physical extermination of *any* other group during the first two-thirds of the twentieth century, although a number of similarly egregious examples—e.g., the Armenians at the hands of the Turks during World War I—were readily available. Even "the gipsies [*sic*]," who were subject to the

same decrees as Jews, and whose proportional extermination by the Nazis was equal to or greater than their Jewish counterparts, receive only a single passing mention (p. 110). In sum, *The Incomparable Crime* is a prime example of how scholarship has been used to obscure rather than reveal the realities of genocide. On the Nazi extermination of Gypsies (Romani), see Ian Hancock, "Responses to the Porrajmos: The Romani Holocaust," in Alan S. Rosenbaum, ed., *Is the Holocaust Unique? Perspectives on Comparative Genocide, 2nd ed.* (Boulder, CO: Westview Press, 2001), 69-95. Also see Vahakn N. Dadrian, *A History of the Armenian Genocide: Ethnic Conflict from the Balkans to Anatolia to the Caucasus* (Providence, R.I.: Berghahn, 1995).

56 Robert Jay Lifton and Eric Markusen, *The Genocidal Mentality: Nazi Holocaust and Nuclear Threat* (New York: Basic Books, 1990). The phrase is taken from the cover of their book.

57 Jack D. Forbes, *Columbus and Other Cannibals: The Wétiko Disease of Exploitation, Imperialism, and Terrorism, rev. ed.* (New York: Seven Stories Press, 2008). For Churchill's use of the term "dis-ease," see, e.g., "I Am Indigenist: Notes on the Ideology of the Fourth World," in his *Acts of Rebellion: The Ward Churchill Reader* (New York: Routledge, 2003), 294.

58 The phrase quoted is the subtitle of William Schabas' *Genocide in International Law*. Although there are sometimes problems with his work—see, e.g., note 55—one of which will be discussed in Chapter 1, Schabas is generally considered to be among the preeminent scholars on the topic.

59 Although the term "[a]uto-genocide has been defined…as 'mass killing of members of the group to which the perpetrators belong'" and "applied primarily to the Cambodian case" in which the Khmer Rouge government exterminated up to a quarter of the country's population during the late 1970s, it should be borne in mind that genocide does not equate simply to mass murder. The concept is far less "curious" when Lemkin's far broader definition is applied, or even the full range of criteria set forth in the Genocide Convention. For the passages quoted, see Martin Shaw, *What is Genocide?* 2nd ed. (Cambridge, UK: Polity Press, 2015), 97-98. On the Khmer Rouge extermination campaign, see generally, Ben Kiernan, *The Pol Pot Regime: Race, Power, and Genocide in Cambodia, 1975-79* 3rd ed. (New Haven, CT: Yale University Press, 2008).

60 As is stated in Common Article 1(1) of the International Covenant on Economic, Social and Cultural Rights (U.N.G.A. Res. 2200 (XXI), 21 U.N. GAOR, Supp. (No. 16) 49, U.N. Doc. A/6316 (1967)) and the International Covenant on Civil and Political Rights (U.N.G.A. Res. 2200 (XXI), 21 U.N. GAOR, Supp. (No. 16) 52, U.N. Doc. A/6316 (1967)), "All peoples have the right to self-determination. By virtue of that right they freely determine their political status and freely pursue their economic, social and cultural development." That this applies to

Indigenous Peoples no less than any others is affirmed in Article 3 of the United Nations Declaration on the Rights of Indigenous Peoples (U.N.G.A. Res. 61/295, Supp. 53, U.N. Doc. A/61/67 and Add. 1 (2007)).

61 While we hardly needed a U.N. declaration to understand this, it's nonetheless nice to see it finally set forth in black letter form, and to thus be able to quote it.

62 One reason I wish to emphasize the point is that Canada, along with several other states—the U.S., Australian, and New Zealand settler-states in particular—spent a quarter-century insisting that Indigenous Peoples should be referred to as "minorities" or "populations" rather than "Peoples" during the drafting process of the U.N. declaration on our rights. Their objective was specifically to avert formal recognition of our right to self-determination, if we were termed "Peoples". See Churchill, "A Travesty of a Mockery of a Sham," 540-46.

63 *Shoah* is a Hebrew word meaning "calamity" or "catastrophe," employed to describe the judeocide since the early 1940s. It has seen increasing usage over the past thirty years as a substitute for—or replacement of—"Holocaust" as a preferred term of reference, especially in Israel. See Jessica Setbon, "'Who Beat My Father'? Issues of Terminology and Translation in Teaching the Holocaust," workshop presentation during the Fifth International Conference on Teaching the Holocaust to Future Generations, Yad Vashem, Jerusalem (June 29, 2006) [pdf online].

64 See Michael Berenbaum, ed., *A Mosaic of Victims: Non-Jews Persecuted and Murdered by the Nazis* (New York: New York University Press, 1990).Also see generally, Richard C. Lukas, *Forgotten Holocaust: The Poles Under German Occupation, 1939-1944* (New York: Hippocrene Books, 1986). Stephen G. Fritz, *Ostkreig: Hitler's War of Extermination in the East* (Lexington: University Press of Kentucky, 2011).

65 See Hancock, "Responses to the *Parrajmos*," 73-75. Also see Michael Stewart, "The 'Gypsy Problem': An Invisible Genocide," in René Lemarchand, ed., *Forgotten Genocides: Oblivion, Denial, Memory* (Philadelphia: University of Pennsylvania Press, 2011), 137-56. It should be noted that *Parrajmos* is a Romani word meaning "devouring," used to connote what they suffered at the hands of the Nazis.

66 Newcomb, *Pagans*, 131; see esp. Newcomb, "Paradigm of Domination"579.

67 Apart from its degrading connotations in the colonial discourse, the word carries significant negative legal implications. See Ward Churchill, "Naming Our Destiny: Toward a Language of American Indian Liberation," in his *Indians Are Us? Culture and Genocide in Native North America* (Toronto: Between the Lines, 1994), 291-357.

68 I am familiar with the idea that the term "Indian," as applied to the Indigenous Peoples of this hemisphere, arose not from Christopher Columbus' poor sense of geography, but rather from his description of us as being "*una gente in Dios*" ("a people in God"). I am also aware that a number of people for whom I hold the deepest respect embrace the term. This obviously includes Ward Churchill—as is readily evidenced by the title of his book *Indians Are Us?*—and the entire membership of the American Indian Movement. For the theory regarding Columbus' terminology, see Peter Matthiessen, *Indian Country* (New York: Viking Press, 1984), 3.

69 No less luminary a figure in anthropology than Claude Levy-Strauss characterized the discipline as "the handmaiden of colonialism." This is quoted in Edward W. Said, *Culture and Imperialism* (New York: Alfred A. Knopf, 1993), 152. For further background, see Kathleen Gough, "Anthropology and Imperialism," *Monthly Review* 19, No. 11 (November 1968): 12-27; Diane Lewis, "Anthropology and Colonialism," *Current Anthropology* 14, No. 5 (December 1973): 581-602.

70 I might of course as easily use the *Anishinaabeg* (Ojibwe) word *shognosh*, the Lakota ("Sioux") word *wasi'chu*, and so on. It appears that all Indigenous languages now include a term for white settlers. The *Kanaka Maoli* (Native Hawaiian) word *haoli*, is one example, the Maori word *paheka* is another.

71 This criticism is actually a smear. It involves a "radical alteration in the role of evidence" in scholarship, allowing anyone making comparisons to or even "asking critical questions" about the genocidal aspects of Nazi policy to be "accused of diminishing and disrespecting the memory of the victims of the Holocaust," a charge that is then offered "as proof of [the 'offender's'] anti-Semitism and Holocaust denial." Dagmar Barnouw, *The War in the Empty Air: Victims, Perpetrators, and Postwar Germans* (Bloomington: Indiana University Press, 2005), 66.

72 See note 55, above. For a powerful rejoinder to this kind of "scholarship," see Lillian Friedberg, "Dare to Compare: Americanizing the Holocaust," *American Indian Quarterly* 24, No. 2 (Fall 2000): 353-80.

73 Although there are any number of articles and books in which this is argued, by far the most exhaustive effort to prove that the "phenomenological uniqueness" of the Nazi judeocide is a 720-page tome by Steven T. Katz, *The Holocaust in Historical Context, Volume 1: The Holocaust and Mass Death before the Modern Age* (New York: Oxford University Press, 1994). Highly-touted for "scholarly rigor" when it was released, the book was soon revealed to be so riddled with logical inconsistencies and factual distortions that it was never reprinted. Nor have the second or third volumes of his announced trilogy ever been published.

74 This can often be quite vicious. One of the more prominent academics voicing this view is Deborah Lipstadt, professor of Judaic Studies at Emory University, who "regards as her enemy anyone who expresses doubt about the utter singularity in all of human history of Jewish suffering at the hands of the Nazis, an enemy situated intellectually and ideologically at one place or another along a posited anti-semitic continuum stretching from those she calls Holocaust 'deniers' to those she labels Holocaust 'relativists' ... For, to Lipstadt, even someone who has no doubt regarding the ghastly horrors of Jewish suffering and death under Hitler—but who has the temerity to dissent from her insistence regarding the unquestionable uniqueness of the Jewish experience—is, in her phrase, merely a not yet denier.... In short, if you disagree with Deborah Lipstadt that the Jewish suffering in the Holocaust was unique, you are, by definition...a crypto-Nazi." David E. Stannard, "Uniqueness as Denial: The Politics of Holocaust Scholarship," in Rosenbaum, *Is the Holocaust Unique?,* 250;

75 Stannard, "Uniqueness as Denial," 245-281.

76 Nicholas Flood Davin, "Report on Industrial Schools for Indians and Half-Breeds" (March 14, 1879), in Sir John A. McDonald Papers, Vol. 91 (Ottawa: National Archives of Canada, Doc. N.A.C. MG 26A), 35428-45. Cited and discussed in John S. Milloy, *A National Crime: The Canadian Government and the Residential School System 1879-1986* (Winnipeg: University of Manitoba Press, 1999), xiv-xv, 7-8, 23-26, 31-32, 51; Also see J.R. Miller, *Shingwauk's Vision: A History of Native Residential Schools* (Toronto: University of Toronto Press, 1996), 101-03. On the U.S. prototype, see generally, David Wallace Adams, *Education for Extinction: American Indians and the Boarding School Experience, 1875-1928* (Lawrence: University Press of Kansas, 1995).

77 *Canada, House of Commons Debates,* 5th Parliament, 1st Session, No 14 (9 May 1883) at 1101 (Hon. John A. MacDonald). Also see the chapter titled "Residential Schools, "Canada, Royal Commission on Aboriginal Peoples, "Chapter 10: Residential Schools," *Looking Forward, Looking Back,* vol 5 (Ottawa: Canada Communication Group, 1996), 312.

Chapter One

1 Ward Churchill, "Introduction: That Little Matter of Genocide: Revisited Contours of a Hidden Holocaust in Native North America" Churchill, *Kill the Indian Save the Man: The Genocidal Impact of American Indian Residential Schools* (San Francisco: City Lights Books, 2004), xliii. The phrase is from the epigraph of Churchill's essay.

2 Raphaël Lemkin, *Axis Rule in Occupied Europe: Laws of Occupation,*

Analysis of Government, Proposals for Redress, 2nd ed. (Clark, NJ: The Lawbook Exchange, 2008).

3 *Convention on the Prevention and Punishment of the Crime of Genocide,* December 9, 1948, 78 U.N.T.S. 277 [Genocide Convention]; "[t]he United Nations General Assembly adopted the Genocide Convention on December 9, 1948, and the Convention entered into force on January 12, 1951. Canada joined the treaty, signing the Convention on November 28, 1949, and subsequently ratifying it on September 3, 1952." As is observed by Jayme Herschkopf and Julie Hunter of a coauthored study prepared for the Truth and Reconciliation Commission under the title *Genocide Reinterpreted: An Analysis of the Genocide Convention's Potential Application to Canada's Indian Residential School System* (New Haven, CT: Allard K. Lowenstein International Human Rights Clinic, Yale University College of Law, April 2011).

4 Lemkin "[i]nitiated the [w]orld movement to [o]utlaw [g]enocide." William A. Schabas, *Genocide in International Law: The Crime of Crimes,* 2nd ed.(Cambridge, UK: Cambridge University Press, 2009), 29. Also see "'Father' of Genocide Convention Nominated for Nobel Prize," *Jewish Telegraphic Agency* March 10, 1952, https://archive.jta.org/1952/03/10/archive/father-of-genocide-convention-nominated-for-nobel-prize.

5 John Cooper, *Raphael Lemkin and the Struggle for the Genocide Convention* (New York: Palgrave Macmillan: 2008), 5. Also see Roland Chrisjohn et al., "Genocide and Indian Residential Schooling: The Past is Present," in *Canada and International Humanitarian Law: Peacekeeping and War Crimes in the Modern Era*, eds. Richard Wiggers and Ann Griffiths, (Halifax, NS: Dalhousie University Centre for Foreign Policy Studies, 2002); In "Forbidding the 'G-Word': Holocaust Denial as Judicial Doctrine in Canada," Ward Churchill examines the U.S. and Canadian roles in deleting entire provisions of the Draft Convention on Genocide; see his *Perversions of Justice: Indigenous Peoples and Angloamerican Law* (San Francisco: City Lights Books, 2003), 249-251 Also see Robert Davis and Mark Zannis, *The Genocide Machine in Canada* (Montréal: Black Rose Books, 1973), 15-27.

6 Lemkin, *Axis Rule*, 79.

7 Samantha Power, Introduction to the First Edition of *Axis Rule in Occupied Europe: Laws of Occupation, Analysis of Government, Proposals for Redress,* by Raphaël Lemkin, 2nd ed. (Clark, NJ: The Lawbook Exchange, 2008), xx; Also see generally Power's "*A Problem From Hell" America and the Age of Genocide* (New York: Harper Perennial, 2002) and Ward Churchill, *A Little Matter of Genocide: Holocaust and Denial in the Americas 1492 to the Present* (Winnipeg: Arbiter Ring, 1998).

8 Schabas, *Genocide,* 30.

9 See Lemkin, *Axis Rule*, 79-95; Schabas, *Genocide*, 30.

10 Ibid, 79.

11 Ibid.

12 Ibid, Lemkin in his title articulates, "Genocide —A New Term and Conception for Destruction of *Nations*" (Emphasis Added).

13 Ibid.

14 Schabas, "Introduction to the Second Edition," in Lemkin, *Axis Rule*, x.

15 Lemkin refers to the Nazi régime's policies as "designed to destroy nations according to a previously prepared plan." Lemkin, *Axis Rule*, 81, 79, and ix.

16 Churchill, *Kill the Indian*, 4.

17 See chapter two, end note 291 for the reference to "domination and dehumanization". The concepts are based on Steven Newcomb's scholarship.

18 Ibid, 3; also see Power, "Introduction to the First Edition" xxi.

19 Ibid; also see Lemkin, *Axis Rule*, 79.

20 Ibid, 4

21 Lemkin, *Axis Rule*, 79.

22 Ibid.

23 Ibid, 80.

24 Power, *Problem from Hell*, 43

25 See Churchill, "Forbidding the 'G-Word,'" 249.

26 Schabas, "Introduction to the Second Edition," x.

27 Ibid.

28 See E. Brian Titley, *A Narrow Vision: Duncan Campbell Scott and the Administration of Indian Affairs in Canada* (Vancouver: University of British Columbia Press, 1986), 50. Duncan Campbell Scott refers to the "body politic". Steven T. Newcomb, *Pagans in the Promised Land Decoding the Doctrine of Christian Discovery* (Golden, CO: Fulcrum, 2008). At pages 15-16 Newcomb explains that the 'body politic' represents the colonial body that assimilates, swallows, and devours original nations/land into its ravenous hungry body.

29 Cooper, *Lemkin*, 56.

30 Timothy Snyder, *Bloodlands: Europe Between Hitler and Stalin* (New York: Basic Books, 2010), 160. Also see John Toland, *Adolf Hitler* (Garden State, NY: Doubleday,1976), 702; Norman Rich, *Hitler's War Aims: Ideology, The Nazi State, and the Course of Expansion* (New York: W.W. Norton, 1973), 8; and Churchill, *A Little Matter of Genocide*, for comparisons of the Nazi invasion and destruction in Eastern Europe to that of Indigenous Peoples in North America.

31 Synder, *Bloodlands*, 160.

32 Cooper, *Lemkin*, 56.

33 Lemkin, *Axis Rule*, ix.

34 Schabas, "Introduction to the Second Edition," v.

35 Lemkin, *Axis Rule*, ix.

36 Ibid, ix.

37 Ibid, xi-xii.

38 Mathew Lippman, "Genocide", vol. 1 of *International Criminal Law*

Source, Subjects, and Contents, ed. M. Cherif Bassiouni, 3rd ed. (Leiden: Martinus Nijhoff, 2008), 404.

39 Ibid .

40 United Nations Codification Division, "Economic and Social Council resolution 47 (IV) of 28 March 1947 (Crime of genocide) (E/437 (E/325), Documents", accessed on 28 December 2017 from the website of the United Nations Audiovisual Library of International Law, http://www.un.org/law/avl.

41 United Nations Economic and Social Council, Summary Record of the Seventieth Meeting, U.N. Doc. E/421 (15 March 1947) [U.N. Doc. E/421], reprinted in Hirad Abtahi and Philippa Webb, *The Genocide Convention: The Travaux Préparatoires* Vol. One, (Leiden: Martinus Nijhoff, 2008) [Travaux], 39-40.

42 See William A. Schabas, "Convention for the Prevention and Punishment of the Crime of Genocide," accessed on 28 December 2017 from the website of the United Nations Audiovisual Library of International Law, http://www.un.org/law/avl.

43 United Nations Economic and Social Council, Draft Convention on the Crime of Genocide, Note by the Secretary General, U.N. Doc. E/476 (18 July 1947), reprinted in Abtahi and Webb, *Travaux*, 283.

44 Schabas, Convention for the Prevention and Punishment of the Crime of Genocide, 1.

45 United Nations Economic and Social Council, Draft Convention on the Crime of Genocide, U.N. Doc. E/447 (26 June 1947) [U.N. Doc E/447], reprinted in Abtahi and Webb, *Travaux*, 209.

46 Churchill, *Kill the Indian*, 5.

47 See esp., United Nations General Assembly, Draft Convention on the Crime of Genocide, U.N. Doc. A/362, (25 August 1947), reprinted in Abtahi and Webb, *Travaux*, 333-334. See for a review of the Draft Convention on Genocide on the Crime of Genocide.

48 See Davis and Zannis, *Genocide Machine*, 19-20; also see Churchill, *Perversions of Justice*, 250.

49 U.N. Doc E/447, reprinted in Abtahi and Webb, *Travaux*, 234. Also see Cooper, *Lemkin*, 90-91. He explains that, "While Professors De Vabres and Pella accepted that there was physical and biological genocide, they were more skeptical about the concept of cultural genocide, stating that the General Assembly should decide this point."

50 Lemkin explained that "cultural genocide was much more than just a policy of forced assimilation by moderate coercion – involving for example, prohibition of the opening of schools for teaching the language of the group concerned, of the publication of newspapers printed in that language, of the use of that language in official documents and in court, and so on. It was a policy which by drastic methods, aimed at the rapid and complete disappearance of the cultural, moral and religious life of a group of human beings." U.N. Doc E/447, reprinted in Abtahi and Webb, *Travaux*, 234-35.

51 "[A]lmost everyone wanted to ignore [his] definition of 'genocide.'" Davis and Zannis, *Genocide Machine*, 24.

52 Chrisjohn *et al.*, "Past is Present," 234. Herschkopf and Hunter *Genocide Reinterpreted,* 11-14; Davis and Zannis, *Genocide Machine*, 15-27; Churchill, "Forbidding the 'G-Word,'" 249-51.

53 United Nations General Assembly, Committee on the Progressive Development of International Law and its Codification: Draft Convention for the Prevention and Punishment of Genocide, U.N. Doc. A/AC. 10/42/Add.1 (10 June 1947), reprinted in Abtahi and Webb, *Travaux*, 133.

54 United Nations Economic and Social Council, Two Hundred and Eighteenth Meeting, U.N. Doc. E/SR.218 (26 August 1948), reprinted in Abtahi and Webb, *Travaux,* 1224.

55 Ibid, 1225.

56 Ibid.

57 Davis and Zannis, *Genocide Machine*, 20.

58 Herschkopf and Hunter, *Genocide Reinterpreted*, 11-14.

59 Ibid, 11.

60 Ibid.

61 United Nations General Assembly, Eighty Third Meeting, Sixth Committee, U.N. Doc. A/C.6/SR.83 (25 October 1948) [U.N. Doc. A/C.6/SR.83], reprinted in Abtahi and Webb, *Travaux*, 1509-1510.

62 Sharon Helen Venne, "The Creator Knows Their Lies and So Should We: Ward Churchill's Pursuit of Juridical Truth," introduction to Churchill, *Perversions of Justice*, xiii.

63 The seminal work using the term "settler" in the sense it is employed herein, is Grenfell Price, *White Settlers and Native Peoples: An Historical Study of Racial Contacts between English Speaking Whites and Aboriginal Peoples in the United States, Canada, Australia, and New Zealand* (Cambridge: Cambridge University Press, 1950).

64 U.N. Doc. A/C.6/SR.83, reprinted in Abtahi and Webb, *Travaux*, 1510.

65 Ibid.

66 Mathew Lippman, "The Global Politics of Genocide Denial" in *United Nations, Commemorating the 60th Anniversary of the Genocide Convention Conference* (The Hague, December 11, 2008), 7.

67 United Nations General Assembly, Sixty-Fourth Meeting, Sixth Committee, U.N. Doc. A/C.6/SR.64 (1 October 1948), reprinted in Abtahi and Webb, *Travaux*, 1301.

68 United Nations General Assembly, Sixty-Fifth Meeting, Sixth Committee, U.N. Doc. A/C.6/SR.65 (2 October 1948) [U.N. Doc. A/C.6/SR.65], reprinted in Abtahi and Webb, *Travaux*, 1312.

69 United Nations Economic and Social Council, Ad Hoc Committee on Genocide Commentary on Articles Adopted by the Committee (U.N. Doc. E/AC. 25/W.1 (26 April 1948)), reprinted in Abtahi and Webb, *Travaux*, 982.

70 Ibid.

71 Davis and Zannis, *Genocide Machine*, 20; citing/quoting the United Nations Economic and Social Council, (U.N. Doc. E/AC. 25/S.R. 1-28).
72 U.N. Doc. A/C.6/SR.83, reprinted in Abtahi and Webb, 1510.
73 Churchill, *Kill the Indian*, 1-3.
74 See, e.g., Michael A. McDonnell and A. Dirk Moses, "Raphael Lemkin as Historian of Genocide in the Americas," *Journal of Genocide Research* 7, No. 4 (December 2005): 501-529, doi: 10.1080/14623520500349951. Also see Colin Tatz, *With Intent to Destroy Reflecting on Genocide* (New York: Verso, 2003) for an example of the genocide denial.
75 Chrisjohn *et al.*, "Past is Present," 234.
76 Ibid.
77 Davis and Zannis, *Genocide Machine*, 22; This citation accrues from Canada, Department of External Affairs, *Canada and the United Nations Report on the United Nations* (Ottawa: 1948), 191; Also see Chrisjohn *et al.*, "Past is Present," 234.
78 *Canada and the United Nations*, 191.
79 U.N. Doc. A/C.6/SR.83, reprinted in Abtahi and Webb, *Travaux*, 1509.
80 Ibid., 1510.
81 Ibid.
82 United Nations General Assembly, Sixty Third Meeting, Sixth Committee, U.N. Doc. A/C.6/SR. 63 (30 September 1948), reprinted in Abtahi and Webb, *Travaux*, 1296.
83 Ibid, 1297.
84 Ibid, 1296; Canada still refuses to condemn Nazism, see http://rabble.ca/blogs/bloggers/roger-annis/2015/11/canada-votes-no-on-un-resolution-condemning-racism-and-neo-Nazism
85 Ibid.
86 Ibid, 1295-97.
87 U.N. Doc. A/C.6/SR.65, reprinted in Abtahi and Webb, *Travaux*, 1318.
88 Ibid, 1319.
89 Ibid.
90 U.N. Doc. A/C.6/SR.83, reprinted in Abtahi and Webb, *Travaux*, 1518.
91 United Nations General Assembly, Eighty-First Meeting, Sixth Committee, U.N. Doc. A/C.6/SR.81 (22 October 1948), reprinted in Abtahi and Webb, *Travaux*, 1479.
92 United Nations General Assembly, Eighty-Second Meeting, Sixth Committee, U.N. Doc. A/C.6/SR.82 (23 October 1948), reprinted in Abtahi and Webb, *Travaux*, 1492.
93 Ibid, 1493.
94 Ibid.
95 Ibid, 1494.
96 Ibid, 1495.
97 U.N. Doc. A/C.6/SR.83, reprinted in Abtahi and Webb, *Travaux*, 1504.
98 Ibid.

99 Churchill, "Forbidding the 'G-Word,'" 250.

100 Herschkopf and Hunter, *Genocide Reinterpreted*, 16.

101 Ibid, 13-14.

102 Schabas, *Genocide*, 172. For a useful outline of the elements of the offence to be proven, see Kurt Mundorff, "Other Peoples' Children: A Textual and Contextual Interpretation of the Genocide Convention, Article 2 (e)," *Harvard International Law Journal* 50, No. 1 (Winter 2009): 84-103.

103 Ibid.

104 John Quigley, "States as Perpetrators of Genocide" in *The Genocide Convention: An International Law Analysis* (Burlington, VT: Ashgate, 2006), 236

105 *Case Concerning the Application of the Convention on the Prevention and Punishment of the Crime of Genocide (Bosnia and Herzegovina v. Serbia and Montenegro)* [2007] ICJ Rep. 43 at 167 [hereinafter Bosnia and Serbia].

106 Genocide Convention, Article III.

107 Schabas, *Genocide*, 499.

108 Genocide Convention, Article II.

109 Schabas, *Genocide*, 176.

110 Ibid, 177.

111 Ibid. Schabas cites *Prosecutor v. Zejnil Delalić,* (Case No. IT-96-21-T), Judgment (16 November 1998) para. 424 (International Criminal Tribunal for the former Yugoslavia, Trial Chamber).

112 Ibid, 182.

113 Ibid, "see esp. *Attorney-General of Israel v. Eichmann* (1968) 36 ILR 5 at 238 (District Court, Jerusalem) [hereinafter Eichmann].

114 *Prosecutor v. Jean-Paul Akayesu,* (Case No. ICTR-96-4-T), Judgment (2 September 1998) paras 503-504 (International Criminal Tribunal for Rwanda, Trial Chamber) [hereinafter Akayesu].

115 *Akayesu*, paras 706; Also see para 707, 711, 712. MacDonald and Hudson list the acts as consisting only of bodily harm. However, paras 707 and 712 of the opinion acknowledge *both* bodily and mental harm. See Macdonald and Hudson, "Genocide Question," 438-39.

116 *Prosecutor v. Milomir Stakić,* (Case No. IT-97-24-T), Judgment (31 July 2003) para 516 (International Criminal Tribunal for the former Yugoslavia, Trial Chamber).

117 See Schabas, *Genocide*, 180-182.

118 Schabas, *Genocide*, 183. He cites the cases of *Krajišnik* and *Krstić* for this determination.

119 *Prosecutor v. Momčilo Krajišnik,* (Case No. IT-00-39-T), Judgment (27 September 2006) para 862 (International Criminal Tribunal for the former Yugoslavia, Trial Chamber) [hereinafter *Krajišnik*].

120 *Prosecutor v. Radislav Krstic,* (Case No. IT-98-33-T), Judgment (2 August 2001) para 513(International Criminal Tribunal for the former

Yugoslavia, Trial Chamber) [hereinafter *Krstic*].

121 *Prosecutor v.Clément Kayishema et al.*, (Case No. ICTR-95-1-T), Judgment (21 May 1999) para 109 (International Criminal Tribunal for Rwanda, Trial Chamber) [hereinafter Kayishema].

122 *Kayishema*, para 108. The court cites *Akayesu*, paras 706-707 and 711-712, but the chamber did not make the distinction in the paragraph cited by the chamber in *Kayishema*.

123 *Akayesu*, paras. 706 -707 and 711-712.

124 *Prosecutor v. Vidoje Blagojević*, (Case No. IT-02-60-T), Judgment (17January 2005) para 647 (International Criminal Tribunal for the former Yugoslavia, Trial Chamber).

125 *Akayesu*, para 731.

126 Ibid.

127 Ibid.

128 Ibid, para 687.

129 Ibid, para 688.

130 Ibid.

131 Ibid.

132 Schabas, *Genocide*, 187.

133 *Krstic*, para. 513.

134 See U.N. Doc. A/C.6/SR.83, reprinted in Abtahi and Webb, *Travaux*, 1504.

135 Schabas, *Genocide*, 202.

136 Ibid, 203 (citing the Elements of Crimes of the International Criminal Court for this definition).

137 Mundorff, "Other Peoples' Children," 96.

138 *Akayesu*, para. 509; originally cited in Mundorff, "Other Peoples' Children," 96.

139 Ibid. He explains that the standard was quite broad until the "ICJ announced a much narrower standard."

140 Ibid, citing *Bosnia v. Serbia*, para. 186.

141 Mundorff, "Other Peoples' Children," 91.

142 Ibid; Mundorff citing Claus Kreβ, "The Crime of Genocide under International Law," *International Criminal Law Review* 6, (2006): 484.

143 Mundorff, "Other Peoples' Children," 91.

144 Australia, Commonwealth, Human Rights and Equal Opportunity Commission, *Bringing Them Home: Report of the National Inquiry into the Separation of Aboriginal and Torres Strait Islander Children from Their Families* (Sydney: Sterling Press, 1997), 275.

145 Cited from Schabas, *Genocide*, 205; See esp. *Bringing Them Home*, 270-75.

146 *Bringing Them Home*, 272-73.

147 Schabas, *Genocide*, 216.

148 Cited from Schabas, *Genocide*, 242; see esp., Article 30 of the Rome Statute of the International Criminal Court, (2187 U.N.T.S. 90 (2002)).

149 Rome Statute, Article 30(3); also cited in Schabas, *Genocide*, 242.
150 Schabas, *Genocide*, 242.
151 Ibid, p. 247; Citing *Prosecutor v. Radovan Karadžić et al.* (Case No. IT-95-5-R61, IT-95-18-R61), Review of the Indictments Pursuant to Rule 61 of the Rules of Procedure and Evidence (11 July 1996) para 94 (International Criminal Tribunal for the former Yugoslavia, Trial Chamber) [hereinafter *Karadžić*].
152 Schabas, *Genocide*, 248.
153 See *Akayesu*, para 524 in which the ICTR cites the ICTY in *Karadžić*, para 94.
154 Schabas, *Genocide*, 260-61; Citing *Bosnia v. Serbia*, para 187.
155 John Quigley, personal communication, September 1, 2017; See also Quigley, *Genocide Convention*, 116-119.
156 Mundorff, "Other Peoples' Children," 101. He writes, "[s]pecific intent in the United States may differ significantly from specific intent in Britain" so his suggestion is to abandon the high standard.
157 Schabas, *Genocide*, 260.
158 Kai Ambos, "What does 'intent to destroy' mean in genocide?" *International Review of the Red Cross* 91, No. 876 (December 2009): 833, doi: 10.1017/S1816383110000056.
159 Quigley refers to the two levels on intent in this manner. On the strict standard of intent, Quigley is concerned "with the use of 'specific' in that it imposes too high an intent requirement with respect to the further intent, which involves intent to destroy a group." Quigley, personal communication; See also Quigley, *Genocide Convention*, 90-136.
160 Schabas, *Genocide*, 270-287.
161 Schabas, *Genocide*, 277.
162 *Akayesu*, paras 497, 498.
163 Ibid, paras 523, 728. Also see Schabas, *Genocide*, 262.
164 Mundorff, "Other Peoples' Children," p. 98; Citing the following at note 214: "*Prosecutor v. Bagilishema* Case No. ICTR-95-1A-T, Judgment 55 (June 7, 2001); *Prosecutor v. Blagojević & Jokić* Case No. IT-02-60-T, Judgment 655-56 (Jan. 17, 2005); Prosecutor v. Brdanin, Case No. IT-99-36-T, Judgment 695 (Sept. 1, 2004); *Prosecutor v. Jelisić* Case No. IT-95-10-A, Judgment 45-46 (July 5, 2001); *Prosecutor v. Rutaganda* Case No. ICTR-96-3-T, Judgment 59 (Dec. 6, 1999); *Prosecutor* v. *Kayishema* Case No. ICTR-95-1-T, Judgment, 91 (May 21, 1999); *Prosecutor v. Stakić* Case No. IT-97-24-T, Judgment 520 (July 31, 2003)."
165 *Kayishema*, para 93.
166 Quigley, *Genocide Convention*, 10.
167 Ibid., 107. This phrase is taken from the subtitle.
168 Ibid; Also see *Akayesu*, paras 520, 521.
169 *Akayesu*, para. 521.
170 *Akayesu*, para. 731.

171 *Krstić*, para. 590.
172 *Akayesu*, para. 523.
173 *Karadzić*, para 95.
174 *Akayesu* para. 524. Citing *Karadzić,* para. 95.
175 *Karadzić*, para. 94.
176 *Akayesu*, para. 728.
177 Ibid, para. 730.
178 Ibid, para. 731.
179 Ibid.
180 Ibid.
181 Schabas, *Genocide*, 188.
182 Mundorff, "Other Peoples' Children," 84-110; Mundorff refers to much academic debate in this section and it will not be elaborated on as this analysis requires only the *actus reus* and the *mens rea* elements to be shown, 93-99.
183 Ibid., 84.
184 Ibid.
185 Mathew Lippman explains that "[t]he debate marked one of the first expressions of an anti-colonial movement among countries in the developing world. Former colonial possessions drew a parallel between the Holocaust and their own exploitation and suffering at the hands of a European country" in his "Development and Drafting of the 1948 Convention and Punishment of the Crime of Genocide: The Politics of Genocide Denial" in *United Nations, Commemorating the 60th Anniversary of the Genocide Convention Conference* (The Hague, December 11, 2008), 6.
186 See especially Newcomb, *Pagans*; More recently, Newcomb, together with Birgil Kills Straight, has described how law and language continue to serve both as protocols and as tools of domination; see their coauthored position paper, "The Doctrine of Discovery and the Protocol of Domination: A Short Essay for the North American Indigenous Caucus Preparatory Meeting for the UN Permanent Forum on Indigenous Issues" (San Diego: Indigenous Law Institute, 2012), 1-8. Martti Koskenniemi advances similar analyses in his *The Gentle Civilizer of Nations: The Rise and Fall of International Law 1870-1960* (Cambridge, UK: Cambridge University Press, 2001), as does Antony Anghie in his magisterial *Imperialism, Sovereignty and the Making of International Law* (Cambridge, UK Cambridge University Press, 2005). Another scholar embracing the view that various aspects of international law have been evolved as a means by which to dominate Indigenous Nations is Ward Churchill. See, as examples, his *Since Predator Came: Notes on the Struggle for American Indian Liberation* (Colorado: Aigis, 1995) and *Struggle for the Land: Native North American Resistance to Genocide, Ecocide, and Colonization* (Winnipeg: Arbeiter Ring, 1999).
187 See Newcomb, *Pagans*.

188 Steven T. Newcomb, "The UN Declaration on the Rights of Indigenous Peoples and the Paradigm of Domination," *Griffith Law Review* 20, No. 3 (2011), 580.

189 Sharon H. Venne, *Our Elders Understand our Rights: Evolving International Law Regarding Indigenous Rights* (Penticton, B.C.: Theytus Books, 1998), 13.

190 Anghie, *Imperialism*, 193.

191 Churchill, *Kill the Indian,* 1. In their article, "Raphael Lemkin as Historian of Genocide in the Americas," Michael A. McDonnell and A. Dirk Moses provide a classic example of exactly this sort of sophistry.

192 Koskenniemi, *Gentle Civilizer,* 106.

193 *Webster's Third New International Dictionary of the English Language Unabridged, sub verbo* "civilization." Cited from Newcomb, "Paradigm of Domination," 581.

194 "Koskenniemi, *Gentle Civilizer,* 106."

195 *Delgamuukw v. British Columbia,* (1991) 79 DLR (4th) 185 at 208.

196 See Ian Mulgrew, "Ian Mulgrew: Busted! Begbie decision, Grand Chief cast pall over top judges' McEachern move" *Vancouver Sun,* June 5, 2017, http://vancouversun.com/opinion/columnists/ian-mulgrew-busted-begbie-decision-grand-chief-cast-pall-over-top-judges-mceachern-move. Mulgrew in critical response to the honoring of the late McEachern's by the law society writes, "In his infamous 1991 decision, *Delgamuukw v B.C.,*, McEachern described the life of First Nations before colonization as 'nasty, brutish, and short' because they had 'no written language, no horses or wheeled vehicles …' His rhetoric reduced elders to tears. He was cribbing from Thomas Hobbes, the 17th-century English philosopher who argued in his 1651 magnum opus Leviathan that the lack of a social contract and the rule of law kept men in 'continual fear and danger of violent death, and the life of man, solitary, poor, nasty, brutish, and short.' McEachern's entire book-length decision reeked of the presumption of European superiority, the lynchpin of colonial cruelties that continues to have ill repercussions for First Nations. He found First Nations' 'oral tradition, did not conform to juridical definitions of truth,' adding he was 'unable to accept adaawk, kungax and oral traditions as reliable bases for detailed history …' McEachern concluded the aboriginal rights of the Gitxsan and the Wet'suwet'en existed only at the 'pleasure of the Crown.'

197 See Abtahi and Webb, *Travaux*, vol 1 and 2 for their most important scholarship. In Herschkopf and Hunter, *Genocide Reinterpreted*, the authors explain that Abtahi's and Webb's work "is the only work to gather together in a single publication the records of the multitude of meetings and statements which led to the adoption of the Convention…" 1.

198 See United Nations General Assembly, Hundredth and Seventh Meeting, Sixth Committee, U.N. Doc. A/C.6/SR.107 (15 November

1948) [U.N. Doc. A/C.6/SR.107], reprinted in Abtahi and Webb, *Travaux*, 1816; also see 1815-1823.

199 For further analysis on the connection see Jean-Paul Sartre, "On Genocide" in Jean-Paul Sartre and Arlette El Kaïm Sartre, *On Genocide and a Summary of the Evidence and Judgments of the International War Crimes Tribunal* (Boston: Beacon Press, 1968), 62-63. Sartre elucidates the connection between the concepts of colonialism and cultural genocide.

200 "In essence, these clauses give the contracting states the freedom of designating those parts of their territories to which the treaty will apply, thereby avoiding the customary presumption in favour of territorial application to all of the territories of a state party, now codified in article 29 of the 1969 Vienna Convention on the Law of Treaties." Marko Milanović, "Territorial Application of the Convention and State Succession," in Paola Gaeta, ed, *The UN Genocide Convention: A Commentary* (New York: Oxford University Press, 2009), 475.

201 Debate on extension of the Convention's protection over non-self-governing territories prompted the Ukrainian SSR to set forth the position quoted at note 204. The Ukrainian SSR maintained the position that "the peoples of non-self-governing territories were most likely to become victims of genocide," U.N. Doc. A/C.6/SR.107, reprinted in Abtahi and Webb, *Travaux*, 1816.

202 Ibid., 1815; also see 1816, 1986-1987, and 2005; also see *Genocide Convention*, Article 12. The current reading of the clause as is provided in Article XII of the UNGC: "any Contracting Party may at any time, by notification addressed to the Secretary-General of the United Nations, extend the application of the present Convention to all or any of the territories for the conduct of whose foreign relations that Contracting Party is responsible;" also see United Nations General Assembly, Ninety-Third Meeting, Sixth Committee, U.N. Doc. A/C.6/SR. 93 (6 November 1948), reprinted in Abtahi and Webb, *Travaux*, 1609. The UK's amendment came up in the discussion on "heads of state" and responsibility for genocide in colonial settings.

203 Ibid., 1816.

204 Ibid.

205 Ibid., 1816-1817.

206 Ibid, 1817.

207 Ibid.

208 Ibid., 1822.

209 See for example U.N. Doc. A/C.6/SR.65, reprinted in Abtahi and Webb, *Travaux*, 1318-1319.

210 United Nations General Assembly, One Hundredth and Seventy Ninth Meeting, Sixth Committee, U.N. Doc. A/PV.179 (9 December 1948), [U.N. Doc. A/PV.179], reprinted in Abtahi and Webb, *Travaux*, 2082.

211 U.N. Doc. A/C.6/SR.83, reprinted in Abtahi and Webb, *Travaux*, 1517.

212 For a review of the debates about cultural genocide during the sixth

committee see Ibid., 1501-1518; for further review of the issues taken up by the USSR on cultural genocide see pp. 1516-1517. The USSR contended that "the physical destruction of members of the group was one way of carrying out that intention, [genocide] and the destruction of the culture of the group was another. The Nürnberg verdicts had shown that the destruction of the culture of certain groups might constitute a method of destroying those groups; there had been examples of that in Czechoslovakia, Poland and Luxembourg."

213 "Union of Soviet Socialist Republics: amendments to the draft convention on the prevention and punishment of genocide proposed by the Sixth Committee (A/760)." The amendment was in response to the final draft proposed by the Sixth Committee. It addressed the USSR's views on the causes of genocide, but was voted down by the General Assembly. See Abtahi and Webb, *Travaux*, 2039.

214 U.N. Doc. A/PV.179, reprinted in Abtahi and Webb, *Travaux*, 2082.

215 U.N. Doc. A/C.6/SR.83, reprinted in Abtahi and Webb, *Travaux*, 1516.

216 United Nations General Assembly, Hundredth and Seventy-Eighth Meeting, Sixth Committee, U.N. Doc. A/PV.178 (9 December 1948), reprinted in Abtahi and Webb, *Travaux*, 2044.

217 Ibid.

218 Ibid., 2045.

219 Ibid.

220 Ibid.

221 Ibid.

222 Ibid., 2046.

223 U.N. Doc. A/PV.179 reprinted in Abtahi and Webb, *Travaux*, 2072.

224 Ibid., 2076.

225 Ibid., 2083.

226 Ibid.

227 Ibid., 2045.

228 Venne, "The Creator Knows Their Lies," xiii.

229 Ibid.

230 U.N. Doc. A/PV 179, reprinted in Abtahi and Webb, *Travaux*, 2083. Whether or not it was intended by the USSR the irony is evident and will be utilized by the author.

231 See especially Newcomb, *Pagans*, 13-15. At page 14 Newcomb explains that "what is referred to as civilization may involve a process of colonization, which is a process by which an empire expands in land, population, wealth, and power." For a review of the domination encoded in the doctrine of discovery that is in the federal Indian law cases such established in federal Indian law such as the Marshall Trilogy read *Pagans* for his succinct analysis.

232 "The German settlers would defend Europe itself at the Ural Mountains, against the Asiatic barbarism that would be forced back to the east. Strife at civilization's edge would test the manhood of coming generations of German settlers. Colonization would make of

Germany a continental empire fit to rival the United States, another hardy frontier state based upon exterminatory colonialism and slave labour. The East was the Nazi Manifest Destiny. In Hitler's view, 'in the East a similar process will repeat itself for a second time as in the conquest of America.' As Hitler imagined the future, Germany would deal with the Slavs much as the North Americans had dealt with the Indians." Snyder, *Bloodlands*, 160. Also see Toland, *Adolf Hitler,* 702; and, see especially, Churchill's *Matter of Genocide* for his comparisons of the American and German colonial invasions.

233 See esp. Greg Bradsher, "The Nuremberg Laws: Archives Receives Original Nazi Documents That 'Legalized' Persecution of Jews," *Prologue Magazine* 42, No. 4 (Winter 2010), http://www.archives.gov/ publications/prologue/2010/winter/nuremberg.html.

234 United State Holocaust Museum, "Holocaust Encyclopedia: NurembergLaws,"https://www.ushmm.org/wlc/en/article.php?ModuleId=10007902; also see Bradsher, "Nuremberg Laws."

235 Mundorff, "Other Peoples' Children," 80; citing "*United States v. Greifelt,(the RuSHA case)*, 4 Trials of War Criminals Before the Nuernberg Military Tribunals Under Control Council Law No. 10, at 610 (1950) (Military Tribunal, Nuernberg, Germany, Oct. 1946-Apr. 1949)" at note 109. At note 110 Mundorff cites Prosecutor Neely in his opening statement, defined a key element of the crime as being that children were abducted for the purpose of being "indoctrinated with Nazi ideology."

236 Ibid.

237 Ibid.

238 Ibid. Cited at note 111 in which Mundorff summarizes Prosecutor Neely. He "provides an overview of Nazi plans to kidnap children from eastern occupied lands…"

239 Ibid, Cited at note 110.

240 Gradual Civilization Act, SC 1857, 20 Vict, c 26.

241 Kent McNeil, "Social Darwinism and Judicial Conceptions of Indian Title in Canada in the 1880s," *Journal of the West* 38, No. 1 (January 1999):71.

242 Ibid. Also see *Canada, House of Commons Debates,* 5th Parliament, *1st Session,* No 14 (9 May 1883) at 1101 (Hon. John A. MacDonald).

243 Ibid.

Chapter Two

1 "Reclaiming History: The Residential School System in Canada," *Where are the Children,* accessed January 5, 2018, http://wherearethechildren.ca/en/timeline/research/. "Following recommendations made in the Davin Report, Sir John A. Macdonald authorizes creation of residential industrial schools in the Canadian West [in 1883]."

2 Hirad Abtahi and Phillipa Webb, *The Genocide Convention: The*

Travaux Préparatoires, vol 2 (Leiden: Martinus Nijhoff Publishers, 2008), 2082.

3 Truth and Reconciliation Canada, "Chapter One: Child welfare: A system in crisis" in *Canada's Residential Schools: The Legacy, The Final Report of the Truth and Reconciliation Commission of Canada Volume 5* (Montreal: McGill-Queen's University Press, 2015), 11. It was explained in the report that "[T]he end of the residential school system did not mean that Aboriginal children were no longer forcibly separated from their families. Child welfare services carried on where the residential schools left off. More Aboriginal children are removed from their families today than attended residential schools in any one year. Following the inquiry into the death of an Aboriginal girl in Manitoba, the Honourable Ted Hughes concluded that the overrepresentation of Aboriginal children in care in Canada is "unconscionable" and "a national embarrassment."

4 See E. Brian Titley, *A Narrow Vision: Duncan Campbell Scott and the Administration of Indian Affairs in Canada* (Vancouver: University of British Columbia Press, 1986), 50; see e.g. John L. Tobias, "Protection, Civilization, Assimilation: An Outline History of Canada's Indian Policy," in Ian A.L. Getty and Antoine S. Lussier ed, *As Long as the Sun Shines and Water Flows*, (Vancouver: University of British Columbia Press, 1983); see also J.R. Miller, *Skyscrapers Hide the Heavens: A History of Indian-White Relations in Canada*, revised ed. (Toronto: University of Toronto Press, 2001) for a review of policy and positions on the Indian problem.

5 See John S. Milloy, *A National Crime: The Canadian Government and the Residential School System, 1879 to 1986* (Winnipeg: The University of Manitoba Press, 1999), 13-22.

6 Quoted in Titley, *A Narrow Vision*, 50.

7 Ibid, p. 50; see especially Steven T. Newcomb, *Pagans in the Promised Land: Decoding the Christian Doctrine of Discovery* (Golden, CO: Fulcrum, 2008), 13-16. Newcomb explains that the 'body politic' represents the colonial body that absorbs, swallows, and consumes original nations and their lands into its ravenous hungry body. The author uses cognitive theory to turn the tables on the western reader.

8 Milloy, *National Crime*, xiv.

9 Canada, Royal Commission on Aboriginal Peoples, "Chapter 10: Residential Schools," *Looking Forward, Looking Back*, vol 5 (Ottawa: Canada Communication Group, 1996), 309.

10 Ibid. Also see Milloy, *National Crime*, xiii-xiv.

11 Milloy, *National Crime*, 7-8.

12 Ibid.

13 RCAP, "Residential Schools," 309.

14 Canada, *House of Commons Debates*, 5th Parliament, 1st Session, No 14 (9 May 1883) at 1107-08 (Hon. John A. MacDonald).

15 RCAP, "Residential Schools", 309.

16 Ibid., 310.
17 Ibid., 313.
18 Ibid.
19 Ibid., 313.
20 Elizabeth Furniss, *Victims of Benevolence: The Dark Legacy of the Williams Lake Residential School* (Vancouver: Arsenal Pulp Press, 1992, 1995), 28. Furniss cites from Canada, Annual Report of the Department of Indian Affairs (Ottawa, Queen's Printer, 1895), xxiii.
21 Milloy, *National Crime*, 19.
22 Raphaël Lemkin, *Axis Rule in Occupied Europe: Laws of Occupation, Analysis of Government, Proposals for Redress,* 2nd ed. (Clark, NJ: The Lawbook Exchange, 2008), ix.
23 See *An Act Further to Amend the Indian Act,* SC 1894, c 32, s 11, ss 137 and 138 which required "the compulsory attendance of children at school. Such regulations, in addition to any other provisions deemed expedient, may provide for the arrest and conveyance to school, and detention there, of truant children and of children who are prevented by their parents or guardians from attending: and such regulations may provide for the punishment, upon summary conviction, by fine or imprisonment, or both of parents or guardians, or persons having the charge of children, who fail, refuse or neglect to cause such children to attend school." These sections are consolidated in the Indian Act, RSC 1906, c 81, ss 9, 10 and 11 and *An Act to amend the Indian Act,* SC 1920, c 50, s 9 and 10.
24 Milloy, *National Crime*, xiii.
25 *Gradual Civilization Act,* SC 1857, 20 Vict, c 26.
26 *British North American Act,* 1867 (UK), 30 & 31 Vict, c 3, now the Constitution Act, 1867.
27 Ibid, section 18. The section reads, "The Privileges, Immunities, and Powers to be held, enjoyed, and exercised by the Senate and by the House of Commons and by the Members thereof respectively shall be such as are from Time to Time defined by Act of the Parliament of Canada, but so that the same shall never exceed those at the passing of this Act held, enjoyed, and exercised by the Commons House of Parliament of the United Kingdom of Great Britain and Ireland and by the Members thereof."
28 Ibid., s. 91 (24).
29 *The Indian Act, SC 1876, 37-38 & 38-39 Vict, c 18 [Indian Act, 1876].*
30 As a prime example of such legislation, see the 1894 version of the *Indian Act.*
31 See Canada, Indian and Northern Affairs, *Statement of the Government of Canada on Indian Policy 1969* (Ottawa: Department of Indian and Northern Affairs, 1969).
32 See Titley, *A Narrow Vision*, 50.
33 See especially, Harold Cardinal, *The Unjust Society* (Toronto: Douglas & McIntyre, 1999).

34 For use of the word "digest" in the sense intended here, see Ward Churchill, "'Nits Make Lice': The Extermination of North American Indians, 1607-1996," in *A Little Matter of Genocide: Holocaust and Denial in the Americas, 1492 to the Present* (San Francisco: City Lights Books, 1997), 245-250; Also see Aimé Césaire, *Discourse on Colonialism*, (New York: Monthly Review Press, 1972), 31; Newcomb, *Pagans*, 16.

35 Kurt Mundorff, "Other Peoples' Children: A Textual and Contextual Interpretation of the Genocide Convention, Article 2(e)," *Harvard International Law Journal*, Vol. 50, No. 1 (Winter 2009), 80.

36 David Wallace Adams, *Education for Extinction: American Indians and the American Boarding School Experience, 1875-1928* (Lawrence: University Press of Kansas, 1995). The phrase is taken from the title of Adam's book.

37 Milloy, *National Crime*, 42; See also Titley, *A Narrow Vision*, 75-93 for a review of Duncan Campbell's Scott's administration with respect to "schooling and civilization."

38 See especially the discussion of the "laws of occupation" in William A. Schabas, Introduction to the Second Edition of *Axis Rule in Occupied Europe: Laws of Occupation, Analysis of Government, Proposals for Redress,* by Raphaël Lemkin, 2nd ed. (Clark, NJ: The Lawbook Exchange, 2008), ix; Compare to Canada's *The Indian Act,* SC 1876 and also see *The Indian Act*, SC 1880 (UK), 42 & 43 Vict, c 28, s 4. The 1880 amendment created the Department of Indian Affairs among many other oppressive measures.

39 RCAP, "Residential Schools," 312.

40 Canada, Office of the Prime Minister, *Statement of Apology to Former Students of the Indian Residential Schools,* (Ottawa: June 11, 2008).

41 MacDonald, *House of Commons Debates*, 1108.

42 Titley, *A Narrow Vision*, 50.

43 *Prosecutor v. Radovan Karadžić et al.* (Case No. IT-95-5-R61, IT-95-18-R61), Review of the Indictments Pursuant to Rule 61 of the Rules of Procedure and Evidence (11 July 1996) para 94 (International Criminal Tribunal for the former Yugoslavia, Trial Chamber).

44 See Ward Churchill, *Kill the Indian Save the Man: The Genocidal Impact of American Indian Residential Schools* (San Francisco: City Lights Books, 2004), 18.

45 See e.g. Agnes Grant, *No End of Grief: Indian Residential Schools in Canada* (Winnipeg, MB: Pemmican, 1996), 209-216.

46 Agnes Jack, ed., *Behind Closed Doors: Stories from the Kamloops Indian Residential School* (Penticton, B.C.: Theytus Books, 2006), xi.

47 Grant, *No End of Grief*, 209.

48 Constance Deiter, *From Our Mother's Arms: The Intergenerational Impact of the Residential Schools in Saskatchewan* (Etobicoke, ON: United Church Publishing House, 1999), 7-8.

49 See Churchill, *Kill the Indian*, 18; see Grant, *No End of Grief*, 209-

216; see Milloy, *A National Crime*, 19.

50 Furniss, *Victims of Benevolence*, 28. Furniss explains that "by 1899, DIA officials reporting that 'the strong disinclination on the part of parents to the separation involved in letting [the students] go to industrial schools…remains more or less widespread.'"

51 J.R. Miller, *Shingwauk's Vision: A History of the Native Residential Schools* (Toronto: University of Toronto Press, 1996), 128.

52 Grant, *No End of Grief*, 210.

53 Sharon Venne, "Understanding Treaty Six: An Indigenous Perspective" in *Aboriginal and Treaty Rights in Canada: Essays on Law, Equality and Respect for Difference*, ed. Michael Asch, (Vancouver: UBC Press, 1997), 194-195.

54 Ibid., 195.

55 Ibid.

56 See Celia Haig-Brown, *Resistance and Renewal Surviving the Residential School* (Vancouver: Tillicum Library, 1989), 43-45.

57 Ibid., 44.

58 Ernie Crey and Suzanne Fournier, *Stolen From Our Embrace: The Abduction of First Nations Children and the Restoration of Aboriginal Communities* (Vancouver: Douglas & McIntyre, 1997), 47.

59 Churchill, *Kill the Indian*, 21.

60 Roland Chrisjohn and Sherri Young, with Michael Maraun, *The Circle Game: Shadows and Substance in the Indian Residential School Experience in Canada* (Penticton: Theytus Books, 2006), 86-94.

61 Chrisjohn and Young, with Maraun, *Circle Game*, 88; citing/discussing Erving Goffman's *Asylums: Essays on the Social Situation of Mental Patients and Other Inmates* (Garden City, NY: Anchor Books, 1961).

62 Ibid.

63 Lemkin, *Axis Rule*, ix. He refers to the techniques of occupation.

64 Ibid., 79.

65 Milloy, *National Crime*, 124; Chrisjohn and Young, with Maraun, *Circle Game*, 86-94.

66 Chrisjohn and Young, with Maraun, *Circle Game*, 89.

67 Ibid, 89-90.

68 Ibid., 88.

69 Ibid., 90; citing Goffman, *Asylums*, 21.

70 Chrisjohn and Young, with Maraun, *Circle Game*, 49-50.

71 Jordan Chittley and Kevin Newman, "Ottawa forced to turn over report of electric chair use at residential school," *CTN News Live*, January 15, 2014), http://knlive.ctvnews.ca/ottawa-forced-to-turn-over-reports-of-electric-chair-use-at-residential-school-1.1641479.

72 Goffman, *Asylums*, 21; see esp. Chrisjohn and Young, with Maraun, *Circle Game*, 90

73 Chrisjohn and Young, with Maraun, *Circle Game*, 93.

74 See generally Milloy, *National Crime*, for a review of the civilizing mission.

75 See especially Chrisjohn and Young, with Maraun, *Circle Game*, 86-99.

76 RCAP, "Residential Schools," 312; see especially McNeil, "Social Darwinism," 71. John A. MacDonald in a statement to the House of Commons openly held that Indian children will "*acquire the habits and modes and thought of white men* [emphasis added]."

77 Haig Brown, *Resistance and Renewal*, 53.

78 *Collins English Dictionary*, 2nd ed., *sub verbo*, "brainwashing."

79 Milloy, *National Crime*, 42.

80 Ibid.

81 Chrisjohn and Young, with Maraun, *Circle Game*, 91.

82 The residential school system, resembling a total institution, was established by "programs of cultural replacement [and cultural synthesis] with the avowed aim of westernizing the Indian children as completely as possible." David A. Nock, A *Victorian Missionary and Canadian Indian Policy: Cultural Synthesis vs. Cultural Replacement* (Waterloo, ON: Wilfred Laurier Press, 1988), 3.

83 Ibid.

84 Ibid., 2.

85 *Webster's Third New International Dictionary of the English Language Unabridged*, *sub verbo* "civilization."

86 Nock, *A Victorian Missionary*, 2.

87 Chrisjohn and Young, with Maraun, *Circle Game*, 91.

88 Ibid., 93.

89 Ibid. Also see Haig-Brown, *Resistance and Renewal,* 53-87; RCAP, "Residential Schools," 309-384.

90 Shauna Troniak, "Background Paper: Addressing the Legacy of the Residential Schools," *Background Paper* (Ottawa: Library of Parliament, Canada, 2011), 2, accessed June 14, 2013 http://www.parl.gc.ca/Content/LOP/Research Publications/2011-76-e.pd.

91 Isabelle Knockwood, *Out of the Depths: The Experiences of Mi'kmaw Children at the Indian Residential School at Shubenacadie , Nova Scotia* (Lockeport, N.S.: Roseway, 1992), 45.

92 Chrisjohn and Young, with Maraun, *Circle Game*, 93; Haig-Brown, *Resistance and Renewal*, 47-49.

93 Ibid; Randy Fred, "Foreward" in Haig-Brown, *Resistance and Renewal*, 14-16.

94 Ibid, 93-94; Knockwood, *Out of the Depths*, 45.

95 Ibid.

96 George E. Tinker, "Tracing a Contour of Colonialism: American Indians and the Trajectory of Educational Imperialism," preface to Churchill, *Kill the Indian*, xviii.

97 See Jack, *Behind Closed Doors*, 117-120; Haig-Brown, *Resistance and Renewal*, 32-51.

98 Haig-Brown, *Resistance and Renewal*, 69.

99 Knockwood, *Out of the Depths*, 30.

100 Jack, *Behind Closed Doors*, 109-110.
101 Ibid., 110.
102 Churchill, *Kill the Indian*, 19; Also see Fred, "Foreword" to *Resistance and Renewal*, 11-20.
103 Haig-Brown, *Resistance and Renewal*, 46.
104 Churchill, *Kill the Indian*, 19; Chrisjohn and Young, with Maraun, *Circle Game*, 88-94; Also see Haig-Brown, *Resistance and Renewal*, 43-52.
105 Ibid., 24-26; Also see Haig-Brown, *Resistance and Renewal*, 53: also see 54-78; Knockwood, *Out of the Depths*, 23-46.
106 Churchill, *Kill the Indian*, 19; Also see Miller, *Shingwauk's Vision*, 204. Miller recounts one students experience, "Her first experience at school was having her braided hat cut short and coal oil poured over her head" upon admission into the Shingwauk Residential School.
107 Troniak, "Addressing the Legacy," 1; Also see Chrisjohn and Young, with Maraun, *Circle Game*, 50; See Haig-Brown, *Resistance and Renewal*, 47.
108 Churchill, *Kill the Indian*, 19; Also see Miller, *Shingwauk's Vision*, 204; RCAP, "Residential Schools," 315. The RCAP Report explains that, "[o]n crossing its threshold, the children were entering a non-Aboriginal world where, with their hair shorn and dressed in European clothes, they would leave behind the 'savage'…."
109 Knockwood, *Out of the Depths*, 28.
110 Churchill, *Kill the Indian*, 19; Also see Milloy, *National Crime*, 124.
111 Troniak, "Addressing the Legacy," 1.
112 Ibid; Knockwood, *Out of the Depths*, 28.
113 Haig-Brown, *Resistance and Renewal*, 53.
114 Milloy, *National Crime*, 39; Also see Churchill, *Kill the Indian*, 22; citing Department of Indian Affairs, *Annual Report* (Ottawa: Supplies and Services, 1895), xxii-xxiii at note 148.
115 Deiter, *From Our Mother's Arms*, 40. Also see Grant, *No End of Grief*, 189-208.
116 Miller, *Shingwauk's Vision*, 205.
117 See RCAP, "Residential Schools," 316, 351-352, 355; see Haig-Brown, *Resistance and Renewal*, 51; see Chrisjohn and Young, with Maraun, *Circle Game*, 50.
118 Milloy, *National Crime*, 38.
119 See George Manuel and Michael Posluns, *The Fourth World: An Indian Reality* (Toronto: Collier-Macmillan, 1974), 63-64.; see RCAP, "Residential Schools," 355; see Knockwood, *Out of the Depths*, 34, 54; see Milloy, A National Crime, 143.
120 Churchill, *Kill the Indian*, 22.
121 Churchill, *Kill the Indian*, 16-76. Churchill accurately classifies the destruction that children endured by classifying it as "slow death measure of starvation", "indirect killing by disease", "slow death measure of forced labour", "torture", "predation."

122 See Deiter, *From Our Mother's Arms*, 66; RCAP, "Residential Schools," 316; Also see Churchill, *Kill the Indian*, 24-26.

123 Jack, *Behind Closed Doors*, 129; Fred, "Foreword" to Resistance and Renewal, 13-14.

124 Deiter, *From Our Mother's Arms*, 66.

125 Ibid., 62.

126 Christian "religion was stuffed down our throats." Fred, "Foreword" to Resistance and Renewal, 14; Also see Haig-Brown, *Resistance and Renewal*, 57-58.

127 See Milloy, *National Crime*, 43; Also see Haig-Brown, *Resistance and Renewal*, 54-69.

128 Troniak, "Addressing the Legacy," 2.

129 Office of the Prime Minister, *Apology to Students..*

130 Churchill, *Kill the Indian*, 27; Also see Haig-Brown, *Resistance and Renewal*, 60-61. The author explains that Shushwap history was not taught and that only European history was important.

131 Haig-Brown, *Resistance and Renewal*, 53; Also see Churchill, *Kill the Indian*, 26-27.

132 Ibid.

133 Ibid, 61.

134 Churchill, Kill the Indian, 27; Also see Milloy, *National Crime*, 33-37.

135 Milloy, *National Crime*, 37. He also writes, "'[T]he symbolic ordering of the world' through which 'actions and objects take on meaning,' is 'inherited from [a child's] parents' and community from the moment of birth. Thus, for example, the child, parent, and community exist in a landscape—a culture's translation of environment into a 'meaning'-filled place."

136 RCAP, "Residential Schools," 312.

137 Chrisjohon and Young, with Maraun, *Circle Game*, 34. XXXXXX

138 Churchill, *Kill the Indian*, 16-76.

139 Milloy, *National Crime*, 129.

140 See Furniss, *Victims of Benevolence*, 62-79, 89-102; Also see Churchill, *Kill the Indian*, 57-60.

141 Ibid., 66-69.

142 Grant, *No End of Grief*, 134.

143 Crey, *Stolen From Our Embrace*, 47.

144 Grant, *No End of Grief*, 135.

145 Chrisjohn and Young, with Maraun, *Circle Game*, 49.

146 Grant, *No End of Grief*, 134.

147 See Grant, *No End of Grief*, 133-138; Churchill, *Kill the Indian*, 34-44.

148 Grant, No End of Grief, 137.

149 Milloy, *National Crime*, 51. In 1922, the principal of St. Joseph's Indian Industrial School reported that "the building could not be properly heated. Parts of it were 'entirely unfit for human habitation."

150 P.H. Byrce, *The Story of a National Crime being an Appeal for Justice to the Indians of Canada* (Ottawa: James Hope and Sons, 1922), 14.

Cited from Milloy, *National Crime*, 51.
151 Milloy, *National Crime*, 77.
152 Ibid.
153 Churchill, *Kill the Indian*, 37; Also see Milloy, *National Crime*, 91-92.
154 Milloy, *National Crime*, 51
155 See RCAP, "Residential Schools," 353-65; Milloy, *National Crime*, 51-107.
156 Milloy, *National Crime*, 51.
157 RCAP, "Residential Schools," 331.
158 Churchill, *Kill the Indian*, 34;citing Michael Burleigh, *Ethics and Extermination: Reflections on the Nazi Genocide* (Cambridge: UK: Cambridge University Press, 1997), 211; See Tinker, "Contour of Colonialism," xxiv; Also see Chrisjohn and Young, with Maraun, *Circle Game*, 94-99.
159 Ibid.
160 See Churchill, *Kill the Indian*, 34-43; Milloy, *National Crime*, 77-107.
161 Dene Moore, "Provinces hand over aboriginal death records from residential school period," *CTV News*, March 28, 2014.
162 See Churchill, *Kill the Indian*, 51-60; see Chrisjohn and Young, with Maraun, *Circle Game*, 44-57; Grant, *No End of Grief*, 225-27; Furniss, *Victims of Benevolence*, 66-70, 109-111.
163 Chrisjohn and Young, with Maraun, *Circle Game*, 50.
164 Furniss, *Victims of Benevolence*, 67-68.
165 Chrisjohn and Young, with Maraun, *Circle Game*, 50.
166 Ibid; Also see Jesse Staniforth, "Cover-up of residential school crimes a national shame," *Toronto Star*, August 25, 2015.
167 Churchill, *Kill the Indian*, 51.
168 Chrisjohn and Young, with Maraun, 50.
169 Ibid; Also see Grant, *No End of Grief*, 131-33.
170 Churchill, *Kill the Indian*, 51.
171 Jack, *Behind Closed Doors*, 123.
172 Ibid., 129.
173 Furniss, *Victims of Benevolence*, 68.
174 Chrisjohn and Young, with Maraun, *Circle Game*, 49-50; Also see Haig-Brown, *Resistance and Renewal*, 76-79.
175 Milloy, *National Crime*, 154-155.
176 Churchill, *Kill the Indian*, 55; also see Milloy, *National Crime*, 140-41.
177 Ibid; Chrisjohn and Young, with Maraun, *Circle Game*, 51
178 Ibid; also see Milloy, *National Crime*, 154-55; Furniss, *Victims of Benevolence*, 109-11.
179 Chrisjohn and Young, with Maraun, *Circle Game*, 51.
180 Milloy, *National Crime*, 130.
181 Ibid.
182 "Battleford Hangings", *Saskatchewan Indian*, 3, no. 7(July 1972), 5, accessed on October 20, 2017, http://www.sicc.sk.ca/archive/

saskindian/a72jul05.htm.

183 Ibid.

184 See Milloy, *National Crime*, 109-127 (esp. 112); Grant, *No End of Grief*, 114-17; Furniss, *Victims of Benevolence*, 66-71; Churchill, *Kill the Indian*, 29-33; Troniak, "Addressing the Legacy," 2.

185 Chrisjohn and Young, with Maraun, *Circle Game*, 50; Also see Knockwood, *Out of the Depths*, 36.

186 Ibid.

187 See Miller, *Shingwauk's Vision*, 294.

188 Ibid., 293-294. Miller describes the unhealthy and unsanitary food that children prepared and were forced to eat.

189 Haig-Brown, *Resistance and Renewal*, 54.

190 Furniss, *Victims of Benevolence*, 67.

191 Ibid.

192 Ibid.

193 Milloy, *National Crime*, 109.

194 Manuel and Posluns, *The Fourth World*, 65*; Cited from* Grant, *No End of Grief*, 114-15.

195 Churchill, *Kill the Indian*, 31.

196 Ibid; Citing from Milloy, *National Crime*, 117-118.

197 Churchill, *Kill the Indian*, 32; Miller, *Shingwauk's Vision*, 294.

198 Ibid.

199 Milloy, *National Crime*, 112.

200 Bob Weber, "Canadian government withheld food from hungry aboriginal kids in 1940s nutritional experiments," *The Globe and Mail*, July 16, 2013.

201 Ibid.

202 Ibid: Also see Ian Mosby, "Administering Colonial Science: Nutrition Research and Human Biomedical Experimentation in Aboriginal Communities and Residential Schools, 1942–1952," *Histoire Sociale/ Social History*, 46, No. 91 (Mai/May 2013): 145-72, DOI: 10.1353/his.2013.0015.

203 Weber, "Nutritional Experiments."

204 Ibid.

205 Ibid; Also see Mosby, "Administering Colonial Science."

206 Evelyne Shuster, "Fifty Years Later: The Significance of the Nuremberg Code," *New England Journal of Medicine*, No. 337 (1997): 1436-1440, DOI: 10.1056/NEJM199711133372006.

207 See Chrisjohn and Young, with Maraun, *Circle Game*, 50; Milloy, *National Crime*, 169-71; Churchill, *Kill the Indian*, 47.

208 Milloy, *National Crime*, 169.

209 Churchill, *Kill the Indian*, 44.

210 Jack, *Behind Closed Doors*, 132.

211 Ibid.

212 Milloy, *National Crime*, 68.

213 Ibid., 169.

214 Churchill, *Kill the Indian*, 47. Also see Furniss, *Victims of Benevolence*, 52-57.

215 Milloy, *National Crime*, 169.

216 See Churchill, *Kill the Indian*, 44-50; Also see Furniss, *Victims of Benevolence*, 52-57.

217 Grant, *No End of Grief*, 228; also see Churchill, *Kill the Indian*, 60-68; also see Miller, *Shingwauk's Vision*, 330-336.

218 Ibid., see esp. *R. v. Plint*, [1995] BCJ No 3060 (QL) at para 14.

219 Ibid.

220 Miller, *Shingwauk's Vision*, 329.

221 Crey, *Stolen From Our Embrace*, 48.

222 Ibid.

223 Jack, *Behind Closed Doors*, 123.

224 Chrisjohn and Young, with Maraun, *Circle Game*, 49; also see Grant, *No End of Grief*, 227-231; also see Knockwood, *Out of the Depths*, 93.

225 Miller, *Shingwauk's Vision*, 329.

226 RCAP, "Residential Schools," 362.

227 Churchill, *Kill the Indian*, 60-68; Milloy, *A National Crime*, 140-156; Chrisjohn and Young, with Maraun, *Circle Game*, 51; Miller, *Shingwauk's Vision*, 337.

228 Churchill, *Kill the Indian*, 60; see also 106 n 407 "One can search, but the search will be in vain, for evidence of a nonwhite presence in jobs other than kitchen help among those employed by either U.S. or Canadian residential schools prior to the 1970s."

229 Ibid., 61; Also see Milloy, *A National Crime*, 146.

230 Ibid; Also see Milloy, *A National Crime*, 140-156.

231 Ibid; Churchill explains "Duncan Campbell's Scott removal of P.H. Bryce from the Indian Service provides an excellent example."

232 Churchill, *Kill the Indian*, 63; Also see Milloy, *A National Crime*, 146-147.

233 Milloy, *A National Crime*, 145.

234 Churchill, *Kill the Indian*, 63; citing Roy MacGregor, *Chief: The Fearless Vision of Billy Diamond* (Toronto: Penguin, 1988), 24.

235 Grant, *No End of Grief*, 229-230.

236 Churchill, *Kill the Indian*, 68.

237 Abtahi and Webb, *Travaux Préparatoires*, 235; also see 1493, 1494, and 1504.

238 See Chrisjohn and Young, with Maraun, *Circle Game*, 95-99.

239 Ibid.

240 Chrisjohn and Young, with Maraun, *Circle Game*, 95.

241 Ibid., 97; see note 176-178 in which Chrisjohn and Young, with Maraun cite from Leo Eitinger, "The Concentration Camp Syndrome and Its Late Sequelae," in Joel Dimsdale (Ed.), *Survivors, Victims, and Perpetrators: Essays on the Nazi Holocaust* ((New York: Hemisphere Publishing, 1980); Metin Basoglu and Susan Mineka, "The Role of Uncontrollable and Unpredictable Stress in Post-Traumatic Stress

Responses in Torture Survivors" in M. Basoglu (Ed.), *Torture and its Consequences: Current Treatment Approaches* (Cambridge: Cambridge University Press, 1992); Albert Memmi, *The Colonizer and the Colonized* (Boston: Beacon Press, 1965) as examples of the scholarship on the subject.

242 Ibid.

243 Ibid.

244 Churchill, *Kill the Indian*, 74.

245 Chrisjohn and Young, with Maraun, *Circle Game*, 96.

246 Phil Fontaine and Bernie Farber, "What Canada committed against First Nations was genocide: The UN should recognize it," *The Globe and Mail*, October 14, 2013.

247 Churchill, *Kill the Indian*, 70.

248 Fournier and Crey, *Stolen From Our Embrace*, 61.

249 Churchill, *Kill the Indian*, 70.

250 Ashely Quinn citing a study entitled "Health and quality of life of Aboriginal residential school survivors, Bella Coola Valley" by S. Barton, H. Thommasen, B. Tallio, W. Zhang, and A. Michalos establish the "intergenerational pervasiveness of the residential school experience" that shows that there are "significant differences" "between Aboriginals and non-Aboriginals concerning overall quality of life." Quinn explains "[The] suggestion is validated by research that has found approximately two-thirds of Aboriginal Peoples have experienced trauma as a direct result of the residential school era." Ashley Quinn, "Reflections on Intergenerational Trauma: Healing as a Critical Intervention," *First Peoples Child and Family Review* 3, No. 4 (2007): 73, https://fncaringsociety.com/first-peoples-child-family-review.

251 See Quinn, "Intergenerational Trauma," 72-73. Chrisjohn and Young, with Maraun, *Circle Game*, 94-99; Churchill, *Kill the Indian*, 68-76; Rosalind Ing, "The Effects of Residential Schooling on Native Child-Rearing Practices," in *Canadian Journal of Native Education*, 18, Supplement (1991): 65-118.

252 Tinker, "Contour of Colonialism," xvii

253 Ibid.

254 Ibid., xxi.

255 Office of the Prime Minister, *Apology to Students.*

256 MacDonald, *House of Commons Debates*, 1107-08; McNeil, "Social Darwinism," 71.

257 Removal of Indigenous children by the provinces was authorized under the 1951 amendment to the Indian Act (Section 88). In 1976, the Supreme Court of Canada "confirmed…that the legal jurisdiction of the Province's ability to extend child welfare services onto reserve, regardless of the provincial incursion into a federal sphere of responsibility." Marilyn Bennett, "First Nations Fact Sheet: A General Profile on First Nations Child Welfare in Canada," *First Nations Child*

and Family Caring Society of Canada, http://www.fncfcs.com/docs/FirstNationsFS1.pdf; citing "*Natural Parents v. Superintendent of Child Welfare*, 1976, 60 D.L.R. 3rd 148 S.C.C;" Also see Leroy Little Bear, "Section 88 of the Indian Act and the Application of Provincial Laws to Indians" in *Governments in Conflict? Provinces and Indian Nations in Canada*, eds. Anthony Long and Menno Boldt (Toronto: University of Toronto Press, 1992), 175-87.

258 Fournier and Crey, *Stolen From Our Embrace*, 81.

259 Patrick Johnston, *Native Children and the Child Welfare System* (Toronto: James Lorimer and the Canadian Council on Social Development, 1983); See Erin Hanson, "Sixties Scoop: The Sixties Scoop and Aboriginal Child Welfare," *Indigenous Foundations*, http://indigenousfoundations.arts.ubc.ca.

260 Sharon Venne, Interview, January 4, 2013. For background, see generally, Fournier and Crey, *Stolen From Our Embrace*; also see Andrew Armitage, "Family and Child Welfare in First Nations Communities" in Brian Wharf, ed., *Rethinking Child Welfare in Canada* (Toronto: Oxford University Press, 1993), 131-71.

261 Fournier and Crey, *Stolen From Our Embrace*, 81.

262 See, e.g., Hanson, "Sixties Scoop."

263 See Cindy Blackstock, "First Nations child and family services: restoring peace and harmony in First Nations communities," in Kufedlt, Kathleen, and Brad McKenzie, eds., *Child Welfare: Connecting Research and Policy* (Waterloo, Ont.: Wilfred Laurier University Press, 2011), 331-42.

264 Jillian Taylor, 'The ultimate goal is to reduce the number of children in care': Indigenous Affairs Minister, *CBC News*, March 27, 2017, http://www.cbc.ca/news/canada/manitoba/manitoba-carolyn-bennett-child-welfare-1.4042484.

265 Statistics Canada, Study: Living arrangements of Aboriginal children aged 14 and under, 2011 (Released at 8:30 a.m. eastern time in The Daily, Wednesday, April 13, 2016.

266 Fournier and Crey, *Stolen From Our Embrace*, 84. The 'changes' that MacKenzie and Hudson refer to is changes to condition or continue to forcibly indoctrinate children in the welfare system. The 'colonial argument' is the objectives of the residential school system.

267 Julia Rand, "Residential Schools: Creating and Continuing Institutionalization among Aboriginal Peoples in Canada," *First Peoples Child and Family Review* 6, No. 1 (2011): 63.

268 Hanson, "Sixties Scoop". Hanson cited from Lavina White and Eva Jacobs, *Liberating our Children, Liberating our Nations: Report of the Aboriginal Committee: Community Panel of Family and Children's Services Legislation Review in British Columbia* (Victoria: Minister of Social Services, 1992), 18-23; see also Fournier and Crey, *Stolen From Our Embrace*, 81-114.

269 Fournier and Crey, *Stolen From Our Embrace*, 111.

270 Darcy Henton, "Deaths of Alberta aboriginal children in care no 'fluke of statistics," *Edmonton Journal*, 8 January 2014, http://www.edmontonjournal.com/life/Deaths+Alberta+aboriginal+children+care+fluke+statistics/9212384/story.html,_No longer available but cited by the First Nations Child and Family Caring Society "Deaths of Alberta aboriginal children in care no 'fluke of statistics' and cited in Truth and Reconciliation Canada, *Canada's Residential Schools: The Legacy The Final Report of the Truth and Reconciliation Commission of Canada The Legacy* vol 5 (Montreal: McGill-Queen's University Press, 2015), 381.

271 Mary Ellen Turpel-Lafond, Representative for Children and Youth, 'Too Many Victims Sexualized Violence in the Lives of Children and Youth in Care: An Aggregate Review '(British Columbia, October 2016).

272 Chinta Puxley, "Manitoba opens Tina Fontaine case to review by children's advocate," *The Globe and Mail,* December 15, 2015, https://www.theglobeandmail.com/news/national/man-accused-in-death-of-tina-fontaine-waives-court-appearance/article27759601/.

273 'Teen in B.C. provincial care dies in fall from hotel window' B.C. children's advocate calls death of Alex Gervais a tragedy, says ministry 'has a lot to answer for,' *CBC News,* September 23, 2015, http://www.cbc.ca/news/canada/british-columbia/teen-in-b-c-provincial-care-dies-in-fall-from-hotel-window-1.3240959.

274 Fournier and Crey, *Stolen From Our Embrace*, 81-142. Also see Hanson, "Sixties Scoop"; White and Jacobs, *Liberating our Children,* 18-23.

275 Hanson, "Sixties Scoop." Also see Raven Sinclair, "Identity Lost and Found: Lessons from the Sixties Scoop," *First Nations Child and Family Law Review*, 3, No. 1 (2007): 65-82.

276 Sinclair, "Identity Lost," 66. Sinclair's paper studies the historical roots of the sixties scoop that resulted in thousands of Indigenous children removed from birth families and placed in non-Indigenous homes. She writes in her Abstract (page 65) that, "Despite literature that indicates adoption breakdown rates of 85-95%, recent research with adults adopted as children indicate that some adoptees have found solace through re-acculturation to their birth culture and contextualizing their adoptions within colonial history."

277 Patrick J. Morrissette, "The Holocaust of First Nations People: Residual Effects on Parenting and Treatment Implications," *Contemporary Family Therapy*, 16, No. 5 (October 1994): 384.

278 Linda Bull, "Indian Residential Schooling: The Native Perspective," in *Canadian Journal of Native Education*, 18, Supplement (1991): 56.

279 Ibid., 58.

280 Ibid., 59.

281 Ing, "The Effects of Residential Schooling on Native Child-Rearing

Practices," 113.
282 Ibid.
283 Ibid., 77-85.
284 Quinn, "Intergenerational Trauma," 73.
285 Ing, "The Effects of Residential Schooling on Native Child-Rearing Practices," 115.
286 Quinn, "Intergenerational Trauma," 73.
287 Ing, "The Effects of Residential Schooling on Native Child-Rearing Practices," 94.
288 Ibid., 95.
289 Ibid.
290 Ibid., 113.
291 See Newcomb, *Pagans*; see Steven T. Newcomb, "The UN Declaration on the Rights of Indigenous Peoples and the Paradigm of Domination," *Griffiths Law Review,* 20 (2011): 578.

Chapter Three

1 Sharon Helen Venne, "The Creator Knows Their Lies and So Should We: Ward Churchill's Pursuit of Juridical Truth," introduction to Ward Churchill, *Perversions of Justice: Indigenous Peoples and Angloamerican Law* (San Francisco: City Lights Books, 2003), xiii.
2 E. Brian Titley, *A Narrow Vision: Duncan Campbell Scott and the Administration of Indian Affairs in Canada* (Vancouver: University of British Columbia Press, 1986), 50.
3 Derrick O'Keefe, "Harper In Denial at G20: Canada has no history of colonialism," Rabble.ca (September 28, 2009), http://rabble.ca/blogs/bloggers/derrick/2009/09/harper-denial-g20-canada-has-no-history-colonialism. For a more accurate appraisal, see Arthur R.M. Lower, *Colony to Nation: History of Canada* (Toronto: Longmans, Green, 1946) esp. the maps by T.W. McLean.
4 Titley, *A Narrow Vision*, 3.
5 See Canada, Office of the Prime Minister, *Statement of Apology to Former Students of the Indian Residential Schools,* (Ottawa: June 11, 2008). Also see Canada, Royal Commission on Aboriginal Peoples, "Chapter 10: Residential Schools," *Looking Forward, Looking Back*, vol 5 (Ottawa: Canada Communication Group, 1996). The RCAP report is widely considered to be the most progressive research undertaken with regard to the residential school system, yet its classification/description of the experience is by no means adequate.
6 Peter d'Errico "Foreword," in Steven T. Newcomb, *Pagans in the Promised Land: Decoding the Christian Doctrine of Discovery* (Golden, CO: Fulcrum, 2008), xii.
7 Newcomb, Pagans, 1.
8 Steven T. Newcomb, "The UN Declaration on the Rights of Indigenous Peoples and the Paradigm of Domination," *Griffiths Law Review*, 20,

No. 3 (2011): 578.

9 Newcomb, Pagans, 14.

10 Newcomb, Pagans, 14. At page 13, Newcomb writes in reference to Price in the above quote, "In his 1882 'Annual Report of the Commissioner of Indian Affairs,' U.S. Indian Commissioner Hiram Price commented on the need for the federal government to cooperate with religious societies in order to 'civilize' the Indians:

> a. One very important auxiliary in transforming men from savage to civilized life is the influence brought to bear upon them through the labors of Christian men and women as educators and missionaries. This I think, has been forcibly demonstrated among the different Indian tribes by the missionary labors of the various religious societies in the last few years. Civilization is a plant of exceeding slow growth…[emphasis added]."

11 Newcomb, *Pagans*, xvi.

12 This understanding about the detriment of words and terminology is from my own experience in law school and learning that the colonial language could trap Indigenous Peoples in a positive rule of law framework, ie. "Crown's underlying title"; see also Roland Chrisjohn and Sherri Young, with Michael Maraun, *The Circle Game: Shadows and Substance in the Indian Residential School Experience in Canada* (Penticton, B.C.: Theytus Books, 2006), 34. The writers refer to the rhetoric as a "word-game."

13 See especially Ashley Montagu, "The Fallacy of the Primitive," in his *Concept of the Primitive* (New York: Collier Macmillan, 1968), 1-6. Also see J.M. Blaut, *The Colonizer's Model of the World: Geographical Diffusionism and Eurocentric History* (New York: Guilford Press, 1993).

14 Canada, *House of Commons Debates*, 5th Parliament, 1st Session, No 14 (9 May 1883) at 1107-1108 (Hon. John A. MacDonald).

15 Steven L. Winter, *A Clearing in the Forest: Law, Life, and Mind* (Chicago: The University of Chicago Press, 2001), 200.

16 The passage quoted appears in the second paragraph of the Prime Minister's 2008 *Apology to Former Students.*

17 See Raphaël Lemkin, *Axis Rule in Occupied Europe: Laws of Occupation, Analysis of Government, Proposals for Redress*, 2nd ed. (Clark, NJ: The Lawbook Exchange, 2008), 79.

18 United Nations General Assembly, Two Hundred and Eighteenth Meeting, Draft Convention on the Crime of Genocide (U.N. Doc. E/794, E/794/Corr. 1 and E/AC. 27/1, (26 August 1948), 710. Poland claimed that the effectiveness of a convention on genocide would depend on its being drafted in such a as to leave no "loopholes of escape for perpetrators of the crime."

19 "No word is more vague and has permitted the commission of more crimes than that of civilization." Martti Koskenniemi, *The Gentle*

Civilizer of Nations: The Rise and Fall of International Law 1870-1960 (Cambridge: UK, Cambridge University Press, 2001), 106.

20 On the cognitive dimension of the process, see Newcomb, Pagans, 1-36.

21 Article II, *Convention on the Prevention and Punishment of the Crime of Genocide*, 9 December 1948, 78 UNTS 277, (entered into force 12 January 1951, signed by Canada 28 November 1949, accession by Canada 3 September 1952).

22 Lemkin, Axis Rule, ix.

23 During the early 1890s, Deputy Superintendent General of Indian Affairs Haytor Reed described the "obliteration" of Indigenous children's sense of cultural identity as being a primary objective of compulsory residential schooling. RCAP, "Residential Schools," 312.

24 The "body politic" referred to by Duncan Campbell Scott calls for the complete absorption of Indian identity into the state. See Titley, *Narrow Vision,* 50. Newcomb explains that the 'body politic' represents the colonial body that swallows, absorbs, or in any case consumes original nations/land into its ravenous hungry body. See Newcomb, *Pagans,* 13-16.

25 Newcomb, Pagans, 4.

26 See especially Thomas Hobbes, *Leviathan: Or the Matter, Forme, & Power of a Common–Wealth Ecclesiasticall add Civill,* ed. Ian Shapiro (California: Yale University Press, 2010). Also see also Robert A. Williams, Jr., *Savage Anxieties: The Invention of Western Civilization* (New York: Palgrave Macmillan, 2012).

27 "[T]he one distinction which Vitoria insists upon and which he elaborates in considerable detail is the distinction between the sovereign Spanish and the non-sovereign Indians. Vitoria bases his conclusion that the Indians are not sovereign on the simple assertion that they are pagans. In so doing he resorts to exactly the same crude reasoning which he had previously refuted when denying the validity of the Church's claim that the Indians lack rights under divine law because they are heathens." Antony Anghie, *Imperialism, Sovereignty and the Making of International Law* (New York: Cambridge University Press, 2004), 29. Also see Robert A. Williams, Jr., *The American Indian in Western Legal Thought: The Discourses of Conquest* (New York: Oxford University Press, 1990).

28 That early conceptions of law and policy were developed according to terms such as "savage" is conveyed quite well by Kent McNeil, "Social Darwinism and Judicial Conceptions of Indian Title in Canada in the 1880s," *Journal of the West*, 38, No. 1 (January 1999): 68-76.

29 For a succinct review of the doctrine of discovery and the problems that arise from the imposition of colonial legal systems, see Sharon H. Venne, "Discovering Peoples in International Law" in *Our Elders Understand our Rights: Evolving International Law Regarding Indigenous Rights* (Penticton, B.C.: Theytus Books, 1998), 1-18.

30 See *Western Sahara: Advisory Opinion* [1975] ICJ Rep 12. Also see Venne, *Our Elders Understand Our Rights*, 45-46.

31 Newcomb, *Pagans*, 19.

32 Ibid.

33 Winter, *Clearing in the Forest*, xiv.

34 Newcomb, *Pagans*, 2.

35 Ibid., 3. The terms of savage or pagan are the foundational to the doctrine of discovery. Newcomb explains that jurists and law "makers have unconsciously and imaginatively applied certain categories, concepts, metaphors and other thought processes to American Indian peoples, some of which, through time have come to be objectified and reified as the 'law'."

36 Newcomb, *Pagans*, xxv. Newcomb highlighting Steven Winter's research in *A Clearing in the Forest* explains that "legal thinking is a product of the human imagination."

37 McNeil, "Social Darwinism", 68. He explains, "Unfortunately, judicial analyses of the St. Catherine's case rarely take into account the impact of the historical context or contemporary attitudes toward the Indian peoples in Canada. While important insights into the case are found in the commentary of historians such as Donald Smith, S. Barry Cottam, and Anthony J. Hall, the case is still cited as a judicial precedent on the meaning of Indian title to land without any consideration of these matters. But one does not have to look very hard to find that the attitudes of Whites toward the Indian peoples in the 1880s were generally based on ignorance of Indian cultures and prejudicial views of human society. Moreover, it is clear that those attitudes influenced judicial conceptions of Indian title to land in the St. Catherine's case, making reliance on that aspect of the case highly problematic."

38 Newcomb, "The UN Declaration on the Rights of Indigenous Peoples," 578.

39 Ibid., 579

40. Ibid., 579-580.

41 Ibid., 578-607.

42 Ibid., 579; see also Anghie, Imperialism.

43 Ibid;

44 Ibid., 579-580.

45 For other views on the effects of colonialism on the colonized see the French-trained Martiniquan psychiatrist Frantz Fanon, who practiced in Algeria during the height of that colony's independence struggle, emphasized the devastating mental effects of colonialism upon the colonized. See, e.g., Frantz Fanon, *The Wretched of the Earth* (New York: Grove Press, 1963), 181-85. Other noteworthy works arising from the same context and pursuing essentially the same theme include Albert Memmi's *The Colonizer and the Colonized* (New York: Orion Press, 1965) and *Dominated Man: Sketches for a Portrait* (New York: Orion Press, 1968).

46 See also Steven T. Newcomb, "On Narratives and Dehumanization," *Indian Country Today*, June 20, 2012, http://indiancountryto¬daymedianetwork.com.

47 Steven Newcomb, personal communication, January 11, 2013. For the material at issue, see René Maunier, *The Sociology of Colonies: An Introduction to the Study of Race Contact* (London: Routledge and Kegan Paul, 1949), 3-36.

48 Newcomb, *Pagans*, 18.

49 Ibid., 17.

50 Ibid.

51 Chrisjohn, Young, with Michael Maraun, *Circle Game* 34.

52 Ibid., 19-23, 34-38, 99-101.

53 On the neo-Nazi use of minimization techniques, see, e.g., Deborah Lipstadt, *Denying the Holocaust: The Growing Assault on Truth and Memory* (New York: Free Press, 1993) esp. 7-8, 52-61, 90-4.

54 Newcomb, *Pagans*, 17.

55 See John S. Milloy, *A National Crime: The Canadian Government and the Residential School System, 1879 to 1986* (Winnipeg: The University of Manitoba Press, 1999) for a review of his analysis that characterizes the residential school as less than the genocidal reality.

56 Steven Newcomb, "A Critique of the Proposed Doctrine of Reconciliation" (San Diego: Indigenous Law Institute, 2012), 1.

57 Newcomb, *Pagans*, xxii.

58 Ibid., 3.

59 Concise Oxford Dictionary (9th ed.), sub verbo "dehumanize."

60 Collins English Dictionary (2nd ed.), sub verbo "colonialism."

61 Ibid., sub verbo "indoctrination."

62 *Webster's New Dictionary and Thesaurus*, sub verbo, "brainwashing."

63 Lemkin, *Axis Rule*, 79.

64 Apart from the several relevant works already cited with respect to the matrices of dehumanization and domination under colonialism, also see Jean-Paul Sartre, "Preface" to Fanon, *Wretched of the Earth*, xliii-lxii; Azzedine Haddour, "Introduction: Remembering Sartre," in Jean-Paul Sartre, *Colonialism and Neocolonialism* (New York: Routledge, 2001), 1-29; Steven Newcomb and Birgil Kills Straight, "The Doctrine of Discovery and the Protocol of Domination: A Short Essay for the North American Indigenous Caucus Preparatory Meeting for the UN Permanent Forum on Indigenous Issues" (San Diego: Indigenous Law Institute, 2012). Relatedly, as concerns Canada in particular, see Dean Neu and Richard Therrien, *Accounting for Genocide: Canada's Bureaucratic Assault on Aboriginal Peoples* (Halifax, N.S.: Fernwood, 2003).

65 United Nations General Assembly, One Hundredth and Seventh Meeting, Sixth Committee, U.N. Doc. A/C.6/SR.107 (15 November 1948) [U.N. Doc. A/C.6/SR.107], reprinted in Hirad Abtahi and Philippa Webb, eds., *The Genocide Convention: The Travaux*

Préparatoires Vol 2, (Leiden: Martinus Nijhoff, 2008) [Travaux], 1816.

66 See Jean-Paul Sartre, "On Genocide" in Jean-Paul Sartre and Arlette El Kaïm Sartre, *On Genocide and a Summary of the Evidence and Judgments of the International War Crimes Tribunal* (Boston: Beacon Press, 1968), 63. Sartre elucidates the connection between the concepts of colonialism and cultural genocide; Also see Jean-Paul Sartre, "Colonialism is a System," in Sartre, *Colonialism and Neocolonialism,* 30-47.

67 Chrisjohn and Young, with Maraun, *Circle Game*, 70.

68 In her *Beyond Blood: Rethinking Indigenous Identity* (Saskatoon: Purich, 2011), Pamela Palmater delineates how colonial law is designed to bring about the "legislative extinction" of Indigenous People. More expansively, See Bruce Clark, N*ative Liberty, Crown Sovereignty: The Existing Aboriginal Right of Self-Government in Canada* (Montréal: McGill-Queen's University Press, 1990).

69 James Crawford, "Foreword" to Antony Anghie, *Imperialism, Sovereignty and the Making of International Law* (Cambridge, UK: Cambridge University Press, 2004), xi. He continues further, "and doing so despite continued professions of idealism and universal values by the (Western) lawyers and leaders who have been dominantly engaged."

70 Crawford, "Foreword," xi.

71 See e.g. Kurt Mundorff, "Other Peoples' Children: A Textual and Contextual Interpretation of the Genocide Convention, Article II(e)," *Harvard International Law Journal* 50, No. 1 (Winter 2009): 61.

72 Ibid., 65-66.

73 Aimé Césaire, *Discourse on Colonialism*, (New York: Monthly Review Press, 1972), 13.

74 Koskenniemi, *Gentle Civilizer,* 106.

75 United Nations General Assembly, Sixty Third Meeting, Sixth Committee, U.N. Doc. A/C.6/SR.63 (30 September 1948) [U.N. Doc. A/C.6/SR], reprinted in Abtahi and Webb, *Travaux,* 1291. Brazil said, "Cultural genocide should be taken to denote the destruction by violence of the cultural and social characteristics of a group of human beings; care should be taken, when dealing with new countries, not to favor [the oppressed] which would tend to oppose the legitimate efforts made to assimilate the [oppressed peoples] by the countries in which they were living.

76 Venne, "The Creator Knows Their Lies and So Should We" introduction to Churchill, *Perversions of Justice*, xiii.

77 United Nations General Assembly, One Hundredth and Seventy Ninth Meeting, Sixth Committee, U.N. Doc. A/PV.179 (9 December 1948) [U.N. Doc. A/PV.179], reprinted in Abtahi and Webb, *Travaux,* 2082-83. See the USSR's discussion on the "doctrines of racial superiority", the removal of "cultural genocide" and "the colonies administered by

the countries who prided themselves on their civilization."

78 Newcomb, *Pagans,* xxiv.

79 Lemkin, *Axis Rule*, ix.

80 See Greg Bradsher, "The Nuremberg Laws: Archives Receives Original Nazi Documents That 'Legalized' Persecution of Jews," *Prologue Magazine* 42, No. 4 (Winter 2010), http://www.archives.gov/ publications/prologue/2010/winter/nuremberg.html; Also see United State Holocaust Museum, "Holocaust Encyclopedia: Nuremberg Laws," https://www.ushmm.org/wlc/en/article.php?ModuleId=10007902.

81 Lemkin, *Axis Rule*, 79.

82 Samantha Power, *A Problem From Hell: America and the Age of Genocide* (New York: Basic Books, 2002), 43.

83 "From the start, the meaning of 'genocide' was controversial. Many people were receptive to the idea of coining a word that would connote a practice so horrid and so irreparable that the very utterance of the word would galvanize all who heard it. They also recognized that it would be unwise and undesirable to make Hitler's crimes the future standard for moving outsiders to act. Statesmen and citizens needed to learn from the past without letting it paralyze them. They had to respond to mass atrocity long before the carnage had reached the scale of the Holocaust. But the link between Hitler's Final Solution and Lemkin's hybrid term would cause endless confusion for policymakers and ordinary people who assumed that genocide occurred only where the perpetrators of atrocity could be shown, like Hitler, to possess an intent to exterminate every last member of an ethnic, national, or religious group." Power, Problem from Hell, 43. It should be noted that Power's pat description of Nazi intentions is questionable, and may well serve simply as a definitional contrivance. For well-supported argumentation to the effect that, rhetoric notwithstanding, even Hitler never literally intended to exterminate "every last member" of a target population (e.g., Jews), see David E. Stannard, "Uniqueness as Denial: The Politics of Genocide Scholarship," in Alan S. Rosenbaum, ed., *Is the Holocaust Unique? Perspectives on Comparative Genocide* (Boulder, CO: Westview Press, 1996), esp. 170-71, 185-89. Relatedly, see Ward Churchill, "Lie for Lie: Linkages between Holocaust Deniers and Proponents of the 'Uniqueness' of the Jewish Experience in World War II," in his *A Little Matter of Genocide: Holocaust and Denial in the Americas, 1492 to the Present* (San Francisco: City Lights Books, 1997), 63-80.

84 On the Nazi agenda in Eastern Europe, see Alexander Dallin, *German Rule in Russia, 1941-1945: A Study in Occupation Policy,* 2nd ed. (London: Macmillan, 1981). With regard to the European performance in North America, see Ward Churchill, "'Nits Make Lice': The Extermination of North American Indians, 1607-1996," in Churchill, *Little Matter of Genocide*, 129-288; David E. Stannard, *American*

Holocaust: Columbus and the Conquest of the New World (New York: Oxford University Press, 1992), esp. 223-46. On the latter process serving as the model for the former, see Norman Rich, *Hitler's War Aims: Ideology, The Nazi State, and the Course of Expansion* (New York: W.W. Norton, 1973), 8; John Toland, *Adolf Hitler* (New York: Doubleday, 1976), 702; Timothy Snyder, *Bloodlands: Europe Between Hitler and Stalin* (New York: Basic Books, 2010), 160; Carroll P. Kakel, III, *The American West and the Nazi East: A Comparative and Interpretive Perspective* (New York: Palgrave Macmillan, 2013).

85 Robert Davis and Mark Zannis, *The Genocide Machine in Canada* (Montréal: Black Rose Books, 1973), 28.

86 Ibid., 29.

87 Ibid.

88 Ward Churchill, *Kill the Indian Save the Man: The Genocidal Impact of American Indian Residential Schools* (San Francisco: City Lights Books, 2004), 78.

89 Ibid; Also see Sartre, "Colonialism is a System," 30-47.

90 Sartre, *On Genocide*, 63-64.

91 Power, *A Problem from Hell*, 43.

92 For the estimate that the North American Indigenous population "surpassed 18 million individuals" circa 1500, see Henry F. Dobyns, *Their Number Become Thinned: Native American Population Dynamics in Eastern North America* (Knoxville: University of Tennessee Press, 1983), 343. For the number of Indigenous people surviving north of the Río Bravo (Rio Grande) circa 1900, see for the U.S., U.S. Bureau of the Census, *Fifteenth Census of the United State, 1930: The Indian Population of the United States and Alaska* (Washington, D.C.: Government Printing Office, 1937) "Table H: Indian Population by Divisions and States, 1890-1930"; for Canada, James H. Mooney, *The Aboriginal Population of America North of Mexico* (Washington, D.C.: Smithsonian Miscellaneous Collections LXXX, No. 7, 1928), 33. The best-known instance of a complete physical extermination is probably that of the Beothuks, but there were many others. On the example given, see L.F.S. Upton, "The Extermination of the Beothuks in Newfoundland," *in Sweet Promises: A Reader on Indian-White Relations in Canada,* ed. J.R. Miller (Toronto: University of Toronto Press, 1991), 68-89. For a close study of the outright extermination of numerous peoples in a specific area during a single brief period, see Brendan Lindsay, *Murder State: California's Native American Genocide, 1846-1873* (Lincoln: University of Nebraska Press, 2012).

93 Stannard, *American Holocaus*t, 281.

94 George E. Tinker, "Tracing a Contour of Colonialism: American Indians and the Trajectory of Educational Imperialism," preface to Churchill, *Kill the Indian*, xiv.

95 Churchill, *Kill the Indian*, 77; quoting/citing p. 15 of Sartre's preface to Fanon's *Wretched of the Earth*; xxiv-xxv of his introduction to

Memmi's *Colonizer and Colonized,* and p. 76 of his 1958 essay, "A Victory," included in Sartre, *Colonialism and Neocolonialism*, 65-77.

96 See Giorgio Agamben, *Homo Sacer: Sovereign Power and Bare Life* (Stanford, CA: Stanford University Press, 1998). Agamben, further holds that the colonized exist in permanent "state of exception" imposed by the colonizing sovereign, whereby they are perpetually subjected to a legislative/juridical process of "inclusive exclusion," i.e., forced into compliance with a legal régime designed to proscribe their traditional ("autochthanous") sociocultural, political, and economic identities while formally demarcating their status as beings "Other"—and less—than members of the colonizing society. He substantially develops and refines this theme in his *State of Exception* (Chicago: University of Chicago Press, 2005). Agamben himself has never directly addressed the issue of Indigenous Peoples, but see Mark Rifkin, "Indigenizing Agamben: Rethinking Sovereignty in Light of the 'Peculiar' Status of Native Peoples," *in Agamben and Colonialism,* eds. Marcelo Svirsky and Simone Bignall (Edinburgh: Edinburgh University Press, 2012), 77-109.

97 McNeil, "Social Darwinism," 71.

98 See Newcomb, *Pagans,* 19.

99 Newcomb, "The UN Declaration on the Rights of Indigenous Peoples," 579.

100 Rarihowkwats, Unpublished speech delivered at the Treaties 1-11 Conference in Regina, Saskatchewan (October 2010).

101 As George Orwell framed the approach in *Nineteen Eighty-Four,* "We shall squeeze you empty, and then we shall fill you with ourselves." The passage is quoted as an epigraph to Part I of Naomi Klein's *The Shock Doctrine: The Rise of Disaster Capitalism* (New York: Alfred A. Knopf, 2007). For a taste of the true horror embodied in brainwashing techniques, see Klein's first chapter, "The Torture Lab: Ewen Cameron, The CIA and the Maniacal Quest to Erase and Remake the Human Mind," 25-48.

102 Ngũgĩ wa Thiong'o, *Decolonising the Mind: The Politics of Language in African Literature* (Portsmouth, NH: James Currey/Heinemann, 1986), 16.

103 Ibid.

104 Ibid., 17.

105 Ibid., 18.

106 Sartre, *On Genocide*, 63.

107 Jean-Paul Sartre, "A Victory" in Sartre, *Colonialism and Neocolonialism*, 76.

108 Thiong'o, *Decolonising the Mind,* 17.

109 Tinker, "Contour of Colonialism," preface to Churchill, *Kill the Indian,* xviii.

110 Churchill, *Kill the Indian*, 77. Also see Fanon, *Wretched of the Earth,* 181-239.

111 Sartre, "Wretched of the Earth," lii. This is a fresh translation of Sartre's earlier-cited "Preface" to *Wretched of the Earth*. It is included in Sartre, *Colonialism and Neocolonialism*, 136-155.

112 Churchill, *Kill the Indian*, 77.

113 Churchill, *Kill the Indian,* 77. Citing from Sartre, "The Wretched of the Earth," in *Colonialism and Neocolonialism*, 142-43.

114 Fanon, *Wretched of the Earth*, 181.

115 Ibid., 181-182.

116 Ibid., 182.

117 Sartre, "The Wretched of the Earth" in *Colonialism and Neocolonialism*, 144.

118 Tinker, "Contour of Colonialism," preface to Churchill, *Kill the Indian*, xvii.

119 Chrisjohn and Young, with Maraun, *Circle Game*, 70. This phrase is taken from the subtitle.

120 Ibid., 99.

121 Ibid., 100.

122 Chrisjohn and his coauthors conclude that the real "Residential School Syndrome" centers in the pathological efforts of the perpetrator society to evade responsibility for what was done in the schools, why, and even that it was done. Among those suffering most acutely from RSS in this diagnosis are those belonging to the "therapeutic establishment" who insist upon pathologizing individual victims as a means of displacing responsibility from the perpetrator society of which they themselves form an integral component. For their position and diagnostic criteria supporting it, see Chrisjohn and Young, with Maraun, *Circle Game*, 101-104. In forming their overall argument, they draw upon a broad range of sources, perhaps most significantly William Ryan's *Blaming the Victim* (New York: Random House, 1971); Thomas Szasz, *The Therapeutic State: Psychiatry in the Mirror of Current Events* (Buffalo, NY: Prometheus Books, 1984), and Andrew Polsky, *The Rise of the Therapeutic State* (Princeton, NJ: Princeton University Press, 1991).

123 Tinker, "Contour of Colonialism ," preface to Churchill, *Kill the Indian*, xvi.

124 Césaire, *Discourse on Colonialism*, 9.

125 Ibid., 18.

126 Chrisjohn and Young, with Maraun, *Circle Game*, 98.

127 Tinker, "Contour of Colonialism," preface to Churchill, *Kill the Indian,* xvi.

128 Joshua David Bellin, *The Demon of the Continent: Indians and the Shaping of American Literature* (Philadelphia: University of Pennsylvania Press, 2001), 1. This is from the realm of American literature with respect to Indigenous Peoples.

129 See Ward Churchill, *Indians Are Us? Culture and Genocide in Native North America* (Maine: Common Courage Press, 2002).

130 Stannard, *American Holocaust*, x.

131 See Paul Johnson, *Birth of the Modern: World Society, 1815-1830* (New York: HarperCollins, 1991). On the subsequent hegemony of legal positivism in the Western juridical and diplomatic thought, see, e.g., Francis Anthony Boyle, *Foundations of World Order: The Legalist Approach to International Relations, 1898-1922* (Durham, NC: Duke University Press, 1999).

132 For a very succinct overview, see Nigel Joseph, "Doing things our way: The "state of nature" in Hobbes and Locke, land appropriation, and the inclusive autonomies of Indigenous people (Unpublished Paper, Assistant Professor, University of Western Ontario). Also see John C. Mohawk, *Utopian Legacies: A History of Conquest and Oppression in the Western World* (Santa Fe: NM: Clear Light, 2000), 152-153.

133 The first tenet of positivism is that "primitive communities have only primary rules and that these are binding entirely because of practices of acceptance. Such communities cannot be said to have 'law,' because there is no way to distinguish a set of legal rules from amongst other social rules. [Only] when a particular community has developed a fundamental secondary rule that stipulates how legal rules are to be identified, the idea of a distinct set of rules, and thus law, is born." Ronald Dworkin, "The Model of Rules I," from Taking Rights Seriously" *in Readings in the Philosophy of Law,* ed. Keith C. Culver, 2nd ed. (Petersborough, ON: Broadview Press, 2008), 152.

134 Perhaps because colonial practice was often to effectively treat Indigenous territories as if they were uninhabited, the term terra nullius is often mistakenly believed to mean "vacant land." The term for the latter, which also has a place in the European legal discourse, is vacuum domicilium. It is used much less frequently because genuinely unoccupied land was a rarity on the planet long before the European expansion began. While Hobbes popularized the term terra nullius, he by no means invented it. The concept originated in Roman law, and was integrated into the so-called Doctrine of Discovery well before 1492. In terms of formal legal theory, it was developed by Hugo Grotius before Hobbes seized upon it, and was subsequently refined to a considerable extent by Emer de Vattel and others. See Olive P. Dickason, "Concepts of Sovereignty at the Time of First Contacts," in L.C. Green and Olive P. Dickason, *The Law of Nations and the New World* (Edmonton: University of Alberta Press, 1989), 221, 235, 239-40. Also see Williams, *American Indian in Western Legal Thought,* 13-15, 43-50. For an example of terra nullius being misconstrued as meaning "empty of people," see Boyce Richardson, People of Terra Nullius: Betrayal and Rebirth on Aboriginal Canada (Vancouver: Douglas & McIntyre, 1993), vii.

135 Williams, *American Indian in Western Legal Thought*, 246-251.

136 Ibid., 248.

137 Ibid., 248, 249.

138 Anthony J. Hall, *Earth Into Property: Colonization, Decolonization,*

and Capitalism: The Bowl With One Spoon, Volume Two (Montréal: McGill-Queen's University Press, 2010).

139 James (Sákéj) Youngblood Henderson, "The Context of the State of Nature," in Marie Battiste, ed., *Reclaiming Indigenous Voice and Vision* (Vancouver: University of British Columbia Press, 2001), 13.

140 *Regina v. The St. Catharines Milling and Lumber Company* (1885), 10 O.R. 196 at 206 (Chancery Division).

141 See, e.g., Churchill, *Kill the Indian*, 77-78; citing/quoting Sartre, *On Genocide*, 62-63; "Preface" to *Wretched of the Earth,* 15; "Wretched of the Earth," 145; "Colonialism is a System," 30-47; and "A Victory," 76.

142 *Delgamuukw v. British Columbia,* (1991) 79 DLR (4th) 185.

143 Ibid., at 208.

144 And look at them now, realizing that their land practices have run amok, turning to Indigenous Peoples as protectors of the land.

145 Williams, *American Indians in Western Legal Thought*, 325.

146 Ibid., 326.

147 For further discussion of the fallout, see Ward Churchill, "The Tragedy and the Tragedy: The Subversion of Indigenous Sovereignty in North America," in Churchill, *Struggle for the Land: Native North American Resistance to Genocide, Ecocide, and Colonization* (Winnipeg: Arbeiter Ring, 1999), 43-53.

148 U.N. Doc. A/PV 179, reprinted in Abtahi and Webb, *Travaux*, 2083. Also see Newcomb, *Pagans*, 13-17.

149 Ibid., 2082

150 Ibid., 2083. Also see Newcomb and Kills Straight, "Doctrine of Discovery," 3-4.

151 Newcomb, *Pagans*, 14. Also see Tzvetan Todorov, *The Conquest of America: The Question of the Other* (New York: Harper & Row, 1984) esp. 42-44, 129-33, 150-51, 248-9.

152 See Agamben, *Homo Sacer.*

153 Colonialism invariably "manifest[s] the agenda of dominating originally free peoples" on the grounds that they are "wild, barbarous, savage, heathen, pagan, infidel, wandering (around free of domination) roaming (free of domination), domesticated, conquered, uncivilized (not yet dominated), minors, tribes, tribal, aborigines, aboriginal, ethnic groups, rude, primitive, ignorant, dirty, and so forth." Newcomb and Kills Straight, "Doctrine of Discovery," 3. For a very strong argument as to why we should reject continued usage of terms like "tribe," see Ward Churchill, "Naming Our Destiny: Toward a Language of American Indian Liberation," in his *Indians Are Us? Culture and Genocide in Native North America* (Toronto: Between the Lines, 1994), 291-357. Churchill himself might of course be open to criticism for using the term "American Indian," although his activism as a member of the American Indian Movement (AIM) may well have left him little choice. In any case, he contends that the term originated

not in a mistaken reference to "India," but from Columbus' initial description of the Indigenous People of "Española" as being "in Dios," which translates as "close to God."

154 The Nazis may well have adopted the term from the title of the acclaimed euroamerican racial theorist Lothrop Stoddard's *The Revolt Against Civilization: The Menace of the Under Man* (New York: Charles Scribner's Sons, 1922). Stoddard's books are known to have been Hitler's favorites, and Stoddard himself was accorded extraordinary access to the Führer and other high-ranking Nazi officials while living in Germany for several months in 1939-40. See Stefan Kühl, *The Nazi Connection: Eugenics, American Racism, and German National Socialism* (New York: Oxford University Press, 1994), 60-61.

155 Newcomb and Kill Straight, "Doctrine of Discovery," 3; Todorov, *Conquest of America*, 133-45.

156 Blaut, Colonizer's Model, 1. The very ideas of "The West" and "Western Civilization" have been characterized as "a fraud" and "a grim farce." "Even the geographic status of 'Europe' is invented. Far from being a continent in its own right—less still 'The Continent,' as most eurocentrists have long-since proclaimed it—Europe, the territorial locus of 'The West,' is, 'geographically speaking[,]... simply a large peninsula of Asia.'" Ward Churchill, "Foreword: The Islamophobic Foundation of 'Western Civilization,'" in Stephen Sheehi, *Islamophobia: The Ideological Campaign Against Muslims* (Atlanta: Clarity Press, 2011), 17; quoting Kenneth C. Davis, *Don't Know Much About Geography: Everything You Need to Know About the World but Never Learned* (New York: William Morrow, 1992), 129. Also see generally, Williams, *Savage Anxieties*.

157 "The very term 'Europe'...originated with the Phoenician word 'erub, connoting 'a place of nether darkness' and ignorance. It is perhaps self-evident that those inhabiting a domain viewed for over a millennium as amounting to no more than a benighted cultural backwater, utterly irrelevant to civilized societies, might well have come to harbor a certain resentment. No less certainly, such resentments were in all likelihood fueled by an ever deepening and more intractable sense of cultural inferiority." The virulence of the collective inferiority complex which marked the formation of "European" or "Western" cultural identity could only be "rectified" in the disordered minds of those afflicted by way of continuous and ferocious assaults upon Others, "not simply [for purposes of] negating the Other's existence...but of claiming the attributes giving shape to the Other's superior status, thereby in effect incorporating the attainments of the Other into its own conception of itself." Although it was already underway, the process may be said to have begun in earnest with the so-called First Crusade in 1095, and has continued ever since. See Churchill, "Islamophobic Foundation of 'Western Civilization,'" 17-20; citing, among other sources, *J.R.S.*

Philips, The Medieval Expansion of Europe (New York: Oxford University Press, 1988); and Jo Ann Hoeppner Moran Cruz, "Popular Attitudes Toward Islam in Medieval Europe," in Michael Frassetto and David R. Blanks, eds., *Western Views of Islam in Medieval and Early Europe: Perception of the Other* (New York: Palgrave, 1999), 55-82. Also see Chrisjohn and Young, with Maraun, Circle Game, 101-104.

158 Blaut, Colonizer's Model, 1. Put somewhat differently, "eurocentrism" is Europe's practice of "contemplating itself as the center of the world, the axis of civilization, [and] the goal of history." Hichem Djaït, *Europe and Islam* (Berkeley: University of California Press, 1985), 5. Also see Samir Amin, *Eurocentrism* (New York Monthly Review Press, 1989), 106-17.

159 "It is the idea that Europe was more advanced and more progressive than all other regions prior to 1492, prior, that is, to the beginning of the period of colonialism, the period in which Europe and non-Europe came into intense interaction.... Therefore: colonialism cannot have been really important for Europe's modernization. Therefore: colonialism must mean, for the Africans, Asians and Americans, not spoliation and cultural destruction, but, rather, the receipt-by-diffusion of European civilization." Blaut, *Colonizer's Model,* 2.

160 See Churchill, *Matter of Genocide*, for a review of numbers estimated in North America; see Stannard, *American Holocaust,* for a review of the numbers estimated in South America.

161 *Western Sahara.*

162 Venne, *Our Elders Understand Our Rights*, 45-46.

163 Ibid., 45.

164 Ibid.

165 Ibid., 46.

166 For the Elders' understanding of treaty review the sources listed below. This book does not refer to Treaties in the context of the Canadian state's policies on land claims (land extinguishment agreements) but rather to the historic treaties (numbered treaties, peace and friendship treaties) negotiated and concluded prior to Canada becoming an independent colony. On that note, Canada is not a party to the Treaty. The states inherited the legal obligations to honour and respect the Treaty. It is also important to recognize that at that time, the nearly 200 Indigenous Nations in what is now called British Columbia never entered into a treaty relationship, though their children, too, were seized and placed in the residential school system. See the following for a review of treaty as international agreements. Miguel Alfonso Martínez,(Special Rapporteur), Final Repot: Human Rights of Indigenous People Study on Treaties, agreements and other constructive arrangements between States and indigenous populations (E/CN.4/Sub 2/1999/20 (1999)); Isabelle Schulte-Tenckhoff, "Reassessing the Paradigm of Domestication: The Problematic of Indigenous Treaties," *Review of Constitutional Studies* 4, No. 2 (1998): 239-89; Sharon Venne, "Understanding Treaty Six: An

Indigenous Perspective" in *Aboriginal and Treaty Rights in Canada: Essays on Law, Equality and Respect for Difference,* ed. Michael Asch (Vancouver: UBC, Press, 1997), 173-207; Sharon Venne, ed., *Honour Bound Onion Lake and the Spirit of Treaty Six: The International Validity of Treaties with Indigenous Peoples* (Copenhagen: International Working Group for Indigenous Affairs Doc. 84, 1997). Andrew Gray, "Onion Lake and the Revitalization of Treaty Six," in Venne, *Honour Bound Onion Lake and the Spirit of Treaty Six*, 19-54.

167 See Sharon H. Venne, "Treaties Made in Good Faith" in *Native and Settlers—Now and Then*, ed. Paul W. DePasquale (Edmonton: University of Alberta Press, 2007), 1-16. Venne reiterated these points when interviewed by the author on January 4, 2013.

168 Martinez, *Study on Treaties*, para. 116.

169 Martinez, *Study on Treaties*, para. 117; also see paras. 122 and 214.

170 See Venne, *Honour Bound.*

171 Venne, "Understanding Treaty Six," 193.

172 Ibid., 192. As UN special rapporteur Miguel Alfonso Martinez concluded, "This observation clearly pertains to all treaty/agreement-related issues. One example is the alleged opposition, in the Canadian context, between treaties of peace and friendship (concluded in the eighteenth century and earlier) and so-called numbered treaties or 'land surrenders' (especially from the second half of the nineteenth century on). This opposition is contradicted by indigenous parties to numbered treaties, who consider that they are parties to treaties of peace, friendship and alliance and that they did not cede either their territories or their original juridical status as sovereigns. Similar discrepancies are to be noted in the United States and New Zealand." Martinez, *Study on Treaties*, para. 122.

173 Venne, "Treaties Made in Good Faith," 9. Lord Denning explained, "There is nothing, so far as I can see, to warrant any distrust by the Indians of the Government of Canada. But in case there should be, the discussion in this case will strengthen their hand so as to enable them to withstand any onslaught. They will be able to say that their rights and freedoms have been guaranteed to them by the Crown—originally by the Crown in respect of the United Kingdom—now by the Crown in respect of Canada—but, in any case, by the Crown. No Parliament should do anything to lessen the worth of these guarantees. They should be honored by the Crown in respect of Canada 'so long as the sun rises and the river flows.' That promise must never be broken." *The Queen v. The Secretary of State for Foreign and Commonwealth Affairs, ex parte: The Indian Association of Alberta, Union of New Brunswick Indians, Union of Nova Scotian Indians,* [1981] 4 CNLR 86 (QL) at para 11.

174 See Venne, "Treaties Made in Good Faith," 1-16, 81-82.

175 Ibid., 2.

176 Quoted in Venne, *Honour Bound*, 93.

177 Chrisjohn and Young, with Maraun, *Circle Game*, 70.

178 Ibid.

179 Agnes Grant, *No End of Grief: Indian Residential Schools in Canada* (Winnipeg: Pemmican, 1996), 210.

180 Quoted in Venne, *Honour Bound*, 93.

181 In our interview Sharon Venne strongly emphasized that the undermining and eventual eradication of Indigenous languages was an intended effect of the residential schools into which the children of Original Nations were forcibly transferred. That our "children continue to be given no choice but to attend schools…submersing [them] in English or French" at the expense of proficiency in their own languages is not only well-documented, but "tantamount to [their] forcible transfer," and thus an ongoing violation of the Genocide Convention. See Andrea Bear Nicholas, "Action needed to stop the destruction of indigenous languages," NB Media Co-Op (November 18, 2013), http://nbmediacoop.org/2013/11/18/action-needed-to-stop-the-destruction-of-indigenous-languages/

182 See especially Venne, *Honour Bound*, for a review of the concern that young people do not understand the Treaty; see generally Venne, "Treaties Made in Good Faith" for the concern that young people do not understand the Treaty.

183 One way the State of Canada individualizes a collective attack against our Nations is by the Residential School Settlement Agreement compensation payouts to settle personal "abuse." Rather the residential school system should be viewed as a grave violation of our Treaties.

184 RCAP, "Residential Schools," 313.

185 See e.g. Michael A. McDonnell and A. Dirk Moses, "Raphael Lemkin as Historian of Genocide in the Americas," *Journal of Genocide Research* 7(4) (December 2005):501-529, doi:10.1080/14623520500349951; see e.g. MacDonald, David, "First Nations, Residential Schools, and the Americanization of the Holocaust: Rewriting Indigenous History in the United States and Canada," *Canadian Journal of Political Science* 40:4 (December 2007): 995-1015, doi:10.1017/S0008423907071107.

186 Mundorff, "Other Peoples' Children," 65-66; discussing Colin Tatz, *With Intent to Destroy: Reflecting on Genocide* (New York: Verso, 2003), 146.

187 Mundorff, "Other Peoples' Children," 66.

188 Newcomb, *Pagans*, 131.

189 Ibid.

190 Ibid.

191 Office of the Prime Minster, *Apology to Students*.

192 Richard Henry Pratt, "The Advantages of Mingling Indians with Whites," *Proceedings and Addresses of the National Education Association, 1895* (Washington, D.C.: National Educational Association, 1895), 761-762; cited in Churchill, *Kill the Indian*, 90.

193 MacDonald, *House of Commons*, 1107-08.

194 "BC residential school survivor says he was starved: At least 1300 aboriginal children were involved in the government run nutrition experiment," CBC Canada (July 17, 2013), http://www.cbc.ca/news/canada/british-columbia/b-c-residential-school-survivor-says-he-was-starved-1.1317712

195 Dene Moore, "Provinces hand over aboriginal death records from residential school period" CTV News (28 March 2014), https://www.ctvnews.ca/canada/provinces-hand-over-aboriginal-death-records-from-residential-school-period-1.1751450

196 Chinta Puxley, "Up to 6,000 children may have died at Canada's residential schools" CTV News (31 May 2015), https://www.ctvnews.ca/canada/up-to-6-000-children-may-have-died-at-canada-s-residential-schools-1.2399586

197 Milloy, *National Crime*, 91; citing P.H. Bryce, *Report on the Indian Schools of Manitoba and the Northwest Territories* (Ottawa: Government Printing Bureau, 1907).

198 Ibid.

199 Tinker, "Contour of Colonialism," preface to Churchill, *Kill the Indian*, xxiv. For comparative data, see Churchill, Kill the Indian, 34.

200 RCAP, "Residential Schools," 312.

201 Quoted in RCAP, "Residential Schools," 331. As evidenced both by Scott's statement and by Bryce's *Report on the Indian Schools*, the responsible officials were by 1907 unquestionably aware of the extreme damage being done to Indigenous children confined in such facilities.

202 Bob Weber, "Government conducted nutrition experiments on hungry, malnourished Aboriginal Children: paper, Researchers in 1942 decided that isolated, dependent people in northern Manitoba would be ideal subjects for tests on the effects of different diets" *National Post* (16 July 2013), http://nationalpost.com/news/canada/government-conducted-nutrition-experiments-on-hungry-malnourished-aboriginal-children-paper.

203 The term "loophole" refers to state representatives, such as Poland and USSR that opposed the removal of the legal concept of "cultural genocide" and their concern that perpetrators of the crime might invoke the loopholes. See for e.g. U.N. Doc. A/PV.179, reprinted in Abtahi and Webb, Travaux, 2082.

204 Truth and Reconciliation Canada, *Honouring the Truth, Reconciling for the Future: Summary of the Final Report of the Truth and Reconciliation Commission of Canada* (Winnipeg, MB: Truth and Reconciliation Commission of Canada, 2015), 1.

205 See Davis and Zannis, *Genocide Machine*, 23.

206 See e.g. RCAP, "Residential Schools," 331.

207 Office of the Prime Minster, *Apology to Students*.

208 Mathew Lippman, "The Global Politics of Genocide Denial" in *United Nations Conference Commemorating the 60th Anniversary*

of the Genocide Convention (The Hague, December 11, 2008); See Churchill, Perversions of Justice.

209 This three-stage formulation was offered in a presentation by Miguel Alfonso Martinez, Working Session on Indigenous Issues Edmonton, Alberta. (September 18, 2009).

210 For use of the term "body politic" in the manner intended here, see Titley, Narrow Vision, 50. For use of the term "colonial body" and "body politic" in the same sense, see Newcomb, *Pagans*, 16.

211 U.S. President Theodore Roosevelt, for example, described the General Allotment Act of 1887, otherwise known as the "Dawes Act"—a centerpiece of his country's assimilation policy—as a "mighty pulverizing engine to break up the tribal mass." Theodore Roosevelt, "The President Defends the Dawes Act" (1901) Digital History, http://www.digitalhistory.uh.edu/disp_textbook.cfm?smtid=3&psid=720. For use of the term in reference to Canada's residential schools, see, e.g., Chrisjohn and Young, with Maraun, *Circle Game,* 72, 98, 251. As regards use of the term "machine," see the title Davis and Zannis, *Genocide Machine.*

212 The process entails clear violations of Article II(b) and (e) of the Genocide Convention.

213 See especially Churchill, Kill the Indian; also see Agnes Jack, ed., Behind Closed Doors: Stories from the Kamloops Indian Residential School (Penticton, B.C.: Theytus Books, 2006); Bernard Schissel and Terry Wotherspoon, *The Legacy of School for Aboriginal People: Education, Oppression and Emancipation* (New York: Oxford University Press. 2003); J.R. Miller, Shingwauk's *Vision: A History of the Native Residential Schools* (Toronto: University of Toronto Press, 1996).

214 See especially Chrisjohn and Young, with Maraun, Circle Game; also see Carl Urion, "Introduction: The Experience of Indian Residential Schooling," Linda Bull, "Indian Residential Schooling: The Native Perspective," and Rosalind Ing, "The Effects of Residential Schooling on Native Child-Rearing Practices," all in *Canadian Journal of Native Education*, Vol. 18, Supplement (1991), i-iv, 1-64, and 65-118, respectively. Also see Isabelle Knockwood, *Out of the Depths: The Experiences of Mi'kmaw Children at the Indian Residential School at Shubenacadie, Nova Scotia* (Lockeport, NS: Roseway, 1992); Constance Deiter, *From Our Mother's Arms: The Intergenerational Impact of the Residential Schools in Saskatchewan* (Etobicoke, ON: United Church Publishing House, 1999); Ernie Crey and Suzanne Fournier, *Stolen From Our Embrace: The Abduction of First Nations Children and the Restoration of Aboriginal Communities* (Vancouver: Douglas & McIntyre, 1997).

215 See Churchill, *Kill the Indian*, front cover and 20. These juxtaposed images can be viewed herein on p. 141. Also see the front cover of Milloy, *National Crime.*

216 Churchill, *Kill the Indian*, 20.
217 Lemkin, *Axis Rule*, 79.
218 Churchill, *Kill the Indian*, 28.
219 MacDonald, *House of Commons,* 1108.
220 For compelling surveys of these horrors, see Churchill, *Kill the Indian*, 16-76; Malloy, *National Crime*, 129-56, 259-93; Chrisjohn, Young, and Maraun, *Circle Game,* 44-57; RCAP, "Residential Schools".
221 Churchill, *Kill the Indian*, 68-82.
222 Office of the Prime Minister, *Apology to Students.*
223 Sartre, "Wretched of the Earth," lii.
224 Churchill, *Kill the Indian*, xlv.
225 In simplest terms, a "total institution" is one designed to strip essential features humanity from human beings, thereby reducing them to a state of "bare life" in Agambenian terms. For the original formulation of the concept, see Erving Goffman, A*sylums: Essays on the Social Situation of Mental Patients and Other Inmates* (Garden City, NY: Anchor Books, 1961). For application to the residential school context, see Chrisjohn and Young, with Maraun, *Circle Game*, 80-104.
226 MacDonald, *House of Commons,* 1107-1108. Also see Newcomb, *Pagans*, 18.
227 Chrisjohn and Young, with Maraun, *Circle Game*, 91.
228 Ibid.
229 *Canadian Oxford Dictionary* (2nd ed.) sub verbo "engine."
230 *The Concise Oxford Dictionary* (9nd ed.), sub verbo "dehumanize."
231 *The Concise Oxford Dictionary* (9nd ed.), sub verbo "engine."
232 Titley, *Narrow Vision*, 50.
233 Newcomb, *Pagans*, 15-16. For purposes of casting it as "the colonizing body," Newcomb adopts Hobbes' metaphor of the state as an "artificial man." William Schabas writes that there is "no doubt that Lemkin understood genocide to be a crime of the state, something, requiring the control, organization and planning that only a state could deliver." William A. Schabas, "Introduction to the Second Edition," in Lemkin, *Axis Rule*, viii.
234 Newcomb, *Pagans,* 16.
235 Ibid. Newcomb explains that "[s]uch conceptions of assimilation are suggestive of COLONIZATION IS EATING, a metaphor that was reflected in a comment made in mid-nineteenth century by Lewis Cass, who was deeply involved in Indian-treaty making in the Great Lakes region. While Cass was a U.S. senator, and before he became secretary of state, he 'once boasted in the Senate that he had 'a capacious swallow for territory'." The term capacious is structured by the CONTAINER image-schema and is derived from the French capere, 'to take or contain' and 'able to contain a great deal.' And swallow refers to the following:

a. 1: to take through the esophagus into the stomach: receive into the body through the mouth and throat…b: to eat hurriedly without careful chewing: gulp down…to cause to disappear: envelop completely: ENGULF, DEVOUR… APPROPRIATE…to receive something into the body through the mouth and throat...syn. see EAT [emphasis original]."

236 Ibid.

237 Ibid; also see Césaire, Discourse on Colonialism, 31; and Ward Churchill, "A Breach of Trust: The Radioactive Colonization of Native North America," in *Acts of Rebellion: The Ward Churchill Reader* (New York: Routledge, 2003), 140 for their uses of the word 'digestion'.

238 Ibid.

239 Churchill, *Kill the Indian*, 12.

240 Newcomb, *Pagans*, 16; For an earlier example of the term being used in this manner, consider the title of Ward Churchill, *Since Predator Came* (Colorado: Aigis Publications, 1995). Churchill credits former AIM leader John Trudell with having introduced him to the idea in a speech delivered during the 1980 Black Hills International Survival Gathering outside Rapid City, South Dakota.

241 Ibid.

242 Titley, *Narrow Vision*, 50.

243 See Theodore Roosevelt, *President Defends the Dawes Act.*

244 See Churchill, *Kill the Indian,* 16-76.

245 MacDonald, *House of Commons*, 1107-1108. Also see McNeil, "Social Darwinism."

246 The Canadian state consumes the land and devours it into its body politic by stripping the land (Mother Earth) of its water, trees, minerals, oil and gas, and so forth. Our Mother Earth is a living being that depends on the 'resources' that the colonial body politic strips and devours into its ravenous hungry greedy body. For further examples of the stripping of our lands see Arthur Manuel and Grand Chief Ronald M. Derrickson, "Sun Peaks to Geneva: Playgrounds and Fortresses' in *Unsettling Canada: A National Wake Up Call* (Toronto: Between the Lines, 2014); see also Winona LaDuke, *Native Struggles for the Land and Life* (Chicago, IL: Haymarket Books, 1999)

247 Indigenous Peoples become swallowed up in a "conceptual system of the dominating society as a means of thinking, speaking and writing about our own existence while challenging certain negative, oppressive, and dominating concepts that have been mentally and, from an indigenous perspective, illegitimately imposed on our existence." Newcomb, *Pagans*, 18. "[T]he fact remains, however, that the ideas used to construct and maintain such patterns of domination are not a physical container, nor a physical object; they are nothing more than mental processes. The paradigm of domination is more and foremost, a

product of the mind." Newcomb, "Paradigm of Domination," 578-606.

248 This was the stated objective of both the government and Christian churches right on into the 1960s, e.g.: "Canada…must increasingly become…a country of white men rooted and grounded in those fundamental conceptions of the individual, of society, [and] of the state…. The Canadian problem in Indian education is not primarily one of schooling Indian children in the same way as other Canadian children are schooled, but of changing the persevering Indian community into a Canadian community." For this purpose, Indigenous children should be isolated "as much as possible from [their] native background, ideally twenty four hours a day and twelve months of the year, to prevent 'exposure' to Indian culture." Fr. Andre Renaud, "Education for Acculturation," in *Oblate Fathers of Canada, Residential Education for Indian Acculturation* (Ottawa: Indian and Eskimo Welfare Commission, 1958), 39, 34. Also see Churchill, *Kill the Indian*, 16-67; Chrisjohn and Young, with Maraun, *Circle Game,* 19-20; and Thiong'o, *Decolonising the Mind*, 16-18.

249 United Nations General Assembly, Eighty-Second Meeting, Sixth Committee, U.N. Doc. A/C.6/SR.82 (23 October 1948) [U.N. Doc. A/C.6/SR.82], reprinted in Abtahi and Webb, *Travaux*, 1494. The representative from Uruguay said, "…there was reason also to condemn measures intended to destroy a new generation through abducting infants, forcing them to change their religion and educating them to become enemies of their own people [emphasis added]."

250 Churchill, *Kill the Indian*, 24.

251 This explanation of the relationship between language, law, and land in Cree tradition derives from that given by Sharon Venne when I interviewed her on January 4, 2013.

252 Venne emphasized this point during our interview. Elsewhere, she quotes elder Alex Twinn of the Louis Bull First Nation explaining how residential school severed him from the teachings that would otherwise have been passed on to him as a child, and elder Alex Bonais of the Little Pine First Nation explaining that by "tak[ing] away our children…the whiteman has broken all our Indian ways." Venne, *Honour Bound*, 90-94.

253 Newcomb, *Pagans*, 19.

254 Venne, Interview.

255 See Churchill, *Kill the Indian*, 68-76; also see Chrisjohn and Young, with Maraun, *Circle Game*, 94-99.

256 See Churchill, Kill the Indian, 19-24.

257 See Chrisjohn, Young, and Maraun, *Circle Game*, 49-51; Churchill, *Kill the Indian*, 51-60; Grant, *No End of Grief*, 225-27.

258 Chrisjohn and Young, with Maraun, *Circle Game*, 49, 255.

259 Steven Newcomb, Interview with Steven Newcomb about his interviews with Elders in the U.S. context of the boarding school system, December 2, 2012.

260 Chrisjohn and Young, with Maraun, *Circle Game*, 91.

261 "There is no explicit reference to child welfare in either the Indian Act or the Constitutional Act, 1867, 1982, it has been subsequently deemed to be the responsibility of the provinces." The Supreme Court of Canada case in which it was "confirmed in 1976 that the legal jurisdiction of the Province's ability to extend child welfare services onto reserve, regardless of the provincial incursion into a federal sphere of responsibility." Marilyn Bennett, "First Nations Fact Sheet: A General Profile on First Nations Child Welfare in Canada" First Nations Child and Family Caring Society,http://www. fncfcs.com/docs/FirstNationsFS1.pdf. Bennett is referring to *Natural Parents v. Superintendent of Child Welfare* (60 D.L.R. 3rd 148 S.C.C. (1976)). Also see Leroy Little Bear, "Section 88 of the Indian Act and the Application of Provincial Laws to Indians" in Anthony Long and Menno Boldt, eds., *Governments in Conflict? Provinces and Indian Nations in Canada* (Toronto: University of Toronto Press, 1992), 175-187.

262 See Aboriginal Justice Implementation Commission, "Child Welfare-The Justice System and Aboriginal People" in *Report of the Aboriginal Justice Inquiry of Manitoba* (Winnipeg: November 1999), http://www.ajic.mb.ca/volume.html; Also see Andrew Armitage, *Comparing the Policy of Aboriginal Assimilation: Australia, Canada and New Zealand* (Vancouver: University of British Columbia Press, 1995); Jacqueline Marie Maurice, Despiriting Aboriginal Children: Aboriginal Children During the 1960s and 1970s Child Welfare Era (unpublished Ph.D. dissertation, University of Toronto Faculty of Social Work, 2003).

263 Statistics Canada, Study: Living arrangements of Aboriginal children aged 14 and under, 2011 (Released at 8:30 a.m. eastern time in *The Daily*, Wednesday, April 13, 2016. The study shows that 48 percent of the children in care are Aboriginal. See National Collaborating Centre for Aboriginal Health, 2013, First Nations and Non-Aboriginal Children in Child Protection Services. Prince George, BC: National Collaborating Centre for Aboriginal Health.

264 See Nico Trocmé, Della Knoke, and Cindy Blackstock, "Pathways to the Overrepresentation of Aboriginal Children in Canada's Child Welfare System," *Social Service Review* 78, No. 4 (December 2004): 577-600, accessed February 3, 2018, https://doi.org/10.1086/424545. These estimates are from 2004; however, they are relevant to contemporary times as they show that even then the numbers of Indigenous children in care at that time were catastrophically high.

265 United Nations General Assembly, Eighty-Third Meeting, Sixth Committee, U.N. Doc. A/C.6/SR.83 (25 October 1948), reprinted in Abtahi and Webb, *Travaux,* 1504.

266 U.N. Doc. A/C.6/SR.82, reprinted in Abtahi and Webb, *Travaux*, 1492; Mundorff explains that "the boundaries between cultural, physical and biological destruction are often indistinct; a cultural mediated form

of destruction, like forcible child transfer, may nonetheless cause a group's physical or biological destruction." Mundorff, "Other Peoples' Children," 63.

267 See generally, Deiter, *From Our Mother's Arms*; Also see Chrisjohn and Young, with Maraun, *Circle Game,* 21-22, 89-101; Churchill, *Kill the Indian*, 71-76; Milloy, *National Crime*, 296, 299-300; Grant, *No End of Grief,* 255-56, 260-62; Ing, "Native Child-Rearing Practices," 65-118.

268 The fallout from the forcible transferring of Indigenous children is incalculable. This list of effects is not exhaustive. For comparison to the people that suffered long term impacts in German concentration camps. See Zdzislaw Jan Ryn, "Long-Term Psychological Morbidity of Incarceration in Auschwitz" No. 6, (April 2000) 6 Echoes of the Holocaust, http://www.holocaustechoes.com/ryn.html, accessed (November 15, 2012). Removed. Copy on file with the author. Zdzislaw Jan Ryn notes that, "the stamp left by experiencing camp stresses seems to be something permanent or even progressive, in both the physical and psychic spheres. The stigma of the concentration camp has been transferred to the second or even third generation."

269 See UN Study on Treaties, para. 135-146 Martinez refers to the land claims process and the domesticating assimilating of the Indigenous Peoples; also see Newcomb, Pagans, 18-20. Newcomb explains the problem is that Indigenous Peoples have been forced to "utilize the language and conceptual system of the dominating society as a means of thinking, speaking and writing about our own existence." From the perspective of this book the forcible indoctrination and effects of genocide is that Original Nations and Peoples enter into agreements that cede and surrender their land under Canada's Comprehensive Land Claims Policy. Indigenous Peoples, who are not raised in accordance with their identities, surrender their lands under this policy. In this regard, if one applies the metaphor in the model, the land and the original peoples become consumed and devoured into the "predator body politic" by the genocidal conditions the state created in the residential schools.

270 See U.N. Doc. A/PV.179, Abtahi and Webb, Travaux, 2028-2083 for a review of how colonialism is masked as a genocidal process.

Chapter Four

1 Elie Wiesel, *Night* (New York: Hill and Wang, [rev. ed.] 2006).

2 For a prime example of the "fence sitting" dimension of the "controversy," see David B. MacDonald and Graham Hudson, "The Genocide Question and Indian Residential Schools in Canada," *Canadian Journal of Political Science* 45, No. 2 (June 2012): 427-449, esp. 429, doi:10.10170S000842391200039X.

3 Article II, *Convention on the Prevention and Punishment of the Crime*

of Genocide, 9 December 1948, 78 UNTS 277, (entered into force 12 January 1951, signed by Canada 28 November 1949, accession by Canada 3 September 1952). Cited from Jayme Herschkopf and Julie Hunter of a coauthored study prepared for the Truth and Reconciliation Commission under the title *Genocide Reinterpreted: An Analysis of the Genocide Convention's Potential Application to Canada's Indian Residential School System* (New Haven, CT: Allard K. Lowenstein International Human Rights Clinic, Yale University College of Law, April 2011), 16. The authors note, ""[T]he United Nations General Assembly adopted the Genocide Convention on December 9, 1948 and the Convention entered into force January 12, 1951. Canada joined the treaty, signing the Convention on November 28, 1948, and subsequently ratifying it on September 3, 1952."

4 See esp. *Criminal Code*, RSC 1985, c C-46, s 318; see also *An Act to amend the Criminal Code*, SC 1970, c C-39, s 267A(2) for the original amendment of Canada's "Hate Propoganda"; also see *An Act to amend the Criminal Code,* SC 1969-70, c C-11, s 281.1(2).

5 Ibid., Article II.

6 An Act Respecting the Criminal Law (R.S., 1985, c. C-46, s. 318; 2004, c. 14, s. 1).

7 Statistics Canada, Study: Living arrangements of Aboriginal children aged 14 and under, 2011 (Released at 8:30 a.m. eastern time in The Daily, Wednesday, April 13, 2016. The report shows that, "[w]hile Aboriginal children represented 7% of all children in Canada in 2011, they accounted for almost half (48%) of all foster children in the country."

8 See generally, *Reservations to the Convention on the Prevention and Punishment of the Crime of Genocide*, Advisory Opinion, [1951] ICJ Rep 15 [hereinafter Advisory Opinion], 23-24. The court found the convention to be universal in scope. Hence, "the universal acceptance by the international community of the norms set out in the Convention since its adoption in 1948 mean that what originated in 'general principles' ought now to be considered a part of customary law." Also see William A. Schabas, *Genocide in International Law: The Crime of Crimes*, 2nd ed. (Cambridge, UK: Cambridge University Press, 2009), 4.

9 Ibid.

10 For a textual analysis of the laws pertaining to genocide, see Schabas, *Genocide*; For a useful discussion of the Convention as a part of international customary law, see John Quigley, *The Genocide Convention: An International Law Analysis* (Burlington, VT: Ashgate, 2006), 80-84.

11 Article 38(1) of the *Statute of the International Court of Justice,* 26 June 1945, 59 Stat 1055, USTS 993 (entered into force 26 October 1945). sets forth the parameters of "international law" as follows: a. international conventions, whether general or particular, establishing rules expressly recognized by the contesting states; b. international

custom, as evidence of a general practice accepted as law; c. the general principles of law recognized by civilized nations; and d., subject to the provisions of Article 59, judicial decisions and the teachings of the most highly qualified publicists of the various nations, as subsidiary means for the determination of the rule of law.

12 *Vienna Convention on the Law of Treaties*, 23 May 1969, 1155 UNTS 331, (entered into force 27 January 1980, accession by Canada 14 October 1970) [hereinafter Vienna Convention].

13 "According to the Vienna Convention, a treaty should be interpreted according to its 'ordinary meaning' unless such a reading 'leaves the meaning ambiguous or obscure'. Therefore, the Genocide Convention's actual text should be considered the preeminent source for assessing genocidal culpability. However, like any statute, the Genocide Convention is unclear in parts, and even where the language appears clear, it is often subject to conflicting interpretations. As a result, recourse to other interpretive sources, including drafting materials, scholarly opinions and genocide case law, is permitted in some circumstances." Kurt Mundorff, "Other Peoples' Children: A Textual and Contextual Interpretation of the Genocide Convention, Article II(e)," *Harvard International Law Journal* 50, No. 1 (Winter 2009):68. He cites *Case Concerning the Application of the Convention on the Prevention and Punishment of the Crime of Genocide (Bosnia and Herzegovina v. Serbia and Montenegro)*, Judgement (26 February 2007) [hereinafter Bosnia v. Serbia] para. 160.

14 Vienna Convention, Article 31

15 Ibid., Article 32.

16 See Hirad Abtahi and Philippa Webb, *The Genocide Convention: The Travaux Préparatoires* (Leiden: Martinus Nijhoff, 2008), Volume 1 & 2 [Travaux]. As is observed by Herschkopf and Hunter, *Genocide Reinterpreted*, 1. The *Travaux* "is the only work to gather in a single publication the records of the multitude of meetings and statements which led to the adoption of the Convention on the Prevention and Punishment of the Crime of Genocide on 9 December 1948. As it includes almost all of the preparatory work leading to the adoption of the Convention, the *Travaux* serves as a 'supplementary means of interpretation' under Article 32 of the 1969 Vienna Convention on the Law of Treaties. The Vienna Convention establishes that the preparatory work of international binding instruments may be consulted in order to help determine the meaning of a treaty when there is ambiguity regarding the actual terms of the agreement."

17 Mundorff, "Other Peoples' Children," 69.

18 Sharon H. Venne, "Discovering Peoples in International Law" in *Our Elders Understand our Rights: Evolving International Law Regarding Indigenous Rights* (Penticton, B.C.: Theytus Books, 1998), 16.

19 MacDonald and Hudson, "Genocide Question," 435.

20 Ibid., 429.

21 See esp., MacDonald and Hudson, "Genocide Question," 436-438. Canadian courts in private law or criminal proceedings claims have "found the UNGC to be inapplicable owing to the principle of non-retroactivity and to its 'political' nature." The court claimed that it cannot make a finding based on a "political code of conduct;" See esp., *Indian Residential Schools, Re*, [2000] 9 WWR 237 at para 73 (ABQB) for further reference

22 Ibid., 436. The authors suggest that the courts use the domestic legislation to strike down the defendants' claims of genocide in *Re Residential Schools*.

23 Ibid., 435.

24 Ibid., 437. See *Re Residential Schools.*

25 Canada, *Debates of the Senate,* 21st Parl, 6th Sess, No 1 (27 May 1952) at 313 (Arthur Roebuck).

26 Ibid.

27 Ibid.

28 See esp., MacDonald and Hudson, "Genocide Question," 436-438.

29 Robert Davis and Mark Zannis, *The Genocide Machine in Canada* (Montréal: Black Rose Books, 1973), 21.

30 Davis and Zannis, *Genocide Machine*, 23.

31 Canada, *House of Commons Debates,* 21st Parl, 6th Sess, No 3 (21 May 1952) at 2436 (Hon L.D Crestohl).

32 Ibid., 2347.

33 Ibid.

34 Ibid., 2438.

35 Canada, *House of Commons Debates,* 21st Parl, 6th Sess, No 3 (21 May 1952) at 2443 (Hon Lester Pearson).

36 Ibid., 2442.

37 The basis of Pearson's claim was an argument by China's UN delegation that Japan administered, "opium to the Chinese people as a means of weakening their resistance in the Sino-Japanese war." Ibid., 2442.

38 Schabas, *Genocide*, 184. Also see MacDonald and Hudson, "Genocide Question," 435.

39 Canada, *Report to the Minister of Justice of the Special Committee on Hate Propaganda in Canada* (Ottawa: Queen's Printer, 1966) [hereinafter cited as Cohen Report] 61. Originally cited/quoted by Davis and Zannis, *Genocide Machine*, 23; see also MacDonald and Hudson, "Genocide Question," 435.

40 Ward Churchill, "Forbidding the 'G-Word,'" in his *Perversions of Justice: Indigenous Peoples and Angloamerican Law* (San Francisco: City Lights Books, 2003), 251; see Chrisjohn, Young, with Maraun, *The Circle Game,* 63-66; see Roland Chrisjohn, Tanya Wasacase, Lisa Nussey, Andrea Smith, Marc Legault, Pierre Loiselle and Mathieu Bourgeois, "Genocide and Indian Residential Schooling: The Past is

Present," in Richard Wiggers and Ann Griffiths, eds., *Canada and International Humanitarian Law: Peacekeeping and War Crimes in the Modern Era* (Nova Scotia: Dalhousie University Centre for Foreign Policy Studies, 2002).

41 Churchill, "Forbidding the 'G-Word,'" 251.

42 Cited in Davis and Zannis, *Genocide Machine*, 23.

43 Ibid.

44 *Cohen Report*, 62.

45 Ibid.

46 Criminal Code, Section 318.

47 Genocide Convention, Article II(b).

48 Ibid., Article II(e).

49 Ibid., Article II(d).

50 Chrisjohn and Young, with Maraun, *Circle Game*, 63; See, e.g., Karen Stote, *An Act of Genocide: Colonialism and the Sterilization of Aboriginal Women* (Halifax, N.S.: Fernwood, 2015), for a review of the issue relating to imposing measures intended to prevent births within the group.

51 Chrisjohn *et al.*, "Past is Present," 235.

52 Chrisjohn and Young, with Mauran, *Circle Game*, 20.

53 Chrisjohn et. al, "Genocide and Indian Residential Schooling: The Past is Present," 230.

54 For examples of the terms in quotes being used in the relevant connection, see Chrisjohn and Young, with Maraun, *Circle Game*, 34; Ward Churchill, "A Breach of Trust: The Radioactive Colonization of Native North America," in *Acts of Rebellion: The Ward Churchill Reader* (New York: Routledge, 2003), 139.

55 Canada, Office of the Prime Minister, *Statement of Apology to Former Students of the Indian Residential Schools,* (Ottawa: June 11, 2008); Truth and Reconciliation Canada. *Truth and Reconciliation Commission of Canada: Interim Report* (Winnipeg, MB: Truth and Reconciliation Commission, 2012), 25-27.

56 See Steven Newcomb, "A Critique of the Proposed Doctrine of Reconciliation" (Kumeyaay Territory: Indigenous Law Institute, 2012), 1

57 RCAP, "Residential Schools," 312.

58 See Chrisjohn and Young, with Maraun, *Circle Game*, 49-50; also see John S. Milloy, *A National Crime: The Canadian Government and the Residential School System, 1879 to 1986* (Winnipeg: The University of Manitoba Press, 1999), 77-156; Agnes Grant, *No End of Grief: Indian Residential Schools in Canada* (Winnipeg, MB: Pemmican, 1996); 221-244; J.R. Miller, *Shingwauk's Vision: A History of the Native Residential Schools* (Toronto: University of Toronto Press, 1996), 317-342; Ward Churchill, *Kill the Indian Save the Man: The Genocidal Impact of American Indian Residential Schools* (San Francisco: City Lights Books, 2004), 16-76.

59 Office of the Prime Minister, *Apology to Students.*

60 Quoted in Churchill, *Kill the Indian*, xliii. Also see Chrisjohn and Young, with Maraun, *Circle Game*, 62-63.

61 Chrisjohn and Young, with Maraun, *Circle Game*, 34.

62 Ibid.

63 Office of the Prime Minister, *Apology to Students.*

64 Ibid, see the 4th and 7th paragraphs.

65 Ibid. On the scale of deaths, see P.H. Bryce, Report on the Indian Schools of Manitoba and the Northwest Territories (Ottawa: Government Printing Bureau, 1907); P.H. Bryce, *The Story of a National Crime being an Appeal for Justice to the Indians of Canada* (Ottawa: James Hope and Sons, 1922); see also *National Crime*; Milloy, *A National Crime*, 91; Churchill, *Kill the Indian*, 34, 43-44.

66 See generally Agnes Jack, ed., *Behind Closed Doors: Stories from the Kamloops Indian Residential School* (Penticton, B.C.: Theytus Books, 2006) for survivor accounts.

67 Vienna Convention, Article II(d).

68 Schabas, *Genocide*, 615.

69 Ibid.

70 Legal Information Institute, *Wex Legal Dictionary*, *sub verbo* "jus cogens," accessed (November 22, 2017), http://www.law.cornell.edu/wex/jus_cogens.

71 United Nations, General Assembly Resolution 96(1) (U.N. Doc. A/Res/96(1) (11 December 1946)); also see Advisory Opinion at 23 in which the ICJ discusses the GA Res 96(1).

72 Advisory Opinion, 16.

73 Ibid., 21.

74 This being tied to the notion of contract, the court contends that in some instances a flexible approach is required as regards to the Genocide Convention and in general a need for flexibility in the operation of multilateral conventions. Ibid.

75 The flexible approach requires the consideration of the "universal character of the United Nations under whose auspices the Convention was concluded." Ibid.

76 Ibid; also see p. 23 in which the ICJ explains that, "[i]n such a convention the contracting States do not have any interests of their own; they merely have, one and all, a common interest, namely, the accomplishment of those high purposes which are the *raison d'être* of the convention."

77 "The origins and characteristics of that Convention, the objects pursued by the General Assembly and the contracting parties, the relations which exist between the provisions of the Convention, *inter se*, and between those provisions and these objects, furnish elements of interpretation of the will of the General Assembly and the parties." Ibid., 23.

78 Ibid. Cited from U.N.G.A. Res. 96(1).

79 Ibid.

80 Ibid.

81 Ibid.

82 Ibid., 24.

83 "It follows that it is the compatibility of a reservation with the object and purpose of the Convention that must furnish the criterion for the attitude of a State in making the reservation on accession as well as for the appraisal by a State in objecting to the reservation. Such is the rule of conduct which must guide every State in the appraisal which it must make, individually and from its own stand point, of the admissibility of any reservation." Ibid.

84 Ibid.

85 Ibid., 29-30.

86 Ibid., 26-27.

87 Ibid., 27.

88 "There is simply no evidence of dishonesty or intentional disloyalty on the part of Canada or the United Church towards the plaintiffs which would make it permissible or desirable to engage the law relating to fiduciary obligations. I include in this conclusion the more general complaints of the plaintiffs relating to linguistic and cultural deprivation. In my view the plaintiffs have failed to demonstrate that either Canada or the Church were acting dishonestly or were intentionally disloyal to the plaintiffs." *Blackwater v. Plint*,[2001] 93 BCLR 228 at para 247 (BCSC). The BCCA upheld this decision pertaining to the plaintiff's claim of loss of language and culture. The point being there is no Canadian Court that has employed the term genocide or acknowledged the application of genocide in international law to government culpability into genocide. *Blackwater v. Plint* [2003] 253 DLR (4th) 60 (BCCA).

89 Australia, Commonwealth, Human Rights and Equal Opportunity Commission, *Bringing Them Home*: *Report of the National Inquiry into the Separation of Aboriginal and Torres Strait Islander Children from Their Families (*Sydney: Sterling Press, 1997), 270.

90 "Genocide is prohibited under customary international law, which provides a distinct source of obligation for both individuals and states." Quigley, *Genocide Convention*, 80.

91 Genocide Convention, Article II.

92 Canada's program of involuntarily sterilizing indigenous women is one example. See, e.g., Stote, *An Act of Genocide: Colonialism and the Sterilization of Aboriginal Women.*

93 Vienna Convention, Article 18.

94 Ibid.

95 Paolo Palchetti, "Article 18 of the 1969 Vienna Convention: A Vague and Ineffective Obligation or a Useful Means for Strengthening Legal Cooperation" in Enzo Cannizzaro ed., *The Law of Treaties Beyond the Vienna Convention* (New York: Oxford University Press, 2011), 26. Palchetti refers to the domestic courts as a possible avenue to

determine the scope of the section; however, given the Criminal Code and jurisprudential analysis in this book, it is questionable whether the domestic courts can answer and determine this question.

96 Palchetti, "Article 18," 25-26.

97 Ibid., 27-31.

98 Ibid., 28.

99 Laurence Boisson de Chazournes, Anne-Marie La Rosa, and Makane Moïse Mbengue, "1969 Vienna Convention: Article 18 Obligation not to defeat the object and purpose of a treaty prior to its entry into force" in Olivier Corten and Pierre Klein, eds., *The Vienna Convention on the Law of Treaties: A Commentary* (Great Britain: Oxford University Press, 2011), 370-372

100 Ibid., 370.

101 Ibid.

102 Ibid.

103 Ibid.

104 Ibid., 370-371. "[I]n the case of International Labour Organization (ILO) the statutes of which were included in the Peace Treaty of Versailles, it is interesting to take into account the reporting obligations with which states have to comply even before the ratification of international labour conventions. From the moment the International Labour Organization (plenary organ of the organization) adopts a convention, every member State has the obligation to submit it to the competent authorities 'for the enactment of legislation or other action'. The member States are also obliged to report to the Director General of the organization on the said measures. If the State obtains consent with a view to ratification it has to communicate it to the Director General and take all measures necessary to render its provision effective. In the case in which a State does not wish to be bound by the obligations contained in an international labour convention, it still remains under a transparent obligation. This transparent requirement is established by requiring States to submit at adequate intervals information to the Director General on, 'the position of its law and practice in regard to the matters dealt with in the Convention, showing the extent to which effect has been given, or is proposed to be given, to any of the provisions of the Convention by legislation, administrative action, collective agreement or otherwise and stating the difficulties which prevent or delay the ratification of such Convention."

105 Ibid., 371.

106 Ibid.

107 Ibid.

108 Ibid., 370.

109 Ibid., 371.

110 U.N.G.A. Resolution 96(1).

111 Ibid.

112 Genocide Convention, Article II; Also see See Raphaël Lemkin, *Axis Rule in Occupied Europe: Laws of Occupation, Analysis of*

Government, Proposals for Redress, 2nd ed. (Clark, NJ: The Lawbook Exchange, 2008), 79-80.

113 Advisory Opinion, 24.

114 Ibid.

115 Ibid., 23.

116 Schabas, *Genocide,* 52-58.

117 See esp, U.N.G.A. Resolution 96(1) and Advisory Opinion.

118 Schabas, *Genocide,* 4.

119 Ibid. Schabas cites the *Case Concerning Armed Activities on the Territory of Congo (New Application: 2002) Democratic, Republic of Congo v. Rwanda, Jurisdiction of the Court and Admissibility of the Application* [2006] ICJ Rep 126 at para 64 [hereinafter cited as Congo v Rwanda].

120 *Congo v. Rwanda*, para 64.

121 Schabas, *Genocide*, 4-5. Schabas cites the *Case Concerning the Application of the Convention on the Prevention and Punishment of the Crime of Genocide (Bosnia and Herzegovina v. Serbia and Montenegro)* [2007] ICJ Rep 43 at para 161 [hereinafter cited as *Bosnia v. Serbia*].

122 *Bosnia v. Serbia*, para 161; Citing from the Advisory Opinion of 1951.

123 Legal Information Institute, *Wex Legal Dictionary*, *sub verbo* "jus cogens."

124 Venne, *Our Elders Understand our Rights,* 15.

125 Ibid.

126 Ian Mosby, "Administering Colonial Science: Nutrition Research and Human Biomedical Experimentation in Aboriginal Communities and Residential Schools, 1942–1952," *Histoire Sociale/Social History*, 46, No. 19 (2013): 145-172; Also see Bob Weber, "Government conducted nutrition experiments on hungry, malnourished Aboriginal Children: paper, Researchers in 1942 decided that isolated, dependent people in northern Manitoba would be ideal subjects for tests on the effects of different diets" *National Post* (16 July 2013), http://nationalpost.com/news/canada/government-conducted-nutrition-experiments-on-hungry-malnourished-aboriginal-children-paper.

127 Quigley, *Genocide Convention*, 80. Quigley explains that "[e]ven if issues of construction of the Genocide Convention can be resolved, there exists a separate, and potentially competing, body of genocide law, namely, genocide under customary international law. Genocide is prohibited under customary international law, which provides a distinct source of obligation for both individuals and states."

128 Criminal Code, s 318.

129 Vienna Convention, Article 18.

130 See *Advisory Opinion.*

131 Chazournes, La Rosa, and Mbengue, "Article 18 Obligation," 371.

132 See MacDonald and Hudson, "Genocide Question," 434-38.

133 Chazournes, La Rosa, with Mbengue, "Article 18 Obligation," 371.

134 Ibid.

135 See Davis and Zannis, *Genocide Machine*, 22.

136 Chazournes, La Rosa, and Mbengue, "Article 18 Obligation," 370.

137 Mosby, "Administering Colonial Science."

138 Chazournes, La Rosa, and Mbengue, "Article 18 Obligation," 371.

139 William Schabas, *Unimaginable Atrocities: Justice, Politics, and Rights at the War Crimes Tribunals* (London: Oxford University Press, 2012) 63.

140 See Schabas, *Unimaginable Atrocities*, 63. For further review, see *Application of the Convention on the Prevention and Punishment of the Crime of Genocide (Croatia v. Serbia)*, Preliminary Objections, Judgment, [2008] ICJ Rep 412 at para. 123; *Application of the Convention on the Prevention and Punishment of the Crime of Genocide (Bosnia and Herzegovina v. Yugoslavia)*, Preliminary Objections, Judgment, [1996] ICJ Rep 595 at para 34.

141 Ibid., 62.

142 The Chair of the Truth and Reconciliation Commission has openly accused Canada of attempting to exempt its actions from assessment under the international legal definition of genocide. Chinta Puxley, "Residential Schools Called a Form of Genocide," *Globe and Mail* (February 17, 2012).

143 Herschkopf and Hunter, *Genocide Reinterpreted*, 11.

144 United Nations General Assembly, Eighty-Second Meeting, Sixth Committee, U.N. Doc. A/C.6/SR.82 (23 October 1948) [U.N. Doc. A/C.6/SR.82], reprinted in Abtahi and Webb, *Travaux*, 1493.

145 Ibid.

146 Ibid., 1495.

147 United Nations General Assembly, Eighty-Third Meeting, Sixth Committee, U.N. Doc. A/C.6/SR.83 (25 October 1948), [U.N. Doc. A/C.6/SR.83] reprinted in Abtahi and Webb, *Travaux*, 1504.

148 U.N. Doc. A/C.6/SR.82, reprinted in Abtahi and Webb, *Travaux*, 1494.

149 See esp. Statistics Canada, "Study: Living arrangements of Aboriginal children aged 14 and under, 2011". The report shows that, "[w]hile Aboriginal children represented 7% of all children in Canada in 2011, they accounted for almost half (48%) of all foster children in the country." Also "In 1959, only one percent of all children in care were of Native ancestry. By the late 1960s, 30-40 percent of all legal wards of the state of Canada were Aboriginal children, even though they formed less than 4 percent of the national population.' At the height of the Scoop, one in four status Indian children were separated from his or her parents for all or part of their childhood." Emily Alston-O'Connor, "The Sixties Scoop Implications for Social Workers and Social Work Education" *Critical Social Work* 11, no. 1 (2010): 54, accessed September 5, 2012, http://www.uwindsor.ca/criticalsocialwork/the-sixties-scoop-implications-for-social-workers-and-social-work-education.

150 Ibid., 59.

151 U.N.G.A. Resolution 96(1).

152 United Nations General Assembly, One Hundredth and Seventy Ninth Meeting, Sixth Committee, U.N. Doc. A/PV.179 (9 December 1948) [U.N. Doc. A/PV.179], reprinted in Abtahi and Webb, *Travaux*, 2082.

153 See The Indian Act, SC 1876, 37-38 & 38-39 Vict, c 18; also see The Indian Act, RSC 1985, c I-5.

154 As a prime example of such legislation, see the 1894 version of *The Indian Act.*

155 ("[I]n the name of efficiency, total institutions "unmake" the people over whom they gain control. It matters little how old an inmate is and how he or she defends and asserts it, must be taken apart and reassembled enough to allow what remains to operate in accordance with the institutional requirements)" Chrisjohn and Young, with Maraun, *Circle Game*, 91.

156 The passages quoted are from Article II, subparagraphs (b) and (e), of the Genocide Convention.

157 Office of the Prime Minister, *Apology to Students.*

158 *Prosecutor v. Jean-Paul Akayesu,* (Case No. ICTR-96-4-T), Judgment (2 September 1998) (International Criminal Tribunal for Rwanda, Trial Chamber) [hereinafter Akayesu]; *Prosecutor v. Radovan Karadžić et al.* (Case No. IT-95-5-R61, IT-95-18-R61), Review of the Indictments Pursuant to Rule 61 of the Rules of Procedure and Evidence (11 July 1996) (International Criminal Tribunal for the former Yugoslavia, Trial Chamber) [hereinafter *Karadžić*].

159 Abtahi and Webb, *Travaux,* 235, see also 1493 1494, 1495, 1504 for further state views on the subject.

160 Kai Ambos, "What does 'intent to destroy' mean in genocide?" *International Review of the Red Cross* 91, No. 876 (December 2009): 833, doi: 10.1017/S1816383110000056.

161 *Bosnia v. Serbia,* para 187.

162 Schabas, *Genocide,* 243-256.

163 *Akayesu,* para 730;

164 Ibid., para 523.

165 Ibid.

166 *Karadzić ,* para 94.

167 *Karadzić,* para 95; also see Akayesu, para 524.

168 *Akayesu,* para 521. The ICTR held, "In concrete terms, for any of the acts charged under Article 2 (2) of the Statute to bea constitutive element of genocide, the act must have been committed against one or several individuals, because such individual or individuals were members of a specific group, and specifically because they belonged to this group. Thus, the victim is chosen not because of his individual identity, but rather on account of his membership of a national, ethnical, racial or religious group. The victim of the act is therefore a member of a group, chosen as such, which, hence, means that the victim of the crime of genocide is the group itself and not only the individual"

169 Ibid., para 728.

170 Ibid., para 504. Also see Schabas, *Genocide*, 182.

171 *Prosecutor v. Radislav Krstić,* (Case No. IT-98-33-T), Judgment (2 August 2001) para 508 (International Criminal Tribunal for the former Yugoslavia, Trial Chamber) [hereinafter *Krstic*].The court finds that the crime is defined to mean "acts of torture, be they bodily or mental, inhumane or degrading, persecution."

172 See Akayesu, para 503. The ICTR cites *Attorney-General of Israel v. Eichmann* (1968) 36 ILR 5 at 238 (District Court, Jerusalem) [hereinafter Eichmann].

173 *Prosecutor v. Milomir Stakić,* (Case No. IT-97-24-T), Judgment (31 July 2003) para 516 (International Criminal Tribunal for the former Yugoslavia, Trial Chamber).

174 *Prosecutor v. Vidoje Blagojević,* (Case No. IT-02-60-T), Judgment (17January 2005) para 647 (International Criminal Tribunal for the former Yugoslavia, Trial Chamber).

175 Ibid.

176 Akayesu, para 731.

177 Ibid.

178 *Krstić*, para 513.

179 Ibid; *Prosecutor v. Momčilo Krajišnik,* (Case No. IT-00-39-T), Judgment (27 September 2006) para 862 (International Criminal Tribunal for the former Yugoslavia, Trial Chamber) [hereinafter *Krajišnik*].

180 Titley, *Narrow Vision*, 50.

181 See Lemkin, *Axis Rule*, 79.

182 Dene Moore, "Provinces hand over aboriginal death records from residential school period" *CTV News* (28 March 2014), https://www.ctvnews.ca/canada/provinces-hand-over-aboriginal-death-records-from-residential-school-period-1.1751450; See chapter three at pages for the discussion on the issue of the death rates. The "official" numbers of children that died are indeed questionable

183 See Lemkin, "Preface," *Axis Rule*, ix for his use of the word "technique."

184 Churchill, *Kill the Indian*, 28.

185 Newcomb, *Pagans*, 16.

186 Titley, *Narrow Vision*, 50; See Newcomb's explanation of the body politic. Ibid.

187 Chrisjohn and Young, with Maraun, *Circle Game*, 59.

188 Churchill, *Kill the Indian*, 16. Also see Grant, *No End of Grief*, 209-220.

189 Grant, *No End of Grief*, 209.

190 Kent McNeil, "Social Darwinism and Judicial Conceptions of Indian Title in Canada in the 1880s," *Journal of the West*, 38, No. 1 (January 1999): 70.

191 Lemkin, *Axis Rule*, 79; see MacDonald, House of Commons.

192 Schabas, *Genocide*, 17.

193 Mundorff, "Other Peoples' Children," 91. He writes, "As Kreβ illustrates, Article 2 (e) does not require the children to be fully integrated into another group. Instead, Article 2 (e) 's requirement that children be transferred 'to another group' should be considered satisfied when the children are in another group's control."

194 Schabas, *Genocide*, 202.

195 *Akayesu*, para 509.

196 Schabas, *Genocide*, 203.

197 Sharon Venne, "Understanding Treaty Six: An Indigenous Perspective" in ed. Michael Asch, *Aboriginal and Treaty Rights in Canada: Essays on Law, Equality and Respect for Difference* (Vancouver: UBC, Press, 1997), 195. Also see Stephanie Cran, "Dark history of Canada's First Nations pass system uncovered in documentary," CBC News, February 29, 2016, http://www.cbc.ca/news/indigenous/dark-history-canada-s-pass-system-1.3454022.

198 Vicki Trerise, *Aboriginal Children and the Dishonour of the Crown: Human Rights Best Interests and Customary Adoption* (unpublished LL.M. thesis, University of British Columbia, 2011), 19; Of particular relevance in this regard is *An Act Further to Amend the Indian Act,* SC 1894, c 32, s 11, ss 137 and 138 which required "the compulsory attendance of children at school. Such regulations, in addition to any other provisions deemed expedient, may provide for the arrest and conveyance to school, and detention there, of truant children and of children who are prevented by their parents or guardians from attending: and such regulations may provide for the punishment, upon summary conviction, by fine or imprisonment, or both of parents or guardians, or persons having the charge of children, who fail, refuse or neglect to cause such children to attend school." These sections are consolidated in *the Indian Act,* RSC 1906, c 81, ss 9, 10 and 11; also see An Act to amend the Indian Act, SC 1920, c 50, s 9 and 10 [hereinafter The Indian Act, 1920].

199 Lemkin, Axis Rule, ix.

200 See Jack, *Behind Closed Doors*, xi.

201 Miller, *Shingwauk's Vision*, 128.

202 Trerise, *Aboriginal Children*, 19.

203 *Eichmann*, 340.

204 Chrisjohn and Young, with Maraun, *Circle Game*, 49.

205 See all for examples of the destruction, Isabelle Knockwood, *Out of the Depths: The Experiences of Mi'kmaw Children at the Indian Residential School at Shubenacadie , Nova Scotia* (Lockeport, N.S.: Roseway, 1992); Elizabeth Furniss, *Victims of Benevolence: The Dark Legacy of the Williams Lake Residential School* (Vancouver: Arsenal Pulp Press, 1992, 1995); Milloy, *A National Crime*; RCAP, "Residential Schools"; Miller, *Shingwauk's Vision*. This list is not exhaustive.

206 *Akayesu*, paras 706, 707, 711, 712.
207 *Stakić*, para 516.
208 Jordan Chittley and Kevin Newman, "Ottawa forced to turn over report of electric chair use at residential school," *CTN News Live*, (January 15, 2014), http://knlive.ctvnews.ca/ottawa-forced-to-turn-over-reports-of-electric-chair-use-at-residential-school-1.1641479.
209 See Chrisjohn and Young, with Maraun, *Circle Game*, 49-50.
210 Weber, "Nutritional Experiments"; Mosby, "Administering Colonial Science."
211 For background, see generally, George J. Annas and Michael A. Grodin, *The Nazi Doctors and the Nuremberg Code: Human Rights in Human Experimentation* (New York: Oxford University Press, 1992).
212 *Akayesu*, para 731.
213 Grant, *No End of Grief*, 229.
214 Ibid., 227-232; Also see Shauna Troniak, "Background Paper: Addressing the Legacy of the Residential Schools," *Background Paper* (Ottawa: Library of Parliament, Canada, 2011), 2, accessed (June 14, 2013) http://www.parl.gc.ca/Content/LOP/Research Publications/2011-76-e.pd; see Churchill, *Kill the Indian*, 60-68; Chrisjohn and Young, with Maraun, *Circle Game*, 50; Harper, *Apology to Students*.
215 *Akayesu*, para 731.
216 Ibid.
217 *Krstić*, para 513; *Krajisnik*, para 862.
218 *Krajisnik*, para 862.
219 "Residential schools linked to suicidal thoughts: Statscan" *The Globe and Mail* (17 March 2017); also see Michael Shulman and Jesse Tahirali, "Suicide among Canada's First Nations: Key numbers" CTV News (16 April 2016); and Allison Crawford, "Suicide among Indigenous Peoples in Canada" last modified September 9, 2016, http://www.thecanadianencyclopedia.ca/en/article/suicide-among-indigenous-peoples-in-canada/
220 Ibid.
221 Alston-O'Connor, "The Sixties Scoop Implications for Social Workers and Social Work Education," 54.
222 *Travaux*, 235,1493, 1494, 1495 1504; Troniak, "Addressing the Legacy," 2-3.
223 Canada, *House of Commons Debates*, 5th Parliament, 1st Session, No 14 (9 May 1883) at 1107-1108 (Hon. John A. MacDonald).
224 Schabas, *Genocide*, 248.
225 *Akayesu, para 523*
226 MacDonald, *House of Commons*, 1107-1108.
227 Milloy, *National Crime*, 19.
228 *Akayesu*, para 524; *Karadzić*, para. 94.
229 *Karadzić*, para 94.
230 *Akayesu*, para 523.

231 RCAP, "Residential Schools," 312.
232 Office of the Prime Minister, Apology to Students.
233 Quigley, *Genocide Convention*, 107; Cited from *Akayesu*, para. 520-521.
234 MacDonald, *House of Commons*, 1107-1108.
235 Ibid.
236 *Akayesu*, para 730.
237 U.N. Doc. A/C.6/SR.83, reprinted in Abtahi and Webb, *Travaux*, 1504.
238 U.N. Doc. A/C.6/SR.82, reprinted in Abtahi and Webb, *Travaux*, 1494.
239 *Krstić*, para 590.
240 See, e.g., RCAP, "Residential Schools," 349-59.
241 *The Indian Act,* 1920, s 10(3).
242 *Akayesu*, para 731.
243 *Akayesu*, para 732.
244 Ibid.
245 As examples, "[I]n 1989…Oblate priest Harold McIntee pled guilty to allegations that he'd molested more than a score of boys as young as five during his years at the St. Joseph's Mission School. In 1991, an Oblate brother, Glen Doughty, who'd also worked at St. Joseph's, did the same, and a year later Hubert O'Connor, a priest who'd been principal of the school before being promoted to serve as Bishop of St. George, went on trial for raping and otherwise molesting several female students…. In 1995, 'Catholic official Jerzy Maczynski [was] sentenced to sixteen years in jail on twenty-eight accounts of sexual abuse at the Lower Post Indian Residential school," Churchill, *Kill the Indian*, 64, also see 62-63; Also see Grant, *No End of Grief*, 229; RCAP, "Residential Schools," 349-59; Troniak, "Addressing the Legacy," 2.
246 Office of the Prime Minister, *Apology to Students.*
247 Chrisjohn and Young, with Maraun, *Circle Game*, 91.
248 Troniak, Addressing the Legacy, 2-3.
249 Removal of Indigenous children by the provinces was authorized under the 1951 amendment to the Indian Act (Section 88). In 1976, the Supreme Court of Canada "confirmed…that the legal jurisdiction of the Province's ability to extend child welfare services onto reserve, regardless of the provincial incursion into a federal sphere of responsibility." Marilyn Bennett, "First Nations Fact Sheet: A General Profile on First Nations Child Welfare in Canada," First Nations Child and Family Caring Society of Canada, http://www.fncfcs.com/docs/FirstNationsFS1.pdf); citing *Natural Parents v. Superintendent of Child Welfare* (60 D.L.R. 3rd 148 S.C.C. (1976)). Also see Leroy Little Bear, "Section 88 of the Indian Act and the Application of Provincial Laws to Indians" in Anthony Long and Menno Boldt, eds., *Governments in Conflict? Provinces and Indian Nations in Canada* (Toronto: University of Toronto Press, 1992), 175-87.
250 See Ashley Quinn, "Reflections on Intergenerational Trauma: Healing as a Critical Intervention," *First Peoples Child and Family Review*

3, No. 4 (2007): 73. She explains that the devastating effects of the residential school system and the destruction of the culture "can be seen in high numbers of children who are removed from their homes and placed into provincial care."

251 See Linda Bull, "Indian Residential Schooling: The Native Perspective," and Rosalind Ing, "The Effects of Residential Schooling on Native Child-Rearing Practices," all in *Canadian Journal of Native Education*, Vol. 18, Supplement (1991): 9-64. Also see Patrick J. Morrissette, "The Holocaust of First Nations People: Residual Effects on Parenting and Treatment Implications," *Contemporary Family Therapy* 16, No. 5 (October 1994): 381-92.

252 Ing, "The Effects of Residential Schooling on Native Child-Rearing Practices," 77-85.

253 Quinn, "Intergenerational Trauma," 73.

254 Ing, "The Effects of Residential Schooling on Native Child-Rearing Practices," 115.

255 Office of the Prime Minister, *Apology to Students,* ninth paragraph.

256 See Erin Hanson, "Sixties Scoop: The Sixties Scoop and Aboriginal Child Welfare," *Indigenous Foundations,* http://indigenousfoundations.arts.ubc.ca, accessed (August 14, 2012). Hanson cites Lavina White and Eva Jacobs, *Liberating our Children, Liberating our Nations: Report of the Aboriginal Committee: Community Panel of Family and Children's Services Legislation Review in British Columbia* (Victoria: Minister of Social Services, 1992), 18-23; also see Ernie Crey and Suzanne Fournier, *Stolen From Our Embrace: The Abduction of First Nations Children and the Restoration of Aboriginal Communities* (Vancouver: Douglas & McIntyre, 1997), 81-114.

257 Darcy Henton, "Deaths of Alberta aboriginal children in care no 'fluke of statistics," *Edmonton Journal*, 8 January 2014 ,http://www.edmontonjournal.com/life/Deaths+Alberta+aboriginal+children+care+fluke+statistics/9212384/story.html, No longer available but cited by the First Nations Child and Family Caring Society "Deaths of Alberta aboriginal children in care no 'fluke of statistics' and cited in Truth and Reconciliation Canada, *Canada's Residential Schools: The Legacy The Final Report of the Truth and Reconciliation Commission of Canada The Legacy* vol 5 (Montreal: McGill-Queen's University Press, 2015), 381.

258 Mary Ellen Turpel-Lafond, Representative for Children and Youth, 'Too Many Victims Sexualized Violence in the Lives of Children and Youth in Care: An Aggregate Review '(British Columbia: October 2016).

259 Kathryn Blaze Baum, Mark Hume and Gloria Galloway, "B.C. report finds indigenous girls in care more likely to face sex abuse," *The Globe and Mail* (4 October 2016), https://www.theglobeandmail.com/news/british-columbia/damning-bc-report-finds-indigenous-girls-in-care-more-likely-to-face-sex-abuse/article32230796/, accessed (December

12, 2017).

260 Ibid.

261 Chinta Puxley, "Manitoba opens Tina Fontaine case to review by children's advocate" The Globe and Mail (15 December 2014), https://www.theglobeandmail.com/news/national/man-accused-in-death-of-tina-fontaine-waives-court-appearance/article27759601/, accessed (September 2, 2017).

262 'Teen in B.C. provincial care dies in fall from hotel window' B.C. children's advocate calls death of Alex Gervais a tragedy, says ministry 'has a lot to answer for' *CBC News* (23 September 2015), http://www.cbc.ca/news/canada/british-columbia/teen-in-b-c-provincial-care-dies-in-fall-from-hotel-window-1.3240959, accessed (August 29, 2017).

263 Fournier and Crey, *Stolen From Our Embrace*, 81-142. Also see Hanson, "Sixties Scoop"; White and Jacobs, *Liberating our Children,* 18-23.

264 Hanson, "Sixties Scoop." Also see Raven Sinclair, "Identity Lost and Found: Lessons from the Sixties Scoop," *First Peoples Child and Family Review* 3, No. 1 (2007): 65-82.

265 Sinclair, "Identity Lost," 66. It is acknowledged that Sinclair's article "explores the history of Aboriginal adoption in Canada and examines some of the issues of transracial adoption through the lens of psychology theories to aid understanding of identity conflicts facing Aboriginal adoptees." She examines the child welfare system in the colonial context and the disproportionate removals of Indigenous children in the child welfare system. The phrase cited refers to "transracial adoptees." This note will verify to the reader that I am using this phrase in the context of the child welfare system.

Conclusion

1 See David B. MacDonald and Graham Hudson, "The Genocide Question and Indian Residential Schools in Canada," *Canadian Journal of Political Science* 45, No. 2 (June 2012): 427-449, doi:10.10170S000842391200039X.

2 As a prime example, see Colin Tatz, *With Intent to Destroy: Reflecting on Genocide* (New York: Verso, 2003).

3 This is just a note to say that not all of the scholars present were engaging in this destructive practice.

4 Ward Churchill, *Kill the Indian Save the Man: The Genocidal Impact of American Indian Residential Schools* (San Francisco: City Lights Books, 2004), 39: For further information see see P.H. Bryce, *Report on the Indian Schools of Manitoba and the Northwest Territories* (Ottawa: Government Printing Bureau, 1907); P.H. Bryce, *The Story of a National Crime being an Appeal for Justice to the Indians of Canada* (Ottawa: James Hope and Sons, 1922).

5 Ibid., 41. An important issue not addressed is the death of Indigenous children in the residential school system. It was acknowledged earlier that this omission is not to deny or purposely exclude this enumerated crime (Article 2 (a) and (c) as this would require an independent study and could be the subject of another study.

6 This refers to the ongoing resource extraction, jobs and employment in social welfare services, legal, courts, penal institutions and so forth.

7 See e.g. *Prosecutor v. Jean-Paul Akayesu,* (Case No. ICTR-96-4-T), Judgment (2 September 1998) para 497 (International Criminal Tribunal for Rwanda, Trial Chamber). The ICTR explained that, "[c] ontrary to popular belief, the crime of genocide does not imply the actual extermination of group in its entirety, but is understood as such once any one of the acts mentioned in Article 2(2)(a) through 2(2)(e) is committed with the specific intent to destroy "in whole or in part" a national, ethnical, racial or religious group."

8 See Raphaël Lemkin, *Axis Rule in Occupied Europe: Laws of Occupation, Analysis of Government, Proposals for Redress*, 2nd ed. (Clark, NJ: The Lawbook Exchange, 2008).

9 Truth and Reconciliation Commission, *Honouring the Truth, Reconciling for the Future: Summary of the Final Report of the Truth and Reconciliation Commission of Canada* (Winnipeg, MB: Truth and Reconciliation Commission of Canada, 2015), 1. The TRC did indeed find cultural genocide. As was already addressed in previous chapters, this is the safety valve, enabling recognition without facing legal culpability due to the legal loopholes herein discussed.

10 Steven Newcomb, personal communication, December 2, 2012; see especially Steven Newcomb, "Reconciliation and the Claim of Crown Sovereignty," *Indian Country Today* (2 May 2016), https://indiancountrymedianetwork.com/news/opinions/reconciliation-and-the-claim-of-crown-sovereignty/

11 Steven Newcomb, "A Critique of the Proposed Doctrine of Reconciliation" (Kumeyaay Territory: Indigenous Law Institute, 2012) 1.

12 George E. Tinker, "Tracing a Contour of Colonialism: American Indians and the Trajectory of Educational Imperialism," preface to Churchill, *Kill the Indian Save the Man*, xxvii.

13 Hirad Abtahi and Philippa Webb, eds., *The Genocide Convention: The Travaux Préparatoires* Vol 2, (Leiden: Martinus Nijhoff, 2008), 1291, 1293, 1295, 1301.

14 Miguel Alfonso Martinez, (Special Rapporteur), *Final Report: Human Rights of Indigenous People Study on Treaties, agreements and other constructive arrangements between States and indigenous populations,* UN Commission on Human Rights, 1999, E/CN.4/Sub 2/1999/20 (1999)), para 206-208. Martinez explains, "It is impossible to determine with any certainty, in 1998, the number of indigenous

peoples which have become extinct since the time of their first encounter with the "discoverers", as the result of the "civilization" imposed on them. Nor is it possible to say how many more will disappear in the not so distant future, unless the circumstances in which they live in multinational States today do not change." And later explains, "To cite just two known examples, according to all indications, the original inhabitants of Catalina Island off the coast of California and the Yanomamis of Roraima should be included in the category of "peoples in danger of extinction". The relentless carving away of their lands as a result of the most varied actions, their expulsion from these lands (either through the use of direct force by the new State or because they could not obtain the resources to continue practising their traditional economic activities or to continuing tilling the soil), draconian restrictions on the use of their own languages and on the practice of their religious beliefs (or the prohibition of one or both) have contributed, historically and currently to this situation."

15 See Steven T. Newcomb, *Pagans in the Promised Land: Decoding the Christian Doctrine of Discovery* (Golden, CO: Fulcrum, 2008), 16. Please review for his metaphor of the predator body politic.

16 Sharon Venne, ed., *Honour Bound Onion Lake and the Spirit of Treaty Six: The International Validity of Treaties with Indigenous Peoples* (Copenhagen: International Work Group for Indigenous Affairs Doc. 84, 1997), 6.

17 Ibid., 6-7. Martinez, *Study on Treaties*, para 256.

18 Martinez, *Study on Treaties,* para 256.

19 Martinez, *Study on Treaties,* para 265.

20 Newcomb, *Pagans,* 18.

21 Churchill, *Kill the Indian*, 82.

Afterword

1 "Manitoba Child Services Seizing a Newborn a Day: First Nations Advocate", The Huffington Post (1 September 2015) online: <http://www.huffingtonpost.ca/2015/09/01/manitoba-child-services-first-nations_n_8072038.html>; see also Chinta Puxley, "Manitoba Child Services Seizing a Newborn a Day: First Nations Advocate", (1 September 2015) online: <http://www.cbc.ca/news/canada/manitoba/cfs-seizes-a-manitoba-newborn-a-day-first-nations-advocate-says-1.3211451>

2 John Coldwell Adams, "Duncan Campbell Scott," *Confederation Voices,* Canadian Poetry, UWO, Web, Mar. 30, 2011.

INDEX

T

U

V

W

Y

Z